Also by Martin E. P. Seligman

with Joanne Hager
THE BIOLOGICAL BOUNDARIES OF LEARNING

HELPLESSNESS: ON DEPRESSION, DEVELOPMENT, AND DEATH

with Jack Maser
PSYCHOPATHOLOGY: EXPERIMENTAL MODELS

with Judy Garber
HUMAN HELPLESSNESS: THEORY AND APPLICATIONS

with David Rosenhan
ABNORMAL PSYCHOLOGY

LEARNED OPTIMISM

WHAT YOU CAN CHANGE AND WHAT YOU CAN'T

What You Can Change and What You Can't

THE COMPLETE GUIDE TO SUCCESSFUL SELF-IMPROVEMENT

MARTIN E. P. SELIGMAN, Ph.D.

Alfred A. Knopf New York 1994

THIS IS A BORZOI BOOK
PUBLISHED BY ALFRED A. KNOPF, INC.

 Published in the United States by Alfred A. Knopf, Inc., New York, and simultaneously in Canada by Random House of Canada Limited, Toronto. Distributed by Random House, Inc., New York.

Owing to limitations of space, acknowledgments for permission to reprint previously published material will be found following the Index.

Library of Congress Cataloging-in-Publication Data
Seligman, Martin E. P.
What you can change and what you can't : the complete guide to successful self-improvement / Martin E. P. Seligman. — 1st ed.
p. cm.
Includes bibliographical references and index.

1. Change (Psychology) 2. Self-actualization (Psychology)
3. Behavior modification. I. Title.
BF637.C4S45 1994
158'.1—dc20 93-14757 CIP

Manufactured in the United States of America

To

NICOLE DANA SELIGMAN

born August 26, 1991,

at the end of a week

in which human beings changed

what for most of this century

had seemed

beyond change.

Born into a new world.

God, grant me serenity to accept the things I cannot change, courage to change the things I can, and wisdom to know the difference.

Attributed to Friedrich Oetinger
(1702–1782), and to Reinhold Niebuhr,
"The Serenity Prayer" (1934)

CONTENTS

PART FOUR

Growing Up—At Last

PART ONE

Biological Psychiatry vs. Psychotherapy and Self-Improvement

O sweet spontaneous
earth how often have
the
doting

    fingers of
prurient philosophers pinched
and
poked

thee
,has the naughty thumb
of science prodded
thy

    beauty ,how
often have religions taken
thee upon their scraggy knees
squeezing and

buffeting thee that thou mightest conceive
gods
    (but
true

to the incomparable
couch of death thy
rhythmic
lover

    thou answerest

them only with

    spring)

e. e. cummings, "O sweet spontaneous," 1923

1

What Changes? What Doesn't Change?

TWO WORLDVIEWS are in collision. On the one hand, this is the age of psychotherapy and the age of self-improvement. Millions are struggling to change: We diet, we jog, we meditate. We adopt new modes of thought to counteract our depressions. We practice relaxation to curtail stress. We exercise to expand our memory and to quadruple our reading speed. We adopt draconian regimes to give up smoking. We raise our little boys and girls to androgyny. We come out of the closet or we try to become heterosexual. We seek to lose our taste for alcohol. We seek more meaning in life. We try to extend our life span.

Sometimes it works. But distressingly often, self-improvement and psychotherapy fail. The cost is enormous. We think we are worthless. We feel guilty and ashamed. We believe we have no willpower and that we are failures. We give up trying to change.

> *Trudy, like tens of millions of Americans, is desperate because she believes, quite incorrectly, that she is a failure. She finds herself even worse off after ten years of trying everything to lose weight.*
>
> *Trudy weighed 175 pounds when she graduated from Brown a decade ago. Four times since, she has slimmed to under 125: Weight Watchers, Nutri-System, six months under the care of a private behavior therapist, and, last year, Optifast. With each regime the weight came off quickly, if not painlessly. Each time the fat returned, faster and more of it. Trudy now weighs 195 and has given up.*

In its faith that we can change anything, the self-improvement movement expects Trudy to succeed in her fight against fat, even though she is such an obvious loser in the weight game. On the other hand, there is a view that expects Trudy to fail. For this is not only the age of self-improvement and therapy, this is the age of biological psychiatry. The human genome will be nearly mapped before the millennium is over. The brain systems underlying sex, hearing, memory, left-handedness, and sadness are now known. Psychoactive drugs—external agents—quiet our fears, relieve our blues, bring us bliss, dampen our mania, and dissolve our delusions more effectively than we can on our own. Our very personality—our intelligence and musical talent, even our religiousness, our conscience (or its absence), our politics, and our exuberance—turns out to be more the product of our genes than almost anyone would have believed a decade ago. Identical twins reared apart are uncannily similar in all these traits, almost as similar as they are for height and weight. The underlying message of the age of biological psychiatry is that our biology frequently makes changing, in spite of all our efforts, impossible.

But the view that all is genetic and biochemical and therefore cannot change is also very often wrong. Many individuals surpass their IQs, fail to "respond" to drugs, make sweeping changes in their lives, live on when their cancer is "terminal," or defy the hormones and brain circuitry that "dictate" lust or femininity or memory loss.

Clay is one of many who ignored the conventional wisdom that his problem was "biological" and found just the right psychotherapy, which worked quickly and permanently.

> *Out of the blue, about once a week, Clay, a software designer, was having panic attacks. His heart started to pound, he couldn't catch his breath, and he was sure he was going to die. After about an hour of terror, the panic subsided. Clay underwent four years of psychoanalysis, which gave him insight into his childhood feelings of abandonment but didn't lessen the panic attacks. Then he was on high doses of Xanax (alprazolam, a tranquilizer) for a year; during that time he only panicked once a month, but he was so sleepy most of the time that he lost his two biggest accounts. So Clay stopped taking Xanax and the panic returned with unabated fury. Two years ago, he had ten sessions of cognitive therapy for panic disorder. He corrected his mistaken belief that the symptoms of anxiety (e.g., heart racing, shortness of breath) are catastrophic: symptoms of an impending heart attack. Since then he hasn't had a single attack.*

As the ideologies of biological psychiatry and self-improvement collide, a resolution is apparent. There are some things about ourselves that can be changed, others that cannot, and some that can be changed only with extreme difficulty.

What can we succeed in changing about ourselves? What can we not? Why did Trudy fail and Clay succeed? When can we overcome our biology? When is our biology our destiny? These are the central questions I will address in this book.

A great deal is now known about change. Much of this knowledge exists only in the technical literature, and it has often been obfuscated by vested commercial, therapeutic, and, not the least, political interests. The behaviorists long ago told the world that everything can be changed—intelligence, sexuality, mood, masculinity or femininity. The psychoanalysts still claim that with enough insight, all your personality traits can be "worked through." The Marxist left, the "politically correct," and the self-help industry added their voices to this convenient chorus. In contrast, the pharmaceutical companies, the biologists mapping the human genome, and the extreme right wing tell us that our character is fixed, that we are prisoners of our genes and the chemicals bathing our brains, that short of powerful drugs, genetic engineering, or brain surgery, nothing basic can change: certainly not mood, or intelligence, or sexuality, or masculinity. These are all ideologically driven falsehoods.

Here are some facts about what you can change:

- Panic can be easily unlearned, but cannot be cured by medication.
- The sexual "dysfunctions"—frigidity, impotence, premature ejaculation—are easily unlearned.
- Our moods, which can wreak havoc with our physical health, are readily controlled.
- Depression can be cured by straightforward changes in conscious thinking or helped by medication, but it cannot be cured by insight into childhood.
- Optimism is a learned skill. Once learned, it increases achievement at work and improves physical health.

Here are some facts about what doesn't change:

- Dieting, in the long run, almost never works.
- Kids do not become androgynous easily.
- No treatment is known to improve on the natural course of recovery from alcoholism.
- Homosexuality does not become heterosexuality.
- Reliving childhood trauma does not undo adult personality problems.

To deal with what we cannot change, the first step, all too often evaded, is to know what about ourselves will not yield. But that is not the end of the matter; there are usually ways of coping. Much of successful living consists of learning to make the best of a bad situation. My purpose here, in part, is not only to point out what will not easily change but to impart the skills for coping with what you cannot change.

This book is the first accurate and factual guide to what you can change and what you cannot change. Since I am going to argue that so many loudly trumpeted claims about self-improvement, psychotherapy, medication, and genetics are not to be believed, that some things about you will not change no matter how much you try, but that other things will change easily, you should know a little about my qualifications.

I have spent the last thirty years working on the question of "plasticity," academic jargon for what changes and what doesn't. I have worked both sides of the street. I started my academic life in the field pretentiously called "learning." Like most of the social sciences of the 1960s, the psychology of learning was enthusiastically environmental, its ideology a reaction to the still-fresh nightmare of the genetically minded Nazis. Just arrange the rewards and punishments right, learning theory held, and the organism (pigeon, adult human, rat, rhesus monkey, or toddler—it mattered so little that we simply called all of them "S's," for "Subjects") would absorb whatever you wanted to teach it.

My years in the learning laboratory taught me that there were many things organisms wouldn't learn no matter how ingenious the experiment. Rats wouldn't learn that tones predicted poisoning, and pigeons wouldn't learn to peck keys to avoid getting shocked. (Humans are even more resistant to change—but more on that later.) My first book, *The Biological Boundaries of Learning* (1972), set out a theory, "Preparedness," of how natural selection shapes what we can and cannot learn.[1] Evolution, acting through our genes and our nervous system, has made it simple for us to change in certain ways and almost impossible for us to change in others.

With the constraints that evolution places on learning very much in mind, I had to pick my problems carefully. I was and I am an unabashed do-gooder. I wanted to discover things that would relieve suffering—leaving knowledge for knowledge's sake to other, purer souls. Some psychological suffering seemed to me unyielding, unchangeable because of biology. Other problems seemed more tractable, solvable if only I was patient enough, worked hard enough, and was clever enough. I had to discover the "plastic" problems on which to work.

I chose to work on helplessness, depression, and pessimism. Each of these, I found, could be learned and could be unlearned. In 1975, I wrote *Helplessness: On Depression, Development, and Death.* Its focus was on how helplessness was learned in the wake of uncontrollable bad events, and how this posture could devastate the rest of one's life. My most recent book, *Learned Optimism* (1991), was very much the opposite. It spelled out fifteen years of my research documenting the bad news: Habits of pessimism lead to depression, wither achievement, and undermine physical health. The good news is that pessimism can be unlearned, and that with its removal depression, underachievement, and poor health can be alleviated. My present research program is trying to prevent America's most costly mental illness—depression—rather than waiting to attempt cures after it strikes. All this is very much in the spirit of the age of self-improvement and the age of therapy.[2]

A recurring theme of this book will be the need for truth in packaging in psychology and psychiatry; so I had best start by laying out my biases and my background.

The nature of the beast. This book is about the psychological beasts: depression, anxiety, stupidity, meanness, traumatic stress, alcoholism, fatness, sexual "perversion." When I was a callow learning theorist, I knew I was stalking after those beasts. I did not then realize that to understand them I had to take into account another beast, the human beast.

My ideology told me that environment is completely responsible for the psychological beasts. Stupidity is caused by ignorance; provide enough books and education, and you will cure stupidity. Depression and anxiety are caused by trauma, particularly bad childhood experience; minimize bad experience, raise children without adversity, and you will banish depression and anxiety. Prejudice is caused by unfamiliarity; get people acquainted, and prejudice will disappear. Sexual "perversion" is caused by repression and suppression; let it all hang out, and everyone will become lusty heterosexuals.

My bias now is that while this is not wholly wrong, it is seriously incomplete. The long evolutionary history of our species has also shaped our stupidities, our fears, our sadness, our crimes, what we lust after, and much else besides. The species we are combines with what actually happens to us to burden us with psychological beasts or to protect us against them. To understand and undo such malevolent effects, we must face the human beast.

No sacred cows. This book walks a political tightrope. On one side is the racist segment of the right, fervently hoping that intelligence, femininity, and criminality are all entirely genetic. On the other side are many aging 1960s liberals and their "politically correct" campus heirs, condemning all who dare to speak ill of victims; failure, they say, results from poverty, racism, a bad upbringing, a malevolent system, underprivilege, deprivation—from anything but oneself.

My loyalty is not to the right or to the left. I have no patience for their sacred cows or their special pleading. My loyalty is to reasoned argument, to the unfashionable positions that deserve a hearing, to the thoughtful weighing of evidence. I realize that much of what I will say in this book is grist for the agendas of both political positions. I believe that facing the beast entails airing unpopular arguments. When the evidence points toward genetic causes, I will say so. When the evidence points toward a bad environment or bad parenting as responsible, I will say so. When the evidence points toward unchangeability, I will say so. When the evidence points to effective ways of changing, I will say that too.

Outcome studies as best evidence. Suppose for a moment that an epidemic of German measles is predicted. You are pregnant and you know that German measles causes birth defects. Two vaccines, Measex and Pneuplox, are on the market. A famous Hollywood star says on TV that she was given Measex and didn't get German measles. An Olympic sprinter also adds her testimonial. Your best friend has heard good things about Measex. Pneuplox, on the other hand, is not advertising. But it has been tested in what is called an *outcome study,* in which it was administered to five hundred people: Only two of these people contracted German measles. Another five hundred received a sham injection: Twenty-eight of them got German measles. Now assume that Measex has not been so tested. Which vaccine do you want? The one that has passed a rigorous outcome test, of course.

Making up your mind about self-improvement courses, psychotherapy, and medications for you and your family is difficult because the industries that champion them are enormous and profitable and try to sell themselves with highly persuasive means: testimonials, case histories, word of mouth, endorsements ("My doctor is the best specialist on *X* in the East"), all slick forms of advertising. Just as this is no way to pick a vaccine or to decide on whether to have chemotherapy versus radiation for cancer, this is no way to decide on whether to try a particular diet, or whether to send your father to a particular alcohol-treatment center, or whether to take a particular drug for depression or to have psychotherapy. Much better evidence—outcome studies—is now often available.

In the collision between self-improvement and biological psychiatry, the two sides have until recently used different sorts of evidence. The biological psychiatrists started with case histories but then built up to outcome studies—comparing a treated group with a group given a sugar pill, a placebo. The self-improvement and psychotherapy advocates still rely, for the most part, on single case histories and testimonials: before and after snapshots of some formerly obese person, a dramatic case report from a professional football player in Alcoholics Anonymous, a case of sudden recovery from profound depression following an angry confrontation with Mother. Case histories make absorbing reading, but they are clinically very weak, and, usually, self-serving evidence. The seller presents the case history that testifies to his product's effectiveness. You never know how many failures there were.

The evaluation of change has improved recently. When the late Gerald Klerman became director of ADAMHA (the Alcohol, Drug Abuse, and Mental Health Administration of the federal government) under President Jimmy Carter, he argued that psychotherapies should be evaluated in the same hard-nosed way that the Federal Drug Administration evaluates drugs. He funded comparisons of drugs and of psychotherapies. Much of what psychology and psychiatry professionals now know comes from many such careful and costly studies. But little of this has filtered down to the general public, partly because of the power of the drug and psychotherapy guilds. For many problems, we can now assert with confidence that some therapies work and some do not. Little of this technology has found its way into the self-improvement industry, but when I make claims about effectiveness, I will lean heavily on outcome studies. I will often use case histories to illustrate important points, but only when they are backed by more substantial evidence.

These, then, are my biases. Now that you know them, you should also know your own. What are your underlying prejudices about self-improvement? Do you think that therapy can change almost all of your personality traits? Or do you think that character is fixed? Do you think that what you do is the product of choice, of the environment, or of genes?

Lisa Friedman Miller, the author of the following survey, has obtained responses from thousands of people in order to explore how different views of change relate to emotions and politics. There are no right or wrong answers, but your score will tell you where you stand on the crucial issue of change. Circle the choice that best fits your view. This survey will take you less than five minutes.

HUMAN PLASTICITY QUESTIONNAIRE[3]

Tom is shopping at a department store when he spots a sweater that he likes. He goes into the dressing room to try it on but notices that it costs too much money. Tom steals the sweater by covering it with his jacket and then walking out of the store.

What accounts for Tom stealing the sweater from the department store?

Your opinion:

1. How much is Tom's behavior influenced by the immediate situation?

Not at all 1 2 3 4 5 6 7 Very much

2. How much is Tom's behavior influenced by more removed situations (e.g., childhood, race, the system)?

Not at all 1 2 3 4 5 6 7 Very much

3. How much is Tom's behavior influenced by the kind of person he is?

Not at all 1 2 3 4 5 6 7 Very much

4. How much is Tom's behavior influenced by his own decision to act that way?

Not at all 1 2 3 4 5 6 7 Very much

Now suppose that you explained to Tom that what he had done was wrong. You suggested that he change. He agreed that he should change and that he wants to change.

5. How completely could Tom change?

Not at all 1 2 3 4 5 6 7 Completely change

Now suppose that you had never approached Tom on the issue of his behavior.

6. How much do you think Tom would have changed anyway?

Not at all 1 2 3 4 5 6 7 Completely changed

John meets a woman at a friend's party and asks her on a date for the next evening. At the end of their date, John says that he wants to have sex with the woman. When she refuses, he presses her against a wall and starts taking off her clothes.

What accounts for John taking off the woman's clothes?

Your opinion:

1. How much is John's behavior influenced by the immediate situation?

Not at all 1 2 3 4 5 6 7 Very much

2. How much is John's behavior influenced by more removed situations (e.g., childhood, race, the system)?

Not at all 1 2 3 4 5 6 7 Very much

3. How much is John's behavior influenced by the kind of person he is?

Not at all 1 2 3 4 5 6 7 Very much

4. How much is John's behavior influenced by his own decision to act that way?

Not at all 1 2 3 4 5 6 7 Very much

Now suppose that you explained to John that what he had done was wrong. You suggested that he change. He agreed that he should change and that he wants to change.

5. How completely could John change?

Not at all 1 2 3 4 5 6 7 Completely change

Now suppose that you had never approached John on the issue of his behavior.

6. How much do you think John would have changed anyway?

Not at all 1 2 3 4 5 6 7 Completely changed

Dave is on his way home from class when he sees a brand-new automobile on the street. Taking his keys from his pocket, Dave deliberately carves three long lines across the hood of the car.

What accounts for Dave defacing the automobile?

Your opinion:

1. How much is Dave's behavior influenced by the immediate situation?

Not at all 1 2 3 4 5 6 7 Very much

2. How much is Dave's behavior influenced by more removed situations (e.g., childhood, race, the system)?

Not at all 1 2 3 4 5 6 7 Very much

3. How much is Dave's behavior influenced by the kind of person he is?

Not at all 1 2 3 4 5 6 7 Very much

4. How much is Dave's behavior influenced by his own decision to act that way?

Not at all 1 2 3 4 5 6 7 Very much

Now suppose that you explained to Dave that what he had done was wrong. You suggested that he change. He agreed that he should change and that he wants to change.

5. How completely could Dave change?

Not at all 1 2 3 4 5 6 7 Completely change

Now suppose that you had never approached Dave on the issue of his behavior.

6. How much do you think Dave would have changed anyway?

Not at all 1 2 3 4 5 6 7 Completely changed

To score your test, simply add up your numbers for each one of the six questions and fill in the total score below. Each of your totals should be between 3 and 21.

Question 1 (Immediate situation) ______
Question 2 (Removed situation) ______
Question 3 (Character) ______
Question 4 (Choice) ______
Question 5 (Change) ______
Question 6 (Change by himself) ______

What do these scores mean?

Question 1 taps your belief that people are pushed around by the immediate situation. If you scored 18 or above, you are in the quarter that believes most in the potency of the immediate situation; 15 is average; if you scored 9 or below, you are in the quarter of Americans who believe least in the power of immediate circumstances. Democrats tend to score 16 and above, whereas Republicans and independents usually score below 15.

Question 2 is about the importance of a person's life history, and the higher you score, the more you endorse its significance. People who score 19 or more are in the quarter that most believes in life history; above 16 is in the top half; and 12 or below is the most skeptical quarter. The higher you score, the more you endorse welfare, affirmative action, and foreign aid; also, the more depressed you tend to be. The lower you score, the more you are for the death penalty, abortion, and military intervention.

Question 3 is about character. People who score 21 or more are in the quarter that most believes in character; 18 or more is in the upper half; and 14 or less is in the lower quarter. The higher your score, test results have shown, the more you believe in welfare, affirmative action, and economic assistance, and the more you believe in the death penalty, military intervention, and abortion. The older you are, the more you believe in character. As you can see, this scale breaks apart liberal and conservative stereotypes.

Question 4 taps your belief in the power of choice and willpower. The top quarter of Americans score 21; above 19 is in the top half; 16 or below is in the quarter that least believes in the power of choice. People who score high are more socially and economically conservative, less depressed, and older.

Question 5 is about how sweeping you think change can be. A score of 20 or above puts you in the top quarter; 16 or above in the top half; and a score of 10 or below puts you in the bottom quarter. People who score high are socially liberal and more in favor of welfare, affirmative action, and foreign aid.

Question 6 taps your belief in change. If you scored 11 or above, you are in the top quarter of those who believe that things naturally change a lot; 8 or above is the top half; 3 marks the quarter of those who most believe things stay the same. People with high scores believe more in foreign aid, welfare, and affirmative action, and are more socially and economically liberal. People with low scores believe more in the death penalty, military intervention, and abortion.

IN THE DOMAIN of human personality, what are the facts? That, of course, is what this book is about. I want to provide an understanding of what you can and what you can't change about yourself so that you can concentrate your limited time and energy on what is possible. So much time has been wasted. So much needless frustration has been endured. So much of therapy, so much of child rearing, so much of self-improving, and even some of the great social movements in our century have come to nothing because they tried to change the unchangeable. Too often we have wrongly thought we were weak-willed failures, when the changes we wanted to make in ourselves were just not possible. But all this effort was necessary: Because there have been so many failures, we are now able to see the boundaries of the unchangeable; this in turn allows us to see clearly for the first time the boundaries of what *is* changeable.

The knowledge of the difference between what we can change and what we must accept in ourselves is the beginning of real change. With this knowledge, we can use our precious time to make the many rewarding changes that are possible. We can live with less self-reproach and less remorse. We can live with greater confidence. This knowledge is a new understanding of who we are and where we are going.

2

Booters and Bootstrappers: The Age of Self-Improvement and Psychotherapy

"The end of our foundation is the knowledge of causes, and the secret motion of things, and the enlarging of the bounds of human empire for the affecting of all things possible."

Inscription over the door of the
House of Solomon—Francis Bacon,
The New Atlantis, 1626

WHAT AMERICANS believe people can change is—in historical perspective—truly astonishing.

We are told from childhood that we can improve ourselves in almost every way. This is what our schools are supposed to help us accomplish. Our children are not just to be filled up with facts but taught to read, to be good citizens, to be lovingly sexual, to exercise, to have high self-esteem, to enjoy literature, to be tolerant of people who are different, to play baseball, to sing on key, to be competitive as well as cooperative, to lead and to follow, to have good health habits, to be ambitious, to use condoms, to obey the law.

The reality may fall short, but that is the mission of American schools.

Improving is absolutely central to American ideology. It is tantamount in importance to freedom in our national identity; indeed, advancement is probably the end for which Americans believe freedom is the means. Every boy and, at last, every girl might be president of the United States—with enough work and ambition.

The reality may fall short, but that is the ideal that Americans profess.

This is more than empty rhetoric. There is an enormous, and profitable, self-improvement industry that plays to your desire to achieve.

Adult Americans spend billions of dollars and pass tens of billions of hours taking courses in

- Selling
- Dieting
- Memory
- Meditation
- Time Management
- Stress Management
- Charm
- Controlling Anger
- Martial Arts
- Negotiation
- Exercise
- Life Extension
- Relaxation
- Snagging a Mate
- Small Talk
- Reading Speed
- Giving Up Alcohol
- Appreciating Wine
- Giving Up Drugs
- Giving Up On People Who Take Drugs
- Talking to Children
- Talking on the Phone
- Loving Yourself
- Overcoming Fear of Flying
- Interpreting Your Dreams
- Asserting Yourself
- Diplomacy
- Etiquette
- Becoming Funny
- Becoming Less Feminine
- Becoming More Feminine
- Overcoming Homosexuality
- Overcoming Homophobia
- Increasing Intelligence Test Scores
- Learning Optimism
- Drawing with the Right Hemisphere
- Taking Other People's Perspectives
- Winning Friends
- Positive Thinking
- Realistic Thinking
- Becoming Richer Spiritually
- Becoming Richer Materially
- Buying
- Loving Better
- Falling out of Love
- Writing
- Controlling Your Family
- Becoming Less Type A
- Being On Time
- Getting Elected
- Public Speaking
- Music Appreciation
- Performing Music
- Fighting Depression
- Letting Go
- Opening Up
- Picking Up Women
- Picking Up Men
- Math Phobia
- Teaching
- Learning
- Listening

This does little more than scratch the surface of what courses are available. But what all these share is the simple premise that we can change, improve, and advance. Is this so obvious as to not need saying? Its very obviousness, how deeply we all accept it, is just the point—because most of humankind over most of history has not believed anything remotely like this.

Traditionally, most people in the West have believed that human character is fixed and unalterable, that people do not and cannot improve, advance, or perfect themselves. The change from a deep belief in the unchangeability of character to an equally deep belief in the capacity to improve is recent, and it represents one of the most fundamental and important revolutions in modern thought. Strangely, this is a history that has gone unwritten.

How did Americans come to believe so strongly in human plasticity? Where did the belief in psychotherapy come from? From where did our faith in self-improvement emanate?

The Seder and the Road to Damascus

How do we hear and retell the great acts of courage of the Judeo-Christian tradition? Let's examine two of them: the Exodus from Egypt and the conversion of Saul. Do you think that the Israelites, hard oppressed by Pharaoh, screwed up their courage, decided they must have freedom, and bravely gathered themselves up and fled? This is what I thought until I listened more closely to the readings at a recent Seder. Here is the story of the Passover as told in the Haggadah. Listen for who did what to whom.

> And he went down into Egypt, compelled by the word of God, and sojourned there. . . . And the children of Israel were fruitful, increased abundantly, multiplied, and became exceedingly mighty. . . . "I have caused thee to multiply like the growth of the field."
>
> And the Egyptians ill-treated us, afflicted us, and laid heavy bondage upon us.
>
> And we cried unto the Eternal. . . . And the Eternal heard our voice. . . . And the Eternal brought us forth from Egypt, with a strong hand and with an outstretched arm, with great terror, and with signs and wonders.[1]

God is the actor, and the Israelites (and, to a lesser extent, the Egyptians) are the acted-upon. There is almost nothing that the Israelites do that is not caused or commanded by God. Their only act without God's command is to complain. This paradigmatic act of liberation is not portrayed as the act of a brave people resolved on freedom. It is not even commanded by a daring general. Moses, in fact, merely quotes God verbatim, as ordered. God says:

> I will be with thy mouth, and with his [Aaron's] mouth, and will teach you what ye shall do. (Exodus 4:15)

Every step of the way, the good events are wholly the doing of God. When the situation improves, it is not by human agency but by God's intervention. Indeed, this is the central message of the tale and why we are supposed to retell it every Passover.

Examine a different major event, one from Christianity—the conversion of Saul. Do you think that Saul rued his mistreatment of Jesus' followers, was fed up with the old religion, understood with blinded insight the promise of Jesus, and decided to convert? This is what I thought until I reread Acts 9:

> And suddenly there shined round about him a light from heaven:
>
> And he fell to the earth, and heard a voice saying unto him, Saul, Saul, why persecutest thou me?
>
> And he said, Who art thou, Lord? And the Lord said, I am Jesus whom thou persecutest: *it is* hard for thee to kick against the pricks.
>
> And he trembling and astonished said, Lord, what wilt thou have me do? And the Lord *said* unto him, Arise, and go to the city, and it shall be told thee what thou must do. . . .
>
> The Lord . . . hath sent me, that thou mightest receive thy sight, and be filled with the Holy Ghost.
>
> And immediately there fell from his eyes as it had been scales: and he received sight forthwith, and arose, and was baptized.

Again, God is the actor and Saul is passively acquiescent. Saul merely inquires, but God commands. There is no decision making, not a wisp of thought or choice or insight on Saul's part.

The Bible is almost devoid of psychology.[2] You will search the Old Testament and the New Testament in vain for feats of human intention—individual choice, decision, and preference. You will search in vain for some hero wreaking change by his own initiative in a world of adversity. You will search in vain for a character who thinks, weighs the pros and cons, and then acts. God commands Abraham to sacrifice Isaac, the son of his old age. Abraham, without a thought, saddles his ass and sets off.[3] So it goes with the entire dramatis personae of the Bible.

The Bible presents a stunning contrast with modern reportage. When any major event occurs today—an earthquake, the World Cup, a battlefield victory, an assassination, a riot in Los Angeles—reporters badger the participants with "How does it feel?" and "What was going through your mind?" It is anachronistic to wonder how Joshua felt upon toppling the walls of Jericho. This impulse was totally alien to those who reported the monumental doings from the time of Abraham to the time of Jesus. What happened—particularly if it was good, an improvement, an advance—was simply God's intervention in human affairs. Human thought, decision, and intention played no role. The Scriptures militantly and uniformly nullify human agency.

This dogma of human implasticity pervades Western civilization from biblical times through the next two thousand years.

Cracks in the Firmament

This dour view of human advancement—that if things improve, it is only through God's grace—went largely unchallenged through the Middle Ages. While the Middle Ages are no longer characterized as utterly stagnant, there undoubtedly was a great slowing of change in human affairs. For eight hundred years, individual character did not change, and the society did not change much. Sons largely did what their fathers did before them. Women were little noted. The poor remained poor. The rich remained rich. Knowledge, coming only from authority, did not accumulate. Except for astronomy describing the heavenly bodies' movements, science did not progress. The Church was at the center, standing immutable on the Rock of Peter. The pace of change mirrored the ideology.

Then three cracks in the firmament appeared—liberty, science, and free will—and the dogma of human implasticity finally shattered. The first crack was the movement toward individual liberty.

Political liberty. On June 15, 1215, at Runnymede, England, a handful of rebellious barons wrested from King John a document, Magna Carta, that protected them from some of the caprices of their king. While it hardly proclaimed universal suffrage, Magna Carta is certainly the forerunner of freedom as we know it:

> No freeman shall be taken, or imprisoned, or disseised [dispossessed], or outlawed, or exiled, or in any way destroyed, nor will we go upon him, nor will we send upon him, except by the legal judgment of his peers or by the law of the land. . . .
>
> All persons are to be free to come and go, except outlaws and prisoners.

The growth of freedom was glacial in its pace, however, and it was more than four centuries before civil war broke out in England, Charles I was beheaded, and the Commonwealth declared. It was almost six centuries before the American Revolution realized John Locke's claim that government derives its power from the consent of the governed. This was followed in 1789 by the even more sweepingly democratic Declaration of the Rights of Man of the French Revolution.

The movement toward liberty had now become a torrent. For our purposes, it is one of the three streams that washed away the dogma that human character cannot change and that individuals cannot, without the intervention of God, improve or advance.

The second crack was the belief that we are not completely at the mercy of nature.

Science can manipulate nature. Until the Renaissance, Western science did little but describe God's creation, though detailed observation of the tides and of the heavenly bodies predicted eclipses, and sometimes even floods, pretty well. Given the prevailing worldview that humans were powerless to change the nature of things and that all knowledge depended upon authority, the feeble science of the era should come as no surprise.

Enter Francis Bacon, one of the truly iconoclastic minds of the Renaissance. Bacon, who it has been speculated wrote the works attributed to Shakespeare and was the bastard son of the Virgin Queen, Elizabeth I, was born in 1561. His father was Nicholas Bacon, keeper of the great seal of England, and his mother was Anne Cooke, lady-in-waiting to Elizabeth. Bacon senior was notable for his social progress: He had been a clerk before Henry VIII established the Anglican church, but when Henry abolished the monasteries, and was short of loyalists to run things, he promoted Nicholas Bacon, among other formerly humble men. Bacon senior leapt social barriers, becoming the first member of his family to rise in class. First the Black Death had destroyed the feudal system; now Henry had disenfranchised many of the gentry, opening up the higher-status jobs that the myriad plague dead and Henry's new enemies had once filled. Whole families scrambled upward. Francis Bacon grew up knowing that the social order is not fixed.

Francis Bacon entered Cambridge at twelve (no artificially prolonged adolescence in this subsistence economy) and immediately loathed the mandatory Aristotelian curriculum that then passed for knowledge. He rebelled against it openly. In a breathtaking break with the past, he urged us to look to nature—not to authority—for knowledge in order to benefit humankind. Science should not be restricted merely to observing nature passively, he said. Humans can actually manipulate nature (just as he had learned that man could alter the social order). We can do experiments. If we want to know why water is boiling, we should not consult Aristotle or the Church. We can experiment and find out. We remove the fire and the boiling stops. We rekindle the fire and the boiling resumes. Fire is the cause.

Science can change things, Bacon told us. Within fifty years Isaac Newton had unlocked the secrets of motion. This was followed rapidly by an explosion of knowledge in medicine, agriculture, and economics. In a burst of activity, the next two centuries witnessed human beings changing their kings, their God, and Nature herself. Perhaps human beings, as individuals, could even change themselves. But for this to become plausible, the final crack in the firmament had to appear. It did, and in deceptively academic guise—in debate among theologians.

Free will. In the 1480s, heretics were burned at the stake all over Europe. The infamous *Malleus Maleficarum,* a guide to detecting witches and torturing them into confessing, was published. With the stench of burning flesh in his nostrils, Giovanni Pico della Mirandola, a young Ferraran aristocrat, arrived in Rome and defied the dogma of human implasticity. In his *Oration: On the Dignity of Man,* Pico's God tells Adam

> Neither a determined dwelling place, nor a unique shape, nor a role that is peculiarly your own have we given you, O Adam, so that you may have and possess what habitation, shape, and roles you yourself may wish for according to your desire and as you decide. The nature of all the rest is defined and encompassed by laws prescribed by us; you, restrained by no limitations, of your own free will in whose hand I have placed you, shall appoint your own nature.[4]

Pico revels in the vision that man is free to choose. Man is endowed by his Creator with the potential of raising himself above all created beings, even above the angels.

The pope condemned Pico and prohibited his writings. Pico wandered barefoot through the world and died of fever at age thirty-one.

But within thirty years, the Protestant Reformation was in full swing. The Catholic church lost its monopoly on the spiritual life of Europe. The Reformation was decidedly not, however, a celebration of free will. Luther dismissed freedom of the will, viewing humanity as having been created vile and powerless: Everyone is fallen, all of us merit damnation.[5]

John Calvin then argued that everyone is damned or saved even before they are born. God predestines some of us to eternal life and the rest of us to eternal death. His elect are kept by God in faith and holiness through their lives. Worldly success can be an emblem of their election. No actions you undertake, no choices you make, will change your fate. Unaided, humans are incapable of choosing good, and human reason is incapable of knowing a single truth beyond the mere existence of God. Good works do not produce grace. Your destiny is sealed before you are born.

If this is so, why should people bother to try to be good? How could people be held responsible for their actions? The theological battle for human agency was engaged. On the outcome of this monumental battle hinged the very fate of the idea that humans can change and advance themselves. By the beginning of the seventeenth century, liberal Dutch Protestants, led by Jacobus Arminius (the latinization of Jacob Harmensen), claimed that man has free will and participates in his election to grace.[6] To be saved we must meet God, if not halfway, some of the way. This was dubbed "the Arminian Heresy."

This debate continued for almost two hundred years, with inroads made by the Arminians in Holland immediately and in England one hundred years later during the Restoration purge of the Calvinists. This "heresy" then became popular through the evangelical preaching of John Wesley, the English cofounder of Methodism, who preached this doctrine of salvation widely. First, Wesley declared, humans have free will:

> He was endowed with a will, exerting itself in various affections and passions; and, lastly, with liberty, or freedom of choice; without which all the rest would have been in vain . . . he would have been as incapable of vice or virtue as any part of inanimate creation. In these, in the power of self motion, understanding, will, and liberty, the natural image of God consisted.[7]

Wesley told the masses who turned out for his sermons that God offers salvation *in general,* but that humans, using free will, actively participate in attaining their own salvation by using the "means":

> The sure and general rule for all who groan for the salvation of God is this—Whenever opportunity serves, use all the means which God has ordained; for who knows in which God will meet thee with the grace that bringeth salvation?[8]

Wesley's charismatic sermons, heard through the cities, towns, and villages of England, Wales, and Northern Ireland, and in the American colonies, and the efficiency of the organizations he set up to keep the converted from backsliding made Methodism a strong and popular religion. Free will now entered popular consciousness. Ordinary people no longer saw themselves as passive vessels waiting to be filled with grace. Ordinary human life could be improved. Ordinary people could act to better themselves. Even the insane, formerly thought hopeless, were now unshackled from their prison walls. In 1792, Philippe Pinel, newly appointed chief physician of La Bicêtre asylum in Paris, boldly struck the chains from his patients in the presence of the leaders of the French Revolution.

SO BY THE BEGINNING of the nineteenth century, the three cracks in the dogma of human implasticity had grown into irreparable fissures. The American and French revolutions had been fought and won; many had attained a large measure of political liberty. It was widely believed that science could change nature, that humans need not sit passively by and let nature grind them down, that human beings have free will. It followed that human beings could change and better themselves. The dogma of human implasticity that had lasted almost two thousand years and had paralyzed human progress was at last overthrown.

The Dogma of Human Plasticity

There was no better soil than that of nineteenth-century America for this new dogma. Rugged individualism was America's answer to the unraveling European mind-set of human implasticity. All of these fed the faith:

- the democratic idea that all men are created equal
- an endless frontier for the poor to find riches
- waves of immigrants, subsistence laborers who were soon clamoring for power
- the gold rush
- the motto "Rags to Riches"
- universal schooling
- the notion of criminal rehabilitation
- public libraries
- the freeing of the slaves
- the drive toward women's suffrage

- a new religious liberalism that emphasized free will and good works as the road to heaven
- the idealization of the entrepreneur—ambition and initiative incarnate

The Federalists, skeptical that the people could govern themselves wisely ("Your people, sir—your people is a great *beast!*" declared Alexander Hamilton), soon lost their hold on power to the Democrats. Few now advocated human implasticity. The first half of the nineteenth century became a great age of social reform. The evangelical religious movement of the American frontier was intensely individualistic, the meetings climaxing with the drama of the choice of Christ. Utopian communities sprang up to achieve human perfection.

It was commonly accepted that humans could change and improve. Andrew Jackson, when he was president-elect, gave voice to it:

> I believe man can be elevated; man can become more and more endowed with divinity; and as he does he becomes more God-like in his character and capable of governing himself. Let us go on elevating our people, perfecting our institutions, until democracy shall reach such a point of perfection that we can acclaim with truth that the voice of the people is the voice of God.[9]

There were two dominant opinions in this era as to who can be the agent of change; both are still very much with us as we enter the next millennium.

The booters and the bootstrappers. The *booters* believed that people can improve, but that *the agent of change must be someone else.* For some of the booters, the means of change was the therapist who guides the patient into change. Freud, the founder of the therapeutic movement, tried self-analysis and gave up.

> My self-analysis remains interrupted. I have realized why I can analyze myself only with the help of knowledge obtained objectively (like an outsider). True self-analysis is impossible; otherwise there would be no neurotic illness.[10]

When the analysand and the analyst are the same, the conflicts that distort thinking and impede insight are insuperable.

For other booters, the means of human advancement was changing the social institutions. These reformers founded public libraries, installed universal schooling, advocated rehabilitation of criminals, urged moral treatment of the insane, marched for women's suffrage and abolition of slavery, and founded Utopian communities. They still march today. Marx epitomized this view of change: Humans are prisoners of the capitalistic economic system; change the economic system, put the means of production into the hands of the workers, and thereby change humanity for the better.

Out of this group, the idea of a "social science" emerged. In the wake of Chicago's Haymarket Riot of 1886, in which seventy policemen were injured and one killed by armed strikers, class warfare became apparent to American opinion makers. Their explanation of bad behavior shifted from bad character (immutable and individual) to poverty and social class (changeable and general). The cure was to improve the environment of the lower class, since the individual perpetrators were not responsible. Theologians asked "not how every individual was responsible, but how they could be responsible for the many who were not."[11] The science of social institutions took this program as its agenda.

For still other booters, the means of change was to manipulate the environmental contingencies that affect the individual. The behaviorists, led by John Watson, told us that the child is totally a product of the environment. Watson said in 1920 that the only way to change

> is to remake the individual by changing his environment in such a way that new habits have to form. The more completely they change, the more the personality changes. Few individuals can do all this unaided.[12]

The science of learning theory was dedicated to this proposition (B. F. Skinner was the most popular recent advocate of this worldview).

All these propositions share the notion that people will change. But they need to be booted into it—by a therapist, by reformed social institutions, by benevolent manipulation of the environment. People can't change on their own. The booters are the heirs of Francis Bacon.

The *bootstrappers* are the heirs of the individualism of Pico, Arminius, and Wesley. The agent of change is the self: Human beings can lift themselves by their own bootstraps.

For some of the bootstrappers, self-improvement had theological roots, derived from Wesley and nineteenth-century liberal Protestantism melded with the American doctrine of "rugged individualism." Norman Vincent Peale's *The Power of Positive Thinking,* published in 1952, and Robert Schuller's present-day Sunday-morning preaching in the Crystal Cathedral have touched the lives of tens of millions of Americans.[13] Individuals believe that they can achieve success in this world by improving themselves, and salvation in the next by good works. Emile Coué, the French pharmacist who urged turn-of-the-century pill takers to accompany their medication with the thought "Every day and in every way, I am becoming better and better," was a worthy secular forerunner of these contemporary religious bootstrappers.

Humanistic psychologists are also bootstrappers. Abraham Maslow urged "self-actualization" as the highest form of human motivation, though it is only when more basic needs—like food, safety, love, and self-esteem—are slaked that we can achieve it. The ideas of will, responsibility, and freedom command center stage in existential and humanistic psychotherapy; patients can even have disorders of will, and therapy emphasizes widening the capacity to choose.

The advocates of Alcoholics Anonymous (AA) are also bootstrappers. In 1935, Dr. Robert H. Smith began AA, and since that time AA has assisted perhaps a million people in giving up alcohol, a problem that had once seemed quite hopeless. AA is not pure bootstrapping, however: One element in recovery is individual determination and will. This is coupled with a belief in assistance from a Higher Power and vigorous social support from the group. In fact, AA is a curious mix of the seemingly conflicting elements of self-improvement and acceding to a higher power, and I will look at its doctrines and its successes and failures more closely in the chapter on alcoholism.

In twentieth-century America, somewhere between the ministrations of the booters and the boosterism of the bootstrappers, the dogma of human implasticity died. The old dogma has been replaced by a new dogma, its opposite, which maintains that human beings can always change and improve—by the agency of others and by themselves. Like the dogma it has usurped, the new one makes sweeping claims. *All* aspects of human character, it says, can, with enough effort, or learning, or insight, yield and change for the better.

Is the dogma of human plasticity true?

The Maximal Self

Many widespread beliefs are true. Some, like the medieval belief that the moon is covered with a crystal sphere, are false: Some are self-fulfilling. The rest of this book is about whether the belief in limitless human plasticity is true. But before evaluating it, I want to emphasize that the belief that we can change ourselves differs from most other beliefs. It has, at the very least, one remarkable self-fulfilling aspect.

The society we live in exalts the self—the self that can change itself and can even change the way it thinks. Our economy increasingly thrives on individual whim. Our society grants power to the self that selves have never had before. We live in the age of personal control.

When the assembly line was created at the turn of this century, we could buy only white refrigerators. Painting every refrigerator the same color saved money. In the 1950s, the development of rudimentary machine intelligence created a bewildering range of choices. It became possible (and profitable, if there was a market for it) to, say, encrust every hundredth refrigerator with rhinestones.

Such a market was created by the glorification of individual choice. Now all jeans are no longer blue; they come in dozens of colors and hundreds of varieties. With the permutation of available options, you are offered a staggering number of different models of new cars. There are hundreds of kinds of aspirin and a thousand kinds of beer.

To create a market for all these products, advertising whipped up a great enthusiasm for personal control. The deciding, choosing, pleasure-preoccupied self became big business. (Now there is even a successful magazine called *Self*.) When the individual has a lot of money to spend, individualism becomes a profitable worldview.

Since World War II, America has become a rich country. Although tens of millions have been left out of the prosperity, Americans on the average now have more buying power than any other people in history. Our wealth is tied to the bewildering array of choices opened to us by the selfsame process that produced the rhinestone refrigerator. We have more food, more clothes, more education, more concerts, more books, and more marketed knowledge to choose from than any other people has ever had.

Who chooses? The self. The modern self is not the peasant of yore, with a fixed future yawning ahead. He (and now she, effectively doubling the market—and add in kids) is a frantic trading floor of options, decisions, and preferences. The result is a kind of self never before seen on the planet—the Maximal Self.

The self has a history. We have seen that until the Renaissance the self was minimal; in a Fra Angelico painting everyone but Jesus looks just like everyone else. With Pico and Bacon the self expanded, and in the works of El Greco and Rembrandt the bystanders no longer look like interchangeable members of a chorus. By Andrew Jackson's time the self, wielding political power, possessing free will, and capable of divine perfectibility, had become elaborate.

Our wealth and our technology have now culminated in a self that, to a degree never experienced before, chooses, feels pleasure and pain, dictates action, optimizes, and even has rarefied attributes—like esteem and efficacy and confidence and control and knowledge. I call this new self, with its absorbing concern for its gratifications and losses, the Maximal Self, to distinguish it from what it has replaced, the Minimal Self, the self of the Bible and of Luther. The Minimal Self did little more than just behave; it was certainly less preoccupied with how it felt. It was more concerned with duty.

Advocating self-improvement would have made no sense before the rise of the Maximal Self. A society that views tornadoes as God's will does not build tornado shelters. Even if it does, people will not go into them or even listen to the radio for tornado warnings. A society that views drinking as stemming from a bad and immutable character will not try to get alcoholics to refrain from drinking. A society that views depression as stemming from bad genes or unfortunate brain chemistry will not attempt to have depressives change what they think when they encounter failure. Notions of therapy, rehabilitation, and self-improvement do not arise in a society of Minimal Selves, which would not be much interested in psychology in the first place. Believing the dogma of human implasticity, the Minimal Self does not act to change itself.

But when a society exalts the self, as ours does, the self, its thoughts, and their consequences become objects of careful science, of therapy and of improvement. This improving self is not a chimera. Self-improvement and therapy often work well, and it is a belief in human plasticity that underlies these strategies. The Maximal Self believes that it can change and improve, and this very belief allows change and improvement. The dogma of human plasticity tends to fulfill itself.

3

Drugs, Germs, and Genes: The Age of Biological Psychiatry

FOR ALL THEIR CURRENCY, self-improvement and psychotherapy are viewed by many with skepticism and even disdain, for this is also the age of biological psychiatry, with its biomedical vision of emotion, personality, and mental illness. It has three basic principles:

- Mental illness is really physical illness.
- Emotion and mood are determined by brain chemistry.
- Personality is determined by genes.

All three run counter to the idea that we can change ourselves—with or without a therapist. Biological psychiatry has a radically different vision of change:

- Curing the underlying physical illness cures mental illness.
- Drugs cure negative emotions and moods.
- Our personality is fixed.

This is the extreme position. There are many compromise positions that refer to the "interaction" of biology and environment, genetic "contribution," "preparedness," and genetic "predispositions." Some of these compromises are just anesthetics, numbing us into thinking that the fundamental dispute between nature and nurture has somehow been solved or is a pseudoquestion. Much of this book is about reasonable in-between positions, but this chapter is not. It lays out the extreme position, and the extreme position is neither frivolous nor is it a straw man. It represents the bedrock beliefs of a very large part of the biomedical world. This view emerges from three momentous discoveries.

The Italian Pox, the French Pox, the English Pox

The worst epidemic of madness in recorded history began a few years after Columbus discovered the New World and continued with mounting ferocity until the beginning of our century. It afflicted the mighty—from Henry VIII to Randolph Churchill, Winston's brilliant, erratic father—along with the ordinary. First there was a weakness in the arms and legs, then eccentricity, then downright delusions of grandeur, then global paralysis, stupor, and death. The malady took its name from its final, paralytic symptom: general paresis.

By 1884, the asylums of Europe burst with men in the final stages of this disease, shrieking obscenities. Controversy swirled over its cause. Established opinion, led by the dean of German psychiatry, Wilhelm Griesinger, held that paresis comes from loose living, especially from inhaling bad cigars. A minority—empirical scientists rather than armchair psychiatrists, among them the young Richard von Krafft-Ebing—held that it comes from syphilis.

Griesinger would have none of this. How could it come from syphilis? Many paretics had had no sexual contact for years. Almost all heatedly denied ever having had syphilis. A few others may have had syphilis, but twenty or thirty years before—a sore on their penises for a week and then the sore disappeared. How could paresis possibly come from syphilis?

Scientists then could not just look into the brain of one of these dead paretics and see if the syphilitic germ was present. In this era, microscopes were still primitive and tissue stains even worse. When you looked into the brain, what you saw was grayish-white mush. Moreover, the syphilitic organism was unknown—it was just a hypothetical germ; no one had ever seen it. The evidence was mounting, however, that paresis was a disorder of the brain: The pupils of paretics' eyes didn't contract when light was flashed on them, and the autopsied brains of dead paretics were shrunken.

It was not only Griesinger who denied that this mental illness is a disease of the body. Unlike today, when we argue that madness is either mental or physical, nineteenth-century common sense held otherwise. Madness was a *moral* defect, the outward manifestation of a bad character. Strange as this sounds to our ears, this belief was an advance over the common sense of earlier centuries, which had held that madness was possession by the Devil.

Krafft-Ebing changed all this. In one of the most daring experiments in psychiatric history, he showed that general paresis is caused by syphilis. He showed this without once looking at the brain, and he showed this thirty years before anyone was to glimpse *Treponema pallidum,* the syphilitic spirochete, through a microscope. He knew, as did all street-wise males, that syphilis, like measles or mumps, was a disease you could not catch twice. If you got a sore on your penis once after intercourse with an infected woman, you would be uncomfortable for a few weeks: Urination stung; you might run a fever. After that you seemed to be safe and could then enjoy unlimited pleasure with even the most notorious whores, and never get another sore.

Krafft-Ebing experimented on nine of his patients, all middle-aged men with delusions of grandeur, all of whom vehemently denied ever having had the shameful "French pox" (the Germans called it the French pox; the French called it the Italian pox; the Italians called it the English pox). He scraped material from the penile sores of men who had just contracted syphilis (no armchair science, this) and injected it into these nine paretics.

Not one of the nine developed a sore. The controversy was settled by one monumental experiment. All nine of these men must already have had syphilis, and the syphilitic germ must therefore cause, by some very slow process, general paresis.

Supporting evidence soon cascaded in. *Treponema pallidum* was discovered, and was found in the brains of paretics. A simple blood test was developed to detect syphilis, and "606," so named because six hundred and five prior concoctions had failed, was created—it killed *Treponema* and thus prevented paresis.

So successful was Krafft-Ebing's work that the most common mental illness of the nineteenth century was eradicated within a generation. (When we look for paretics in Philadelphia—where I teach at the University of Pennsylvania—to instruct present-day medical students, it is very hard to find one.) But Krafft-Ebing, this scientist of courage and genius, accomplished more than just discovering the cause of paresis. With this discovery, he convinced the medical world of something much more global: *Mental illness is just an illness of the body.* This became the first principle, the rallying cry, and the agenda for the new field of biological psychiatry. A century of research on schizophrenia, depression, Alzheimer's, and many other problems hypothesized as stemming from some underlying brain disorder followed. Schizophrenia is now seen as caused by too much of a neurotransmitter in the brain; depression by too little of another neurotransmitter; Alzheimer's by the deterioration of certain nerve centers; overweight by the underactivity of another center (the verdict is in on none of this).

It follows for all mental illness that real change is possible only after eliminating the physical illness. Kill the spirochetes, for example, and the mental deterioration ends. Raise the neurotransmitter level and cure depression; lower the level and cure schizophrenia. Lobotomize—cut out the appropriate brain centers—and cure the anxiety disorders. Reset the appetite center with a drug and cure overweight. Psychotherapy for a biological illness, from this point of view, is sentimental nonsense. At best, it might be cosmetic: A therapist might help a paretic adjust to his worsening mental and physical state; a therapist might urge a schizophrenic not to forget to take his pills and not to tell his boss about his delusions.

Drugs and Emotion

Here is what florid psychosis look like:

> *Lester shows up at his father's dry-goods store one morning in a terrifying costume. He is stark naked, painted a dull brownish red from head to toe, and is daubed with slime. There is an enormous barbed fishhook sticking out of his cheek.*[1]
>
> *"I'm a worm!" he babbles as he crawls along the floor. The cashier calls the police, and Lester is dragged off to Baptist Memorial Hospital.*
>
> *In the hospital, Lester is floridly schizophrenic. He hallucinates the sounds of fish in a feeding frenzy. He believes that he is the object of their frenzy. He retains the singular delusion that he is a worm, probably related to his despair over his girlfriend's walking out on him ("You worm!" she shouted as she slammed the door). His mood fluctuates wildly from terror to giddy mania to deep sadness.*
>
> *Lester is as crazy as they come. But what happens next seems little short of a miracle. It is the late summer of 1952. One of the residents at Baptist Memorial has just returned to Memphis from a year in France. Before he left Europe, he had heard a startling paper delivered in Luxembourg at the French Congress of Psychiatrists and Neurologists. Professor Jean Delay, chief psychiatrist at the Hôpital Sainte-Anne in Paris, announced a breakthrough in the treatment of psychosis.*

Psychosis: the most ferocious mental illness. In 1952, the back wards of mental hospitals in Paris, New York, Moscow, and Memphis were filled beyond their capacities with patients like Lester. These wards were called "snake pits." The inmates were hallucinating and unreachable, or mutely catatonic, or wild with delusions and straitjacketed, or giggling out word salad, or simply broken, with their faces turned toward the wall. Everything was tried on these schizophrenics: electroshock therapy, artificial hibernation, lobotomy, insulin shock, cocktails of drugs. Nothing worked. The psychotic might have some remissions, but his future was widely believed to be hopeless.

Delay announced a cure. He and Pierre Deniker had tested a new antihistamine, synthesized for hay fever by the Rhone-Poulenc drug company two years earlier. Their patients became amazingly calm: Delusions dissolved in a matter of days, like shakos of snow melting slowly off a tree after an ice storm on a warm winter morning. The psychotics' contact with the real world resumed.

At Lester's case conference there is a heated quarrel. The psychoanalysts advocate psychotherapy. They believe that his delusion is caused by homosexual panic. All schizophrenia is "latent homosexuality," they say. Drugging Lester will only be cosmetic, and, worse, it may impede his gaining insight into his underlying conflict. But the resident fresh from Paris is dogged. He reiterates Delay's findings and he prevails. Lester is injected with this new drug, chlorpromazine. He relaxes immediately. (The new drug was described as a "major tranquilizer.") By the weekend, Lester is aghast at his garb and washes off all traces of the paint. The idea that he is a worm now seems as crazy to him as it does to us. Within three weeks, Lester is back at work as a stock boy.

The new drug exploded across the psychiatric world. At every major medical center, chlorpromazine was used for psychotic patients, and, by and large, it worked. Most got better in a few weeks. Many got astonishingly better. Even some patients who had vegetated mutely in the back wards for a decade or more recovered and were discharged within months. The back wards emptied out, and psychiatric beds became readily available for the first time in years.

Thus began the drug revolution, dubbed "the third revolution" in psychiatry. The first had been Pinel's striking the shackles of the insane; the second was Freud's invention of psychoanalysis. The premise of the drug revolution is that *disordered mood and emotion reflect disordered brain chemistry. Correct the chemistry of the brain with drugs, and correct mood and emotion.*

The drug revolution spread rapidly. Drugs were compatible with the venerable disease model. Giving drugs rescued psychiatrists from the disdainful skepticism of their more traditionally scientific medical colleagues. Drugs were cheap and quick. Drugs were very big business, and there was a huge lobby to sell them to physicians, to Congress, to the media, and to the public.

And drugs worked. Case histories poured in. Outcome studies of the new antipsychotics were done, and the drugs were usually more effective than sugar pills given to control groups. Perhaps 60 percent of the patients improved, though few recovered completely.[2]

Depression, mania, and anxiety. As the fervor for drugging psychotics grew, new drugs were tried on patients suffering from other maladies. The first antidepressant was discovered by accident: A new drug had been tried on tuberculosis. The patients improved. They were pleased. Enormously pleased. They danced in the corridors and shouted in ecstasy. The drug—iproniazid—was primarily a euphoriant. It also relieved depression. The first year it was available, 1957, 400,000 patients were treated with it.[3] Unfortunately, iproniazid is toxic, even occasionally lethal. It was soon outsold by milder antidepressants, called tricyclics, as the drug companies fell over each other to mint new, slightly different (and therefore patentable) versions. These also worked, and their side effects were subtler. About 65 percent of patients became less depressed.[4] Prozac, hyped as "A Breakthrough Drug for Depression" on the cover of *Newsweek* in 1990, works at just the same rate as the earlier medications, but milder side effects were claimed.[5] Prozac seized the lion's share of the market.

The antidepressants were moderately helpful. In contrast, a true "miracle" drug—lithium carbonate—was discovered for mania. John Cade, an Australian physician, working alone and under primitive conditions, found that the urine of his manic patients killed guinea pigs: The rodents trembled, twitched violently, collapsed, and died. He injected them with lithium, an element known to be a poison, and the guinea pigs became calm and lethargic—and they survived injections of the manics' urine. Cade then tried lithium on the manic humans whose urine was so lethal. Within days their agitation, their racing thoughts, their distractibility, and their euphoric excitement gave way to calm.[6]

By 1970, psychiatrists prescribed lithium routinely for manic-depression. Before lithium, manic-depression was a crippling and hopeless illness: 15 percent of manic-depressive patients killed themselves, and most—many manic-depressives are very talented—could not hold jobs. So obnoxious are manics that their families were universally miserable, and 60 percent of their marriages ended in divorce (in the days when divorce was rare). With lithium, this is no longer so. Roughly 80 percent of manic-depressives are helped by it, most of them markedly.[7]

The biggest splash was made with the anti-anxiety drugs. Anxiety has usually been thought of as an inevitable, if uncomfortable and disorganizing, part of life we all face. Freud thought of it as the fundamental emotion, and the first half of this century was dubbed the age of it. When extreme and out of control, however, anxiety is indisputably a clinical problem.

In the mid-1950s, Miltown (meprobamate) was first used with anxious patients, to phenomenal effect: Frenzied patients relaxed almost to jelly in a few minutes, but they remained conscious; and their troubles, which moments before had overwhelmed them, now seemed pleasantly far away. Sleep came easily.

Predictably, Miltown was used promiscuously. The industry race was on. Librium (chlordiazepoxide) replaced Miltown and became the world's number one prescription drug. Valium (diazepam), five times stronger, soon displaced Librium. These drugs presently rival alcohol in their everyday use by Americans. If your troubles make you anxious and you can find a cooperative physician, taking Valium four times a day is quite acceptable.[8] Ours is no longer the Age of Anxiety. It is the Age of Tranquilizers.

The second principle of biological psychiatry seems firmly in place. Drugs, claim their advocates, have conquered psychosis and mania and eliminated the more commonplace moods of depression and anxiety. Emotion and mood are nothing but brain chemistry. If you don't like yours, you can change them with the right drug.

The Seamy Side of Drugs

I have tried to make as sympathetic a case as I can for drugs. I had to restrain myself. Drugs do work on emotion. Mania can be greatly dampened. Depression can be moderately relieved. Anxiety can be almost instantly dispelled. Psychotic delusions can be chemically dissolved.

But there is another side to the story. Why in general do drugs work?

You might entertain the naïve image that the drug swoops down on the invading foreign disease and kills it, like a falcon attacking a rabbit. I have a different image of how a lot of drugs work, and while controversial, it may help you understand the seamy side. In my image, drugs are themselves foreign invaders, just like diseases. Your body regards the drug as a toxin, and your natural defenses are mobilized to fight it off. A side effect is that these mobilized defenses happen to kill off the disease. The true side effect of a drug is to arrest the disease. The main effect of the drug is to produce the unwanted lesser illnesses, euphemistically dubbed side effects.

General paresis itself was first arrested by just such a tactic. In 1917, Julius Wagner von Jauregg, an Austrian psychiatrist, intentionally gave paretics malaria. He reasoned that the "minor" disease of malaria, producing high fever and marshaling other defenses, might kill the major disease of paresis. So it did, and Wagner von Jauregg was awarded the Nobel Prize in 1927, becoming the only psychiatrist ever so honored. In my view, Wagner von Jauregg's tactic was not a peculiar medical tactic. Drugs usually work the same way: by inducing a lesser malady to cure a greater malady.

Psychosis. Antipsychotic drugs seem to "work" about 60 percent of the time, although, surprisingly, well-done outcome studies are scarce. A large minority of patients do not benefit[9] (though "benefit" is not exactly a straightforward term, even when the drugs *do* work—the drugs *relieve* the symptoms, but the patients do not recover completely). Schizophrenics become more manageable—quieter, less bizarre, more docile—but they are still schizophrenics. This is convenient for hospital staff and can easily be mistaken for a cure.

Lester still finds himself with strange thoughts, but they are not as compelling as they once were. He has also learned not to talk about being a worm, though he often still thinks he really is one.

Sadly, Lester, plagued once again by delusions, has returned to the hospital for monthlong bouts of delusions six times since 1952.

Back-ward overcrowding was ended by the drugs, but it was replaced with a "revolving door." Many of the people we see lying on grates in large American cities got there by being released, again and again, from mental hospitals by virtue of the antipsychotic drugs. Out on the street, they deteriorate once more—either because they stop taking their drugs or because their drugs lose effect—and the police soon bring them back to the hospital.

Psychotics do not stop taking their medication only because of confusion or absentmindedness. I once was a "pseudopatient" and got myself admitted to the locked men's ward of Norristown (Pennsylvania) State Hospital. I noticed a rush to the bathroom at medication time and followed my fellow patients. There I found a long line of patients who had hidden their pills under their tongues and were, one by one, depositing their pills into the toilet bowl.[10]

The antipsychotic drugs produce nasty side effects. The most noticeable are cardiac arrhythmia; low blood pressure; uncontrollable restlessness and fidgeting; immobility of the face, robbing the patient of the ability to smile; tremor; and a shuffling gait. A few patients die. A devastating, and especially hideous, side effect is tardive dyskinesia, when the drugs destroy something (as yet unknown) in the brain's control of movement. Its victims suck and smack their lips uncontrollably.

> *Lester's family pretends not to notice. But Lester often looks like a frog catching flies.*

Between one-quarter and one-third of drugged patients develop this deformity. The longer you take the drug, the more likely it is that tardive dyskinesia will develop. And once it starts, it is completely irreversible.[11]

Depression. Antidepressant drugs work about 65 percent of the time. Like the antipsychotics, they are cosmetic. Once you stop taking them, you are just as likely to relapse or have a fresh attack of depression as you were before. They do not alter the deep pessimism and helplessness characteristic of depressives. When you recover from depression using a drug, you have acquired no new skills and no new insights into how to handle life's recurrent setbacks. You credit your recovery to a drug or to a benevolent physician, not to yourself.

Antidepressants, like antipsychotics, have nasty side effects. The monoamine-oxidase (MAO) inhibitors, a once commonly used type of antidepressant, can be fatal. The tricyclics are milder, but they can produce cardiac problems, mania, confusion and memory loss, and extreme fatigue; a large minority of patients cannot tolerate them. The newest entry—Prozac—produces less drowsiness, dry mouth, and sweating than the older ones, but it produces more nausea, nervousness, and insomnia. Eli Lilly, its maker, may now be reaping the consequences of premature media hype, for there are case histories suggesting that Prozac causes unprecedented suicidal preoccupation. No controlled study has yet been done.[12]

Anxiety. Anti-anxiety drugs relieve anxiety. They relax you dramatically and make life seem rosier. But like the antidepression and antipsychotic drugs, they are cosmetic. Once you stop taking them, anxiety returns in full force. Worse, when the anxiety stems from a real problem, you find you have done nothing in the meantime to surmount it. To the extent that anxiety is a message to do something about your life, anti-anxiety drugs prevent your getting the message. In addition, these drugs are overused in anxiety disorders: They are probably useless for panic disorder and for generalized anxiety disorder.[13]

Anti-anxiety drugs do not have the nasty side effects that the antipsychotics and antidepressants have. They probably won't kill you, even in megadoses. But unlike the others, the antianxiety drugs become less potent the longer you take them, and they probably are addictive.[14]

Mania. Lithium works well on mania. The main problem with lithium is that many manics refuse to take it because they like staying manic. In past centuries lithium had been used as a drug, but it was in disrepute (because it produced heart attacks) when John Cade, the Australian researcher, revived it by discovering its anti-manic property. Unlike the rest of the aforementioned drugs, lithium therefore generated few unpleasant surprises.[15] The medical field was forewarned, and from the outset, patients who took lithium to relieve manic-depression were carefully monitored by their physicians.

Your Genes and Your Personality

The final principle of biological psychiatry is that personality is genetic. This is so contrary to the political sensibility of our times that its rediscovery is a shock to the system. How did biological psychiatry come to believe in such an "unenlightened" idea? Consider the fashionable explanation of child abuse.

Andy is a terrible two. Steven, his father, beats him whenever Andy throws a tantrum—not just a spanking: Black eyes and broken fingers result. Once Steven starts, he can't stop. Andy's crying eggs his father on, and Steven doesn't stop until Andy is whimpering quietly. All this came out when Andy's mother took him, suffering from a "fall," to the emergency room. Steven was arrested.

Steven was mercilessly beaten by his own father through most of his childhood, and Steven remembers his father claiming to have been beaten by his own father when he was a boy.

Social scientists tell us that this cycle of child abuse is learned. Steven learned to beat Andy by being beaten by his father, and his father learned it the same way. It is quite possible that the children of abusers beat up their own children more often than do children who were not beaten up by their parents. But this evidence is equally compatible with another theory, one that is so unfashionable as to be omitted as a possibility by the social scientists who discovered the generational transmission of child abuse.[16]

What evolution works on. The alternative explanation is that aggression is inherited, and that more aggressive people have "more aggressive genes." People who beat little children are loaded with them, this theory suggests. If these little children are the abusers' biological children, they will, in turn, grow up aggressive—not because they "learn" anything while being beaten, but because they inherit their parents' aggressive tendencies.

Does Steven beat Andy because he inherited an aggressive disposition (which he has passed on to his doubly unfortunate son), or did he learn to beat up children from his own childhood beatings? How can this question be answered?

We are used to the idea of genes controlling simple characteristics like eye color. But can something complex, like a personality trait—aggression, for example—be inherited? To approach this question, it is useful to think about evolution: What does evolution work on and what gets selected?

I believe that genes, the particular molecular string of DNA, and simple traits like eye color are selected only *indirectly.* These get selected because their owner is more successful at reproducing and surviving than the owners of different strings of DNA. What gets directly selected, however, are the characteristics that cause their owner to outreproduce and outsurvive the competition. It is complex, "molar" traits like beauty, intelligence, and aggression that are the primary material of natural selection, which cares only about "modules," the traits that lead directly to reproductive success. This means that complex trait selection is the normal mechanism of evolution.

Molecular biology has it backward. This field looks exclusively at simple traits and molecular building blocks (DNA strings), which can be measured—respectable, quantitative science. But this does not mean that nature is at all interested in simple traits or their molecular constituents, or that the inheritance of simple traits illuminates the inheritance of the more fundamental, complex traits.

Evolution, for example, has certainly worked on the complex trait of "beauty,"[17] which is passed on from one generation to the next, as is the propensity to be attracted to it. Natural selection sees to it that attractive people have higher reproductive success than people less so. Beauty in turn is made up of traits like eye color, and eye color in turn has building blocks—for example, a particular chain of DNA. But beauty, like automobiles, comes in many models, and its definition changes within limits over time and culture. There are many ways to be attractive: many combinations of eye color, teeth, and hair. More important, a greater number of combinations will be ugly and will thus be eliminated from the gene pool. If there are myriad kinds of beauty, then there are myriad molecular ways to construct "beauty," all of which get selected.

The upshot is that there is unlikely to be a molecular biology of beauty. There will not be "beauty genes," or there will be so many combinations of genes underlying beauty as to be scientifically unwieldy. But beauty will still be subject to natural selection and will still be inherited. So too with intelligence, aggression, and all complex traits.[18] It follows that the notion of "aggressive genes" may not make much sense, but that the notion of the heritability of aggression makes good, scientific sense.

How the inheritance of personality is studied. Beauty, aggression, nervousness, depression, intelligence, and the ability to make up limericks all run in families. But if you can't find the genes underlying a personality trait, how can you possibly find out if it is inherited rather than learned? This formidable question has a surprisingly simple answer: Study twins and study adopted children.

Identical twins are genetically identical. They always have, for instance, the same color eyes. Fraternal twins have, on average, half their genes in common. Sometimes one twin is green-eyed and the other blue-eyed. They are no more alike genetically than any other two siblings. When identical twins are more similar for some trait than fraternal twins, we say that the trait is *heritable.*

This is true for eye color, but how about more complex traits, like limerick composing? Even if identical twins have the same limerick-composing ability (or its lack), and fraternal twins are not as similar, this talent could still be the result of child rearing. Everyone knows that identical twins are raised more similarly: Their parents dress them the same, they share the same bedroom more often, they take the same classes, and so on. Identical twins reared apart have the same genes, but they grow up in vastly different environments. If they are similar for some personality trait, it must be heritable and not learned. The study of identical twins reared apart is the best way to untangle the effects of child rearing from the effects of genetics.[19]

Indeed, if you want to attach a number for degree of heritability, simply take the correlation for identical twins reared apart: When that correlation is 1.00, the trait is completely determined genetically; when it is lower, say .50, this means that the trait is half genetic and half nongenetic in origin.

Identical twins reared apart.

Tony and Roger were given up for adoption as infants. Tony grew up in a warm and effusive working-class Italian home in Philadelphia. Roger was raised in Florida by austere, highly educated Jewish parents. While in his twenties, Tony, a traveling salesman, was eating at a restaurant in New Jersey when he was accosted by a very insistent woman diner. "Roger, how have you been? You haven't called." With effort, Tony was able to convince her that he wasn't Roger and that he knew no such Roger. But he was intrigued and tracked Roger down. When they traded birth dates, each discovered he had a twin brother.

The similarity was spooky. Of course, they looked and sounded identical. But their IQ was also exactly the same. They used the same toothpaste. They had both been atheists since grade school. Their school grades had been the same. They both smoked Lucky Strikes and wore Canoe after-shave. They had the same politics. They had similar jobs and liked similar types of women. On their next birthday, they sent each other surprise gifts by mail: identical sweater-and-tie sets.

Over the last twelve years, a diligent group of University of Minnesota psychologists led by Tom Bouchard, David Lykken, and Auke

Tellegen has studied the psychological profiles of twins. The group started with the "Jim" twins (both were named Jim), a pair whose reunion was written about in the press in the 1970s. The project snowballed. People who knew they had a long-lost twin came to the University of Minnesota for help in finding their twins. Minnesota has now accumulated 110 pairs of identical twins reared apart and 27 pairs of fraternal twins reared apart. Many of these twins' very first reunions have taken place in the Minnesota laboratory. The stories of spooky similarity are repeated over and over (e.g., two identicals who each divorced a Linda to marry a Betty; another pair who named their sons James Allen and James Alan, respectively). Could it just be coincidence? Unlikely: These "coincidences" do not seem to occur in the lives of fraternal twins reared apart.

To scientists, the degree of heritability and the range of personality traits that are heritable are more impressive than the anecdotes. All of the following are strongly related in identical twins reared apart, and are much less related in fraternal twins reared apart:[20]

- IQ
- Mental speed
- Perceptual speed and accuracy
- Religiosity
- Traditionalism
- Alcohol and drug abuse
- Crime and conduct
- Job satisfaction
- Actual choice of jobs
- Cheerfulness (positive affectivity)
- Depression (negative affectivity)
- Danger-seeking
- Authoritarianism
- Extraversion
- Neuroticism
- Amount of television viewing
- Well-being
- Self-acceptance
- Self-control
- Dominance

These findings have been duplicated in another massive study carried out with five hundred pairs of Swedish twins, identical and fraternal, reared apart and reared together, and now middle-aged.[21] The results are similar, but you can add to the list:

- Optimism
- Pessimism
- Hostility
- Cynicism

Adopted children. In addition to studying identical twins reared apart, there is a second way to separate the effects of genes from those of child rearing: by comparing adopted children to their biological parents versus comparing them to their adoptive parents. Hundreds of adoption studies have been done: Denmark keeps complete records of adoptions (and complete criminal records as well), so the Danish Population Register is a gold mine for untangling childrearing from biology. The criminal records (or their absence) for the fathers, both biological and adoptive, of all the adopted boys born in Copenhagen in 1953 and the criminal records of the sons have been scrutinized.

If neither the natural nor the adopted father had ever been convicted of a crime, 10.5 percent of the sons turned out to be criminals. If the adopted father was a criminal, but the natural father was not, 11.5 percent of the sons were criminals, an insignificant difference. So having a criminal rearing a child does not increase the child's risk of himself becoming a criminal.

If the natural father (whom the child had not seen since he was, at most, six months old) was a criminal, but the adopted father was not, 22 percent of the sons were criminals. Crime rate is doubled by having "criminal genes." If both natural and adopted fathers were criminals, the sons' crime rate was 36.2 percent—more than triple the rate of the sons of upstanding fathers.

This means that there is a biological predisposition to commit crime (and to get caught). If it is present and you are reared by a criminal father, you are at very high risk. Merely having a criminal father rear you, without the biological predisposition, does not increase your risk.[22]

So crime, astonishingly, is heritable. Similar adoptive studies strongly confirm the findings of the twin studies: Most of human personality has a strong genetic component.

The other major finding of the adoption studies is that two children raised in the same family are almost as different from each other as any two random kids—on almost every measure of personality and intelligence—once you take genes into account. There is no similarity between two children adopted into the same family; everyone who has raised two adopted kids knows this, but others who have only ideology to guide them greatly overestimate the importance of the family environment. This revolutionary finding—which suggests that many of our labors in childrearing are simply irrelevant—will be discussed later.

But for every one of these heritable traits, the degree of heritability is much less than 1.00. Generally, it hovers a bit below .50. This means that our personality is not utterly determined by our genes—far from it—but it also means that much of what we are *is* contributed to by our genes.

Conclusion and evaluation. So the final principle of biological psychiatry is firmly in place: A massive body of research in the last ten years has shown that personality is heritable. Add this to the principles that mental illness is physical illness and that drugs change our emotions and mood, and you arrive at a powerful view of human nature.

Biological psychiatry, as a philosophy of mental illness, must be taken seriously. But I have three caveats—one for each principle.

First: That mental illness is physical illness has been demonstrated for only one mental illness—general paresis. The claims for schizophrenia, Alzheimer's, and manic-depression are plausible but unproven—no biochemical causes have yet been located. The claims for depression, anxiety, sexual problems, overweight, and post-traumatic stress disorder are merely part of an ideological agenda, with very modest evidence to back them up.

Second: The claim that mood and emotion are just brain chemistry and that to change you merely need the right drug must be viewed with skepticism. The basic drug discoveries to date warrant only modest enthusiasm. There are indeed drugs that alter mood for some—but not all—people. All of these drugs are cosmetic, however, and all of them produce unwanted side effects, some of which are awful.

Third: The claim that personality is inherited has strong evidence behind it. But, at most, personality is only partly genetic. The degree of heritability hovers below .50 for all personality traits (except for IQ, which may be around .75). Even by the most extreme estimates, at least half of personality is not inherited. This means that, at most, half of personality is fixed.[23] The other half of personality comes from what you do and from what happens to you—and this opens the door for therapy and self-improvement.

Which half you can change and which you cannot is what the rest of this book is about.

PART TWO

Changing Your Emotional Life: Anxiety, Depression, and Anger

The mind is a city like London,
Smoky and populous: it is a capital
Like Rome, ruined and eternal,
Marked by the monuments which no one
Now remembers. For the mind, like Rome, contains
Catacombs, aqueducts, amphitheatres, palaces,
Churches and equestrian statues, fallen, broken or soiled.
The mind possesses and is possessed by all the ruins
Of every haunted, hunted generation's celebration.

Delmore Schwartz, "The Mind Is an Ancient
and Famous Capital," 1959

4

Everyday Anxiety

EVERY DAY WE EXPERIENCE, at least momentarily, three emotions we don't like: anxiety, depression, and anger. These are the three faces of *dysphoria*—bad feeling. These same three common emotions, when out of control, cause most "mental illness." When we experience one, we want to get rid of it. Indeed, that is their very point. In this chapter, I will discuss what you can and cannot change about anxiety. In later chapters in this part, I will discuss depression and anger. But before exploring the exorcising of these emotions, we should first ask what they are doing in your life in the first place.

There are two kinds of "wisdom to distinguish the one from the other" at issue here. One is what you can and cannot change about dysphoria—a central topic of this book. The other, however, comes first.

When should you *not try changing?* When should you listen to the message of your negative emotions, as uncomfortable as it may be, and change your external life rather than your emotional life?

Bad weather inside. People, by and large, are astonishingly attracted to the catastrophic interpretation of things. Not just "neurotics," not just depressives, not just phobics, not just explosive personalities, but most of us, much of the time.

Goethe said that in his entire life he had only a couple of completely happy days. I am astonished that when my own life is going smoothly—work, love, and play all in place, which is not very often—I begin to fret about anything I can find that is wrong. What, the microwave is on the blink? This disaster is followed by repeated, angry calls to the appliance service; worrying at four a.m.; busy signals, cursing, and blaming. I experience just about as much total dysphoria over this triviality as I do when the big things, all of them, go badly. I call this common irrationality *conservation of dysphoria.*

Why is dysphoria so common? Why is it conserved? Why do anxiety, anger, and sadness pervade so much of our lives—concurrent with so much success, wealth, and absence of biological need in the lives of privileged Americans? The Russian psychologist Blyuma Zeigarnik discovered early in this century that we remember unsolved problems, frustrations, failures, and rejections much better than we remember our successes and completions.

Why do we hurt on the inside so much of the time? Here is an evolutionary approach: The last geological epoch save one was the Miocene—tropical savannas, fruit on the trees, good weather, a Garden of Eden. Peace of mind, satisfaction, and optimism—all of which mirrored the good weather outside—being adaptive were selected and flourished during this twenty-million-year-long paradise. The last hundred thousand years, the Pleistocene epoch, however, have seen bad weather: ice, flood, drought, famine, heat, more ice, hurricanes, more ice; one catastrophe after another. Who survives this ordeal? What kind of emotional life is selected by climatic disaster? Perhaps one that broods, worries, is "future-oriented" (this euphemism disguises the fact that future-orientation is not lotus-eating contemplation of the future, but a state fraught with anxiety). A person with this mentality always considered the catastrophic interpretations and could always see the cloud that the silver lining hides behind; he even woke up at four in the morning to make sure he hadn't overlooked some subtle, awful portent. His brain endured because, by and large during the Pleistocene, he was right—disaster *was* just around the corner. This prudent neurotic passed his genes on. His blithe-spirited Miocene-brained brothers and sisters were washed away in a flash flood, froze under the apple tree, or were trampled by mastodons.

Here is a radical proposal: *Homo dysphorus,* our species, evolved during the Pleistocene from *Homo sapiens,* our predecessor. It is fascinating that the "big" brain (1,200- to 1,500-cubic-centimeter cranial capacity) first appeared about six hundred thousand years ago. But *Homo sapiens* sat on the savanna, wrote no books, planted no corn, spoke little, and built no cathedrals. Not until recent times, ten thousand or so years ago, did progress—agriculture, civilization, the accumulation of knowledge—first dawn. Why the long delay?

Maybe a big brain, sapience, is not enough. Dysphoria, bad weather on the inside, is needed to galvanize mere intelligence into action. Discontent, worry, depression, a pessimistic view of the future (but, as we will see, one with the underlying Miocene belief that a happy ending awaits), are necessary for agriculture, for culture, for civilization.

Each emotion of the dysphoric triad bears—no, *is*—a message—insistent, uncomfortable, hurting—goading us to change our lives. With our daily dysphoria, we are in touch with the very state that makes civilization possible, that transforms berry-gathering into agriculture, cave painting into *Guernica,* eclipse-gaping into astronomy, and, alas, ax handles into Stealth bombers. Each emotion has specific content and goads for specific action.

- Anxiety warns us that danger lurks. It fuels planning and replanning, searching for alternative ways out, rehearsing action.
- Depression marks the loss of something very dear to us. Depression urges us to divest, "decathect," fall out of love, mourn, and ultimately resign ourselves to its absence.
- Anger, highly opinionated, warns that something evil is trespassing against us. It tells us to get rid of the object, to strike out against it.

In light of this speculation, how should we regard our own everyday dysphorias?

Your mental tongue. Attend to your tongue—right now. What is it doing? Mine is swishing around near my lower right molars. It has just found a minute fragment of last night's popcorn (debris from *Terminator 2*). Like a dog at a bone, it is worrying the firmly wedged flake. Now that I am attending to the popcorn flake, it is hard to go back to writing.

Attend to your hand, the one not holding this book—right now. What's it up to? My left hand is boring in on an itch it just discovered under my left earlobe.

Your tongue and your hands have, for the most part, a life of their own. You can bring them under voluntary control by consciously calling them out of their "default" mode to carry out your commands: "Pick up the phone," or "Stop picking that pimple." But most of the time they are on their own. They are seeking out small imperfections. They scan your entire mouth and skin surface, probing for anything going wrong. They are marvelous, nonstop grooming devices. They, not the more fashionable immune system, are your first line of defense against invaders. You thought your electric toothbrush was neat. It is

Stone Age compared to the preventative maintenance, cleaning, waste detection, and debris removal that your tongue is so often carrying out on your teeth and gums.

Anxiety is your mental tongue. Its default mode is to search for what may be about to go wrong. It continually, and without your conscious consent, scans your life—yes, even when you are asleep, in dreams and nightmares. It reviews your work, your love, your play—until it finds an imperfection. When it finds one, it worries it. It tries to pull it out from its hiding place, where it is wedged inconspicuously under some rock. It will not let go. If the imperfection is threatening enough, anxiety calls your attention to it by making you uncomfortable. If you do not act, it yells more insistently—disturbing your sleep and your appetites.

Do you find your tongue's swishy officiousness irritating now that I have called your attention to it? Do you now find twirling your hair as you read vexatious? There are behavioral techniques for reducing these activities, and there is even a drug that dampens such "tics."[1]

Similarly, there are things you can do to reduce daily, mild anxiety. You can numb it with alcohol, Valium, or marijuana. You can take the edge off it with meditation or progressive relaxation. You can beat it down by becoming more conscious of the automatic thoughts of danger that often trigger anxiety, and then disputing them effectively.

But do not overlook what your anxiety is trying to do for you. In return for the pain it brings, it prevents larger ordeals by making you aware of their possibility and goading you into planning for and forestalling them. It may even help you avoid them altogether. Think of your anxiety as the "low oil" light, flashing on the dashboard of your car. Disconnect it, and you will be less distracted and more comfortable for a while. But this may cost you a burned-up engine.[2] Our dysphoria should, some of the time, be tolerated, attended to, even cherished.

Guidelines for *when* to try to change anxiety. Enough praise for everyday anxiety—much of anxiety is wasted and needs relieving. Few scientists have researched the question of when we should try to change our anxiety level rather than attend to its message. But I can give you my own guidelines. What distinguishes most of the advice in the rest of this book from that in self-help books generally is that mine consists of my integration of vats of serious research leavened with a dollop of clinical wisdom. My advice in this case, in contrast, has more fallible backing some clinical lore and some common sense.

Some of our everyday anxiety, depression, and anger go beyond their useful function. Most adaptive traits fall along a normal spectrum of distribution, and the capacity for bad weather inside for everyone some of the time means that some of us will have terrible weather all of the time. In general, when the hurt is pointless and recurrent—when, for example, anxiety insists we formulate a plan but no plan will work—it is time to take action to relieve the hurt. There are three hallmarks indicating that anxiety has become a burden that wants relieving:

First, is it *irrational?*

We must calibrate our bad weather inside against the real weather outside. Is what you are anxious about out of proportion to the reality of the danger? For some of you, living in the shadow of terminal illness, violence, unemployment, or poverty, anxiety is often founded in reality. But for most of you, daily anxiety may be a vestige of a geological epoch you are no longer living in.

Is your anxiety out of proportion to the reality of the danger you fear? Here are some examples that may help you answer this question. All of the following are *not* irrational:

- A fire fighter trying to smother a raging oil well burning in Kuwait repeatedly wakes up at four in the morning because of flaming terror dreams.
- A mother of three smells perfume on her husband's shirts and, consumed by jealousy, broods about his infidelity, reviewing the list of possible women over and over.
- A woman is the sole source of support for her children. Her co-workers start getting pink slips. She has a panic attack.
- A student who has failed two of his midterm exams finds, as finals approach, that he can't get to sleep for worrying. He has diarrhea most of the time.

The only good thing that can be said about your fears is that they are well-founded.

In contrast, all of the following are irrational, out of proportion to the danger:

- An elderly man, having been in a fender bender, broods about travel and will no longer take cars, trains, or airplanes.
- An eight-year-old child, his parents having been through an ugly divorce, wets his pants at night. He is haunted with visions of his bedroom ceiling collapsing on him.
- A college student skips her final exam because she fears that the professor will look at her while she is writing and her hand will then shake uncontrollably.
- A housewife, who has an MBA and who accumulated a decade of experience

as a financial vice president before her twins were born, is sure her job search will be fruitless. She delays preparing her résumé for a month.

The second hallmark of anxiety out of control is *paralysis.* Anxiety intends action: Plan, rehearse, look into shadows for lurking dangers, change your life. When anxiety becomes strong, it is unproductive; no problem-solving occurs. And when anxiety is extreme, it paralyzes you. Has your anxiety crossed this line? Some examples:

- A woman finds herself housebound because she fears that if she goes out, she will be bitten by a cat.
- Consumed by the fear that his girlfriend is unfaithful, a young swain never calls her again.
- A salesman broods about the next customer hanging up on him and makes no more cold calls.
- A fourth-grader is often chosen last for teams and refuses to go to school anymore because "everybody hates me."
- A writer, afraid of the next rejection slip, stops writing.

The final hallmark is *intensity.* Is your life dominated by anxiety? Dr. Charles Spielberger, a past president of the American Psychological Association, is also one of the world's foremost testers of emotion. He has developed well-validated scales for calibrating how severe anxiety and anger are. He divides these emotions into their *state* form ("How are you feeling right now?") and their *trait* form ("How do you generally feel?"). Since our interest is change in personality, with Dr. Spielberger's kind permission I will use his trait questions.

SELF-ANALYSIS QUESTIONNAIRE[3]

Read each statement and then mark the appropriate number to indicate *how you generally feel.* There are no right or wrong answers. Do not spend too much time on any one statement, but give the answer that seems to describe how you *generally* feel.

1. I am a steady person.

Almost never	Sometimes	Often	Almost always
4	3	2	1

2. I am satisfied with myself.

Almost never	Sometimes	Often	Almost always
4	3	2	1

3. I feel nervous and restless.

Almost never	Sometimes	Often	Almost always
1	2	3	4

4. I wish I could be as happy as others seem to be.

Almost never	Sometimes	Often	Almost always
1	2	3	4

5. I feel like a failure.

Almost never	Sometimes	Often	Almost always
1	2	3	4

6. I get in a state of tension and turmoil as I think over my recent concerns and interests.

Almost never	Sometimes	Often	Almost always
1	2	3	4

7. I feel secure.

Almost never	Sometimes	Often	Almost always
4	3	2	1

8. I have self-confidence.

Almost never	Sometimes	Often	Almost always
4	3	2	1

9. I feel inadequate.

Almost never	Sometimes	Often	Almost always
1	2	3	4

10. I worry too much over something that does not matter.

Almost never	Sometimes	Often	Almost always
1	2	3	4

Scoring. Simply add up the numbers under your answers to the ten questions. Be careful to notice that some of the rows of numbers go up and others go down. The higher your total, the more the trait of anxiety dominates your life. Adult men and women have slightly different scores on average, with women being somewhat more anxious generally.

If you scored 10–11, you are in the lowest 10 percent of anxiety.

If you scored 13–14, you are in the lowest quarter.

If you scored 16–17, your anxiety level is about average.

If you scored 19–20, your anxiety level is around the seventy-fifth percentile.

If you scored 22–24 and you are male, your anxiety level is around the ninetieth percentile.

If you scored 24–26 and you are female, your anxiety level is around the ninetieth percentile.

If you scored 25 and you are male, your anxiety level is at the ninety-fifth percentile.

If you scored 27 and you are female, your anxiety level is at the ninety-fifth percentile.

THE AIM of this section is to help you decide if you should try to change your general anxiety level. There are no hard-and-fast rules, but to make this decision, you should take all three hallmarks—irrationality, paralysis, and intensity—into account. Here are my rules of thumb:

- If your score is at the ninetieth percentile or above, you can probably improve the quality of your life by lowering your general anxiety level—regardless of paralysis and irrationality.
- If your score is at the seventy-fifth percentile or above, and you feel that anxiety is either paralyzing you or that it is unfounded, you should probably try to lower your general anxiety level.
- If your score is 18 or above, and you feel that anxiety is both paralyzing you and that it is unfounded, you should probably try to lower your general anxiety level.

Lowering Your Everyday Anxiety

Everyday anxiety level is not a category to which psychologists have devoted a great deal of attention. The vast bulk of work on emotion is about "disorders"—helping "abnormal" people to lead "normal" emotional lives. In my view, not nearly enough serious science has been done to improve the emotional life of normal people—to help them lead better emotional lives. This task has been left by default to preachers, profiteers, advice columnists, and charismatic hucksters on talk shows. This is a gross mistake, and I believe that one of the obligations of qualified psychologists is to help members of the general public try to make rational decisions about improving their emotional lives. Enough research has been done, however, for me to recommend two techniques that quite reliably lower everyday anxiety levels. Both techniques are cumulative, rather than one-shot fixes. They require twenty to forty minutes a day of your valuable time.

The first is *progressive relaxation,* done once or, better, twice a day for at least ten minutes. In this technique, you tighten and then turn off each of the major muscle groups of your body, until you are wholly flaccid. It is not easy to be highly anxious when your body feels like Jell-O. More formally, relaxation engages a response system that competes with anxious arousal. If this technique appeals to you, I recommend Dr. Herbert Benson's book *The Relaxation Response.*[4]

The second technique is regular *meditation.* Transcendental meditation (TM) is one useful, widely available version of this. You can ignore the cosmology in which it is packaged if you wish, and treat it simply as the beneficial technique it is. Twice a day for twenty minutes, in a quiet setting, you close your eyes and repeat a *mantra* (a syllable whose "sonic properties are known") to yourself. Meditation works by blocking thoughts that produce anxiety. It complements relaxation, which blocks the motor components of anxiety but leaves the anxious thoughts untouched. Done regularly, meditation usually induces a peaceful state of mind. Anxiety at other times of the day wanes, and hyperarousal from bad events is dampened. Done religiously, TM probably works better than relaxation alone.[5]

There also exists a quick fix. The minor tranquilizers—Valium, Dalmane, Librium, and their cousins—relieve everyday anxiety. So does alcohol. The advantage of all these is that they work within minutes and require no discipline to use. Their disadvantages outweigh their advantages, however. The minor tranquilizers make you fuzzy and somewhat uncoordinated as they work (a not uncommon side effect is an automobile accident). Tranquilizers soon lose their effect when taken regularly, and they are habit-forming—probably addictive. The same is true of alcohol, and it is even more clearly addictive. Alcohol, in addition, produces gross cognitive and motor disability in lockstep with its anxiety relief. When taken regularly over long periods, deadly liver and brain damage ensue.

I am, incidentally, no puritan about drugs or about quick fixes, so when I advise you against their use—as I do here—it is not out of

The Right Treatment

ANXIETY SUMMARY TABLE*

	Meditation	*Relaxation*	*Tranquilizers*
IMPROVEMENT	▲▲▲	▲▲	▲▲▲
RELAPSE	▲▲▲	▲▲	▲
SIDE EFFECTS	▼	▼	▼▼▼
COST	inexpensive	inexpensive	inexpensive
TIME SCALE	weeks/months	weeks	minutes
OVERALL	▲▲▲	▲▲	▲

*Throughout this book, I will give my overall evaluation of both psychotherapy and drugs for each problem in *The Right Treatment* summary tables. I will use an upward and downward pointer system, where ▲▲▲▲ means the best and ▼▼▼▼ means the worst.

IMPROVEMENT

▲▲▲▲ = 80–100% markedly improved or symptom free
▲▲▲ = 60–80% markedly improved
▲▲ = at least 50% moderately improved
▲ = probably better than placebo
o = probably useless

RELAPSE (after discontinuation of treatment)

▲▲▲▲ = 10% or fewer relapse
▲▲▲ = 10–20% relapse
▲▲ = moderate relapse rate
▲ = high relapse rate

SIDE EFFECTS

▼▼▼▼ = severe
▼▼▼ = moderate
▼▼ = mild
▼ = none

OVERALL

▲▲▲▲ = excellent, clearly the therapy of choice
▲▲▲ = very good
▲▲ = useful
▲ = marginal
o = probably useless

priggishness. If you crave quick and temporary relief from acute anxiety, either alcohol or minor tranquilizers, taken in small amounts and only occasionally, will do the job. They are, however, a distant second-best to progressive relaxation and meditation, which are each worth trying before you seek out psychotherapy or in conjunction with therapy. Unlike tranquilizers and alcohol, neither of these techniques is likely to do you any harm.[6]

I urge you to weigh your everyday anxiety. If it is not intense, or if it is moderate and not irrational or paralyzing, live with it. Listen to its dictates and change your outer life, rather than your emotional life. If it is intense, or if it is moderate but irrational or paralyzing, act now to reduce it. In spite of its deep evolutionary roots, intense everyday anxiety is often changeable. Meditation and progressive relaxation practiced regularly can change it permanently.

But anxiety, when intense and unremitting, can be a sign of a *disorder* that requires exorcising rather than just acknowledgment. The next three chapters are about the three anxiety disorders we know the most about—panic, phobia, and obsession—and what is changeable and not changeable about them.

5

Catastrophic Thinking: Panic

S. J. RACHMAN, one of the world's leading clinical researchers and one of the founders of behavior therapy, was on the phone. He was proposing that I be the "discussant" at a conference about panic disorder sponsored by the National Institute of Mental Health (NIMH). This meeting would pit the established biological psychiatrists against the Young Turk cognitive therapists.

"Why even bother, Jack?" I responded. "Everyone knows that panic is a biological illness and that the only thing that works is drugs."

"Don't refuse so quickly, Marty. There is a breakthrough you haven't yet heard about."

Breakthrough was a word I had never heard Jack use before. Very British, he had recently immigrated to Canada from England, where he had run Europe's premier anxiety clinic at the University of London's Maudsley Hospital. Understatement and modesty are Jack's strong suits.

"What's the breakthrough?" I asked.

"If you come, you can find out."

So I went.

I HAD KNOWN about and seen panic patients for many years, and had read the literature with mounting excitement during the 1980s. I knew that panic disorder is a frightening condition that consists of recurrent attacks, each much worse than anything experienced before. Without prior warning, you feel as if you are going to die. Here is a typical case history:

The first time Celia had a panic attack, she[1] was working at McDonald's. It was two days before her twentieth birthday. As she was handing a customer a Big Mac, she had the worst experience of her life. The earth seemed to open up beneath her. Her heart began to pound, she felt she was smothering, she broke into a flop sweat, and she was sure she was going to have a heart attack and die. After about twenty minutes of terror, the panic subsided. Trembling, she got in her car, raced home, and barely left the house for the next three months.

Since that time, Celia has had about three attacks a month. She does not know when they are coming. During an attack she feels dread, searing chest pain, smothering and choking, dizziness, and shakiness. She sometimes thinks this is all not real and she is going crazy. She always thinks she is going to die.

Panic attacks are not subtle, and you need no quiz to find out if you or someone you love has them. As many as 5 percent of American adults probably do. The defining feature of the disorder is simple: recurrent, awful attacks of panic that come out of the blue, last for a few minutes, and then subside. The attacks consist of chest pains, sweating, nausea, dizziness, choking, smothering, or trembling. They are accompanied by feelings of overwhelming dread and thoughts that you are going to die, that you are having a heart attack, that you are losing control, or that you are going crazy.

The Biology of Panic

There are four questions that bear on whether a mental problem is primarily "biological" as opposed to "psychological":[2]

- Can it be induced biologically?
- Is it genetically heritable?
- Are specific brain functions involved?
- Does a drug relieve it?

Inducing panic. Panic attacks can be created by a biological agent. For example, patients who have a history of panic attacks are hooked up to an intravenous line. Sodium lactate, a chemical that normally produces rapid, shallow breathing and heart palpitations, is slowly infused into their bloodstream. Within a few minutes, about 60 to 90 percent of these patients have a panic attack. Normal controls, subjects with no history of panic, rarely have attacks when infused with lactate.[3]

Genetics of panic. There may be some heritability of panic. If one of two identical twins has panic attacks, 31 percent of the co-twins also have them. But if one of two fraternal twins has panic attacks, none of the co-twins are so afflicted. More than half of panic-disorder patients, moreover, have close relatives who have some anxiety disorder or alcoholism.[4]

Panic and the brain. The brains of people with panic disorders look somewhat unusual upon close scrutiny. Their neurochemistry shows abnormalities in the system that turns on and then dampens fear. In addition, PET scan (positron-emission tomography), a technique that looks at how much blood and oxygen different parts of the brain use, shows that patients who panic from the infusion of lactate have higher blood flow and oxygen use in relevant parts of their brain than patients who don't panic.[5]

Drugs. There are two kinds of drugs that relieve panic: tricyclic antidepressant drugs and the anti-anxiety drug Xanax, and both work better than placebos. Panic attacks are dampened, and sometimes even eliminated. General anxiety and depression also decrease.[6]

Since these four questions had already been answered "yes," when Jack Rachman called, I thought the issue had already been settled. Panic disorder was simply a biological illness, a disease of the body that could be relieved only by drugs.

A few months later, I was in Bethesda, Maryland,[7] listening once again to the same four lines of biological evidence. An inconspicuous figure in a brown suit sat hunched over the table. At the first break, Jack introduced me to him—David Clark, a young psychologist from Oxford. A few moments later, Clark began his address.

"Consider, if you will, an alternative theory, a cognitive theory." He reminded us that almost all panickers believe that they are going to die during an attack. Most commonly, they believe that they are having a heart attack. Perhaps, Clark suggested, this is more than just a symptom. Perhaps it is the root cause. Panic may simply be the *catastrophic misinterpretation of bodily sensations.*

For example, when you panic, your heart starts to race. You notice this, and you see it as a possible heart attack. This makes you very anxious, which means your heart pounds more. You now notice that your heart is really pounding. You are now sure it's a heart attack. This terrifies you, and you break into a sweat, feel nauseated, short of breath—all symptoms of terror, but for you, they're confirmation of a heart attack. A full-blown panic attack is under way, and at the root of it is your misinterpretation of the symptoms of anxiety as symptoms of impending death.[8]

This psychological theory handles the biological findings well.

- Sodium lactate induces panic because it makes your heart race. It creates the initial bodily sensations that you then misinterpret as catastrophe.
- Panic is partially heritable because having a particularly noticeable bodily sensation, such as heart palpitations, is heritable, not because panic itself is directly heritable.
- Brain areas that prevent the dampening of anxiety are active because this activity is a mere symptom of panic.
- Drugs relieve panic because they quiet the bodily sensations that get interpreted as a heart attack.

I was listening closely now as Clark argued that an obvious sign of a disorder, easily dismissed as a mere symptom, is in fact the disorder itself. This kind of argument had been made only twice before in history, and both times the argument had revolutionized psychiatry.

In the early 1950s, Joseph Wolpe, a young South African psychiatrist, astounded the therapeutic world, and infuriated his colleagues, by finding a simple cure for phobias. Established thinking held that phobia—an irrational and intense fear of certain objects, for instance, cats—was just a surface manifestation of a deeper, underlying disorder. The psychoanalysts said a phobia was the buried fear that your father would castrate you in retaliation for lusting after your mother. The biological psychiatrists, on the other hand, claimed that it was some as-yet-undiscovered brain-chemistry problem. What both groups had in common was the belief that some deeper disorder lay underneath the symptoms. Treating only the patient's fear of cats would do no more good than it would to put rouge over measles.

Wolpe, however, claimed that the irrational fear isn't just a symptom; it is the whole phobia. If the fear could be removed (and it could be), this would extinguish the phobia. The phobia would not, as the psychoanalytic and biomedical theorists claimed, return in some displaced form. Wolpe and his followers routinely cured phobias in a month or two, and the fears did not reappear in any form. For his impertinence—for implying that there was nothing deep about this psychiatric disorder—Wolpe was ostracized.

The other precedent for David Clark's assertion involved the founding of cognitive therapy. In 1967, Aaron Beck, a University of Pennsylvania psychiatrist, wrote his first book about depression. Depressives, he noted, think awful things about themselves and about their future. Beck speculated that maybe that is all there is to depression. Maybe what looks like a symptom of depression—gloomy thinking—is the cause. Depression, he argued, is neither bad brain chemistry nor anger turned inward (Freud's claim) but a disorder of conscious thought. Lightening the gloom of conscious thought should cure depression. This simple theory remade the field of depression and founded a new, effective form of therapy.

David Clark, unassuming of demeanor and only thirty-two years old, was now making the same bold argument for panic. My head was spinning. If he was right, this was a historic occasion. All Clark had done so far, however, was to show that the four lines of evidence for a biological view of panic could be fit equally well with a misinterpretation view. But Clark soon told us about a series of experiments he and his colleague Paul Salkovskis had done at Oxford.

First, they compared panic patients with patients who had other anxiety disorders and with normals. All the subjects read the following sentences aloud, but the last word was presented blurred. For example:

If I had palpitations, I could be ***dying.*** / ***excited.***

If I were breathless, I could be ***choking.*** / ***unfit.***

When the sentences were about bodily sensations, the panic patients, but no one else, saw the catastrophic endings fastest. This showed that panic patients possess the habit of thinking Clark had postulated.

Next, Clark and his colleagues asked if activating this habit with words would induce panic. All the subjects read a series of word pairs aloud. When panic patients got to "breathlessness-suffocation" and "palpitations-dying," 75 percent suffered a full-blown panic attack—right there in the laboratory. No normal people had panic attacks, no recovered panic patients (I'll tell you more in a moment about how they got better) had attacks, and only 17 percent of other anxious patients had attacks.

The final thing Clark told us was the "breakthrough" that Rachman had promised.

"We have developed and tested a rather novel therapy for panic," Clark continued in his understated, disarming way. He explained that if catastrophic misinterpretations of bodily sensation are the cause of a panic attack, then changing the tendency to misinterpret should cure the disorder. His new therapy, as he described it, was straightforward and brief:

Patients are told that panic results when they mistake normal symptoms of mounting anxiety for symptoms of heart attack, going crazy, or dying. Anxiety itself, they are informed, produces shortness of breath, chest pain, and sweating. Once they misinterpret these normal bodily sensations as an imminent heart attack, their symptoms become even more pronounced because the misinterpretation changes their anxiety into terror. A vicious circle culminates in a full-blown panic attack.

Patients are taught to reinterpret the symptoms realistically, as mere anxiety symptoms. Then they are given practice right in the office, breathing rapidly into a paper bag. This causes a buildup of carbon dioxide and shortness of breath, mimicking the sensations that provoke a panic attack. The therapist points out that the symptoms the patient is experiencing—shortness of breath and heart racing—are harmless, simply the result of overbreathing, not a sign of a heart attack. The patient learns to interpret the symptoms correctly.

One patient, when he felt somewhat faint, would have a panic attack. He became afraid that he would actually faint and collapse, and interpreted his anxiety as a further symptom of imminent fainting. This escalated to panic in a few seconds.

"Why," Clark asked him, "have you never actually fainted?"

"I always managed to avoid collapsing just in time by holding on to something," replied the patient.

"That's one possibility. An alternative explanation is that the feeling of faintness you get in a panic attack will never lead you to collapse, even if you don't control it. In order to decide which possibility is correct, we need to know what has to happen to your body for you actually to faint. Do you know?"

"No."

"Your blood pressure needs to drop," said Clark. "Do you know what happens to your blood pressure during a panic attack?"

"Well, my pulse is racing. I guess my blood pressure must be up," the patient responded.

"That's right. In anxiety, heart rate and blood pressure tend to go together. So you are actually less likely to faint when you are anxious than when you are not," said Clark.

"But why do I feel so faint?"

"Your feeling of faintness is a sign that your body is reacting in a normal way to the perception of danger. When you perceive danger, more blood is sent to your muscles and less to your brain. This means there is a small drop in oxygen to the brain. That is why you feel faint. However, this feeling is misleading because you will not actually faint since your blood pressure is up, not down."

The patient concluded, "That's very clear. So next time I feel faint, I can check out whether I am going to faint by taking my pulse. If it's normal or quicker than normal, I know I won't faint."[9]

"This simple therapy appears to be a cure," Clark told us. "Ninety to one hundred percent of the patients are panic free at the end of therapy. One year later, only one person had had another panic attack."

At this point in the meeting, Aaron Beck, the father of cognitive therapy, spoke up. "Clark's results are not a fluke. We have run the same study with the same therapy in Philadelphia. We also find complete remission with almost no recurrence of panic attacks one year later."

This, indeed, was a breakthrough: a simple, brief psychotherapy with no side effects showing a 90-percent cure rate of a disorder that a decade ago was thought to be incurable. In a controlled study of sixty-four patients, comparing cognitive therapy to drugs to relaxation to no treatment, Clark and his colleagues found that cognitive therapy is markedly better than drugs or relaxation, both of which are better than nothing. Such a high cure rate is unprecedented. I could not recall a single instance in the annals of psychotherapy or drug therapy where a treatment produced almost complete cure with almost no recurrence. Lithium for manic-depression, at 80 percent effectiveness (with dangerous side effects), was the closest I could remember.

How does cognitive therapy for panic compare with drugs? It is more effective and less dangerous. Both the antidepressants and Xanax produce marked reduction in panic in most patients, but drugs must be taken forever; once the drug is stopped, panic rebounds to where it was before therapy for perhaps half the patients.[10] The drugs also sometimes have severe side effects, including drowsiness, lethargy, pregnancy complications, and addictions.

After this bombshell, my "discussion" was an anticlimax. I did make

The Right Treatment

PANIC SUMMARY TABLE[11]

	Cognitive Therapy	*Drugs*
IMPROVEMENT	▲▲▲▲	▲▲▲
RELAPSE	▲▲▲▲	▲◢
SIDE EFFECTS	▼	▼▼▼
COST	inexpensive	inexpensive
TIME SCALE	weeks	days/weeks
OVERALL	▲▲▲▲	▲▲

IMPROVEMENT

▲▲▲▲	= 80–100% markedly improved or symptom free
▲▲▲	= 60–80% markedly improved
▲▲	= at least 50% moderately improved
▲	= probably better than placebo
o	= probably useless

RELAPSE (after discontinuation of treatment)

▲▲▲▲	= 10% or fewer relapse
▲▲▲	= 10–20% relapse
▲▲	= moderate relapse rate
▲	= high relapse rate

SIDE EFFECTS

▼▼▼▼	= severe
▼▼▼	= moderate
▼▼	= mild
▼	= none

OVERALL

▲▲▲▲	= excellent, clearly the therapy of choice
▲▲▲	= very good
▲▲	= useful
▲	= marginal
o	= probably useless

one point that Clark took to heart. "Creating a cognitive therapy that works, even one that works as well as this apparently does, is not enough to show that the *cause* of panic is cognitive." I was niggling. "The biological theory doesn't deny that some other therapy might work well on panic. It merely claims that panic is caused at bottom by some biochemical problem. Is there any differential prediction that the catastrophic-misinterpretation theory makes that the biological theory must deny?"

Two years later, I had my answer. Clark carried out a crucial experiment that tested the biological theory against the cognitive theory. The main pillar of the biochemical theory is panic attacks produced with infusions of lactate. Carbon dioxide, yohimbine (a drug that stimulates the brain's fear system), and overbreathing all induce panic as well. There is no known neurochemical pathway that all these have in common. The cognitive theory, on the other hand, claims that the common element is their production of bodily sensations that get misinterpreted as catastrophe.

The cognitive theory predicts that you should be able to block lactate-induced panic attacks merely by countering the misinterpretation. The biological theory, in contrast, predicts that lactate is sufficient to produce panic attacks. Clark gave the usual lactate infusion to ten panic patients, and nine of them panicked. He did the same thing with another ten patients, but added special instructions to allay the misinterpretation of the sensations. He simply told them: "Lactate is a natural bodily substance that produces sensations similar to exercise or alcohol. It is normal to experience intense sensations during infusion, but these do not indicate an adverse reaction." Only three out of the ten panicked. This confirmed the theory crucially.

The therapy works very well, as it did for Celia:

> *Celia's story has a happy ending. She first tried Xanax, which reduced the intensity and the frequency of her panic attacks. But she was too drowsy to work, and she was still having about one attack every six weeks. She was then referred to Audrey, a cognitive therapist who explained that Celia was misinterpreting her heart racing and shortness of breath as symptoms of a heart attack, that they were actually just symptoms of mounting anxiety, nothing more harmful. Audrey taught Celia progressive relaxation, and then she demonstrated the harmlessness of Celia's symptoms by having her breathe rapidly into a paper bag. Audrey pointed out that Celia's heart was racing and that she felt she was suffocating, normal symptoms of overbreathing. Celia then relaxed in the presence of the symptoms and found that they gradually subsided. After several more practice sessions, therapy terminated. Celia has gone two years without another panic attack.*

6

Phobias

BEFORE I DISCUSS PHOBIAS, I must lay the groundwork for the role of evolution in what we can change about ourselves. Some of what resists change does so because it was an adaptive trait for our ancestors and is the product of natural selection. Phobias, and much else in our emotional lives, are like this.

The *sauce béarnaise* phenomenon. *Sauce béarnaise* used to be my favorite sauce until one evening in 1966, when I had a delicious meal of filet mignon with *sauce béarnaise.* About midnight I became violently ill, retching until there was nothing left to throw up. After that, *sauce béarnaise* tasted awful to me; just thinking about it set my teeth on edge.

At the time, I was a fledgling learning theorist. I was familiar with Pavlovian conditioning, and this seemed like an instance. Pavlovian conditioning is, of course, the science of how we learn what signals what. A child hears a dog growl, but she is undisturbed. Then the dog bites her. After that, she is afraid whenever she sees a dog. She has learned, by Pavlovian conditioning, that growling signals hurt, and she is now afraid of dogs. How can this be explained?

Pavlov's dogs, you will remember, first had the conditional[1] stimulus (CS) of the sight of Pavlov paired with their unconditional response (UR) of salivating for the unconditional stimulus (US) of food. After half a dozen such pairings, they began to salivate just on seeing Pavlov. Salivating to Pavlov was the conditional response (CR). Pavlovian conditioning worked because the dogs associated the sight of Pavlov with the response of salivating to food.

Some events turn us off or turn us on the very first time we encounter them: Thunder is frightening the first time it happens; stroking of the genitals is exciting the first time *it* happens. Other events have to acquire their emotional significance. The emotional significance of the face of our mother or of the words "Your money or your life" must be learned. All of our emotional life that is not inborn might be Pavlovian conditioning. This idea had placed Pavlovian conditioning among the most exciting fields in all of psychology by the mid-1960s.

My *sauce béarnaise* aversion seemed to fit. The taste was the CS, and sickness was the UR. This pairing rendered future encounters with *sauce béarnaise* nauseating. At any rate, this was what I mused about over the next month.

What focused my musings was a remarkable paper published a month after this incident. John Garcia, a young radiation researcher, published an experiment with findings so anomalous that—once accepted—they revolutionized learning theory. So hard to swallow were these findings for learning theorists that the leading textbook writer in that field said at the time that they were no more likely to be true than that "you would find bird shit in a cuckoo clock"![2]

Garcia was an obscure investigator studying radiation sickness in a government laboratory. He noticed that when his rats got sick, they went off their food. After they recovered, they still wouldn't eat their old chow. Otherwise, though, they looked completely unperturbed. This was bewildering, but it also looked like Pavlovian conditioning, with the taste of the chow the CS, sickness the UR, and coming to hate their chow the CR. But if the rats were conditioned by being sick, why only a taste aversion? Why not a more widespread aversion—to their handlers, to lights going off, to doors opening, to everything else that occurred with their illness? Garcia was bewildered—for the same reason I was bewildered about *sauce béarnaise.*

Garcia then carried out a classic experiment, my candidate for the most significant experiment conducted during my lifetime in the psychology of learning:

Every time his rats licked at their drinking spouts, they tasted saccharin, and a burst of light and noise came on. This is called a *compound CS*—bright, noisy saccharin water. Then a burst of X rays occurred. Within a few hours the rats were sick to their stomachs. When the rats recovered, Garcia tested the elements of the compound CS separately to see what the rats had learned to fear. They now hated saccharin, but they were completely unperturbed by the bright noise. When they got sick, they blamed it on the taste and ignored everything else.

Maybe they had just failed to notice the bright noise during conditioning? So Garcia counterbalanced the experiment. Other rats were given the same bright, noisy saccharin paired now with foot shock instead of stomach illness. What did they learn? They now cringed in fear of bright noise, but they still loved saccharin. When they suffered pain, they blamed it on the bright noise and ignored the taste.

So both the bright noise and the saccharin were noticeable, but only the taste became aversive when the rats became nauseated, and only the bright noise became aversive when the rats suffered pain. How could this be? Both the Garcia findings and the *sauce béarnaise* aversion looked like Pavlovian conditioning. But they did not fit the laws of conditioning. There were five problems:[3]

First, Pavlovian conditioning is not selective: Any CS that is present when any UR occurs should get conditioned. Pavlov was there when the dogs were fed, and so he became exciting (so, presumably, did his voice, his after-shave lotion, and his white coat). But this didn't work for Garcia's rats. Only the saccharin became aversive with stomach illness, and only the bright noise became aversive with pain.

Similarly with *sauce béarnaise;* it had selectively absorbed the badness of the incident—at the expense of other potential CSs. The *sauce béarnaise,* and nothing else, became nauseating. There were plenty of other stimuli present that should have been conditioned, since conditioning works by sheer contiguity between co-occurring events. But no other stimulus became aversive. I still liked beef. I still liked my wife, who was there the whole time. The white plates I ate the sauce off and the Danish stainless-steel silverware still looked okay to me, though they were paired with illness. So, too, was the toilet bowl I threw up into, and it didn't look unusually noxious to me afterward, either.

The second violation of known laws was that Pavlovian conditioning bridges only very short time gaps. If you hear a burst of noise and an electric shock follows it by one second, you will become afraid of the noise. If the shock doesn't happen until a minute later, however, you will not become afraid of the noise. A single minute's delay between CS and US is too long for conditioning to bridge. The delay between the saccharin and the radiation sickness was much longer, just as was the delay between tasting the *sauce béarnaise* and getting sick: not seconds, but hours—hundreds of times longer than in any successful conditioning experiment.

The third problem was that Garcia's rats hated saccharin after just one dose of X rays, and I came to dislike *sauce béarnaise* with just a single experience. Normal Pavlovian conditioning almost never takes in just one trial. It took Pavlov repeated feeding of his dogs to get them to salivate to his presence. It takes about five noise-shock pairings to get someone sweating over noise. This is true even when the shock is very painful.

The fourth problem was that ordinary Pavlovian conditioning is rational: Its laws follow the growth and decline of conscious expectations. Pavlov's dogs learned to expect food when Pavlov showed up, and so they salivated. Once Pavlov stopped feeding them, they stopped salivating when they saw him—this is called *extinction. Sauce béarnaise* didn't work this way, however. The day after I got sick, I called my closest collaborator to apologize for not showing up at the lab. He asked me if I had come down with the stomach flu that was sweeping the department. After that I "knew" that the sauce was innocent; the stomach flu, not the sauce, had caused the illness. I did not expect that I would throw up if I were to eat *sauce béarnaise* once more. But knowledge didn't help; *sauce béarnaise* still tasted bad.

The same irrationality is true of Garcia's phenomenon. Consciousness, the whole elaborate apparatus that dominates much of our life, is irrelevant to learning a taste aversion. In one experiment, rats tasted saccharin and were then made unconscious with anesthesia. While asleep, brief stomach illness was induced. After the rats woke up, they hated saccharin.[4]

The last problem was that Pavlovian conditioning extinguishes easily, a side effect of its being a conscious expectation. All Pavlov had to do was show up but not feed his dogs a few times, and they stopped salivating when they saw him. But my dislike of *sauce béarnaise* lasted a decade, and remained alive through a dozen dinner parties in which skeptical psychologists gave me *sauce béarnaise* to sample. I can eat it now, twenty-five years later, but still, I had to change from Craig Claiborne's recipe to Julia Child's.

The message from Garcia. All these problems *can* be reconciled with Pavlovian conditioning, because evolution is at work. For millions of years our ancestors repeatedly encountered, among their other woes, stomach illness. Plants and animals they ate sometimes contained poison, their food sometimes spoiled, the streams they drank out of sometimes carried germs. Each of these challenges could have killed them; but if they got sick and survived, they had to learn to avoid the toxin in the future.

The problem is: What to avoid? Toxins in nature are avoidable only because they have distinctive tastes, as do the foods that carry them. Those of our ancestors who after stomach illness learned rapidly and well to hate the most distinctive taste that accompanied sickness passed on their genes. Those who didn't died out.

We are *prepared* by our evolutionary history to learn some things well. We learn, as I did, that *sauce béarnaise* goes with illness—in one trial and across long delays. This learning occurs at levels deeper and less fallible than rationality, is very strong, and is illogical. It took years for me to start liking *sauce béarnaise* again.

We do not "know" any of these things when we are born—they are not "instinctive." Garcia's rats loved saccharin, and I loved *sauce béarnaise* the first time I tasted it. If we have but a single aversive experience with prepared associations, however, we absorb it immediately and will not easily let it go. Evolution has shaped our sensory apparatus, and it has shaped our response system. A keen sense of taste and the response of retching are both the product of natural selection. We have known this ever since Darwin. What Garcia told us that was new is that how quickly we learn something or how slowly we learn it—or whether we learn it at all—is subject to natural selection. Learnability itself is shaped by evolution.

In response to Garcia's findings, a long and bitter quarrel ensued in the journals, perhaps the bitterest in the history of learning theory. It is still not over. Most psychologists now accept the idea that our genes constrain learning, but for the staunch hard core, this is still heresy, for two reasons: The first is a special-interest-group concern, and the second is a fundamental concern.

The guild of behaviorists had by 1965 painted itself into a corner. We did experiments on pigeons pecking disks for grain, on rats pressing bars for Purina pellets, on rats becoming afraid of tones, and very little else. But we dubbed our findings, grandly, "the laws of learning"—not "the laws of hungry pigeon learning" or "the laws of rat learning." We declared our laws to be as universal as Newton's gravity. Garcia, very much not a member of the guild, told us that the kind of stimulus (taste) and its evolutionary relation to the response (stomach illness) mattered a lot. This, he contended, produced a violation of the laws: one trial learning over long delays. This meant that all the years that B. F. Skinner, Clark Hull, Ivan Pavlov, and their followers had put in on rats, pigeons, and dogs might have yielded mere laboratory curiosities—not general laws. All the work of the guild might be unimportant.

But the real reason the rest of psychology was glued to this controversy was more basic. American psychology as a whole is militantly environmentalistic, and Garcia challenged this premise. The underpinnings of American environmentalism are very deep, both intellectually and politically.

John Locke, David Hume, and the British empiricists began this tradition by arguing that all knowledge comes through the senses. These sensations are tied together by associations, they averred, and so everything we know, everything a human being is, is simply the buildup of associations. If you want to understand a person, all you need know is the details of his upbringing. Behaviorism generally, and Pavlovian conditioning in particular, captured the imagination of American psychology because it was a testable version of Locke's environmentalism. Environmentalism is not just at the heart of behaviorism; it is the core of the dogma of human plasticity.

And make no mistake about the political side. It is no coincidence that Locke fathered both the idea that all knowledge is associations and the idea that all men are created equal. The behaviorists, scientific Lockeans all, dominated academic psychology from the end of World War I to the Vietnam era. John Watson began the behaviorist movement in the era of the melting pot. His popularity was in part the result of his covert message: The new immigrants were not inferior to the people already in America; they could be molded into the same high-quality stuff that the WASPs already were. The defeat of Hitler added fuel to American environmentalism: The genocide of the concentration camps filled my generation with determination never again to countenance genetic explanations of human psychology.

We may have been working on rats and pigeons, but in doing so we were trying to show that human beings were the product of their upbringing and their culture, not of their race. The civil rights movement, feminism, the anti–Vietnam War protests (white people killing yellow people), all fed into and fed on this sacred, covert premise of American psychology.

Militant environmentalism allowed behaviorism to dominate American academic psychology. Garcia denied its most basic premise: that we are wholly the creation of our environment, not of our genes. Viewed from afar, the message from Garcia does not seem very earthshaking. He did not claim that we are a product of our genes or that our upbringing was unimportant. He claimed only genetic *predisposition.* He claimed that our genes *limited* what we could learn. But this opened—

just a crack—the door that environmentalists wanted shut forever. The door has stayed open, and it has provided a fresh way to look at the many things that are learned, among them birdsong, aggression, language, imprinting, sexual-object choice, and, not the least, phobias.

Phobia and Fears

A phobia is an intense fear that is out of proportion to the real danger of the object that causes it. In its milder form, phobia is common, afflicting about 10 percent of the adult population. In its extreme form, so intense as to keep sufferers housebound, it is rarer—well under 1 percent of adults.[5] The most common kinds of phobias are agoraphobia (literally, fear of the marketplace), which is the fear of crowded places, open spaces, and travel; social phobia, the fear of humiliation and embarrassment while being observed by other people; and nosophobia, the fear of a specific illness, like AIDS or breast cancer. Also common are the object phobias, which include the fear of animals, insects, heights, airplanes, enclosure, or bad weather. There are rare phobias, like fear of thirteens (triskaidekaphobia) or snow, and I even once came across a patient who had trouble dealing with exhaust pipes (mufflerophobia).

About half of the cases of phobia begin with a traumatic incident, usually in childhood. Susan's severe fear of cats began with a trauma.

> *"Don't let Boycat in!" Susan, four years old, shrieked to her mother, pointing to the kitchen door. Outside sat the proud family cat, covered in rabbit blood and gnawing a partly eaten bunny. Susan cried hysterically for an hour. After this she would never again stay in the same room with Boycat or any other feline.*
>
> *As she grew up, her aversion to cats intensified. But this fall, at age thirty-one, it climaxed. She can't leave the house. The house next door was vacant for the summer, and Susan glimpsed a cat in the unmown grass. She now fears that if she goes out, she will be attacked and mauled by a cat. Her first thought on waking is of what cats she might meet today. Every sudden noise and movement in the house startles her—it might be a cat. Her last thought as she falls asleep, exhausted, is dread—of the cats she will meet in her nightmares.*

Successful therapy. It is normal for four- and five-year-old children to "break out" in strong object fears, particularly of animals. Ninety-five percent of these fears simply disappear as the child grows up. A few, like

Susan's, persist into adulthood, and when they do, they are unremitting and will not wane of their own accord. But there is one brand of therapy for phobias that works reliably: behavior therapy. Here is the theory of why it works:

A phobia is an instance of ordinary conditioning with a particularly traumatic UR (unconditional response). Some neutral object, like a cat, happens to be around when a trauma, like Susan's terror on seeing a mangled bunny, occurs. The cat is the CS (conditional stimulus), and Susan's trauma is the UR. By virtue of this pairing, the CS becomes terrifying.

If phobias are simply Pavlovian conditioning, it should be easy to eliminate them. Therapy needs only to accomplish Pavlovian extinction—by getting the patient to stay in the presence of the CS, but arranging to have no UR occur. Until Joseph Wolpe came along in the 1950s, no one had ever tried this straightforward approach. Psychotherapy at that time was dominated by psychoanalysis, whose practitioners tried, without success, to get phobics to gain insight into the sexual and aggressive conflicts that allegedly caused their phobias. By the mid-1960s, however, psychoanalysts knew that insight therapy on phobias was "never easy."[6]

Two behavior therapies, both of which are forms of extinction, are now used with success on phobias.

The first, *systematic desensitization,* is Wolpe's original. In it, the patient first learns progressive relaxation. The patient then constructs a fear hierarchy, with the worst, full-blown phobic situation at the top, and a situation that produces only the slightest phobic fear at the bottom. Susan, for example, picked meeting someone named Katz for the bottom rung, and seeing *cat* in the word *catsup* on a label on the next rung. At the top was having a real cat sit on her lap—her worst-imaginable situation.

Next, the patient goes into her practiced state of relaxation and imagines vividly the situation on the bottom rung. So Susan lay there flaccidly and imagined being introduced to an Ada Katz. She repeated this until she felt no fear at all while visualizing this. In the subsequent session, the patient once again relaxes and imagines the next-most-fearsome scene—seeing the word *cat,* in Susan's case. She visualizes this, while relaxing, until she feels no fear at all. In about a dozen sessions, the patient will have reached the top of the hierarchy—in her imagination—without feeling fear. Once the top rung is achieved, most cat phobics find they can go from imagining cats fearlessly to actually facing real cats with little fear.

What has happened here is Pavlovian extinction. Susan repeatedly imagined the feared CS in the absence of the UR (the bodily state of relaxation precludes fear). This broke the association between cats and fear.

The other therapy, *flooding,* uses this same extinction principle. Flooding is more dramatic, but briefer. Here the phobic is thrown into the phobic situation: A claustrophobe will agree to be locked in a closet; a cat phobic will sit in a room full of cats; the agoraphobe is dropped off, in the company of the therapist, at a shopping center. In each case, the patient waits an agreed-upon length of time—it may seem an eternity, but it is actually usually around four hours—without leaving. At first the patient is terrified, but inevitably, after an hour or so, the fear starts to dissipate when she sees that no harm comes to her. After about four hours the patient is not in a state of fear anymore. She now is in the presence of the CS, but in the absence of the UR. She is exhausted and drained, but the phobic fear has extinguished.

The opposite of relaxation is used for blood phobias with marked success. In this common phobia (about 3 percent of the population has it), the victim's heart rate and blood pressure drop sharply, and she faints at the sight of blood. *Applied tension* is taught to blood phobics. They learn to tense the muscles of the arms, legs, and chest until a feeling of warmth suffuses the face. This counterconditions the blood-pressure drop and fainting, just as relaxation counterconditions anxious tension.[7]

These therapies work at least 70 percent of the time. After a brief course of such therapy, usually about ten sessions, most patients can face the phobic object. Applied tension with blood phobia works even better: Remission is lasting; former phobics rarely come to like the object, but they no longer fear it.

Unsuccessful therapy. After extinction therapy, symptoms do not manifest themselves elsewhere. This lack of symptom substitution is important, since both psychoanalytic and biomedical theories claim that eliminating the phobia directly is merely cosmetic. The underlying conflict or the underlying biochemical disorder still exists untouched, these schools of thought have it, and symptoms must appear elsewhere. But, in fact, they do not.

Psychoanalysis does not work on phobias. Cognitive therapy, in

The Right Treatment

PHOBIA SUMMARY TABLE

OBJECT PHOBIA

	Extinction Therapy	*Drugs*
IMPROVEMENT	▲▲▲	▲
RELAPSE	▲▲▲▲	▲
SIDE EFFECTS	▼	▼▼▼
COST	inexpensive	inexpensive
TIME SCALE	weeks/months	days/weeks
OVERALL	▲▲▲▲	▲

SOCIAL PHOBIA

	Extinction Therapy	*Drugs (Tricyclics, MAO inhibitors)*
IMPROVEMENT	▲▲▲	▲▲▲
RELAPSE	▲▲▲	▲
SIDE EFFECTS	▼	▼▼▼
COST	inexpensive	inexpensive
TIME SCALE	weeks/months	days/weeks
OVERALL	▲▲▲	▲▲

AGORAPHOBIA

	Extinction Therapy	*Drugs (Tricyclics)*	*Combination*
IMPROVEMENT	▲▲	▲▲	▲▲▲
RELAPSE	▲▲▲	▲	▲▲▲
SIDE EFFECTS	▼	▼▼▼	▼▼▼
COST		all are inexpensive	
TIME SCALE	weeks/months	weeks	weeks/months
OVERALL	▲▲	▲◢	▲▲▲

IMPROVEMENT

▲▲▲▲	= 80–100% markedly improved or symptom free
▲▲▲	= 60–80% markedly improved
▲▲	= at least 50% moderately improved
▲	= probably better than placebo
o	= probably useless

RELAPSE (after discontinuation of treatment)		SIDE EFFECTS	
▲▲▲▲	= 10% or fewer relapse	▼▼▼▼	= severe
▲▲▲	= 10–20% relapse	▼▼▼	= moderate
▲▲	= moderate relapse rate	▼▼	= mild
▲	= high relapse rate	▼	= none

OVERALL	
▲▲▲▲	= excellent, clearly the therapy of choice
▲▲▲	= very good
▲▲	= useful
▲	= marginal
o	= probably useless

---

which patients look at the irrationality of their phobias ("What really is the probability of an airplane crash?" or "Look here—no adult in Philadelphia has ever been mauled by a cat") and learn to dispute these irrational thoughts, does not seem to be of much use for specific phobias.[8] Cognitive therapy for panic may be useful in agoraphobia, however, when panic is a central problem.[9]

Drugs are not very useful with object phobias. The anti-anxiety drugs produce calm when taken in high doses in the phobic situation itself, though the calm is accompanied by drowsiness and lethargy. So for an airplane phobic who must suddenly fly, a minor tranquilizer will help, but only temporarily. The calm is cosmetic: Once the drug wears off, the phobia is intact.

The combination of drugs and extinction therapy for object phobias is also probably not useful. For extinction to work, it seems necessary to experience anxiety and then have it wane. Anti-anxiety drugs block the experience of anxiety and so block extinction of anxiety. The phobia therefore remains intact.

Drugs do not seem very useful with social phobia. MAO inhibitors (strong antidepressants) have been used with some success. About 60 percent of patients improve while on these drugs. But the success is temporary and the relapse rate high once the drugs are discontinued. Remember also that MAO inhibitors have dangerous side effects (see chapter 3). Somewhat lower improvement (around 50 percent) occurs with the strong anti-anxiety agents, like Xanax, and with beta-blockers. But, again, the relapse rate is very high and the drugs have marked side effects. A high relapse rate upon drug discontinuation suggests only a cosmetic effect on phobic anxiety.[10]

Agoraphobia, in contrast, is helped by antidepressant drugs, and in a noncosmetic way. Antidepressants seem to work to almost the same extent as extinction therapies, and they are particularly useful in combination with extinction therapies.[11] What is probably crucial is that agoraphobia, unlike most other phobias, typically involves panic attacks. Indeed, a panic attack is usually the precipitating incident in agoraphobia. Antidepressants suppress panic attacks without sedating the patient.

This is one drug effect that makes Pavlovians happy. Pavlovian theory tells us that agoraphobia starts when the CS of being in the marketplace, the agora, coincides with the UR of the panic attack. This conditions the agora to terror. When a patient is administered the combination of drug and extinction therapy, she ventures out and does not experience another panic attack, because she is drugged. She is now exposed quite effectively to the CS of the agora in the absence of the UR of panic, so Pavlovian extinction occurs.

Thus the case for phobias resulting from Pavlovian conditioning looks quite strong: Some innocent object conjoined to a terrifying trauma imbues that object with terror. As predicted, extinction therapies work quite well.

Phobias and evolution. There are too many loose ends, however: three, to be exact. Each of these makes phobias look more like the *sauce béarnaise* phenomenon and taste aversions than like ordinary Pavlovian conditioning.

First, ordinary Pavlovian conditioning is not selective. Any CS that happens to coincide with any trauma gets conditioned. But phobias are, in fact, highly selective:

> *A seven-year-old on a picnic sees a snake crawling through the grass. She is interested but not disturbed by it. An hour later she returns to the family car and has her hand smashed in the car door. She develops a lifelong phobia—not of car doors, but of snakes!*[12]

There are in fact only about two dozen common phobic objects, most prominently open spaces, crowds, animals, insects, closed spaces, heights, illness, and storms. By and large these are all objects that were occasionally dangerous to our ancestors during the progress of evolution. Even the exceptions, like airplanes, are usually traceable to more primitive fear objects, like falling, suffocating, or being trapped.[13]

Arne Ohman, one of Sweden's leading psychologists, decided to find out if phobias were more like taste aversions than like ordinary Pavlovian conditioning. He performed the Garcia experiment with human fear, giving student volunteers Pavlovian conditioning with electric shock as the unconditional stimulus (US). The conditional stimulus (CS) was either an *evolutionarily prepared* object, a picture of a spider, or an *evolutionarily unprepared* object, a picture of a house. A prepared phobic object is one that has actually been dangerous to humans over evolutionary time; an unprepared object is one that has not. The students were not afraid of the spider to begin with, but after just one pairing of the spider and shock, they broke into a sweat when the spider was shown. The picture of the house induced fear—and only mildly so—only after many pairings. Unlike ordinary conditioning, then, phobic conditioning in the laboratory, the *sauce béarnaise* phenomenon, and human phobias in nature are all selective.[14]

The second problem with the Pavlovian view is that conditioning requires short delays and explicit pairing of CS and US to work. Phobias don't. There was an hour delay between the snake and the hand smashed in the car door; yet the phobia bridged this gap. Even more telling, while about 60 percent of phobics relate a story of explicit pairing of the object with a trauma to explain how it started, 40 percent do not. Rather, these phobics relate a much vaguer, more social story of the origin of their phobia: for example, they had heard that their best friend was bitten by a dog, and after that dogs always terrified them.[15]

The Swedes again forged the link. Ohman showed his students the prepared object, a slide of a scorpion, and they looked at it without any fear. No explicit trauma followed. No electric shock came on. Rather, one of the students, a confederate, jumped up and raced out of the room, shrieking "I can't stand it!" After that, the subjects sweated when they saw the slide of the scorpion.

With another group, Ohman then repeated the scenario, but with an unprepared object, a slide of a flower. Again, a shrieking student ran out in horror. But this time the subjects showed no fear at all of the flower. Evolutionarily prepared objects—though not unprepared objects—become fearful without pairing with trauma; merely seeing someone else traumatized is enough to endow them with fear.[16]

The deepest problem is that ordinary Pavlovian conditioning is rational. It produces a conscious expectation that the CS will be followed by the US. But phobias are decidedly irrational. Telling a phobic that her fears are irrational ("Flying is the safest way to travel") doesn't dent a phobia. All of a phobic's relatives have told her this for years, and she knows the statistics more accurately than anyone. She knows that her fears are unfounded. Cognitive therapy, unsurprisingly, does not extinguish phobias, because they are lodged in less fragile housing than reason; their roots lie deep in the unconscious. They are like my *sauce béarnaise* aversion, undented by my knowledge that the sauce was innocent and the flu guilty. Phobias can be undone, but not by talk.

Phobias, unlike panic disorders, are from Missouri. Their extinction requires the presentation of the phobic object without the UR of terror. Their extinction requires demonstration of harmlessness—flooding and desensitization.

I was a subject in one of Ohman's crucial experiments in Sweden, the one demonstrating that prepared conditioning is irrational whereas ordinary conditioning is rational. He strapped my hand to a shock electrode and showed me a slide of a flower. Twenty seconds later, I felt a brief burst of shock. He repeated this five times. The next time the flower appeared, I was calm during the first few seconds. After about ten seconds, I began to tense up. My unease mounted so that by the nineteenth second I was sweating. I expected to be shocked after twenty seconds, and my fear had timed the interval. I showed ordinary Pavlovian conditioning. Very logical of me.

Ohman then showed me a picture of a python. Sort of repulsive, I thought, but I felt no fear. Twenty seconds into the picture, the same burst of shock came on. Just one pairing of shock and snake. A couple of minutes later, Ohman flashed the slide of the python a second time and I almost jumped out of my chair.

So thanks to John Garcia and Arne Ohman, we now have an accurate picture of what phobias are and what they are not. They are not instances of ordinary Pavlovian conditioning, but instances of prepared Pavlovian conditioning. They do not come about when an innocent object happens to be around precisely when a trauma befalls us. Phobias come about when certain evolutionarily prepared objects coincide roughly with danger. They are not created culturally: Man-made dangerous objects, which do not have an evolutionary history—knives and guns, for instance—condition like houses and flowers, not like dangerous objects from evolution—snakes, spiders, and scorpions.[17] Just as phobias select their objects, they also select their victims. Some of us get phobias more easily than others; relatives of people with anxiety disorders, for example, are more susceptible to phobias. Phobias lurk in each of us. They are the rekindling of dark, primordial fears.

There is a profound and global message in this account. Some of what we are—our darkest fears, for example—originated early in the evolution of our species. Often we find that other parts of us resist change, even though all that is rational in us insists we change. When this happens, our evolutionary heritage is one place to find the source of the resistance. For we are not creatures of our upbringing and our culture only.

Some of what is difficult to change ties us to the life-and-death struggles of our ancestors. And it is not only our fears that are prepared. The sexual objects that we spend our lives pursuing, the aggression and competition we have such difficulty suppressing, our prejudice against people who look different from us, our masculinity or femininity, and those recurring obsessions we can't get out of our minds are all examples of psychological links to our biological past.

Being evolutionarily prepared does not justify something. Some of what our evolution demands of us is just a vestige of pressures that no longer exist. Some of it is morally repulsive. But closing our eyes to the biological side of our nature is worse than useless. For when we work against our evolutionary heritage, we had better be aware that we are doing so. We should know that change in this arena is never easy. Sometimes, as we will see, change is impossible, and so we must learn to live with aspects of ourselves we don't like. Other times, change is possible, but reason alone will not usually produce change. Aided by techniques that work at levels more fundamental than reason, however, we can sometimes succeed. We have just seen two such examples. We will see more as we turn to obsessions, to depression, to anger, and to post-traumatic stress.

7

Obsessions

> What do we plant when we plant the tree?
> We plant the ship that will cross the sea. . . .
> What do we plant when we plant the tree?
> We plant the houses for you and me.[1]

This song is running through my mind now and has been for about two hours. It began when I was singing this jingle from my childhood to my two-year-old, Lara, as we were picking tomatoes. It won't go away.

The jingle channel. Everyone has a jingle channel. For some people there are ditties on it, but not everyone has music. Others have phrases repeated over and over. The words often rhyme, they sometimes have a beat, and they are always simple: "Step on a crack and break your mother's back." For others who are less verbally inclined, there is no audio, only video; the same images recur repeatedly: the Little Mermaid swimming toward Prince Eric, or Lee Harvey Oswald being shot by Jack Ruby. Some people have a mixture of words, songs, and images. Left alone, the content shifts slowly, but with an external prompt, like your roommate humming a tune, it can jump.

Your jingle channel is slightly below consciousness, but once you know about it, it is easy to tune in and listen. Some people have a louder channel than others. You can sometimes tell how this hour's contents started: a radio ad, a phrase from your boss, a new rock song on MTV.

Once you tune in, you will discover that the jingle channel has a life of its own. It is very hard to change voluntarily. When it intrudes and you can't turn it off, it becomes quite a vexation. Mark Twain discovered this, over a century ago, when he heard this ditty for streetcar conductors and could not rid himself of it for days.

A blue trip slip for an eight-cent fare.
A buff trip slip for a six-cent fare.
A pink trip slip for a three-cent fare
Punch in the presence of the passenjare.

Punch, brothers! punch with care!
Punch in the presence of the passenjare.[2]

Civilization has often taken advantage of the channel. Before the modern media bombardment, poetry (epic poetry, no less), catechisms, and the Bible were probably featured. I like to think that human mental furniture was classier then. Astonishingly, psychological researchers have shown no interest in this channel. It is broadcast by an unknown and uninvestigated part of the brain.

The nightmare channel. Much of emotional life is carried on the jingle channel. For many, the jingle channel is not a pleasant and elevating experience. Sometimes the lyrics are about loss and hopelessness. "She's gone, she's gone, she's gone, and she's never coming back" or "I'm a born loser" are the sort of phrases that intrude when we are in a low mood. When these kinds of jingles are dominant and recurrent, we call the listeners *depressed,* and their thoughts have been named *ruminations* or *automatic thoughts.* For others, the jingle channel is a nightmare channel, a production of Stephen King that may feature ferocious animals or poisonous insects, or scenes of humiliation. These people are called *object phobics* or *social phobics,* respectively. For others, the channel features thoughts of a heart attack or of going crazy or of losing control: These people's problem is called *panic disorder.*

For still others, when they tune into their jingle channel, what they hear is alien, repugnant, fearful, and depressing. Worse, they have a loud channel that frequently intrudes unbidden on them during work and play. Their most common themes are dirt and contamination, checking for danger, and doubt. These people have a problem called *obsessive-compulsive disorder* (*OCD*), which is named for the two elements that make it up. Their obsession is a thought or image that recurs, and their compulsion is the ritual act performed to neutralize the thought. When thoughts of dirt dominate the jingle channel, the person will wash his hands for an hour, or scrub her baby's room from floor to ceiling three times a day, or open doors only with her feet to avoid having her hands contaminated by the germs on the doorknob.

> Howard Hughes was a brilliant tycoon. Toward the end of his life he had such severe obsessions about germs that he became a recluse. He wrote a continual stream of memos to his staff worrying about contamination and instructing them in how to prevent "back transmission" of germs to him. Hughes was wealthy and powerful enough to have an entire staff to carry out his cleaning compulsions: In one three page memo he instructed his staff in how to open a can of fruit to prevent germ "fallout":
>
> "The man in charge then turns the valve in the bathtub on, using his bare hands to do so. He also adjusts the water temperature so that it is not too hot nor too cold. He then takes one of the brushes, and, using one of the bars of soap, creates a good lather, and then scrubs the can from a point two inches below the top of the can. He should first soak and remove the label, and then brush the cylindrical part of the can over and over until all particles of dust, pieces of paper label, and, in general, all sources of contamination have been removed."[3]

Washing and cleaning rituals can take up large swaths of the day when, unlike Hughes, you have to do them yourself. One fourteen-year-old had to wake up at four-thirty every morning in order to clean herself thoroughly and make the bed so that it was exactly right before she left for school at eight. She was plagued with the severe skin rashes and abrasions that result when you wash your hands for an hour or more at a time.

"Checkers" find themselves waking many times each night to make sure that the gas in the kitchen is off, or that all the doors and windows are locked. One man drove to a crossroads near his house ten times a day for months to make certain that there was no corpse lying there that he had run over and failed to notice on the last trip. Another woman always peered down into the toilet bowl to make sure that there was no baby in danger of being flushed away. Toilets, incidentally, are often featured on the OCD jingle channel: One otherwise successful and healthy dentist always had to flush in multiples of three—9, 27, 81, or 243 times—before carrying on. He wasn't much fun to go drinking with.

Do you or someone you love have obsessive-compulsive tendencies? How can you tell if what you hear on your jingle channel is in the normal range or if it is in need of changing? Self-diagnosis is always hazardous, and this book is not a diagnostic manual. Rather, my intention is to alert you to a variety of problems, and if they seem to apply to you, I want to point you in the right direction for help. Some problems don't require a lot of sophistication for you to be aware of what they are: Panic attacks and phobias are two examples. Other problems, like obsessions, require an experienced professional to diagnose. There are three problems that should alert you to a need for help:

- Are the thoughts unwelcome and repugnant, and do they intrude?
- Do they arise from within, with no external stimulus?
- Do you find it very hard to distract yourself or dismiss the thoughts?

In addition to these hallmarks, here is a validated test:

THE MAUDSLEY OBSESSIVE-COMPULSIVE INVENTORY

Jack Rachman and Ray Hodgson, two of the world's experts on obsessions, have developed a questionnaire that can tell you if you have a problem you should act to get rid of. With their kind permission I reproduce it here.[4]

Please answer each question by putting a circle around the "TRUE" or "FALSE" following the question. There are no right or wrong answers, and there are no trick questions. Work quickly and do not think too long about the exact meaning of the question.

1. I avoid using public telephones because of possible contamination.
TRUE FALSE

2. I frequently get nasty thoughts and have difficulty in getting rid of them.
TRUE FALSE

3. I am more concerned than most people about honesty.
TRUE FALSE

4. I am often late because I can't seem to get through everything on time.
TRUE FALSE

5. I worry unduly about contamination if I touch an animal.
TRUE FALSE

6. I frequently have to check things (e.g., gas or water taps, doors) several times.

TRUE FALSE

7. I have a very strict conscience.

TRUE FALSE

8. I find that almost every day I am upset by unpleasant thoughts that come into my mind against my will.

TRUE FALSE

9. I worry unduly if I accidentally bump into somebody.

TRUE FALSE

10. I usually have serious doubts about the simple everyday things I do.

TRUE FALSE

11. At least one of my parents was very strict during my childhood.

TRUE FALSE

12. I tend to get behind in my work because I repeat things over and over again.

TRUE FALSE

13. I use more than an average amount of soap.

TRUE FALSE

14. Some numbers are extremely unlucky.

TRUE FALSE

15. I check letters over and over again before mailing them.

TRUE FALSE

16. I take a long time to dress in the morning.

TRUE FALSE

17. I am excessively concerned about cleanliness.

TRUE FALSE

18. One of my major problems is that I pay too much attention to detail.

TRUE FALSE

19. I can use well-kept toilets only with hesitation.

TRUE FALSE

20. My major problem is repeated checking.

TRUE FALSE

21. I am unduly concerned about germs and diseases.

TRUE FALSE

22. I tend to check things more than once.

TRUE FALSE

23. I stick to a very strict routine when doing ordinary things.

TRUE FALSE

24. My hands feel dirty after touching money.

TRUE FALSE

25. I usually count when doing a routine task.

TRUE FALSE

26. I take quite a long time to complete my washing in the morning.

TRUE FALSE

27. I use a great deal of antiseptics.

TRUE FALSE

28. I spend a lot of time every day checking things over and over again.

TRUE FALSE

29. Hanging and folding my clothes at night takes up a lot of time.

TRUE FALSE

30. Even when I do something very carefully, I often feel that it is not quite right.

TRUE FALSE

Each TRUE answer counts for 1 point. The most severe total score is 30. There is a Checking Scale (questions 2, 6, 8, 14, 15, 20, 22, 26, and 28) with a maximum of 9, and a Dirt and Contamination Scale (questions 1, 4, 5, 9, 13, 17, 19, 21, 24, 26, and 27) with a maximum of 11. If your total score exceeds 10, you are in the range of clinically diagnosed obsessive-compulsives. If your Dirt and Contamination score is 2 or greater or your Checking score is 4 or greater, you are also within the clinical range. Scores this high mean you should have professional help. Later in this chapter, I will discuss what kind of professional help is best and how much change is likely to ensue.

There are two viable approaches to OCD: the biological and the behavioral. Each has a theory and each has evidence in its favor. Each has also generated a therapy that helps the majority of people with OCD. Neither is wholly satisfactory.

The Biological Viewpoint

Biological psychiatrists claim that OCD is a brain disease.

Their first line of evidence is that OCD, once in a great while, develops right after a brain trauma.

> *Jacob, eight years old, was playing football in the backyard. He collapsed and went into a coma with a brain hemorrhage. When he came out of brain surgery, which went very well, he was plagued by numbers. He had to touch everything in sevens. He swallowed in sevens and asked seven times for everything.*[5]

Sometimes OCD begins with epilepsy, and after the great sleeping-sickness (a viral brain infection) epidemic of 1916–18 in Europe, there was an apparent rise in the number of OCD patients. There is also some marginal evidence for a genetic factor in OCD. It runs in families: 30 percent of all adolescents with OCD have a parent or sibling with OCD.

The second line of biological evidence comes from brain-scan studies of patients with OCD. Two areas of the brain show higher activity in OCD patients: These two areas are related to filtering out irrelevant information and perseveration of behavior. When patients improve with drugs or behavior therapy, activity in these areas diminishes.[6]

The third line of evidence concerns the specific content of the OCD jingle channel. What goes on there is not arbitrary. Like the content of phobias, which is mostly objects that were once dangerous to the human species, the content of obsessions and of the compulsive rituals is also narrow and selective. The vast majority of OCD patients are obsessed with germs or with violent accidents, and they wash or they check in response. Why such specific and peculiar themes? Why not obsessions about particular shapes, like triangles, or about socializing only with people of the same height? Why no compulsions about push-ups, or about handclapping, or about crossword puzzles? Why germs and violence; why washing and checking?

During the course of evolution, washing and checking have been very important and adaptive. The grooming and physical security of one's self and one's children are constant primate concerns. Perhaps the brain areas that kept our ancestors grooming and checking are the areas gone awry in OCD. Perhaps the recurrent thoughts and the rituals in OCD are deep vestiges of primate habits, run amok.[7] This would mean, as it does for phobias, that it would not be easy to get rid of OCD, that we would not be able to talk people out of their obsessions and compulsions. This is true: Neither psychoanalysis nor cognitive therapy appears to work on OCD.

Effective therapy is, indeed, the final line of evidence for the biological theory. Anafranil (clomipramine) is a drug that has been used successfully with thousands of OCD sufferers, in more than a dozen controlled studies. Anafranil is a potent antidepressant drug, a serotonin-reuptake inhibitor. When OCD victims take Anafranil, the obsessions wane and the compulsions can be more easily resisted.

It is not a perfect drug. A large minority of patients (almost half) taking Anafranil do not get better, or they cannot take it because of side effects including drowsiness, constipation, and loss of sexual interest. Those who benefit are rarely cured: Their symptoms are dampened, but the obsessive thoughts are usually lurking and the temptation to ritualize remains. When those who do benefit go off the drug, many—perhaps most—of them relapse completely. But Anafranil is decidedly better than nothing.[8]

The Behavioral Viewpoint

There is something magnetic about horrible thoughts and images (the popularity of horror films testifies to this). Some of us are better than others at dismissing these thoughts or distracting ourselves from them. When we are depressed or anxious (as most people inclined to OCD are), such thoughts are even more difficult to stop. Indeed, when people are shown films of, for instance, gruesome woodworking accidents, those viewers who are most upset are the ones who have the most trouble discarding the images.[9]

Behavior therapists argue that people who are not very good at distracting themselves or dismissing thoughts are most prone to OCD. Once a horrible thought starts, if you cannot dismiss it, it makes you upset. The more upset you get, the harder it is to dismiss the thought. You get even more anxious, and a vicious circle is under way. If thought stopping by ordinary means doesn't work for you, you can perform a ritual, a *compulsion,* that relieves the anxiety. So if you have mounting horrible thoughts about germs, you can wash your hands thoroughly; if you are obsessed with burglars, you can check the locks. This relieves the anxiety temporarily, but when the thought returns, the temptation to perform the ritual will be even stronger because it has been reinforced by anxiety reduction. This theory fits the subjective experience of OCD quite well.

A therapy follows directly: exposure and response prevention. If you expose the patient to the feared situation and then prevent her from engaging in her ritual, she should become very anxious at first. If she continues to refrain, however, and finds out that the expected harm does not befall her—that she does not become infected by germs, that a gas explosion does not occur—the thoughts should wane and the ritual should extinguish. Thousands of OCD patients have been helped by this therapy. Here is a dramatic instance:

> *Jackie had obsessions about broken glass cutting her vagina. She kept her panties in a separate, locked drawer. She searched minutely for glass around chairs before sitting down. She could not use public toilets, and she would never wear flared skirts. Her most awful thought was of having to wear a tampon.*
>
> *She entered behavior therapy and agreed to a response-prevention treatment. With her therapist's help, she sat down on unfamiliar chairs without checking. She used public toilets. After she was able to do these things with increasing comfort, she sat on the floor while bottles were broken around her. Finally, with her therapist's encouragement, she was able to use a tampon. Her obsessions and compulsions disappeared and have not returned.*[10]

Between half and two-thirds of patients improve markedly after exposure and response prevention, and for most of those who improve, relief

The Right Treatment

OBSESSIVE-COMPULSIVE DISORDER SUMMARY TABLE

	Behavior Therapy	*Anafranil*
IMPROVEMENT	▲▲◢	▲▲◢
RELAPSE	▲▲▲	▲◢
SIDE EFFECTS	▼	▼▼▼
COST	inexpensive	inexpensive
TIME SCALE	weeks/months	weeks/months
OVERALL	▲▲◢	▲▲

IMPROVEMENT

▲▲▲▲ = 80–100% markedly improved or symptom free
▲▲▲ = 60–80% markedly improved
▲▲ = at least 50% moderately improved
▲ = probably better than placebo
o = probably useless

RELAPSE (after discontinuation of treatment)

▲▲▲▲ = 10% or fewer relapse
▲▲▲ = 10–20% relapse
▲▲ = moderate relapse rate
▲ = high relapse rate

SIDE EFFECTS

▼▼▼▼ = severe
▼▼▼ = moderate
▼▼ = mild
▼ = none

OVERALL

▲▲▲▲ = excellent, clearly the therapy of choice
▲▲▲ = very good
▲▲ = useful
▲ = marginal
o = probably useless

There is insufficient evidence as yet about the *combined* effects of Anafranil (clomipramine) and behavior therapy to know if it is superior to either alone. See I. Marks, P. Lelliott, M. Basoglu, et al., "Clomipramine, Self-Exposure, and Therapist-Aided Exposure for Obsessive-Compulsive Rituals," *British Journal of Psychiatry* 152 (1988): 522–34.

---

is lasting. At the end of therapy, however, the patient is usually not completely normal: The thoughts still lurk. A clear minority, it must be said, fail to improve. OCD patients who are depressed, who have delusions, or who secretly perform their rituals usually will not improve.[11]

People with OCD have worry and depression as the dominant emotions on their jingle channel. People with other emotional problems have a different dominant emotion on their channel. People with object phobias have terror accompanying horrific scenes of encounters with the feared object. People with panic attacks have recurrent images of heart attack, stroke, and death accompanied by incipient panic. People with agoraphobia feel panic and terror as they tune in on scenes of going outside, of getting sick and being helpless with no one coming to their aid.

That we have a jingle channel is a fact we cannot change. It is an aspect of mental life so important that evolution wants to make sure it goes on incessantly. It is too important to be left to any conscious decision of whether or not to tune in. But its content may be changeable, and its volume is surely changeable. Changing the content, or at least adjusting the volume, can relieve some of our emotional problems. Cognitive therapy for panic probably removes heart attacks and dying as content on the jingle channel. Extinction therapy for any phobia and antidepressant drug therapy for agoraphobia turn the volume from loud to soft on the feared encounters. Both Anafranil and response prevention turn the volume from very loud to moderate in OCD. Changing the volume of the channel, while not simple, can now be effectively done with all these problems. My best guess, however, is that after successful treatment for OCD—and probably for phobias, too—the old jingles are still there—quieter and less insistent perhaps, but still lurking.

8

Depression

WE LIVE in an age of depression. Compared with when our grandparents were young, depression is now ten times as widespread in the United States, and the rate is climbing. Nowadays, depression first strikes people ten years younger, on average, reaching into late childhood and early adolescence for its youngest victims. It has become the common cold of mental illness.

Every age has a dominant emotion. The first half of this century was the Age of Anxiety, and its emotional tone was captured by Sigmund Freud. Freud lived through the death throes of the Hapsburg Empire and then through the horrors of World War I and its chaotic aftermath. Freud watched a world order that had stood for hundreds of years dissolve and a new one struggle to be born. Times when old values crumble and the future is unpredictable are times fraught with anxiety. Anxiety was the dominant emotion Freud saw in his patients, and it was the dominant theme of contemporary writing, film, and painting. Small wonder that Freud believed that all neuroses and almost all human action stemmed from anxiety. All the other emotions—depression, awe, anger, embarrassment, shame, and guilt—were just footnotes.

Our age, in contrast, is an age of uncontrollability and helplessness. Our values are stable, but the struggle by individuals and groups never before enfranchised to emerge from helplessness and achieve power dominates our politics, our literature, what now passes as the humanities, and what therapists see in the clinic. Depression is the emotion that comes in the wake of helplessness, individual failure, and unrealized attempts to gain power. For our age, depression and sadness are the dominant emotions, and anxiety, while more important than a footnote, has yielded center stage.[1]

TEST YOUR DEPRESSION

To determine how depressed you are, take this widely used test called the CES-D (Center for Epidemiological Studies-Depression). It was developed by Lenore Radloff at the Center for Epidemiological Studies of the National Institute of Mental Health. Circle the answer that best describes how you have felt *over the past week.*

1. I was bothered by things that usually don't bother me.

 0 Rarely or none of the time (less than 1 day)

 1 Some or a little of the time (1–2 days)

 2 Occasionally or a moderate amount of the time (3–4 days)

 3 Most or all of the time (5–7 days)

2. I did not feel like eating; my appetite was poor.

 0 Rarely or none of the time (less than 1 day)

 1 Some or a little of the time (1–2 days)

 2 Occasionally or a moderate amount of the time (3–4 days)

 3 Most or all of the time (5–7 days)

3. I felt that I could not shake off the blues even with help from my family and friends.

 0 Rarely or none of the time (less than 1 day)

 1 Some or a little of the time (1–2 days)

 2 Occasionally or a moderate amount of the time (3–4 days)

 3 Most or all of the time (5–7 days)

4. I felt that I was not as good as other people.

 0 Rarely or none of the time (less than 1 day)

 1 Some or a little of the time (1–2 days)

 2 Occasionally or a moderate amount of the time (3–4 days)

 3 Most or all of the time (5–7 days)

5. I had trouble keeping my mind on what I was doing.

 0 Rarely or none of the time (less than 1 day)

 1 Some or a little of the time (1–2 days)

 2 Occasionally or a moderate amount of the time (3–4 days)

 3 Most or all of the time (5–7 days)

6. I felt depressed.

 0 Rarely or none of the time (less than 1 day)

 1 Some or a little of the time (1–2 days)

 2 Occasionally or a moderate amount of the time (3–4 days)

 3 Most or all of the time (5–7 days)

7. I felt that everything I did was an effort.

 0 Rarely or none of the time (less than 1 day)

 1 Some or a little of the time (1–2 days)

 2 Occasionally or a moderate amount of the time (3–4 days)

 3 Most or all of the time (5–7 days)

8. I felt hopeless about the future.

   0 Rarely or none of the time (less than 1 day)

   1 Some or a little of the time (1–2 days)

   2 Occasionally or a moderate amount of the time (3–4 days)

   3 Most or all of the time (5–7 days)

9. I thought my life had been a failure.

   0 Rarely or none of the time (less than 1 day)

   1 Some or a little of the time (1–2 days)

   2 Occasionally or a moderate amount of the time (3–4 days)

   3 Most or all of the time (5–7 days)

10. I felt fearful.

   0 Rarely or none of the time (less than 1 day)

   1 Some or a little of the time (1–2 days)

   2 Occasionally or a moderate amount of the time (3–4 days)

   3 Most or all of the time (5–7 days)

11. My sleep was restless.

   0 Rarely or none of the time (less than 1 day)

   1 Some or a little of the time (1–2 days)

2 Occasionally or a moderate amount of the time (3–4 days)

3 Most or all of the time (5–7 days)

12. I was unhappy.

0 Rarely or none of the time (less than 1 day)

1 Some or a little of the time (1–2 days)

2 Occasionally or a moderate amount of the time (3–4 days)

3 Most or all of the time (5–7 days)

13. I talked less than usual.

0 Rarely or none of the time (less than 1 day)

1 Some or a little of the time (1–2 days)

2 Occasionally or a moderate amount of the time (3–4 days)

3 Most or all of the time (5–7 days)

14. I felt lonely.

0 Rarely or none of the time (less than 1 day)

1 Some or a little of the time (1–2 days)

2 Occasionally or a moderate amount of the time (3–4 days)

3 Most or all of the time (5–7 days)

15. People were unfriendly.

0 Rarely or none of the time (less than 1 day)

1 Some or a little of the time (1–2 days)

2 Occasionally or a moderate amount of the time (3–4 days)

3 Most or all of the time (5–7 days)

16. I did not enjoy life.

0 Rarely or none of the time (less than 1 day)

1 Some or a little of the time (1–2 days)

2 Occasionally or a moderate amount of the time (3–4 days)

3 Most or all of the time (5–7 days)

17. I had crying spells.

0 Rarely or none of the time (less than 1 day)

1 Some or a little of the time (1–2 days)

2 Occasionally or a moderate amount of the time (3–4 days)

3 Most or all of the time (5–7 days)

18. I felt sad.

0 Rarely or none of the time (less than 1 day)

1 Some or a little of the time (1–2 days)

2 Occasionally or a moderate amount of the time (3–4 days)

3 Most or all of the time (5–7 days)

19. I felt that people disliked me.

0 Rarely or none of the time (less than 1 day)

1 Some or a little of the time (1–2 days)

2 Occasionally or a moderate amount of the time (3–4 days)

3 Most or all of the time (5–7 days)

20. I could not get "going."

0 Rarely or none of the time (less than 1 day)

1 Some or a little of the time (1–2 days)

2 Occasionally or a moderate amount of the time (3–4 days)

3 Most or all of the time (5–7 days)

This test is easy to score. It is simply an aggregation of the symptoms of depression. The more you have, the more likely it is that you are depressed. Add up the numbers you circled. If you couldn't decide and circled two numbers for the same question, count only the higher of the two. Your score will be someplace between 0 and 60.

Before interpreting your score, you should know that a high score is not the same thing as a diagnosis of depression. A few people who get high scores are not in fact depressed, and people with low scores can still have a "depressive disorder." A full-blown diagnosis of depression depends on other things, such as how long your symptoms have lasted and whether they have some primary source other than depression. A diagnosis can be made only after a thorough interview with a qualified psychologist or psychiatrist. Rather than giving a diagnosis, this test gives an accurate indication of your level of depression right now.

If you scored from 0 to 9, you are in the nondepressed range, below the mean of American adults; 10 to 15 puts you in the mildly depressed range; and 16 to 24 puts you in the moderately depressed range. If you scored over 24, you are probably severely depressed.

If you scored in the severely depressed range, *I urge you to seek treatment.* If you believe that you would kill yourself if you had a chance, regardless of the rest of your answers, *I urge you to see a mental health professional right away.* If you scored in the moderately depressed range and, in addition, you often think about killing yourself, you should see a professional right away. If you scored in the moderately depressed range, take the test again in two weeks. If you still score in that range, make an appointment with a mental health professional.

After you have read the rest of this chapter about what treatments work for depression, and if you have trouble finding a qualified professional in your area, I welcome your writing me at the Department of Psychology, University of Pennsylvania, Philadelphia, PA 19104. I will try to send you the names of some of the qualified people in your area who do the therapies that work.

THE SYMPTOMS of depression in the questionnaire fall into four clusters.

First, the way you *think* when you are depressed differs from the way you think when you are not depressed. When you are depressed, you have a dour picture of yourself, the world, and the future. Your future looks hopeless, and you attribute this to a lack of talent. Small obstacles seem like insurmountable barriers. You believe that everything you touch turns to ashes. You have an endless supply of reasons why each of your successes is really a failure. A pessimistic *explanatory style*[2] is at the core of most depressed thinking. You see the causes of your tragedies and your setbacks as permanent, pervasive, and personal ("It's going to last forever, it's going to undermine everything I do, and it's me"), and you see the causes of good events in the opposite way.

The second group of symptoms is a negative change in *mood.* When you are depressed, you feel awful: sad, discouraged, sunk in a pit of despair. You may cry a lot, or you may even be beyond tears. Life loses its zest. Formerly enjoyable activities become flat. Jokes are no longer funny, but unbearably ironic. Sadness is not the only mood of depression; anxiety and irritability are often present. And when depression gets intense, anxiety and hostility drop away and the sufferer becomes numb and blank.

The third cluster of symptoms of depression concerns *behavior:* passivity, indecisiveness, and suicide. Depressed people often cannot get started on any but the most routine tasks, and they give up easily when thwarted. A novelist can't get her first word written. When she finally does manage to get going, she quits writing when the screen on her word processor flickers, and she doesn't return to her work for a month. Depressed people cannot decide among alternatives. A depressed student phones for a pizza, and when asked if he wants it plain or with a topping, he stares paralyzed at the receiver. After fifteen seconds of silence, he hangs up. Many depressed people think about and attempt suicide.

In depression, even your body turns on you—the fourth cluster of symptoms, *somatic.* The more severe the depression, the more bodily symptoms. Your appetites diminish. You can't eat. You can't make love. Even sleep is affected: You wake up too early and toss and turn, trying unsuccessfully to get back to sleep. Finally the alarm clock goes off, and you begin the new day not just depressed but worn out, too.

To be depressed, you needn't have symptoms from all four clusters, and it is not necessary that any particular symptom be present. But the more symptoms you have and the more intense each is, the more certain you can be that the problem is depression.

For some of us, these symptoms are rare, descending on us only when several of our best hopes collapse at once. For many, depression is more familiar, a state that descends every time we are defeated. For still others, it is a constant companion, souring even our sweetest times and darkening the grayer times to an unrelieved black.

Until recently, depression was a mystery. Who is most at risk? Where does depression come from? How do you make it lift? All were enigmas. Today, thanks to thirty years of intensive scientific research by thousands of psychologists and psychiatrists in dozens of laboratories and hundreds of clinics around the world, the shape of the answers is known. If someone has severe symptoms of depression, that person might have one of two very different disorders: *unipolar* or *bipolar* depression. These provide everyday work for clinical psychologists and psychiatrists. What determines the difference between them is whether mania is involved.

Mania is a psychological condition that looks like the opposite of depression: Its symptoms are unwarranted euphoria, grandiosity, frenetic talk and action, little sleep for days on end, and inflated self-esteem. Bipolar depression always involves manic episodes; it is also called manic-depression (with mania as one pole and depression as the other). Unipolar depressives never have manic episodes. Another difference between the two is that bipolar depression is much more heritable. If one of two identical twins has bipolar depression, there is a 72 percent chance that the other also has it. (This is true of only 14 percent of fraternal twins.) Bipolar depression is exquisitely responsive to lithium carbonate. In more than 80 percent of cases, lithium will relieve the mania to a marked extent and the depression to a lesser extent. Taken continually, it tends to prevent new episodes. Manic-depression is an illness, appropriately viewed as a disorder of the body and treated medically. It is similar to unipolar depression only in appearance.

Now, therapists are not usually sued for malpractice when they use an outdated or ineffective therapy, and a poor therapist can always find some other guild member who does the same kind of therapy to testify that their therapy is a "usual" procedure. But so clear are the data that lithium usually works and that any form of psychotherapy alone usually does not that manic-depressives who are not treated with lithium should, I believe, be able to win malpractice lawsuits. At any rate, if you have manic-depression and are being treated with any form of psychotherapy only, drop your therapist. It is simply wrong to do psychotherapy on bipolar depression, except as an adjunct to drug therapy.

More common than manic-depression—probably ten to twenty times as common—is unipolar depression. This is the disorder that so many of us know well. It springs from the pain and loss that are inevitable parts of being creatures who think about the future. We don't get the jobs we want. Our stocks go down. We get rejected by people we love. Our spouses die. We give bad lectures and write books that flop. We age. When such losses occur, what happens next is regular and predictable: We feel sad and helpless. We become passive and lethargic. We believe our prospects are bleak and that we lack the talent to make them brighter. We don't do our work well, and we may not even show up. The zest goes out of activities we used to enjoy, and we lose our interest in food, company, sex. We can't sleep.

But after a while, by one of nature's benevolent mysteries, we start to improve. Mild forms of this depression (called *normal* depression) are extremely common. I have repeatedly found that at any given moment, approximately 25 percent of us are going through an episode of mild depression.

There is sharp disagreement about whether unipolar depression (a certified disorder) and normal depression are related. I believe they are the same thing, differing only in the number of symptoms and their severity. One person may be diagnosed as having unipolar depression and be labeled a patient, while another with just the same symptoms may be held to be suffering from acute symptoms of normal depression and not be a patient. The distinction between these two diagnoses is shallow, often no more than a matter of how readily a person will seek therapy, or whether his insurance policy covers unipolar depression, or how comfortably he can bear the stigma of being labeled a patient.

My view differs radically from prevailing medical opinion, which holds that unipolar depression is an illness and that normal depression is simply passing demoralization of no clinical interest. This view is the dominant one in spite of strong evidence that unipolar depression is just severe normal depression. No one has established the kind of distinction between the two that has been established between, for instance, dwarfs and short normal people—a qualitative distinction.

Most crucial, I feel, is that normal depression and unipolar depression are recognized in exactly the same way: Both involve negative change in thought, mood, behavior, and the body.

Epidemic

It is very important to know that this kind of depression is rampant today and that its usual victim is a woman.

In the late 1970s, under the leadership of the visionary biological psychiatrist Gerald Klerman, the United States government sponsored two major studies of mental illnesses; the findings were startling. In the first, 9,500 people were randomly picked as a cross section of adult Americans. Each was given the same diagnostic interview that a troubled patient who walks into a knowledgeable professional's office would get.

Because such a large number of adults of different ages were interviewed, the study gave an unprecedented picture of mental illness over many years and made it possible to trace the changes that had taken place over the twentieth century.[3] One of the most striking changes was in the lifetime prevalence of depression, that is, the percentage of the population that has had it at least once. Obviously, the older you are, the more chance you have to get the disorder. The lifetime prevalence of broken legs, for instance, goes up with age, since the older you are, the more opportunities you have to break a leg.

It was expected that the earlier in the century a person was born, the higher would be the person's lifetime prevalence for depression—that is, the more episodes of depression she would have had. Someone born in 1920 would have had more chances to suffer depression than someone born in 1960. Before the statisticians looked at the findings, they would have stated confidently that if you were twenty-five years old at the time you were interviewed for the study—which meant that you were born around 1955—there was, say, about a 6 percent chance that you had had at least one episode of severe depression, and that if you were between twenty-five and forty-four years old, your risk of depression would have climbed—say, to about 9 percent—as any sensible cumulative statistic should.

When the statisticians actually looked at the findings, though, they saw something odd. The findings showed that the people born around 1925 hadn't suffered much depression; not 9 percent but only 4 percent had had an episode. And when the statisticians looked at the findings for people born even earlier—before World War I—they found something even odder: Again, the lifetime prevalence had not climbed; in fact, it had nosedived to a mere 1 percent. This meant that people born in the second half of the century were ten times likelier to suffer depression than people born in the first half.

One study, however—even one as well done as this—does not entitle scientists to shout "epidemic." Fortunately, another major study was done at the same time. This time, the people were not randomly selected; they were chosen because they had close relatives who had been hospitalized for depression.[4]

Again, the findings turned expectations upside down. They showed a strong increase in depression over the course of the century—again, more than ten to one. For instance, when the women of the World War I generation were thirty (the age women born during the Korean War now were), only 3 percent of them had ever suffered a severe depression, while by the time the women born during the Korean War period had turned thirty, 60 percent of them had had an episode of depression—a twentyfold difference. The statistics for the men in the study showed the same surprising reversal. Though the men suffered only about half as much depression as the women (a crucial fact I'll discuss in a moment), they also displayed the same strong percentage increase over the decades.

Not only is severe depression much more common now; it also attacks its victims much earlier in their lives. If you were born in the 1930s and at any point thereafter had a depressed relative, your own first depression, if you had one, would strike between the ages of thirty and thirty-five, on average. If you were born in 1956, your first depression would strike between twenty and twenty-five—ten years sooner. Since severe depression recurs in about half of those who have had it once, the extra ten years of exposure to depression amounts to an ocean of tears.[5]

This trend toward more depression at a younger age continues into the 1990s. Dr. Peter Lewinsohn of the Oregon Research Institute recently interviewed 1,710 adolescents, half born between 1968 and 1971, the other half born between 1972 and 1974. The older ones have an alarming rate of depression: By the time they were fourteen, 4.5 percent had had a full-blown episode of depression. The younger ones were even worse off: By fourteen, 7.2 percent had had an episode. It is shocking that Americans, on average, may be victims of unprecedented psychological misery in a nation with unprecedented prosperity, world power, and material well-being.[6]

In any case, this is enough to warrant shouting "epidemic."

Women and Men

Study after study has found that across the twentieth century, depression strikes women more often than men.[7] The ratio is now two to one.

Is it because women are perhaps more willing to go to therapy than men and thus show up more frequently in the statistics? No. The same preponderance shows up in door-to-door surveys.

Is it because women are more willing to talk openly about their troubles? Probably not. The two-to-one ratio manifests itself in both public and anonymous conditions.

Is it because women tend to have worse jobs and less money than men do? No. The ratio stays at two to one even when groups of women and men are matched for the same jobs and the same income: Rich women have twice as much depression as rich men, and unemployed women twice as much as unemployed men.

Is it some sort of biological difference that produces more depression? There may be some biological differences that contribute, but probably not enough to make for a two-to-one ratio. Studies of premenstrual and postpartum emotion show that while hormones do affect depression, their effect isn't nearly big enough to create so large a disparity.

Is it a genetic difference? Careful studies of how much depression occurs among the sons versus the daughters of male and female depressives show that there is substantial depression among the sons of male depressives. Considering the way chromosomes are passed from father to son and from mother to daughter, there is too much male depression in this study for it to be true that genetics causes the lopsided sex ratio. While there is some evidence of a genetic contribution to depression, genetics probably does not cause the lopsided sex ratio.

Is it sex-role pressure? Probably not. There *are* more conflicting demands on women than on men in modern life, and a woman nowadays not only has the traditional role of mother and wife but often must hold down a job as well. This extra demand could produce more strain than ever before and therefore more depression. Sounds plausible, yet like many ideologically congenial theories, this one dashes against the rocks of fact. On average, working wives are less, not more, depressed than wives who do not work outside the home. So sex-role explanations do not seem to account for the female preponderance.

This leaves three plausible explanations:

The first is *learned helplessness.* In our society, it is argued, women receive abundant experience with helplessness over the whole of their lives. Boys' behavior is lauded or criticized by their parents and their teachers, while girls' is often ignored. Boys are trained for self-reliance and activity, girls for passivity and dependence. When they grow up, women find themselves in a culture that deprecates the role of wife and mother. If a woman turns to the world of work, she finds her achievements given less credit than men's. When she speaks in a meeting, she gets more bored nods than a man would. If despite all this she manages to excel and is promoted to a position of power, she is seen as being out of place. Learned helplessness manifests itself at every turn, and learned helplessness reliably produces depression.[8]

The second explanation of why women are more depressed than men involves *rumination.* This theory says that when trouble strikes, men act, whereas women think. She gets fired from her job and she tries to figure out why; she broods and she relives the event over and over. A man, upon getting fired, goes out and gets drunk, beats someone up, or otherwise distracts himself from thinking about it. He may even go right out and look for another job, without bothering to think through what went wrong. If depression is a disorder of thinking, rumination stokes it. The tendency to analyze feeds right into it; the tendency to act breaks it up—at least in the short run.

In fact, depression itself sets off rumination more in women than in men. When we find ourselves depressed, what do we do? Women try to figure out where the depression came from. Men play basketball or head for the office to work in order to distract themselves. It is a fascinating fact that men have more alcoholism and drug abuse than women do, perhaps even enough for us to be able to say: Men drink, women get depressed. Women, ruminating about the source of the depression, will only get more depressed, whereas men, by taking action, may cut depression off at the knees.

The rumination view might explain the depression epidemic as a whole, as well as the lopsided sex ratio. We now live in an age of rationality and self-consciousness. We are encouraged to take our problems more seriously and analyze them endlessly rather than act. Since depression is amplified by negative thinking, more depression might well be the result.[9]

The third possible explanation is the *pursuit of thinness.* To a much greater extent than men, women in our society have been caught up in the notion that being very thin is beautiful. The thin ideal is biologically almost impossible to achieve, however. If you are one of the majority—dieting constantly to achieve the ideal—you are set up for depression. Either you will fail to keep the extra pounds from coming back, like 95 percent of women (and then failure and frequent reminders that you are "too fat" will depress you), or you will succeed and become a walking anorexic, starving constantly (see chapter 12) and suffering one of the major side effects of starvation—depression.

Around the world, every culture that has the thin ideal has more depression in women and also has eating disorders. All cultures that do not have the thin ideal do not have eating disorders, and they do not have more women depressed than men.[10]

In a study of several hundred seventh-graders I participated in, we tried to predict which girls, as they came into puberty, would be at risk for depression. We found discontent with developing body shape to be a major risk factor. When boys go through puberty, they become more muscled and more like the "ideal" man. But when girls go through puberty, they develop soft fat, which fashion dictates is unsightly. They have been brainwashed into thinking that voluptuous is ugly. Before puberty, boys are more depressed than girls, but as puberty sets in, the girls become more depressed.[11]

So there are three factors that make women more depressed than men: more training in helplessness, more rumination, and the vain pursuit of thinness. These are all changeable. Changing the thin ideal is largely a matter of changing societal practices. Changing rumination and changing the indoctrination of girls into helplessness is a matter of changing childrearing and of therapy.

Treatments for Depression That Work

Most of the time, depression can be markedly shortened in duration and considerably relieved in intensity by treatment. There are four therapies that work: two biological, drugs and electroconvulsive shock (ECS); and two psychological, cognitive therapy (CT) and interpersonal therapy (IPT). All four have been subjected to rigorous testing involving tens of thousands of depressed people. They all work to about the same extent—moderately well.

Beware of any other form of treatment offered for unipolar depression.

Drugs. The main kinds of drugs are tricyclics (for instance, Elavil, Tofranil, and Sinequan), MAO inhibitors (Marplan, Nardil, and Parnate), and serotonin-reuptake inhibitors (Prozac). All of these drugs take between ten days and three weeks to start working. When they do work, they relieve depression markedly about 65 percent of the time. That is the good news.

Here is the bad news: First, about a quarter of depressed people cannot or will not take drugs, usually because of side effects. Second, once you go off the drug, your risk for the relapse, or recurrence, of depression is considerable, probably just the same as your risk was before taking the drug. In order to prevent further depression or relapse, you should keep taking the drug—maybe for the rest of your life.[12]

ECS. Electroconvulsive shock is scary. It has worse press than it deserves, but it is far from innocuous. Most of the time it is rapid and highly effective. It relieves severe depression about 75 percent of the time, usually in a series of ECSs that take a few days. Many lives have undoubtedly been saved by its use, particularly the lives of acutely suicidal people.

The bad news is identical to that for drugs. Many people will not agree to ECS because of its considerable side effects—memory loss, cardiovascular changes, and confusion—and because it is a major medical procedure. Even more important, there is no evidence that it cuts down the recurrence of depression. Rather, it provides acute relief.[13]

So both biological treatments bring quite effective relief. Both also have serious side effects, and both are only cosmetic—they don't solve the underlying problems, and depression is likely to return unless you keep taking medication.

Cognitive therapy (CT). Cognitive therapy, which seeks to change the way the depressed person consciously thinks about failure, defeat, loss, and helplessness,[14] employs five basic tactics.

First, you learn to recognize the automatic thoughts—the very quick phrases, so well practiced as to be almost unnoticed and unchallenged—that flit through consciousness at the times you feel worst.

> *A mother of three children sometimes screams at them as she sends them off to school. She feels very depressed as a consequence. In CT, she learns to recognize that right after these screaming incidents she always says to herself, "I'm a terrible mother—even worse than my own mother." She learns to become aware of these automatic thoughts.*

Second, you learn to dispute the automatic thoughts by focusing on contrary evidence.

> *The mother reminds herself that when the kids come home from school, she plays football with them, tutors them in geometry, and talks to them sympathetically about their problems. She marshals this evidence and sees that it contradicts her first thought that she is a bad mother.*

Third, you learn to make different explanations, called *reattributions,* and to use them to dispute your automatic thoughts.

> *The mother learns to say: "I'm fine with the kids in the afternoon and terrible in the morning. Maybe I'm not a morning person."*

That is a much less permanent and pervasive explanation for screaming at the kids in the morning. As for the chain of negative explanations that goes "I'm a terrible mother, I'm not fit to have kids, therefore I don't deserve to live," she learns to interrupt it by inserting the new explanation: "It's completely illogical to infer that I don't deserve to live because I'm not a morning person."

Fourth, you learn how to distract yourself from depressing thoughts. Rumination, particularly when one is under pressure to perform well, makes the situation even worse. Often, in order to do your best, it is better to put off thinking. You learn to control not only what you think but also when you think it.

Fifth, you learn to question the depression-sowing assumptions governing so much of what you do:

- "I can't live without love."
- "Unless everything I do is perfect, I'm a failure."
- "Unless everybody likes me, I'm a failure."
- "There is a perfect right solution for every problem. I must find it."

These kinds of premises set you up for depression. If you choose to live by them—as so many of us do—your life will be filled with blue days and weeks. You can, however, choose a new set of more forgiving premises to live by:

- "Love is precious but rare."
- "Success is doing my best."
- "For every person who likes you, one person doesn't like you."
- "Life consists of putting my fingers in the biggest leaks in the dam."

CT works quite well, bringing considerable relief to about 70 percent of depressed people. It is roughly as effective as the typically prescribed drugs, but somewhat less effective than ECS. It takes about a month to start working, and therapy is brief—usually a total of a few months, once or twice a week. In one way, CT is clearly superior to a single course of drugs or ECS: It lowers your future risk of depression by teaching you new skills of thinking that you can use the next time really bad things happen to you. While CT lowers future risk more than drugs, it does not lower your risk of recurrence even close to zero.[15]

My main reservations about CT are, first, that it may work better on moderate depression than on severe depression—for which drugs should probably be tried first; second, cognitive therapy has mostly been used with educated people who are "psychologically minded"—aware of their thoughts and how thinking affects their emotions. Little is known about how well it works for less educated and less sophisticated people; third, there is so much recurrence of severe depression, even with

CT, that there is a long way to go before anything more than "moderate relief" can be claimed.

Interpersonal therapy (IPT). Interpersonal therapy focuses on social relations. It has become important because in the major NIMH-sponsored outcome study of depression, it was intended to be a placebo treatment but proved just as effective as tricyclics and at least as effective as CT in relieving depression.[16]

This therapy has its origins in the long-term psychoanalytic treatments devised by Harry Stack Sullivan and Frieda Fromm-Reichmann. But IPT is decidedly not psychoanalytic. In contrast, it does not deal with the childhood underpinnings, the decades-old defenses. IPT is also not long-term; rather, it consists of twelve to sixteen sessions, usually once a week.[17]

IPT sees depression in a medical model, asserting that depression has many causes, biological as well as environmental. Salient among the causes are interpersonal problems. IPT hones in on the here-and-now problems of getting along with other people. Current disputes, frustrations, anxieties, and disappointments are the main material of this therapy. IPT looks at four problem areas in the current life of the patient: grief, fights, role transitions, and social deficits.

When dealing with grief, IPT looks for abnormal grief reactions. It brings out the delayed mourning process and helps the patient find new social relationships that can substitute for the loss. When dealing with fights, the IPT practitioner helps determine where the disrupted relationship is going: Does it need renegotiation? Is it at an impasse? Is it irretrievably lost? Communication, negotiation, and assertive skills are taught. Role transitions include retirement, divorce, and leaving home. When dealing with these, the IPT practitioner gets the patient to reevaluate the lost role, to express emotions about the loss, to develop social skills suitable for the new role, and to establish new social supports. When dealing with social deficits, the IPT practitioner looks for recurrent patterns in past relationships. Emotional expression is encouraged. Both abiding social strengths and weaknesses are uncovered. When weaknesses are found, role playing and enhanced communication skills are encouraged.

The main virtues of IPT are that it is brief (a few months) and inexpensive, it has no known adverse side effects, and it has been shown to be quite effective against depression, bringing relief in approximately

The Right Treatment

UNIPOLAR DEPRESSION SUMMARY TABLE

	CT	*IPT*	*Drugs*	*ECS*
IMPROVEMENT	▲▲▲	▲▲▲	▲▲▲	▲▲▲◢
RELAPSE	▲▲◢	▲▲◢ ?	▲◢	▲◢
SIDE EFFECTS	▼	▼	▼▼▼	▼▼▼▼
COST	all are inexpensive			
TIME SCALE	months	months	weeks	days
OVERALL	▲▲▲	▲▲▲	▲▲◢	▲▲◢

CT = Cognitive therapy, IPT = Interpersonal therapy, Drugs = Tricyclics, MAO inhibitors, and serotonin-reuptake inhibitors, ECS = Electroconvulsive shock.

IMPROVEMENT

- ▲▲▲▲ = 80–100% markedly improved or symptom free
- ▲▲▲ = 60–80% markedly improved
- ▲▲ = at least 50% moderately improved
- ▲ = probably better than placebo
- o = probably useless

RELAPSE (after discontinuation of treatment)

- ▲▲▲▲ = 10% or fewer relapse
- ▲▲▲ = 10–20% relapse
- ▲▲ = moderate relapse rate
- ▲ = high relapse rate

Side Effects

- ▼▼▼▼ = severe
- ▼▼▼ = moderate
- ▼▼ = mild
- ▼ = none

OVERALL

- ▲▲▲▲ = excellent, clearly the therapy of choice
- ▲▲▲ = very good
- ▲▲ = useful
- ▲ = marginal
- o = probably useless

70 percent of cases. Its main drawback is that it is not very widely practiced (it is very hard to find an IPT practitioner outside of New York City). This means that little research has been done to find its active ingredients and to replicate its benefits for depression.

Everyday Depression

Your score on the depression test was probably below the moderate-to-severe range; most people score between 5 and 15. If that is true for you,

you are probably not in need of therapy for depression. It may be true that you are sad quite a bit, that most of your life is not filled with gusto, that you get fatigued pretty easily, that setbacks hit you pretty hard, that you suck up energy from social gatherings rather than adding life, and that you are not optimistic about your future. But you probably do not have a depressive disorder.

If the last paragraph describes your state, you should try to do something to change this state of affairs, for even mild depression poisons everyday life. The same four groups of symptoms—sadness, pessimism, passivity, and muted physical appetites—occur when depression is mild, only with less force. When mild depression has become a life-style, it is pointless, and it should be changed.

Mild depression is usually caused by pessimistic habits of thinking. The pessimist sees the causes of failure and rejection as permanent ("It's going to last forever"), pervasive ("It's going to ruin everything"), and personal ("It's my fault"). These habitual beliefs are just that, mere beliefs. They are often false, and they are often inaccurate catastrophizings. The main lesson of cognitive therapy is that this way of thinking can be permanently changed—even in severe depressions. Mild depressives can usually change it without therapy.

The main skill of optimistic thinking is disputing. This is a skill everyone has, but we normally use it only when *others* accuse us wrongly. If a jealous friend tells you what a lousy executive or bad mother you are, you can marshal evidence against the accusation and spit it back in his or her face. Mild depressives make the same sorts of accusations to themselves, *about* themselves, many times a day. You walk into a party and you say to yourself, "I have nothing to say. No one is going to like me. I look terrible." When these accusations issue from inside, you treat them as if they were unimpeachable. But the automatic pessimistic thoughts you have are just as motivated and irrational as the ravings of a jealous rival. They originate not in hard fact but in the criticisms your parents made of you in anger, your big sister's jealous mocking, and your priest's unbending rules, all absorbed passively when you were much younger.

You can, with some discipline, learn to become a superb disputer of pessimistic thoughts. I wrote a book about this, *Learned Optimism* (1991). It has exercises in it that should prove useful to you. This is not the place to repeat its contents, but I commend it to you. Once you acquire the skills of optimism, they stay. This regimen is not like dieting, which, as we shall see in chapter 12, almost always undoes itself after a time. Staying on a diet, continuing to refuse the food you love, is no fun. Disputing your own negative thoughts, in contrast, *is* fun. Once you are good at it, it makes you feel better instantly. Once you start doing it well, you want to keep doing it. If you have a low mood almost every day, you can choose to change the way you think. When you do so, you will find that your life is more worth living.

9

The Angry Person

For some of the large indignities of life, the best remedy is direct action. For the small indignities, the best remedy is a Charlie Chaplin movie. The hard part is knowing the difference.

Carol Tavris, *Anger: The Misunderstood Emotion*

THE DISHWASHER FIGHT
Akron, Ohio, 8:15 p.m.

KATE: *Scrape the gunk off the plates before you hand them to me, puhllease.*
JONAH: *Look, I'm rinsing them off first.*
KATE: *Rinsing isn't enough. I've told you a hundred times: Dishwashers don't scour plates.*
JONAH: *Yeah, I have to wash the dishes before you wash the dishes.*
KATE: *Can't you just be a little help around here before you start complaining?*
JONAH: *You don't seem to realize that I've had a hard day at work. I don't need this shit when I come home!*
KATE: You've *had a hard day! What do you think two teenagers and a six-month-old to take care of are? May Day at Bryn Mawr? I need a man who pitches in, not a black hole.*
JONAH: *Black hole, eh? Who went to my promotion party last week and did nothing except scowl? You ungrateful bitch.*
[Jonah storms out. Kate bursts into tears of helpless rage.]

The dishwasher fight is an all-too-common experience. This couple lives a balance of recriminations. All it takes is some innocent issue, like the dishwasher, to bring the simmering resentments to the surface. The underlying issues don't seep out then; they emerge in volcanic form.

Because they explode, both Kate and Jonah are taken by surprise, and neither can be coolheaded enough to be anything but aggressive and defensive. Nothing gets resolved, and now, yet another incident is added to the ever-mounting mass of things to fight about next time.

Do you often find yourself in "dishwasher fights" with people you care about? Do the issues mount with nothing getting resolved? Are you a grudge collector? Let's find out if you are an angry person—relatively speaking. I want you to take an anger inventory. There is nothing tricky or deep about this quiz. Your score will tell you where you stand relative to other adults.

ANGER INVENTORY[1]

Read each statement and then mark the appropriate number to indicate *how you generally feel.* There are no right or wrong answers. Do not spend too much time on any one statement, but give the answer that seems to describe how you *generally* feel.

1. I am quick-tempered.

Almost never	Sometimes	Often	Almost always
1	2	3	4

2. I have a fiery temper.

Almost never	Sometimes	Often	Almost always
1	2	3	4

3. I am a hotheaded person.

Almost never	Sometimes	Often	Almost always
1	2	3	4

4. I get angry when I am slowed down by others' mistakes.

Almost never	Sometimes	Often	Almost always
1	2	3	4

5. I feel annoyed when I am not given recognition for doing good work.

Almost never	Sometimes	Often	Almost always
1	2	3	4

6. I fly off the handle.

Almost never	Sometimes	Often	Almost always
1	2	3	4

7. When I get mad, I say nasty things.

Almost never	Sometimes	Often	Almost always
1	2	3	4

8. It makes me furious when I am criticized in front of others.

Almost never	Sometimes	Often	Almost always
1	2	3	4

9. When I get frustrated, I feel like hitting someone.

Almost never	Sometimes	Often	Almost always
1	2	3	4

10. I feel infuriated when I do a good job and get a poor evaluation.

Almost never	Sometimes	Often	Almost always
1	2	3	4

Scoring. Simply add the numbers attached to your answers for the ten questions. The higher your total, the more anger dominates your life.

If you scored 13 or below, you are in the least angry 10 percent of people.

If you scored 14–15, you are in the lowest quarter.

If you scored 17–20, your anger level is about average.

If you scored 21–24, your anger level is high, around the seventy-fifth percentile.

If you scored 29–30 and you are male, your anger level is around the ninetieth percentile.

If you scored 25–27 and you are female, your anger level is around the ninetieth percentile.

If you scored above 30 and you are male, your anger level is at the most hotheaded ninety-fifth percentile.

If you scored above 28 and you are female, your anger level is at the ninety-fifth percentile.

People mellow as they age. If you are under twenty-three years old, a score of 26 or more puts you in the most angry 10 percent. But if you are over twenty-three years old, a score of only 24 or more puts you in the top 10 percent.

If you scored in the top half of the anger inventory, anger is an emotion you know well.

ANGER has three components:

There is a *thought,* a very discrete and particular thought: "I am being trespassed against." Often, events get out of hand so quickly that you will not be conscious of this thought. You may simply react—but the thought of trespass is lurking there nonetheless. Kate's underlying thought was "Jonah never helps; he just bitches." Jonah's was "Kate doesn't appreciate me."

There is a *bodily reaction.* Your sympathetic nervous system and your muscles mobilize for physical assault. Your muscles tense. Your blood pressure and heart rate skyrocket. Your digestive processes stop. Brain centers are triggered and your brain chemistry goes into an attack mode. All this is accompanied by subjective feelings of anger.

Third—and this is what the first two phases ready you for—you *attack.* Your attack is directed toward ending the trespass—immediately. You lash out. What you are doing is nothing less than trying to wound or kill the trespasser. If you are well socialized, you will attack verbally, not physically; and if you are very well socialized, you will usually be able to control the attack somewhat. You will mute it, or suppress it, saving it for a more opportune moment. You might even turn the other cheek altogether.

The question of what happens to anger when you control the attack phase is an area of major controversy. It is fundamental to Freudian psychology that emotion is hydraulic (the very meaning of *dynamic* in Freudian *psychodynamics*). Emotion is like a liquid in a closed system: If anger is dammed up or pushed down in one place, it will inevitably push its way up in some other, unwelcome place. If you don't vent your anger when you are angry, it will increase your blood pressure, or eat an ulcer into your stomach, or cause self-hate, or be *displaced* until you come across a less dangerous victim—like your three-year-old daughter. Anti-Freudians claim that anger unexpressed simply dissipates. If you count to four hundred or turn the other cheek, before you know it the anger will be muted. Then it will be gone. Before this chapter is over, we will have a better idea of which view is correct.

What Anger Does for You

Your anger has a long history, one that goes back before your childhood and before your parents' childhoods. It goes back to the life-and-death struggles of your early human ancestors, and further still to our primate ancestors and *their* forebears. Nature "red in tooth and claw" is a popular view of survival of the fittest. And while not completely accurate, the human capacity for anger is one of the principal reasons we—and not some other primate line—are the dominant species on earth.

Robert Ardrey, a theorist of human evolution, argued that our primate ancestors were not the peaceful vegetarian apes whose big brains were adaptive because they made tools, a sentiment so dear to the politics of most anthropologists. Rather, our forebears succeeded because they were carnivorous apes, selected because they made weapons and had the explosive anger to wield them well. Ardrey's school of thought holds that we are descended from a line of nonpareil killers. In the two poles of the evolution of intelligence postulated in the musical, cooperative spacemen of *Close Encounters of the Third Kind* versus the supreme predators in *Alien,* Ardrey's theory claims that the human species embodies the latter.[2]

This kind of anger is most effectively aroused in defense of our own territory, and this is the principal thing—never to be forgotten—that anger does for us. The focal thought is, after all, "My domain is being trespassed against." It is a military postulate that people attacked on their own territory will defend themselves with vigor—nay, with astonishing ferocity. When we defend our children, our land, our jobs, our privileges, or our lives, we are transformed from shepherds, teachers, accountants, and mothers into street fighters and terrorists and Amazons. When we are drafted to fight on somebody else's turf, we are just doing a job, weighing the likely outcome of each move, quite ready to cut and run when the fight seems lost. Not so when it is our domain and we are desperate and angered. Vietnam, Algeria, the Warsaw ghetto, and Ireland are memorable lessons of this postulate.

Another benefit is that anger aims for revenge and restitution—for justice as we see it. It helps to right wrongs and to bring about needed change. When we fight with our spouse, for example, we usually think, "I am right and he is wrong." Anger, unlike fear or sadness, is a moral emotion. It is "righteous." It aims not only to end the current trespass but to repair any damage done. It also aims to prevent further trespass by disarming, imprisoning, emasculating, or killing the trespasser.

When someone advises us to turn the other cheek, to "acknowledge it and let it go," or to weigh the cost versus the benefits of fighting, we may resist this advice. We think that it would be wrong, that if we didn't fight, we would be sacrificing justice. We would be cowards, and evil would triumph again.

There is another moral aspect to anger. We deem it honest to express our anger. We live in an age that tells us to "let it all hang out." If we feel anger, we should not suppress it.

It is important to recognize that this doctrine is not universal. The rituals that submissive baboons go through in the presence of an alpha, that is, dominant, male, the trouble Americans have discerning whether a Japanese is furious, the subtle way in which one Englishman cuts another to the core, all testify to the fact that the expression of anger is malleable. Time and place and custom enormously influence whether it is a virtue to show naked anger or a virtue to hide it. Our "ventilationist" view is no more than a fashion, a fashion that has several sources: a reaction to the global censoring of emotion by Victorian society, the social homogenization of American life urging us to "get down to the nitty-gritty," and the Electronic Age taste for headlines and sound bites, allowing us to dispense with the mannerly and time-consuming rituals of masked emotions.

So anger helps us defend threatened territory—it is just, and it is honest. Not only that—it is healthy. It is widely believed that bottling up anger can kill us, slowly and in three different ways.

First, if we suppress our anger, it turns inward against us. Anger turned against the self produces self-loathing, depression, and, ultimately, true self-destruction in the form of suicide.

Second, anger bottled up produces high blood pressure and heart disease. So compelling is this theory that we can almost feel it at work. Imagine yourself insulted by someone you hate. Force yourself to take it and remain in this uncomfortable state. Grit your teeth, clench your fists, go red in the face. You can almost feel your blood pressure surge. Indeed, in experimental studies, blood pressure subsides faster after insult when you retaliate against the person who insulted you. In field studies, the Type A personality—hostile, competitive, and time-urgent—has more heart attacks than the more relaxed Type Bs do.[3]

Finally, anger suppressed is said to cause cancer. There is a "cancer-prone personality," a Type C. Type C people control their emotional reactions because they believe that it's useless to express their needs. They do not express anger, but suffer silently and stoically; they do not kick against cruel fate. Type C women, particularly, have a higher rate of malignant breast cancer than do women who express their emotions.[4] Moreover, when women with malignant breast cancer receive psychotherapy in which they are encouraged to ventilate their emotions, they live for somewhat longer periods.[5] No wonder we have become a people who anger easily. We protest, we shout, we litigate. We do not suffer trespass stoically. The heroes of many of our movies are Rockys, Rambos, and Dirty Harrys who explode violently: "Go ahead, make my day."

Anger is the effective defense of what belongs to us, the springboard to justice, the emblem of honesty, the path to rosy health. What a splendid emotion!

The Pros of Anger Revisited

Not so fast. In spite of anger being so deeply enshrined in our culture, many of its virtues are myths based on Freudian ideology or on distortions of evidence.

Anger: the unhealthy emotion. Is it true that anger unexpressed leads to more cancer, more heart disease, and more depression?

Cancer. The evidence that suppression of anger leads to cancer is very weak. The Type C personality, allegedly a predisposer to cancer, is made up of several characteristics confounded with one another. The Type C woman, for instance, fails to express her anger. But she is also more helpless and hopeless, has more anxiety and more depression, is more fatalistic, and has little fighting spirit. Which of these is the active ingredient? Lack of anger expression is one possibility, but hopelessness, helplessness, and depression are more likely to be the real culprits. Each of these last three has been linked to tumor growth, but anger suppression has not. Indeed, the inventors of Type C theory also found that "exploders," people who have frequent outbursts of temper, also have more cancer than normal people.[6] Examining the cancer evidence, I cannot determine if anger expression is worse, or better, or of no account in cancer.

Heart disease. The Type A personality—heart-attack prone—is also made up of three confounded traits: hostility, time urgency, and competitiveness. Type A researchers, unlike Type C researchers, have tried to separate the components. Hostility, the overt expression of anger, is probably the real culprit. Time urgency, competitiveness, and the suppression of anger do not seem to play a role in Type As getting more heart disease. In one study, 255 medical-school students took a personality test that measured overt hostility. The angriest of them went on—twenty-five years later—to have roughly five times as much heart disease as the least angry ones. In another study, men who had the highest risk of heart attacks were the ones with especially explosive voices, more irritation when forced to wait, and more outwardly directed anger. In an exploration of the mechanism by which anger expression might damage the heart, the eighteen men in this study angrily recounted incidents that annoyed them. The pumping efficiency of their heart dropped by 5 percent on average, suggesting a drop in blood flow to the heart itself. Pumping efficiency was not changed by other stressors.[7]

Studies find that blood pressure stays high when anger is bottled up only among male students bottling up their anger at other male students, that is, only males of the same status. When a student bottles up his anger against a professor, blood pressure goes down, and it goes up if he decides to express his anger. And anger expression does not lower blood pressure for women; expressing hostility *raises* female blood pressure. In contrast, friendliness in reaction to trespass lowers it.[8]

I have a very simple theory of how emotion affects heart disease. It may well be wrong, but it is compatible with most of the facts. Your heart is a pump, and like any mechanical pump, there is a limit, or *rating,* on how many times it can beat before it wears out. So, for example, your heart might be rated at 100 million beats. Once your rating is exceeded, you are very likely to have a heart attack—if something else hasn't killed you first. Ratings vary from person to person and from family to family, with the limit set by such factors as constitutional strength, exercise, and childhood diseases.

Some emotions, the ones that raise your heart rate and blood pressure, use up your allotted beats more quickly than others. Anger and fear are two such emotions: They mobilize the sympathetic nervous system in just this way. Relaxation and calm have the opposite effect.

People who often get angry use up their allotted beats faster. Several times a day, they go into a rage; their heart races and their blood pressure soars. On a bad day, they may use up two days' allotment. Fearful and paranoid people who see the world as a threatening place get triggered into massive sympathetic activity more often and so also use up their allotment faster. The habit of ventilating your anger—as opposed to suppressing it—uses up your allotment and so contributes to heart disease.[9]

The evidence is clear: Overt anger, contrary to popular belief, is bad for your heart.

Depression. The view that depression is anger turned inward is false. Freud spun this theory out of whole cloth some eighty years ago. Unsupported as it was, his theory of depression, along with his theory of repressed sexuality, was among the main forces that legitimized our present ethic of promiscuous emotional expression.

By the 1950s, therapists were having a field day with this ethic. One of the main treatments for depression was to encourage patients to get angry. Therapists helped depressed people to shout about the times they had been victimized and to rage over how bad their lives were. When I first learned how to treat depression, in the early 1970s, this was one of the techniques I was taught. But something quite shocking occurred when we prodded depressed people into getting angry and remembering long-forgotten abuse.

Keep in mind that depressed people are often quiet, shy, and withdrawn. They are often reluctant to talk about their troubles. With our Freudian-oriented prodding, we got them to talk, and talk, and talk. They began to complain. They remembered how bad life was. They wallowed. Encouraged, they dredged up more and more tragic material. They wept. Not infrequently, they would unravel, and then we had a great deal of trouble getting them together again. What might have started as an ordinary case of mild depression sometimes escalated into a severe case—with a suicide attempt thrown in.

Put another way, there is simply no evidence that depression is anger turned inward. Getting the anger out of depressives, who are often well defended against many of the bad things that have happened to them, sometimes worsens depression. Contrary to the Freudian theory, when you measure anger during depression, hostility increases during the depression and continues after the depression is gone.[10]

So I conclude that venting your anger is not good for your health. It has no clear relation to cancer, it may increase—rather than decrease—your risk for coronary heart disease, and it can exacerbate depression.

Anger: honest? just? effective? We deem it honest to tell the object of our anger just what we think. This is, after all, the truth, and we should tell the truth. But there is a difference between honesty and truth. Anger, specifically, and emotion, generally, color evidence. This may be one of emotion's reasons for existing. By biasing the evidence, emotion readies us to act in certain ways that may be highly adaptive when we are in the right niche. Emotion places colored lenses on the spectacles through which we usually view the world. Anxiety makes the world look more frightening than it is; fear lowers our threshold for seeing danger, and makes us more apt to flee. When we are watching a horror movie on the VCR, a real cat leaping from behind a desk momentarily terrifies us.

Depression colors the world, too, and so gets us to give up, turn inward, and sit in our cave conserving our energy until happier times materialize. To a depressed person, the world often seems bleaker than it actually is (one of the most objectionable aspects of the latest best-selling suicide manual is that it fails to recognize that wanting to kill yourself may be based on a temporary distortion of the evidence, not on rational evaluation). Anger readies us to attack—innocent actions seen through its lens appear to be trespass. Our perceptual threshold for affront lowers. When a clumsy fifth-grader accidentally drops his lunch tray on a bully, the bully interprets the action as aggressive and intentional. This "hostile-attribution bias" characterizes the way aggressive boys think all the time, and the way normal people think when they are angry.[11]

So while it may be honest to be angry, it is not truthful. The judgments we make when we are angry are often far off the mark, coloring evidence in a hostile and threatening manner.

The same can be said for justice. Anger moves us toward justice—*as we see it.* Anger is not an emotion that helps us see things from our attacker's point of view. Rather, it imposes a protective, self-interested lens of trespass on the world. Sometimes it is correct, and it punishes the trespasser most fittingly. Other times it wreaks revenge on innocent people or demands overly severe punishment for minor transgressions. When in the heat of anger you make the mistake of punishing a small child severely, you may create excessive damage. An accurate description of the moral tone of red-hot anger is "self-righteous" rather than "righteous."

Finally, the effectiveness of anger is not all it is cracked up to be. Certainly, in a desperate, back-against-the-wall, physical fight on our own territory, anger gives us the strength of many. But we are almost never in that situation. A rival insults us. A co-worker slights our efforts. Our spouse flirts with another man. Our two-year-old disobeys us. A voyeur peeks at us. How effective is an outburst of temper in these situations?

Anger galvanizes some people into clever repartee and resourceful argument—they become masters of the "last word." For most of the rest of us, anger is a very disorganizing emotion. We fume and we sputter. We forget our most important points. We are reduced to shouting epithets. We regret what we said when the argument is over. We wish we hadn't gotten angry.

The Cons of Anger

> If you are patient in one moment of anger, you will escape a hundred days of sorrow.
>
> Chinese proverb

First and foremost, anger is the emotion that fuels violence. A society like ours, which urges the expression of anger, sanctions it, and makes movies about its virtues, is a violent society. It should be sobering to "ventilationists" that America has five times the rate of violent crime as Japan, an anti-ventilationist society. Murder, assault, and violent rape occur in unprecedented numbers in America. Child abuse and spouse battering are rampant. Strangely, though there are disorders of anxiety and depression, the nosologists have seen fit to designate no certified disorders of anger. The outmoded category "explosive-personality disorder" and the rare category "paranoid disorder (without schizophrenia)" are as close as the taxonomy of mental problems now comes. But out-of-hand anger ruins many lives. More, I believe, than schizophrenia, more than alcohol, more than AIDS. Maybe even more than depression.

A second impact of anger is subtler, but almost as shattering: Serious turmoil between parents is the most depressing ordinary event that children witness. We have followed the lives of some 400 children for the last five years, focusing on children whose parents fight (20 percent) and those whose parents divorce or separate (15 percent).[12] We watched these 140 children carefully and contrasted them to the rest of the children. What we saw has important implications for our society at large and for how married couples should deal with anger.

The children of fighting families look the same—that is, just as bad—as the children of divorce: These children are more depressed than the children from intact families whose parents don't fight. We had hoped the difference would diminish over time, but it didn't. Three years later, these children were still more depressed than the rest of the children.

Once their parents start fighting, these children become unbridled pessimists. They see bad events as permanent and pervasive, and they see themselves as responsible. Years later this pessimism persists, even after they tell us their parents are no longer fighting. Their worldview has changed from the rosy optimism of childhood to the grim pessimism of a depressed adult. I believe that many children react to their parents' fighting by developing a loss of security so shattering that it marks the beginning of a lifetime of dysphoria.

It is important to realize that these are averaged results. Some of the children do not become depressed, some of the children do not become pessimists, and some of the children recover over time. Divorce or fighting does not doom a child to years of unhappiness; it only makes it much more likely.

Many more bad life events occur to children whose parents divorce or fight. This continued disruption could be what keeps depression so high among such children. Among these bad events are

- Classmates act less friendly
- Parent hospitalized
- Child fails a course at school
- Parent loses job
- Child himself hospitalized
- A friend dies

This adds up to a nasty picture for the children of parental turmoil.

Parents' fighting may hurt children in such a lasting way for one of two reasons.

The first possibility is that parents who are unhappy with each other fight and separate. The fighting and separation directly disturb the child, causing long-term depression and pessimism.

The second possibility is the traditional wisdom: Fighting and separation themselves have little direct effect on the child, but awareness of parents' unhappiness is the culprit—so disturbing as to produce long-term depression.

Only future research can clarify this, but although there is nothing in our data to tell us which of these two is right, I lean toward the first. I don't believe that children are subtle creatures with "unhappiness in parents" detectors; in fact, I think that most children see their parents in a very positive light and that it takes real upheaval or deprivation to make a child notice how rotten things are. Fighting and violence between the two people the child most depends on for his or her future is just such upheaval.

Many people are, of course, in rocky marriages, filled with strife and conflict. Less dramatic, but more common, is this situation: After several years of marriage, many people don't like their spouses anymore, which breeds resentment and is fertile ground for fighting. But at the same time, both marriage partners are often overwhelmingly concerned with the well-being of their children. It seems to be a plain fact—at least statistically—that either separation or fighting in response to an unhappy marriage is likely to harm children in lasting ways. If future research tells us that it is parents' unhappiness and not the overt fighting that is the culprit, then I would suggest marital counseling aimed at coming to terms with the shortcomings of the marriage. This sometimes works. But if future research determines that it is the act of fighting and the choice to separate that are responsible for children's depression, very different advice would follow. All of us save money for our children. We put off the trip to Hawaii now, and perhaps forever, so that our children might lead better lives than we do. Are you willing to forgo separation from a spouse you don't like anymore? An even harder challenge: Are you willing to choose to refrain from fighting—on just the same grounds—for the sake of your children?

There may be something to be said for couples' fighting. Sometimes justice is achieved for you. But as far as your children are concerned, there is very little to be said in favor of parents' fighting. Therefore, I choose to go against the prevailing ethic and recommend that it is not your well-being, as much as it is your child's, that is at stake.[13]

Physical violence and childhood depression are the two major costs of venting anger, but there is a third—milder but much more commonplace. It is the most persuasive, however, because it is so obvious: Anger damages relationships.

Anger is hot and quick. Its content, uncensored, is destructive. An angry person never sees things from his target's point of view. Judgment, in contrast, is cool and long. Because there is such weak restraint nowadays on expressing anger, because our society is no longer "well mannered," we often do and say things we regret. Words and brash acts, unlike thoughts, cannot be erased. In a lifetime, most of us wreck dozens, even hundreds, of relationships in the heat of anger. Examples are legion:

- In his last tantrum of childhood, an eleven-year-old boy screams "I hate you" at his doting father. Wounded, and unskilled at handling anger or rejection himself, the father never again expresses warm affection to his son.
- A shy woman, used to her husband taking the sexual lead, makes her first direct advance. He, however, is preoccupied with his income-tax forms and gruffly rejects her advances. She never tries again.
- A brilliant psychology undergraduate bursts excitedly into his professor's office, interrupting an important phone call, to tell her his new theory of anger management. With obvious irritation, the professor says, "Go make an appointment with my secretary." Hurt, he switches his major to physics instead.
- A woman slaps her fiancée, infuriated by his flirting at a party. Rejected and furious himself, he storms off, and the flirtation becomes a bedding. The engagement is broken off. Both regret it for years to come.

Some say that telling the other person off clears the air, or that blowing off steam makes you feel less angry. This is the "catharsis" theory of anger expression, and it is one of the pillars of the ventilationist ethic. Catharsis may happen once in a while, but statistically, the opposite is more often the case. Seymour Feshbach, an early pioneer of experiments on anger, explored catharsis by working with a group of young boys who were not aggressive or destructive. He encouraged them to kick furniture and play with violent toys. They did so—exuberantly. Did this drain the boys of aggression? No, it amplified it. The boys became more hostile and destructive, not less. The same holds with adults: Telling someone off typically makes you feel more hostile, not less hostile, toward the target.[14]

Can Anger Be Changed?

I'm not sure. Concerted research and clinical efforts have been mounted to relieve the two other major negative emotions, anxiety and depression. Because each of these is a certified disorder, millions of dollars have been spent and tens of thousands of patients treated with an adventurous variety of tactics. Control groups have been run, and major outcome studies performed. I am therefore entitled to claim, as I did in the last several chapters, that panic is curable, that depression can usually be relieved and shortened, and that obsessions can often be alleviated. Anger, however, is not a certified disorder. Pitifully little research has been focused on it. There are only a few hundred patients who have been treated, and only a handful of tactics have been tested. There is not a single major outcome study on how to change anger. So my advice about anger mixes what is known with more than a dollop of the clinical wisdom.

Let us assume you scored in the upper 10 percent of the anger inventory. Your short fuse is a vexation to others around you and to your spirit as well. After reading this chapter, you are now convinced that the cost of venting your anger clearly outweighs the gain. What should you do?

A good first step is to keep an "anger diary" for a week.[15] Divide it into five columns. Here is what an entry might look like:

Time	*Trigger*	*Intensity*	*Duration*	*Action & Sequel*
10:15	Lens fell out of new glasses	8 (of 10)	10 min.	Called optician. Yelled at her secretary. Felt guilty.
12:30	No mayo on BLT	9	2 min.	Cursed waitress. Got mayo, dirty looks.

Doing this will allow you to see patterns in your anger. What kind of incidents set it off? Trivial ones? Threats to income? Romantic thwarting? Interruption at unimportant tasks? Does shouting make it worse or better? Do you feel guilty? Does it go away quickly even if you don't do anything? Do people seem to like you less afterward? Do you accomplish the goal?

Once you are on top of some of your patterns, you should learn about how clinicians dampen anger. All of their tactics are simple, and you can use them yourself. Anger consists of three aspects: the thought—trespass; the feeling—fury, blood pressure up, heart racing, muscles tensing; and the behavior—attack. There are separate tactics for dampening each of the three.

Thought. When we are provoked, the time interval between the trigger and our attack is often terribly brief. This is as it should be, since it reflects the evolutionary need for instantaneous defense. It is an old saw to "count to ten." This is very sensible advice—as far as it goes. Such advice attempts to buy time between the provocation and the response.

But time for what? The count-to-ten advice assumes that time itself dampens the impulse to hit back. There is some truth in that, but we can do more than just count—the thought "I am being trespassed against" can be directly modified during the lengthened interval. By all means, count; count not to just ten but through twenty breaths. (Better yet: Sleep on it.) But during that time, challenge and reinterpret the thoughts of trespass and affront.

Imagine yourself as a fish swimming along. Numerous fishhooks, in the form of insults, appear in your path. Each offers you the choice of whether or not to bite.[16] Ask yourself: Is this actually a trespass? Try to see yourself from the provoker's point of view. Try to reframe the provocation:

- Maybe he's having a rough day.
- There's no need to take it personally.
- Don't act like a jerk just because he is.
- He couldn't help it.
- This could be a testy situation, but easy does it.

Use humor if you can. For example: You have just been cut off by a reckless driver who did not signal his sudden change of lane. You think, "What an ass!" Visualize a pair of buttocks steering the car ahead of you. Decorate them with some feathers. Get into the image.

Above all, during the interval, change from "ego orientation" to "task orientation." Think: "I know this seems like a personal insult, but it is not. It is a challenge to be overcome that calls on skills I have." Visualize yourself as a bomb disposer. Your job is to slowly and coolly defuse the bomb. Make a plan for defusing the attacker.

Feelings. Use the lengthened time interval to become aware of your feelings. Conscious awareness of arousal makes it easier to regulate anger. Use the feelings as a signal to remind you to cope without antagonism.

- My muscles are tense. Time to relax.
- My breath is coming fast. Take a deep breath.
- He would probably like me to explode. Well, I'm going to disappoint him.[17]

These techniques will help once you are trapped in the situation. But if you find yourself in these situations all too frequently, you need to prevent anger. There are two long-term ways of doing this: progressive relaxation and meditation. Practiced regularly (twice a day), relaxation or meditation prevents angry arousal. (A review of these techniques can be found on pages 56–58.) The techniques are just as useful for angry persons as for anxious persons.

Action. Once the interval is over, you must do something. There are alternatives to attacking. Turning the other cheek is one. A huge smile with a humorous story is another ("You know, there's an old Jewish proverb about . . ."). Creating a rich defusing repertoire is another; it's a splendid alternative to a repertoire of clever put-downs. In her book *Anger: The Misunderstood Emotion,* Carol Tavris quotes a telephone operator who is able to bypass the rude ventilation of some of her customers: "I just say, in my most genuine way, 'Boy, you must be having a rough day.' They immediately calm down, realize how they must have sounded, and apologize." Write down and use sets of two good "defusing" lines, each pair tailored for your spouse, your boss, a difficult co-worker, or your children.

In many anger situations, you want to get your own way in the face of a roadblock. There are technologies for how to overcome such roadblocks more effectively than by attacking. They are called "negotiation training" and "assertiveness training." There are courses and books on these skills, and they work. My preferred book is Sharon Bower's *Assert Yourself.*[18] Bower breaks down assertion into four manageable steps—she calls them D, E, S, and C—which should be done in order.

- *D–Describe.* Describe—with no emotion and no evaluation—exactly what is bothering you. Don't exaggerate. Don't say *always* when you mean *twice.* This bloodless step must come first.
- *E–Express.* Express how this makes you feel. Don't accuse, don't evaluate the other person, just identify which emotion you feel.
- *S–Specify.* Specify exactly what you want your target to do.
- *C–Consequence.* End by saying just what you will do if your target does not comply. Be accurate. Don't threaten, don't menace, and don't bluff.

Recall the fight between Kate and Jonah. Neither had the DESC skills. But if either had, the fight would not have gotten out of hand.

> KATE: *Scrape the gunk off the plates before you hand them to me, puhllease.*
> JONAH: *Look, I'm rinsing them off first.*
> KATE: *Rinsing isn't enough. I've told you a hundred times . . .*

Here's the place where DESC would help. Kate should do it right here, when she first feels her muscles tense and her anger rise.

> KATE [describing]: *The last two times we did the dishes, you said you didn't want to rinse and scrape the dishes. I said that if the dishes weren't scraped, they wouldn't come out clean.* [expressing] *Your saying this again now makes me feel that you don't listen to me. And that makes me sad and angry.* [specifying] *Next time we do the dishes, I want you to scrape them off before you hand them to me—without comment.* [Consequence] *If you don't, I'd prefer to do them alone.*

Or Jonah could have done it.

> KATE: *Rinsing isn't enough. I've told you a hundred times: Dishwashers don't scour plates.*
> JONAH: *Yeah, I have to wash the dishes before you wash the dishes.*
> KATE: *Can't you just be a little help around here before you start complaining?*
> JONAH: *You don't seem to realize that I've had a hard day at work. I don't need this shit when I come home!*

The crucial spot. His temper is flaring. Jonah should now use this as a signal to deploy his DESC skills.

> JONAH [describing]: *The last time we did the dishes we got into a fight.* [expressing] *This makes me feel sad and hopeless. It also makes me feel angry.* [specifying] *Next time we do the dishes, I want you to rub my shoulders while I scrape and rinse them.* [consequence] *If you don't want to do this, I'll just do the dishes alone next time.*

A final bit of advice, concerning fighting in front of your children: I am not naïve enough to think that even if you take this chapter to heart, you will never again fight in front of your children. Fights happen. There is one solid piece of research on the subject of fighting in front of your children—if you must. It concerns resolution. Children who watch films of adults fighting are much less disturbed when the fight ends with a clear resolution. When you fight, go out of your way to resolve the fight, unambiguously and in front of your child.

10

Post-traumatic Stress

I want to live so that my life cannot be ruined by a single phone call.

Federico Fellini, *La Dolce Vita*

THIS IS the saddest chapter of all.

"How's your son, Tommy, doing?" inquired an old customer of Hector's. Hector had sold him an insurance policy a few years before, and they hadn't run into each other since. Hector burst into tears.[1]

Although it had been five years since that awful October evening, the memory and the pain were ever fresh. Tommy, fourteen, had been the center of Hector's and Jodi's lives. The family ate breakfast together every morning, and Hector and Jodi included Tommy in almost everything they did. Every Saturday was Tommy's special day with Hector: just Tommy and Hector all day long.

Norma Sue, Tommy's seventeen-year-old cousin, was always in trouble in her hometown of Chicago, so her parents sent her to live with Hector and Jodi in their small Iowa town to straighten her out. Tommy was particularly enthused about helping Norma Sue, and tried to get her active in the church youth group.

One Monday evening, Tommy persuaded Norma Sue to go to a youth-group meeting with him. She drove. About an hour later, Jodi dropped by her office and took a call from Hector. Hector said that there had been a small car accident, but that both kids were okay. To put her mind at ease, Jodi called the hospital and was told to come right over. Jodi went there and waited, and when Hector arrived with the police, she saw that he was hysterical. She knew immediately that Tommy was dead.

The five years since have been an unending hell for Jodi and Hector.

Jodi, formerly ebullient, has been suicidally depressed ever since. She has lost all motivation to do anything. She never went back to her office, and now barely keeps house. Once or twice a week she wakes up from terrifying nightmares, which often depict Tommy surrounded by "bad" kids, pleading with his mother to protect him. She relives that Monday evening every day of her life.

Hector has barely hung on to his sales job. He used to be a regular member of the million-dollar club, but he hasn't come close since Tommy died. Weekends are even worse for him because that was the time he always devoted to Tommy. Every time the phone rings, Hector almost jumps out of his skin. He can't talk to anyone—especially Jodi—about Tommy because it would hurt too much.

Last month, Hector moved out and Jodi filed for divorce.

Tragedy used to be a part of everyone's life—the human condition. Until this century in the West, more than half the population thought life was a vale of tears. Not so now. It is not unusual to go through an entire lifetime without tragedy. Bad things still happen to us all too frequently: Our stocks go down, our aged parents die, we don't get the job we had hoped for, people we love reject us, we age and die. But we are usually prepared for many of these losses, or at least we know ways to soften the blow. Once in a while, however, the ancient human condition intrudes, and something irredeemably awful, something beyond ordinary human loss, occurs. We are then reminded how fragile the upholstered cubicles we dwell in really are.

So devastating and long-lasting are the effects of extraordinary loss that it has finally been given a name and a diagnostic category of its own: *post-traumatic stress disorder* (*PTSD*). No jargon, no euphemism, no psychobabble, can camouflage that this is the saddest disorder of them all. Distress is universal. Many—but, assuredly, not all people—display the hallmarks of PTSD for months or years afterward:

- **Reliving:** The victim persistently relives the trauma in dreams or in intrusive flashbacks (or has the opposite reaction: He can't recall the event). Not a day went by for years afterward when Hector and Jodi did not ruminate about Tommy's death. They both repeatedly dreamed variations on Tommy's death.
- **Anxiety:** The victim avoids anything connected with the trauma. He has difficulty falling asleep and staying asleep. He can't concentrate. He startles easily. He becomes passive and continually anxious. Hector couldn't bear to talk to anybody about Tommy, and he jumped whenever the phone rang.
- **Numbness:** The victim becomes numb to life. She may feel detached and estranged from people. She may lose the ability to love anybody. Jodi quit her job, Hector lost his ambition, and their marriage fell apart.

The worst of the common tragedies is, by all statistics, the death of a child. Each year in the United States, 150,000 people are killed accidentally. Accidents are the number one killer of children. Thus there are hundreds of thousands of parents in our country today bereaved by the worst loss of all. Unexpected death of a spouse is a close second.

Bereavement: Common lore tells us that it is difficult, but that time heals all wounds. Doesn't it? Only some wounds, it turns out. When your spouse of many years dies, bereavement takes a predictable course: six months to two years of mourning, sadness, even depression, and an elevated risk of death yourself. And then, your life poorer, you pick up and go on. Not so for extraordinary losses.

It used to be thought that victims recovered briskly. Among the first psychiatric studies of the aftermath of disaster was one that focused on the Cocoanut Grove nightclub fire of 1942. Interviews with the survivors and the families of the dead led to an optimistic picture. An "uncomplicated grief reaction" was supposed to dissipate in four to six weeks.[2] This has remained the lore ever since. When people take longer than a few weeks to adjust after their lives have been devastated, it is considered "abnormal." In order to qualify for a certified diagnosis of PTSD, the symptoms have to last at least one month.

Dr. Camille Wortman, a social psychologist, has single-handedly changed the lore. She went through the microfilm records of every auto fatality in Michigan between 1976 and 1979. She randomly chose thirty-nine people who had lost a spouse and forty-one couples who had lost a child. She interviewed them at length and compared them to matched controls.

The parents and the spouses were in decidedly poor shape four to seven years later: They were much more depressed than the controls, were less optimistic about the future, and did not feel good about their lives. They were more "worn-out," "tense," and "unhappy." More of them had died than had the controls. While they had not differed from the controls in income before their child died, the bereaved parents now earned 25 percent less. Twenty percent were divorced (versus 2 percent of the controls). The bereaved people were just as bad off seven years later as four years later, so there did not seem to be a natural healing process at work. Almost everyone asked "Why me?" Sixty percent could find no answer to this wrenching question.[3]

There are some clear cases of what counts as a loss "outside the normal range of human experience": spending years in a concentration camp where you are forced to aid in the killing of fellow prisoners, watching your child be tortured, being the only survivor in your family of a collision with a truck, living through a catastrophic flood that decimates your community, being pinned down in a foxhole for days surrounded by corpses, being kidnapped and held hostage. Such horrific experiences routinely produce PTSD.

> *Dora, a Polish Jew, was sent to Auschwitz with her husband and three sons after the uprising in the Warsaw ghetto. Her husband and her baby perished in the first few hours, but she lived on until the end of the war, watching her two other sons worked to death; she survived by giving sexual favors to camp guards. Dora found her way after the war to distant relatives in Pittsburgh.*
>
> *An old lady now, she has not recovered. She has never worked, and she stays in her attic room listening to classical music most of the time. When she goes out, the sight of men in uniform—policemen, even mailmen—frightens her. She thinks constantly of her dead family and feels guilty that she lived and they died. Her contact with the present is minimal. Every night she dreams of her baby burning to death in an oven. It has been forty-five years of life in Auschwitz.*

Prisoners of war can show lifelong symptoms of PTSD. Forty years after captivity, 188 World War II POWs underwent diagnostic interviews in Minneapolis. Sixty-seven percent had suffered PTSD during some of the previous forty years. Of these, nearly 35 percent still had moderate or severe symptoms, and 40 percent still had mild symptoms.[4]

If PTSD were only about the clear cases, like Dora's and like the POWs', it would be of interest only to specialists and to voyeurs. But PTSD, I believe, is much more widespread and is set off by more commonplace losses than the diagnostic criteria allow. I believe that the objective definition of "extraordinary" loss masks what takes place in the minds of the victims; what takes place does not reside in the objective awfulness of the event.

Bad things, though maybe not as objectively awful as the horrors above, happen to most of us. Some of us react to our losses with resilience. After a few weeks we go about our lives, look for a new family, a new job, a new country, or a new reason for living. Many others of us are more brittle. Major loss changes our way of looking at ourselves and the world forever. We find ourselves beyond consolation. Most people, living through what Dora did, would suffer PTSD. But many people endure the same symptoms when a child dies suddenly.

Some people suffer it when they are mugged or raped. And a few suffer it when they are abandoned by a spouse or, merely, sued.

The Rape-Trauma Syndrome

Rape is distressingly frequent in our society. About 100,000 rapes are reported every year, and possibly seven times as many go unreported. As many as one out of every three to five women will be raped in her lifetime.[5] Rape is even more frequent in poorer societies. Using "extraordinary" as a criterion, rape, and the death of a child as well, would not qualify for PTSD. But it is clear that the death of a child usually, and rape sometimes, set off just the same symptoms as war, torture, and earthquake almost always do.

> *Ms. T., twenty-eight, was asleep in her apartment when she was awakened by a man with a knife. He told her not to turn over and look at him, and threatened to kill her if she fought. He then raped her and fled. Ms. T. reported the crime, accepted physical help and psychological counseling, and even volunteered for work at a rape-crisis hot line.*
>
> *She showed full-blown PTSD. She was afraid to fall asleep and for a month could only sleep at friends' homes—even then, only in daylight. She had nightmares in which she relived the rape. She had a pervasive fear of being watched by the rapist whenever she went outside. Her relationship with her boyfriend deteriorated and ended. She felt numb to love and sex. Eighteen months later, she still had sleep difficulties and nightmares. She felt that her career and her love life had been ruined by the rape.*[6]

When a woman is raped, her first reaction is called the phase of *disorganization.* She shows one of two emotional styles: expressive—fear, anger, crying; or controlled—a calm exterior. The symptoms of PTSD usually soon follow. As many as 95 percent of the victims may show PTSD within two weeks.[7] The victim relives the rape time and again, in waking life and in dreams. Sleep disturbance, both trouble getting to sleep and sudden awakening, sets in. Ms. T. woke up screaming out of deep sleep for months after the rape (in which, you will recall, her assailant woke her out of deep sleep). Rape victims startle easily. Ms. T., a year and a half later, still startled when male strangers talked to her. Normal sexual activity is hard to resume, and a total phobia about sex sometimes develops.

Most victims go through the phase of disorganization and, in time, enter *reorganization.* They change their phone numbers and where they live. They read about rape, write about their experience, and become active in helping other victims.

Four to six years later, about 75 percent of rape victims say they have recovered. More than half of these say that recovery occurred in the first three months, the rest say within two years. Victims with the least fear and the fewest flashbacks in the week following the rape recover more quickly. The very distressed or benumbed victims have a poor outcome. The degree of violence of the assault and how life-threatening it was also predict long-term outcome. The worst news is that 25 percent of rape victims say they have not recovered, even after four to six years. Seventeen years later, 16 percent still had PTSD.[8]

Severity of the objective circumstances is not that good a predictor of PTSD in either rape or physical injury. In a study of forty-eight victims of severe physical injuries, the severity of the injury did not predict who got PTSD, and it did not predict the amount of distress. Rather, how much psychological distress they felt after the injury predicted PTSD.[9] PTSD should, I believe, be defined by the reaction of the victim and how long it lingers, not by the objective "extraordinariness" of the loss. A better criterion is "Do they believe it ruined their lives?"

Vulnerability

As you read this chapter, your reaction is probably like mine as I wrote it: "Please, God, not me." Your risk of enduring some truly catastrophic event is very small. But your risk of experiencing rape or a child dying or the death of your spouse is larger. And even if you escape these, a few people succumb to PTSD from lesser traumas like lawsuits, divorce, mugging, prison, and job loss. There are expert opinions as to who among us is particularly at risk.

Psychologists comb disasters looking for the people who survive them well, without signs of PTSD, and those who crumble most readily. Here is what they have found:

- A prior life history free of mental problems predicted who did best after a catastrophic factory explosion in Norway.
- Among 469 fire fighters caught in a disastrous Australian brushfire, those most at risk for getting chronic PTSD scored high on neuroticism and had a family history of mental disorders. These were better predictors than how much physical trauma each one experienced.

- After the Lebanon war, Israeli combat casualty veterans who were the children of Holocaust survivors (called "second-generation casualties") had higher rates of PTSD than control casualties.
- Among Israeli combat veterans of two wars, those who came down with PTSD after the second war had more combat-stress reactions during the first war.

What can be concluded from this is that people who are psychologically most healthy before trauma are at least risk for PTSD. This may be of some consolation—if you are lucky enough to be one of those people. But if the bad event is awful enough, previous good psychological health will not protect you.[10]

A Hard-Hearted Caution

What I have presented so far is grim. Extreme trauma reliably produces devastating symptoms that last for years. Lesser trauma produces devastation, but in a smaller percentage of victims. Even minor trauma can produce devastation in some people.

Some are skeptical about these "facts." Almost all PTSD victims have an ax to grind, critics contend. The "victims" stand to gain from prolonged symptoms. PTSD, interestingly, got its name and diagnostic status in the wake of the Vietnam War. Veterans came home complaining of all sorts of ills and ruin; not only the veterans who were physically wounded, but even the veterans who participated in atrocities—on the delivery, not the receiving, end. A sample of men interviewed six to fifteen years after violent combat in Vietnam now led lives full of problems. They had more arrests and convictions, more drinking problems, more drug addiction, and more stress than veterans who did not see combat. (Before Vietnam, these two groups did not differ.) Men who took part in atrocities were now in particularly bad shape.[11] All these veterans receive compensation for combat-related disability, and PTSD is now a reimbursable disability. It is in the victims' interests, the skeptics say, to prolong their symptoms.

Given our litigious society, this is not only true of veterans. Hector and Jodi are involved in a lawsuit against Norma Sue's parents. The survivors of the 1972 Buffalo Creek flood in the mountains of Appalachia, from whom some of the most extensive data on chronic PTSD were gathered, were suing the Pittston Company—whose dam had burst and flooded their valley—for many millions as they narrated their stories to social scientists.[12]

There is probably something to this skepticism. It is hard to estimate the true duration and severity of symptoms among survivors who stand to gain by displaying a severe, prolonged, and ruinous picture. But a similar picture also emerges from victims who have little or nothing to gain: Concentration-camp survivors and rape victims have little more than sympathy to gain, and that hardly seems worth the price of living the life of a PTSD victim.

Therapy

Can there be a therapy for people who have had their lives ruined by "one phone call"? Therapists have tried drugs. In the best controlled study, forty-six PTSD Vietnam veterans were administered antidepressants or a placebo. Some of the symptoms of PTSD relented: Nightmares and flashbacks decreased, but not into the normal range. Numbing, a sense of distance from loved ones, and general anxiety did not decrease. More than a quarter of the veterans refused to take the drugs, and it is not known what happened to the improvement of those who agreed to take the drugs when they were withdrawn. In another study, antidepressant drugs produced some relief, but at the end of treatment 64 percent of the drugged group and 72 percent of the placebo group still had PTSD. Relapse is frequent. Overall, antidepressants and anti-anxiety agents produce some symptom relief for some patients, but drug researchers have concluded that drug treatment alone is "never sufficient to relieve the suffering in PTSD."[13]

Several brands of psychotherapy have been tried, one growing from James Pennebaker's important work on silence. Pennebaker, a health psychology researcher, has found that Holocaust victims and rape victims who do not talk about their trauma to anyone afterward suffer worse physical health than those who do confide in somebody. Pennebaker persuaded sixty Holocaust survivors to open up and describe what had happened to them. They related to others scenes that they had relived in their heads thousands of times over the previous forty years.

> They were throwing babies from the second-floor window of the orphanage. I can still see the pools of blood, the screams, and the thuds of their bodies. I just stood there, afraid to move. The Nazi soldiers faced us with their guns.

The Right Treatment

POST-TRAUMATIC STRESS DISORDER SUMMARY TABLE

	*Cognitive-Behavioral**	*Antidepressants & Anti-anxiety Drugs*
IMPROVEMENT	▲◢	▲
RELAPSE	▲▲▲	▲▲
SIDE EFFECTS	▼▼	▼▼▼
COST	inexpensive	inexpensive
TIME SCALE	weeks/months	weeks
OVERALL	▲◢	▲

IMPROVEMENT

▲▲▲▲ = 80–100% markedly improved or symptom free
▲▲▲ = 60–80% markedly improved
▲▲ = at least 50% moderately improved
▲ = probably better than placebo
o = probably useless

RELAPSE (after discontinuation of treatment)

▲▲▲▲ = 10% or fewer relapse
▲▲▲ = 10–20% relapse
▲▲ = moderate relapse rate
▲ = high relapse rate

SIDE EFFECTS

▼▼▼▼ = severe
▼▼▼ = moderate
▼▼ = mild
▼ = none

OVERALL

▲▲▲▲ = excellent, clearly the therapy of choice
▲▲▲ = very good
▲▲ = useful
▲ = marginal
o = probably useless

*Matters are changing rapidly for the better because of the cognitive-behavioral treatment of rape victims using exposure treatment combined with stress-inoculation training. If psychologist Edna Foa's latest results are borne out and extended to victims of other traumas, this mode of treatment will warrant two or three stars overall (see chapter 10, note 17).

The interviewers had nightmares after hearing these long-buried stories, but the health of the disclosers improved. Similarly, Pennebaker persuaded students to narrate their secret traumas—sexual abuse by a grandfather, the death of a dog, a suicide attempt—in writing. The immediate consequence was increased depression. But in the long run, these students' number of physical illnesses decreased by 50 percent, and their immune system strengthened.[14]

Prolonged *exposure* is the therapy that follows. In exposure treatment, victims relive the trauma in their imagination. They describe it aloud, in the present tense, to their therapist. This is repeated session after session. In the best-executed study of exposure treatment, Edna Foa, a pioneering behavior therapist, and her colleagues treated forty-five rape victims who had PTSD. They compared this treatment to *stress-inoculation training,* which includes deep muscle relaxation, thought stopping for countering ruminations, and cognitive restructuring. Another group received supportive counseling, and a fourth group received no treatment.

All groups, including the no-treatment control, improved. Immediately after the five weeks of treatment, stress-inoculation training relieved PTSD symptoms most, but after another four months, exposure had shown the most lasting effects.[15]

Psychological treatment, then, produces some relief. But one-third of all PTSD patients refused treatment or dropped out, and the PTSD and depression symptoms were still well above normal after treatment.[16]

But there is hopeful news from an ongoing study of Foa's. She is finding that the combination of stress inoculation and prolonged exposure produces very good results. After five weeks of treatment (nine sessions), 80 percent of the victims were no longer showing PTSD, and symptoms were markedly reduced. No significant relapse was found. These new findings are the best outcome yet for rape patients. If replicated, they should encourage victims, who are usually quite reluctant to pursue treatment because they want to avoid thinking about the rape, to seek out this treatment promptly.[17]

Overall, the results for both drugs and cognitive-behavioral therapies are encouraging and call for more research, but with the exception of new cognitive-behavioral treatments for rape victims, these gains are very modest: some symptom relief, but many dropouts, and almost no cures. Of all the disorders we have reviewed, PTSD is the least alleviated by therapy of any sort. I believe that the development of new treatments to relieve PTSD is of the highest priority.

PART THREE

Changing Your Habits of Eating, Drinking, and Making Merry

11

Sex

OUR EROTIC LIFE has five layers, each grown around the layer beneath it.

The core is *sexual identity.*[1] Do you feel yourself to be a man or a woman, a boy or a girl? Sexual identity is almost always consistent with our genitals: If we have a penis, we feel ourselves male; if we have a vagina, we feel female. But scientists know that sexual identity has a separate existence of its own because of the rare and astonishing dissociation of sexual identity and sexual organs. Some men (we call them men because they have penises and 46XY chromosomes) are utterly convinced that they are women trapped in men's bodies by some cosmic mistake, and some women (with vaginas and 46XX chromosomes) are utterly convinced that they are men trapped in women's bodies. Both are called *transsexuals,* and they provide the key to understanding the deepest layer of normal sexual identity.

Laying just over our core sexual identity is our basic *sexual orientation.* Do you love men or women? Are you heterosexual, homosexual, or bisexual? To answer this question, we need not explore our sexual history but, instead, should look to our fantasy life. If you have had erotic fantasies only about the opposite sex, you are exclusively heterosexual. If you have had masturbatory fantasies only about members of your own sex, you are exclusively homosexual. If you have often masturbated to both fantasies, you are bisexual.

The third layer is *sexual preference.* What parts of the body and what situations turn you on? What scenes do you masturbate about? What is on your mind at the moment of orgasm? For most men, the most erotic parts of the body are the female face, breasts, buttocks, and legs. For most women, the preferred body parts are the male chest and shoulders, arms, buttocks, and face. Caressing a member of the opposite sex, seeing him or her naked, dancing, intimate conversation, subdued lighting, and music are common arousing situations.

But these are not—by any means—universal. Many people crave nonstandard objects and situations: Common ones are feet, hair, ears, the belly button; silken and rubbery textures, panties, stockings, jeans; peeping, flashing, receiving and inflicting pain. Animals, children, urine, and even an amputee's stumps are rarer and more bizarre. Lust-murder and arranging one's own death are the most erotic acts for the extremely rare person. If any of these are your turn-ons, forget the bizarreness of the object for a moment, and ask yourself this important question: "Does the object of my passion get in the way of an affectionate, erotic relationship between myself and another consenting human being?" When the panties or the pain become more important than your partner, you have crossed a line.

The fourth layer, the one next to the surface, is our *sex role.* Do you do what most men do or what most women do? Most people who feel they are male adopt male sex roles, and most females adopt female roles. But we know of the separate existence of sex roles by the not-uncommon dissociations of identity and role. For example, some women become truck drivers—dominant, aggressive, and tough. Some men become nurses—caring, gentle, and compassionate. The term *sex role* makes role sound arbitrary, a mere costume that can be shed at will and easily replaced with one more suitable to the moment. In this view, sex roles are creations of fashion: The macho male and bimbo female stereotypes are just accidents of the way Americans now happen to be raised. And as accidents of socialization, they can be changed simply by altering the way we raise our children or by some other act of will. We shall see if this is really so or if this is just ideological fantasy.

The surface layer is *sexual performance,* how adequately you perform when you are with a suitable person in a suitable erotic setting. Normal performance consists of arousal and orgasm. Do you have problems in either of these areas? Frigidity and impotence (what pejorative words!) are common problems, as are premature ejaculation for men and absence of orgasm for women.

I have ordered your erotic life into five layers for one basic purpose—to answer the questions of what changes and how easily it changes. Lack of change, I believe, corresponds to *depth;* the deeper the layer, the harder it is to change. (This is a preview of the global theory I will put forward in chapter 15.) My theory of sex is that transsexuality is a problem at the identity level and simply will not change; sexual orientation, the next deepest layer, very strongly resists change; sexual preference, once acquired, is strong, but some change can be wrought; sex role can change quite a bit, but change is by no means as easy as feminist ideologues contend, nor as difficult as antifeminists would like; correcting sexual performance is painful, but because performance problems are at the surface layer, you should be very hopeful that they will change.

Layer I: Sexual Identity and Transsexuality: What Are You?

Transsexuals are biologically normal. An average transsexual man has a penis in good working order, 46XY chromosomes, hair on his face and body, lots of testosterone, and a deep voice. An average transsexual woman has a vagina, working ovaries, 46XX chromosomes, breasts, and all the rest of the female physical features. Transsexuals are physically indistinguishable from average men or women. Yet psychologically, they are as abnormal as anyone can be. By the three major criteria of abnormality—irrationality, suffering, and maladaptiveness—transsexuals top the chart. They believe—irrationally, it seems—that they are trapped in the body of the wrong sex. They are miserable: depressed, suicidal, and self-mutilating—some try to cut off their sex organs. They almost never marry or reproduce.

Transsexuals have had their "wrong sex" belief for as long as they can remember. And they are doomed to have it for the rest of their lives. Every kind of psychotherapy has been tried on transsexuals. So rare is any success that the single clear case in the archives of successful change calibrates just how intractable this problem is.[2]

> *John was born in 1952 and always thought of himself as a girl. He was the baby of the family, frail and delicate beside his tomboy older sister. When he was four, he started to wear makeup and was delighted when his sister started school because she got lots of new clothes for him to dress up in. [Transsexuals always cross-dress. But they are transvestites only by a technicality. A transvestite male wears women's clothes to get turned on sexually; a transsexual male wears them because he believes he is a woman.]*
>
> *John envied his mother and sister, and loathed his maleness. He went to school, but did badly. Isolated and lonely, he occupied himself with*

cooking and housekeeping. As a teenager, he read about transsexualism and about the important discoveries being made at the Johns Hopkins Medical School. He took estrogen and felt tranquil and calm for the first time in his life. He was also delighted that he no longer got erections. He took a job at a fried-chicken stand and started to save up for sex-change surgery. It was at this time that he was seen by a psychiatric team and formally diagnosed as a transsexual.

He took the name "Judy" and began to live as a woman, preparing for surgery. He passed well as a woman, and with hormone treatment wore bikinis to the beach. Just as surgery was to begin, Judy disappeared.

Several months later, Judy reappeared at the chicken stand. But not as Judy—as John. When he subsequently presented himself to the psychiatric team, he wore a three-piece suit and short hair, had clipped fingernails, and strutted manfully. He related his story enthusiastically:

On his way to surgery, he kept a promise to the stand owner to check in with a local physician who was a member of a fundamentalist religion (John was a lapsed Baptist with no religious interest). The physician told John that he could make it as a woman, but that his real problem was possession by evil spirits. The physician performed a three-hour exorcism with prayers, exhortations, incantations, and the laying-on of hands. John fainted several times, but when it was over, the physician said he had removed twenty-two evil spirits, and John was free of the delusion of being a woman for the first time in his life. He was followed closely for the next two and a half years by the psychiatric team and was clearly male—psychologically as well as physically. He did well in his job, was promoted, and was looking forward to marrying—a woman.

Sex change. Psychotherapy changes sexual identity rarely, if ever.[3] The only thing that reliably works is to change the body to conform to the unshakable sexual identity. This is why sex-change operations were developed. Once a headline-making novelty, these operations are now routine. Tens of thousands have been done. Once the patient convinces the diagnosticians that his or her transsexual identity is unshakable, the long process of changing the body to conform begins. In the more common male-to-female (MF) case, the person first lives for a few months in the female role, changing his name, and dressing and acting like a woman. Hormonal treatment is begun, and breasts grow, the voice changes, and facial hair disappears. Surgery itself is then undertaken. The testicles are removed and the penis is cut off—though its skin is preserved to line the new vagina, making pleasurable intercourse and even orgasm possible.

In the female-to-male (FM) transformations, hormone treatment and multiple surgery (breast removal, ovary removal, and, ultimately, the construction of a penis) are done over several years. The penis cannot naturally become erect, however, and prosthetic devices must be used for intercourse.

As radical as surgery is, long-term follow-up of hundreds of patients suggests that while far from ideal, it is the treatment of choice. Most patients are much happier and adapt fairly well to their new lives, living comfortably in their new bodies, dating, having intercourse, and marrying. Any children, of course, are adopted, since no surgery can transplant viable internal sex organs. Those patients who do poorly psychologically are the ones who have had the poorest surgical results.[4]

The origin of sexual identity. Of the entire nosology, transsexualism is the deepest disorder. I know of no other psychological problem so intractable. We do not know how to change the psyche to conform to the body, so as a last resort we change the body to conform to the psyche. The depth of this disorder reflects the fact that sexual identity is the core layer of sexuality, and perhaps the very core of all of human personality.

Why is sexual identity so deep? I want to go well beyond the data to present a theory of the origin of sexual identity. My speculation is that most of sexual identity—both normal and transsexual—comes from an unknown hormonal process in the second to fourth months of pregnancy.

I start with a simplified version of how a fetus becomes male or female. The embryo has both potentials. Very early, both sets of internal organs—male and female—are present. The fetus would always go on to become female but for the next, crucial step: Two masculinizing hormones are secreted from the male fetus's testes. The female internal organs then wither, the male internal organs grow, and the external male organs develop. In the absence of the masculinizing hormones at this stage, the male internal organs wither, and female internal and external organs develop. All this happens roughly at the end of the first trimester.[5]

I want to speculate that there is something else happening at this stage: The masculinizing hormones have a psychological effect. They produce male sexual identity (or, in their absence, female sexual identity). They also guide the development of the corresponding sexual organs, but this is a separate process. In this theory, sexual identity is present in the fetus. There is no way of asking a fetus if he feels like a male or a female, however, so this is not an easy theory to test. But there are four startling "experiments of nature" in which sexual identity is dissociated from sexual organs—all of which support my thesis.

You already know about two of them: MF transsexuals and FM transsexuals. In this theory, some as-yet-unknown disruption of the sexual-identity phase, but not the organ-development phase, takes place. For the MF transsexual, the psychological phase of masculinization does not occur, but the other phase—the masculinization of the sexual organs—goes normally. For the FM transsexual, the psychological phase goes awry, and masculinization occurs; the other phase—feminization of the sexual organs—goes normally, and herein may lie the tragedy.

There are two mirror-image conditions that show remarkable parallels to the two transsexualisms and that are much better understood—the *adrenogenital syndrome (AGS)* and the *androgen-insensitivity syndrome (AIS)*. They may be the key to understanding transsexualism.

The adrenogenital syndrome has a profound effect on the 46XX fetus (a chromosomally normal female): It bathes her in masculinizing hormones. As a result, she is born with the internal organs of a female (since they were differentiated before the bath), but she is also born with what seems to be a penis and scrotum. The penis and scrotum look convincing, but they are actually an enormously enlarged and penile-shaped (foreskin and all) clitoris. The scrotum contains no testicles. Many AGSs are declared boys and raised as boys. Since the hormonal bath continues, their voice deepens, and face and body hair sprout at puberty. These AGSs *grow up as normal men.* They feel like they are male, they pursue women romantically, they have intercourse as men, and they become good husbands and fathers (by adoption or artificial insemination). There is a complete absence of bisexual fantasy or action. In contrast, when an AGS is surgically feminized and then reared as a girl, as sometimes happens, problems often ensue: She may feel and act like a man; bisexual fantasy and action are common.[6]

In my theory, AGSs reared as males are "first cousins" of FM transsexuals. Both are 46XX fetuses who are masculinized psychologically. But the transsexual misses the next phase—the masculinization of her external organs. She is therefore born psychologically male but with a vagina, and so is declared and raised as a girl. Her life is a constant misery thereafter. It gets even worse after puberty, because unlike her AGS cousin, she sprouts breasts and has periods. Her AGS cousin is psychologically male, but was fortunate enough also to be born with the appearance of a penis and scrotum and so is declared a boy. His life works out because what everyone thinks he is (by virtue of the appearance of a penis at birth and, later, by his deep voice and facial hair) is the same as he thinks he is—a man.

The tragic difference between an AGS reared as a male and an FM transsexual is that only one phase—psychological masculinization as a fetus—goes awry for the transsexual. All the other phases go correctly, locked unfortunately to the chromosomal sex and not to sexual identity. For the AGS, all phases—fortunately—go awry, and so everything corresponds not to *her* chromosomal sex, but to *his* sexual identity.

The other disorder is AIS, the androgen-insensitivity syndrome. AISs are chromosomally male: 46XY. They are insensitive to masculinizing hormones, however. So AISs are born with male internal organs (which differentiate before the ineffective masculinizing bath) and with a vagina, though the vagina is actually a dead end. All AISs are declared girls and raised as girls. They all grow up feeling female, pursue men, and have intercourse as women. In my theory, they don't get masculinized psychologically, and, fortunately, their external organs don't look masculine. Like AGSs, they have an added piece of good fortune: When puberty arrives, they grow breasts under the influence of the normal male amount of estrogen secreted by the testes (which they have deep inside), and so they look like women.[7]

AISs are the first cousins of MF transsexuals. Both are 46XY fetuses with male internal organs who are feminized psychologically at the end of the first trimester. But the transsexual has a normal next phase—the external organs get masculinized. Therefore, though he is psychologically female, he is born with a working penis and so is declared and raised as a boy. He is miserable ever after—or until he loses his penis surgically. His AIS cousin is psychologically female, and was fortunate enough to be born with the appearance of a vagina and so is declared a girl. Her life works out because what everyone thinks she is (by virtue of her vagina and, later, her breasts) is the same as she thinks she is—a woman.

Again, the tragic difference between an AIS female and an MF transsexual is that only one phase—psychological feminization—goes awry for the transsexual. All the other phases proceed correctly, locked to the chromosomal sex and not to sexual identity. For the AIS, all phases go awry and wind up corresponding not to *his* chromosomal sex but to *her* sexual identity.

My theory speculates that sexual identity—both normal and abnormal—is so deep because it has its origin in a fundamental hormonal process that occurs around the end of the first trimester of fetal development. Fetal hormones are not the only influence on sexual identity. Rearing, pubertal hormones, sex organs, and being mocked also play a role. But at most, these later influences can reinforce—or disturb—the core identity with which we are stuck from well before the moment of our birth.

Layer II: Sexual Orientation: Do You Love Men or Women?

Sexologists use the term *object choice* to denote how we come to love what we love. Gay activist groups, on the other hand, say we have no choice at all. I think the truth is in between, although much closer to the gay activists than to the sexologists. I therefore call this layer sexual *orientation* rather than sexual *object choice.* The basic sexual orientations are homosexual and heterosexual.[8] When does a person become heterosexual or homosexual? How does it happen? Once sexually active, can he or she change?

Exclusive homosexuality. We must distinguish between *exclusive* homosexuals on the one hand and bisexuals (*optional homosexuals*) on the other. Most men who have sex with other men are bisexuals. About 15 percent of American men report that they have had orgasms with members of both sexes, but the figure may now be lower in the wake of AIDS. A large minority of men who are homosexual, in contrast to bisexuals, are exclusively homosexual. They number between 1 and 5 percent of all men. As far back as they can remember, they have been erotically interested only in males. They have sexual fantasies only about males. They fall in love only with males. When they masturbate or have wet dreams, the objects are always males. The orientation of the exclusive homosexual—and that of the exclusive heterosexual—are firmly made and deep.

Sexual orientation may even have its origin in the anatomy of the brain. In a highly publicized and technically well done study, brain researcher Simon Levay looked at the brains of newly dead homosexual men, heterosexual men, and heterosexual women. Most had died of AIDS. He focused his autopsies on one small area, the middle of the anterior hypothalamus, which is implicated in male sexual behavior and where men have more tissue than do women. He found a remarkably large difference in tissue: Heterosexual men have twice as much as homosexual men, who have about the same small amount of tissue as women. This is fascinating because this is just the area that controls male sexual behavior in rats; this area develops when the brains of male rats are hormonally masculinized before birth.[9]

So it is possible to speculate that exclusive homosexuality in males is an attenuated form of MF transsexuality, which is in turn an attenuated form of AIS. In this theory, the sexual organs, sexual identity, and sexual orientation for the 46XY male may each have its own separate masculinizer, and so three separate levels of hormonal failure can occur.[10] It might be three different hormones, or it might be a matter of how much hormone. So, for example, with complete hormonal failure, no masculinization occurs: The baby is a chromosomal male with external female organs, female identity, and whose sexual orientation will be toward men—AIS. With grossly insufficient masculinizing hormone, the baby is a chromosomal male, with male organs, but whose sexual orientation will be toward men and whose sexual identity will be female as well—an MF transsexual. With somewhat insufficient hormone, a chromosomal male results, with male organs and male identity but whose sexual orientation will be toward men—an exclusively homosexual male.

In this speculation, the subsequent hormonal events (as yet undiscovered) occur commonly during gestation: A 46XY (normal) male is insufficiently masculinized. He is masculinized enough, however, to have a male identity and to have male external organs. The main effect is to prevent the growth of the medial anterior hypothalamus and so to change just one aspect of erotic life: Sexual orientation is prevented from ever being toward women.

It is important to note that identical twins are more concordant for homosexuality than fraternal male twins, and that male fraternal twins are more concordant than nontwin brothers: Out of fifty-six pairs of identical twins in which one was established as homosexual, 52 percent turned out both to be homosexual, as opposed to 22 percent of male fraternal twins. Only 9 percent of nontwin brothers were concordant for homosexuality. The difference between the identical twins and the fraternal twins means that there is a genetic component to homosexuality. But nontwin brothers and male fraternal twins share exactly the same percentage (50 percent) of genes. That male fraternal twins, who share the uterine world, are more concordant than nontwin brothers points to fetal hormones as an additional cause. What they all might be concordant for, in any case, is a withered medial anterior hypothalamus.[11]

It is tempting to put forward the same theory for female homosexuality, viewing it as slight masculinization of a 46XX female fetus. I will resist the temptation for now. Too little research has been done on lesbians to know. It is possible, but still uncertain, that lesbianism is the mirror image of male homosexuality. There is evidence for a sizable genetic contribution to lesbianism: Out of a sample of more than one hundred female twins, one of whom was lesbian, the second twin was lesbian in 51 percent of the identical twins, but only in 10 percent of the fraternal twins. There is no evidence as yet, however, that the anterior hypothalamus is larger in lesbians than in straight women. No one has looked because lesbians, fortunately, are not dying in great numbers from AIDS. Even the rat evidence is clearer for male than for female rats. Finally, there are no outcome studies of change of sexual orientation in therapy with lesbians.[12]

Homosexuality and therapy. Can exclusive male homosexuality change? Many homosexuals are happy with their sexuality and don't want to change. In contrast, a man who is unhappy with his homosexuality is called an *ego-dystonic* homosexual, and he typically comes to therapy depressed, desperately wanting to change his sexual orientation. He wants to have children, he can't bear the stigma of being "queer," and he despises the promiscuity he perceives in the single, homosexual world. Twenty-five years ago, behavior therapists gave this problem their best effort, ignoring the clinical lore declaring that psychotherapy has no effect on homosexuality.

They tried using sexually arousing pictures of naked men flashed on a screen followed by a long, painful electric shock. When the shock went off, the picture of an attractive woman appeared. The idea was to make sex with men aversive and sex with women more attractive by pairing women with relief.

"Hopelessly naïve," you're probably thinking. Actually, it worked surprisingly well. Around 50 percent of men so treated lost interest in men and began having sex with women. A great burst of enthusiasm about changing homosexuality swept over the therapeutic community. On closer inspection, the findings turned out to be flawed—but revealingly so. When a man was bisexual—sometimes had sexual fantasies about women—therapy usually worked. But when a man was exclusively homosexual, therapy usually failed.[13]

Exclusive homosexuality and exclusive heterosexuality are very deep. Lack of change in therapy, lifelong fantasies of one sex only, anterior hypothalamus withered, high concordance of identical twins, and fetal development all point to an inflexible process. Homosexuality is not quite as deep and unchangeable as transsexuality, however. MF transsexuals almost never marry women and have natural children, whereas homosexual men sometimes marry and have children. They manage this feat by a trick of fantasy. During sex with their wives, they manage to stay aroused and climax by having fantasies about homosexual sex (just as heterosexual men restricted to homosexual release in prison do). So some measure of flexibility is available to exclusively homosexual men—they can choose whom they perform with sexually, but they cannot choose whom they *want* to perform with.

Layer III: Sexual Preference: Breasts, Buttocks, and Bisexuals

Do you remember the first time you saw an oyster, glistening slimily on half its shell, and somebody suggested that you eat it? "What, put that repulsive thing in my mouth?" you probably thought, and shriveled inwardly. Yet once you were cajoled, pressured, or shamed into trying one, you discovered that oysters taste good. Eating oysters, like many forms of human activity, has on its face a disgusting aspect that prevents most people from indulging too casually—until social pressure, curiosity, or sheer bravado get them to try it out. Once tried, however, all the good things about eating oysters—its reinforcers—become apparent, and you may well become an oyster addict.

This important phenomenon, *inhibitory wrapping,* is not confined to human practices. There are two kinds of rats: mouse-killers and nonkillers. When natural mouse-killers—about half of all rats—see a mouse for the first time, they jump on it and kill it. The other half—the nonkillers—either pay no attention to the mouse or even run away. But an experimenter can induce a reluctant rat to kill, by starving the rat and then parading a mouse in front of him. When this happens, a nonkiller will, out of desperation, kill. Once a nonkiller has killed for the first time, once he loses his mouse-killing virginity, he becomes a habitual killer. Thereafter, whenever he sees a mouse, hungry or not, he will jump on it and kill it.[14]

Now remember when you were a child and you first found out about sexual intercourse or, later, about oral sex. "What a disgusting thing to do," you probably thought. "My mother and father don't do that. I know I never will." But as the hormones of adolescence began to seep through your body, or as peer pressure built, or out of bravado or curiosity or rebellion, you found yourself prodded into such acts. You discovered, in doing them, all the good things about them. You soon sought them out and even began to crave them. Most human sexual preferences are like this: a strong inhibitory wrapping around a delicious core. So too with what we eat, with substance abuse, and—I sadly suspect—with violence.

The oyster-eating and mouse-killing stories warn us that there once might have lurked inside us the potential to become erotically attached to any of a large variety of things. That we are breast men, or willing spankees, or women turned on by cheek-to-cheek dancing and sympathetic listening is, while not wholly an accident, a product of what we happened to sample when we were young. I suspect that if we had sampled peeping or rubber clothes, for example, we might have come to crave these instead.

There are two morals to the oyster tale. The first comes from knowing that the potential for arousal by almost anything in the whole gamut of erotic objects lies in each of us: This moral is sexual tolerance. The second moral is caution: The early sexual decisions we make—or are cajoled, seduced, pressured, or forced into making—are matters of real moment for us; more moment, for example, than whom we marry or where we go to college. For once the inhibitory wrapping is torn open, we want the sweet core again and again. What we start doing sexually as teenagers will, by and large, be what we want for the rest of our lives. Yet we make these decisions almost accidentally. As a young person, you should be armed to answer the question "Why not?" with "Do I really want to live my whole life this way?"

Sexual orientation—heterosexual or homosexual—is a close neighbor of sexual identity in its depth and inflexibility, and it is deeper than sexual preference. Once orientation is dictated, the sexual preferences are elaborated around it: breasts or bottoms, peeping, lace panties, calves or feet, rubber textures, the missionary position or sixty-nine, sadism, blond hair, bisexuality, spanking, or high-heeled shoes. These preferences, like mouse-killing, are not, once acquired, easily shelved. Unlike exclusive heterosexuality or homosexuality, they surely do not arise in the womb (the fetus may "know" men from women, but he doesn't know from spiked heels). Rather, our sexual preferences have their beginnings in late childhood as the first hormones of puberty awaken the dormant brain structures that were laid down in the womb.

At this time, play begins to lose its innocence and becomes tinged with sex. Dreams and fantasies do, too. In a survey of third-graders, I found that only about 5 percent could recall having a "love" dream (e.g., dreaming that they are cuddling a boy or girl their own age), though they all recalled monster dreams. On the other hand, the vast majority of sixth-grade children had love dreams, and the monster dreams were on the wane. Most sexologists believe that the intense dreams and fantasy and play at this age are just coincidental with sexual development, or that they simply reflect what the facts of underlying sexuality are. I have a different view: I believe that these events are the crucible out of which our sexual preferences are forged. I believe that the content of dreams, play, and fantasy has a causal role in creating our sexual preferences.

> *Leopold was eight when his half sister taught him to masturbate while they were playing "doctor." As he came, she accidentally touched his penis with her slipper. Within a year, he began masturbating regularly. His masturbatory fantasies revolved around girls' feet and shoes. He got in trouble at school for caressing his teacher's shoes. He eventually married, but was unable to have intercourse unless he was caressing his wife's feet or fantasizing about shoes. Leopold took a job as a shoe salesman in an expensive boutique, and spent his days in a constant state of arousal as he assisted female customers with their footwear.*

> *Sammy was ten when he had his first wet dream. In this never-to-be-forgotten event, his playmate Susan had taken off her bathing-suit bottom and let him rub his penis between her buttocks. It felt great and he came. He woke up gooey, confused, and shocked. Up until that dream he had not the slightest intimation that his penis was for anything except peeing. When he began to masturbate three years later, he found that his fantasies focused on girl's bottoms, particularly as climax neared. As a thirty-five-year-old, he ejaculates only during intercourse from behind. Everything else is foreplay.*

These two stories are typical of the histories men give when asked how they come by their sexual preferences. The stories fit the prepared conditioning theory we used to explain why phobias are selective and so resistant to change. Like phobias, the objects of sexual preference are selective. Panties, feet, hair, breasts, velvet, spanking, and about a dozen other objects are the common ones. Phrases like "whatever turns you on" and "polymorphous perversity" miss the mark. Almost all objects of male sexual preference are somehow related to female body parts and to intercourse. Colors, sounds, flowers, and food are never fetishes. Occasionally, as with phobias, a truly bizarre proclivity sneaks in: dead bodies or feces, for example. But these are usually the fetishes of psychotic people. Also like phobias, the sexual preferences, once acquired, endure.

The prepared conditioning view holds that there is a "short list" of evolutionarily significant stimuli that are potential sexual objects for men. Once there happens to be a pairing of one of these conditional stimuli (feet for Leopold, buttocks for Sammy) with a sexual unconditional stimulus (masturbation for Leopold, wet dream for Sammy), conditioning begins. Late-childhood sex play and wet dreams provide ample opportunity for pairing of the prepared objects with sexual excitement. Once this happens, the objects themselves become imbued with sexual excitement.

Masturbation is the answer to why your sexual preferences continue for a lifetime once they start. After these objects have become arousing, you start to masturbate about them. Masturbation in men is always accompanied by fantasy. You are again in the presence of the conditional stimulus, and you have an orgasm. This is yet another conditioning trial—and it happens a dozen times a week in the lives of most adolescent males. That's a lot of practice. Usually, intercourse for men is either accompanied by variations on the core fantasy, or it actually enacts the fantasy. That's a lot more practice. In my view, evolution has selected masturbation and its concomitant, fantasy, for the purpose of investing men, lastingly, in the erotic practices of their tribe, their race, and their culture.

Females and fetishes. Evidence suggests that women acquire sexual preferences by a subtler process. The major difference between the sexes is that almost all men are "fetishists." When the preference is frowned upon, intrusive, illegal, or hurts others, we label it a "fetish." When the preference is socially acceptable, practiced between consenting adults, and legal, it has no name ("behind closed doors"?). But the process is just the same. Both fetishists and "normal" men harbor highly specific erotic images. These images are the core of their masturbatory fantasies and of their actual sexual pursuits. Many of the preferences are acceptable, and so, with reasonable impulse control, men who are turned on by large breasts or sleek buttocks or being spanked or ripping lace panties or wearing rubber underthings don't get into trouble. Those men whose preferences are socially unacceptable, immoral, illegal, or injurious (or are otherwise acceptable but are pursued by men with little impulse control) get labeled with the nasty name "fetishist." In my view, these men have the same process of sexual preference as normal men, but they differ in the peculiarity or unacceptability or hurtfulness of their preferences, or in their inability to delay gratification, or in getting caught.

Nearly two-thirds of a random sample of rural Oregon college men admitted (under conditions of anonymity) to sexual misconduct: sex with children, forced sex with women, peeping, or frottage (rubbing up against a stranger in a crowd). Even more of them wanted to commit improper acts.[15] These figures testify to the social definition of "fetish" and to the stereotyped, concrete nature of male sexual preferences.

It is not just that *almost all men* are fetishists that distinguishes male preferences from female ones. Rather, it is that *almost no women* are fetishists. Clinical lore has it that absolutely no women are fetishists.[16] I think this is an overstatement. There are rare reports of fetishism in women in the journals, and at least one systematic exploration.[17] In this study, a group of enterprising academics advertised in an S-M magazine, soliciting sadists and masochists. There were 182 responses, 25 percent of them from women—excluding professional dominatrixes. The respondents took a sex questionnaire. Some important average differences emerged between the men and women of the "velvet underground." The men said they acquired their preference when they were boys; the women said their preference took hold when they were adults. The women said they were introduced to S-M by another person, but the men said it was a natural, spontaneous interest from childhood. The men were heterosexual, while the women tended to be bisexual or homosexual (androgenized women?).

I believe that men and women are vastly different in their erotic preferences and maybe even in the process of getting their preferences. Men easily—perhaps universally—acquire very strong arousal to specific, concrete objects. It is the look, the feel, and the smell of these objects that turns men on. Many a man centers his whole life on pursuing them. The objects of male preference are at a lower level than a whole person (Cher's legs are more of a turn-on than Cher). This happens rarely—perhaps never—to women. Women, rather, acquire erotic preferences for subtler scenarios, involving plot lines, intimacy, and character. The essence is that female sex objects are not objects at all; they are at the level of the whole person, and they focus on personal relationships.

I don't know why this is so. The proposed theories are little short of silly. One claims that men know when they are aroused (because the hard penis protrudes), and so they can easily find out that something has turned them on. Women, in contrast, have no external signal to tell them they are aroused, and so they cannot easily be conditioned. This theory explains neither why the objects that come to arouse men are so selective nor why women select very different, more social situations.

Another theory—unsatisfying but not silly—says that women, having to bear and raise children, must, if they wish to pass on their genes, be very selective as to the character and prospects of men (with regard to fathering). Muscular forearms, swarthy complexion, shapely calves—in short, appearance—are very poor predictors of successful fathering and sheltering. Sympathetic conversation, wealth, success, social rank (remember Henry Kissinger's aphorism: "Power is the world's greatest aphrodisiac"), love songs, vows, and poetry about eternal devotion augur better that the man will help parent the children and not abandon them when the woman's childbearing is over. Women who adopt this reproductive strategy are more likely to pass on their genes than women who get aroused by superficial appearance. Men, so this theory continues, merely want to spread their sperm around as far as it will go, and being guided by a pretty face, wide hips, nubility, and large breasts ensures the most offspring.[18] This explains the facts, but provides no mechanism.

Changing sexual preference. In the natural course of life, the sexual preferences of adolescence abide, though new ones can be added. Bisexuals, for example, often start out having heterosexual experience only. In their twenties or thirties, however, they begin to act on their secret fantasies, happen into a homosexual encounter, and become actively bisexual. Married couples are introduced to group sex by other "swingers" and sometimes acquire a taste for it.

The old preferences, however, which rarely die of their own accord, can—with explicit therapy—sometimes be altered. There have been extensive studies on the power of therapy to change sexual preference, but their subjects are mostly atypical men: sex offenders. An exhibitionist (flasher) or a pedophile (child molester) may be arrested and then have therapy mandated in addition to, or instead of, jail. Similarly, men who are overcome with guilt and shame or who want to undo their preferences to avoid jail seek out such therapy. In all these cases, there is strong external pressure to change.

The treatment of flashers is typical, and all of the following are used extensively, alone or in combination:

- *electric shock or chemical nauseants:* The patient reads aloud, in the first person, an exciting sequence of vignettes about flashing. When he gets to the climax—exposing his erect penis—painful shock, or smells that are so bad they produce retching, are delivered. As the climactic act becomes aversive, the aversive stimulus is now delivered earlier and earlier in the sequence.
- *orgasmic reconditioning:* The man masturbates, narrating his fantasies aloud. As he comes, he substitutes a more acceptable scene for the flashing fantasy.
- *masturbatory satiation:* He continues to masturbate for half an hour after ejaculation—a deadly and humiliating task—while rehearsing every variation of flashing aloud.

These are mildly effective. In one study with a six-year follow-up, only 40 percent of treated men continue to flash, whereas 60 percent of untreated men reoffend. More recently, therapists have started to treat this problem cognitively. For example, the patient carries cards with exciting vignettes about flashing. On the back of each card is a horrible consequence of flashing and getting caught. Whenever the flasher is tempted, he reads a sequence, turns the card over, and then ruminates on the awful consequences. This may drop reoffending to about 25 percent.[19]

Patients report changes both in their overt behavior and in their desire to flash. I believe, however, that what they *want* is largely unchanged. But what they *do* is substantially changed. It is very much in the interest of the offender to tell the therapist, the judge, his probation officer, and the world that he no longer wants to flash, and so his reports are not completely believable. But the objective record documents that he actually flashes less. I suspect the offender learns in therapy to restrain himself from acting on his wants. While not a cure, this is all to the good.

It also suggests that some change—perhaps not in desire but in action—can occur in sexual preferences.

There is a substantially more effective way to curtail sex offenders: castration. It is used in Europe for very serious offenses—brutal rape and child molesting. Castration is done surgically—cutting off the testicles—or with drugs that neutralize the hormone produced by the testicles. In four studies of more than two thousand offenders followed for many years, the reoffense rate drops from around 70 percent to around 3 percent. Drug castration, which is reversible, works as well as surgical castration.[20] In America, castration is called "cruel and unusual punishment" and is not done. When I consider all the wasted years in prison, the high likelihood of repeating the offense, and the special hell that other prisoners reserve for child molesters, castration seems less cruel to me than the "usual" punishment.

Layer IV: Sex Role: Social Behavior, Personality, and Ability

Are men different from women? Are boys different from girls? Can sex differences be narrowed?

These are loaded questions, fraught with political overtones. To the feminist, they evoke impatience. They are just scientific code for attempts to claim that women are inferior and to justify continued male oppression. To the sexist, also, they evoke impatience—for the opposite reason: They are part of the long history of left-leaning scientists' manipulating evidence to bolster their pet social theories—touting whatever congenial evidence they can muster, for example, against capital punishment, for abortion on demand, against IQ testing, or for school busing, while ignoring uncongenial evidence. In this incarnation they are attempts to justify narrowing the huge differences between men and women that do exist and should exist, because these differences are at the very foundation of the social order.

Whatever these questions are politically, substantively they are questions about sex *role.* There are a large number of sex differences: anatomy, health, brain makeup, and life span, to name a few. But only three kinds of differences are directly relevant to sex role: the social differences, the personality differences, and the ability differences. The existence or nonexistence of some of these alleged differences is too shrouded by conflicting evidence for me to foist off on you my own opinion. Other differences, however, are clear—based on hundreds of studies and thousands of subjects. So I will present those that are clear and about which most workers, male and female, in these fields agree—however uncongenial to someone's politics the differences might be. There is, in fact, surprising consensus about sex differences.

One point of agreement is that there are huge sex-role differences between very young boys and girls:

- By age two, boys want to play with trucks and girls want to play with dolls.
- By age three, children know the sex stereotypes for dress, toys, jobs, games, tools, and interests.
- By age three, children want to play with peers of their own sex.
- By age four, most girls want to be teachers, nurses, secretaries, and mothers; most boys want to have "masculine" jobs.[21]

In most cultures, young children categorize the world according to sex and organize their lives around the categories. No one has to teach them sex-role stereotypes: They invent them spontaneously. This is hardly a surprise, and the pat explanation is that they learn sex roles from their parents. After all, parents behave differently with daughters than with sons. For example, parents decorate the rooms of girls in pink and put dolls in their cribs. Boys get blue cribs and toy guns.

What is surprising is that kids reared androgynously retain their stereotypes as strongly as kids not so reared. Young kids' preferences bear no relationship to their parents' attitudes or to their parents' education, class, employment, or sexual politics. Kids' play is strongly sex-stereotyped, regardless of their parents' attitudes or their parents' own sex-role behavior.

It is not that boys are simply indifferent to their parents' lessons about *androgyny* (from the Greek for "both male and female"). Boys don't just ignore their parents' telling them it's okay to play with dolls; they actively resist. Having a teacher try to persuade a child to give up a "sex-appropriate" toy produces resistance, anxiety, and backlash, particularly among boys. (Remember how devastating the label "sissy" or, worse, "queer" was?) Watching videotapes of other kids playing joyfully with "sex-inappropriate" toys doesn't work. Intensive home programs of androgynous toys, songs, and books with mother as the teacher produce no changes. Extensive classroom intervention produces no movement toward androgyny—outside the classroom.[22]

These findings should be particularly disturbing to those of you who staunchly hold that social pressure creates sex roles in the first place. If social pressure creates them, intense social pressure by committed parents and teachers should diminish them. But it doesn't.

Since social pressure does not play a measurable role in creating sex roles, the determinant might just be fetal hormones, at least in part. There are two lines of evidence: In one study, conducted in the 1970s, seventy-four mothers had taken prescription drugs during their pregnancies to prevent miscarriage. These drugs had the common property of disrupting the masculinizing hormone androgen. The games their offspring liked to play were compared to those preferred by matched controls when the children were ten years old. The boys' games were less masculine and the girls' more feminine. Similarly, there is a disease (congenital adrenal hyperplasia [CAH]) that bathes girls with extra androgen as fetuses. As young children, these girls like boys' toys and rough-and-tumble play, and they are more tomboyish than matched controls. These findings are tantalizing. They suggest that one source of boys' wanting to play with guns and girls' wanting to play house reaches into the womb.[23]

You might be tempted to conclude that sex roles are deep and unchangeable. You would be wrong. As children grow up, stereotypes weaken and are easier to defy. In late childhood, children begin to have stereotypes about crying, dominance, independence, and kindness. But they are much weaker than the early-childhood toy and job stereotypes. In fact, the only really consistent difference between the behavior of boys and girls as they mature is aggression, with boys much more aggressive than girls. As children grow up, even the difference in aggression gets smaller. The greater aggression in boys may come from socialization (boys are more rewarded for aggression and competition than girls are). But it might also have its origin in fetal hormones: Both the sons and daughters of mothers who took the androgenizing antimiscarriage drugs are more contentious and combative than their unexposed sibs.[24]

Ironically, while pressuring kids to become androgynous does not work immediately, it may have a delayed effect. As children mature into adults, sex-role stereotypes begin to disappear. When children grow up, those raised by androgynous parents tend to become androgynous themselves. Supporting intellectual interests for daughters and warmth and compassion for sons, exposing children to a range of roles, may work, but only in the long run.

This is important, it makes sense, and it is good news. Young children see the world in black-and-white terms: "I'm either a boy or a girl. There's nothing in between. If I like dolls, I'm a sissy. Everyone hates a queer." These are deeply held convictions. Young kids seem to play out a sex-role program fueled by a drive to conform that may have its roots in the fetal brain. As a child matures, however, considerations of morality, of justice, of fairness, come into play, and tolerance can start to displace blind conformity. He or she now *chooses* how to behave. Decisions about androgyny, about unconventionality, about rebellion, are conscious decisions based on a sense of what is right and what an adolescent wants for the future. As such, the choice of androgyny requires a mature mind and a conscience; it is not a product of simple training.

Spatial, math, and verbal abilities. In addition to the clear personality and social-behavior differences between males and females, there are ability differences. The huge amount of information about scholastic ability has yielded three generalities upon which all investigators agree:

- Males are better at spatial and math tasks.
- Females are better at emotional tasks and, perhaps, at verbal tasks.
- There are more males with extreme (very low or very high) scores.

There have been at least two hundred studies of sex differences in these three basic components of "intelligence." The spatial score derives from rotating three-dimensional objects mentally, and the like; the math score from arithmetic, algebra, and geometry; the verbal score from vocabulary, analogies, and reading comprehension. There is near unanimity about spatial and math scores: Males do better on average, but the difference is only moderate. To calibrate what a "moderate" difference is, assume that to become an engineer you should rank in the top 5 percent of spatial ability. The scores show that 7.4 percent of men and 3.2 percent of women rank this high. This means that there should be about two male engineers for every female engineer in the real world. The actual ratio is twenty to one.[25]

Females might be better than males on verbal tests. Based on 165 recent studies, there is a small but fairly consistent difference. Twenty years ago, there was a clear female advantage, but based on recent SATs, males have closed the gap.

On average, females are clearly better at emotional problems than males are. They judge emotion in the face more accurately, they decode nonverbal cues better, they recognize faces better, and they express emotion with nonverbals better. They also have more expressive faces. All of these differences are moderate in degree (the degree is somewhat bigger than that between males and females in spatial abilities). You should keep in mind that even the largest sex differences in ability are smaller than the average height difference between the sexes. Those who believe that the superior math and spatial scores of men suggest that men should dominate engineering and science must be prepared to accept the reverse argument for psychiatry, psychology, and personnel management.[26]

Perhaps the most intriguing difference between the abilities of men and women is a subtle but, I believe, important one. Usually, when scholars compare ability differences, they look at average differences: for example, the average woman is better than the average man at decoding emotion. For the most part, average sex differences are not large. How about the extremes, however? If you want to know who is likely to be very good or very bad—a great scientist or a great poet or a violent criminal or a person profoundly retarded—average differences won't tell you. Extreme scores will, and there is a startling difference between the sexes in extreme scores. The ability scores of men tend to lie at the extremes more often than do the scores of women. The distribution of ability scores is bell-shaped for both sexes, but the women's scores bunch up in the middle, while the men's scores spread out with long tails at each end. Put another way, the average score for reading comprehension on the California Achievement Test, for example, is quite similar for girls and boys, with a small female advantage. But if you look way out in the tails, there are many times the number of boys at both ends.[27]

People often puzzle over why there are so many more men who are math geniuses, CEOs, Nobel Prize winners, champion chess players, great violinists, and world-class chefs. The answer may be that there are more men at the extremely high end of the relevant skill distribution. When we wonder why there are so many more retarded boys than girls and more male school dropouts, the answer may be because there are many more males at the extreme low end.

This answer, while describing the facts accurately, hardly ends the debate, however. Some say there are more men at the extremes because of social learning, with talented men receiving more special attention from mentors while talented women have competing domestic responsibilities or are ignored or discouraged. This may be, but it doesn't explain why there are more retarded men. Others say biological evolution can explain the difference: Women have been selected to be stable and reliable, whereas men have been selected for the potential of being different. This explanation collapses when one looks across cultures, however. There is more male variability in the United States, but more female variability in such countries as the Philippines and South Africa.[28] If variability is an evolutionary trait, it should be the same worldwide. I believe the explanation for this difference at the extremes remains the single most important unanswered question in the study of sex differences.

Can these ability differences change? My answer is a qualified yes. At an individual level, verbal, mathematical, and spatial skills are trainable. This is what school, as well as *Sesame Street,* is about. Any girl's spatial skill can be boosted with good teaching, as can any boy's verbal skill. Emotional skill is trainable also. This is what I do as director of training in clinical psychology at the University of Pennsylvania. Our aim is to take talented young psychologists and train them to be much better at emotional problem solving—for their own benefit and for that of their future patients.

But can *group* sex differences be shrunk? Will women, on average, catch up with men at rotating three-dimensional objects in their head? Will men catch up with women at detecting masked anger? I don't know. But there is a hint of change. Many of the skill differences between the sexes have narrowed in the last twenty-five years, and this coincides with our society's treating boys and girls more similarly.[29]

To summarize Layer IV: Sex roles can change—within limits. The sex roles young boys and young girls adopt differ radically. They are fixed and stereotyped. Raising boys to be more like girls, and vice versa, is fruitless—in the short run. In the long run, however, it may work. When they mature, children raised with parental examples of tolerance for a range of sex roles become more androgynous. There are some clear ability differences between the sexes: On average, girls are worse at spatial and mathematical tasks, but better at emotional tasks. With teaching, however, all these skills can be markedly upgraded, and there is some evidence that the *group* sex differences shrink when we treat boys and girls more similarly.

Layer V: Sexual Performance: Correcting Sexual Dysfunction

Assume that the first four layers of your sexuality are in good working order: You have an identity, a fixed orientation, set preferences, and a clear sex role. You are with someone who fits with your desires and you are in an erotic situation. Tonight's the night. What can go wrong now?

Plenty. Your sexual performance can falter. If you are a man, you might

- fail to maintain an erection (*impotence*)
- climax within the first few seconds (*premature ejaculation*)

If you are a woman, you might

- fail to get aroused (*frigidity*)
- not reach orgasm

These problems are called sexual *dysfunctions.* They are agonizing and quite common problems. Until twenty years ago, they were largely unsolvable: People endured them. Marriages were strained to the breaking point. Love soured. Self-loathing and deep depression ensued. When quiet desperation became unbearable, people sought therapy, which usually failed. But thanks to a major breakthrough, these problems are, today, for the most part, curable.

Adequate sexual performance is exactly parallel in men and women. It consists of two phases: arousal and orgasm. During female arousal, a woman feels excited. Her vagina lubricates and swells to just the size to "glove" a penis. Her clitoris erects. Her uterus enlarges. Her nipples swell. During male arousal, a man feels excited. The penis hardens (the blood vessels of the penis widen dramatically, blood flows in, and a set of valves close to block it from leaving).

Arousal is the natural prelude to orgasm. In men, after enough penile stimulation a plateau of orgasmic inevitability is reached. If no interruption occurs, semen is soon released (*emission*) and is immediately pumped out by a set of rhythmic (at 0.8-second intervals) contractions by powerful muscles at the base of the penis (*ejaculation*). This is accompanied by extremely intense, spasmodic pleasure. Orgasm in women is triggered by the clitoris and is then expressed by a series of rhythmic (you guessed it: 0.8-second intervals) contractions of the muscles around the vagina. It is accompanied by ecstatic and rhapsodic feelings.

As we ponder the "unbridgeable" chasm between the sexes, I find it powerfully consoling to know that the underlying biology of sexual arousal and orgasm is completely parallel for men and women. He is probably feeling what you are feeling.

Men and women can break down at either phase, and where you break down defines your particular sexual dysfunction. Whatever the specific problem, it is always complicated by *spectatoring*. When things go wrong, or when you worry that things will go wrong, you start to watch your own lovemaking—from the outside. This gets in the way of losing yourself in the act, and so worsens the specific problem. Spectatoring creates additional anxiety, thereby starting a vicious circle. This is a clue as to what goes on in every sexual dysfunction. Arousal and orgasm are the result of biological systems that can get shut off by negative emotion. Anxiety, anger, and depression all interfere with arousal and orgasm, and spectatoring worsens all the sexual dysfunctions because it heightens anxiety.

If a woman is frightened or angry during sex, her arousal or her orgasm may be blocked. There are many commonplace sources. She may fear she will not reach orgasm, she may feel helpless and exploited, she may be ashamed of her excitement, she may expect physical pain during intercourse, she may fear pregnancy, she may find her partner unattractive, or she may think he is the wrong man. The sources of sexual blocking are parallel for men.

In the late 1960s, William Masters and Virginia Johnson invented *direct sexual therapy* for these then intractable problems. Their therapy was revolutionary, and it differs in three ways from the sex therapies that had gone before:

- It does not label you "neurotic" or otherwise deeply troubled because you are frigid or a premature ejaculator. Rather, it formulates the problem as local (my Layer V), not global.
- It treats the problem as the problem of a couple, not just of an individual: People are seen in pairs. (In some variations, if no partner shows up, there is a surrogate.)
- The couple directly practices sex with the advice and instructions of the therapist. Typically, you spend one or two weeks in daily therapy. Instruction occurs during the day, and then the couple retires to the privacy of a hotel to practice what is prescribed. They report their progress the next morning.

Direct sex therapy is not a do-it-yourself affair, and therapists can now be found in almost all major American population centers. Ask your prospective therapists if they use Masters and Johnson techniques. The treatment of all the dysfunctions is similar, so I will illustrate only one.

> *Cindy has never had an orgasm, and her marriage to Bob is starting to unravel. They travel to Philadelphia to work with two therapists at the Marriage Council. In the second session, Cindy is taught how to masturbate with a vibrator. Afterward, alone, she has her first orgasm. This builds her confidence and dissolves some of her fear of the unknown. Next, Bob is instructed to start participating—gradually. That night, he just watches Cindy climax. The following night, he holds the vibrator. The night after that, he touches her clitoris lightly with his lubricated finger while she masturbates. Cindy begins to spectate at this phase and is encouraged to have wild sexual fantasies to distract herself. That hurdle past, Cindy and Bob go on to* sensate focus, *a graduated sequence of reciprocal caresses in which giving and receiving is emphasized. This culminates in* nondemand *intercourse—intercourse with no expectation or pressure to have orgasm. Cindy has two orgasms during the first session of nondemand intercourse. Six years after therapy, Cindy almost always has orgasms during intercourse.*

Direct sexual therapy treats all of the major sexual dysfunctions, except for retarded ejaculation in men, with high success rates—70 to 95 percent. Once successful treatment is accomplished, not much relapse occurs.[30]

Conclusion

The idea of *depth* organizes our erotic life and affects how changeable it is. Sexual identity and sexual orientation are very deep and don't change much, if at all. Sexual preference and sex role are of middling depth and, accordingly, change somewhat. Sexual dysfunction is a surface problem that with proper treatment can change readily. This is the beginning of a global theory, and what depth really means and how it applies across all of our lives is the topic of chapter 15.

I want to end here with the most common and least understood sexual problem. So ordinary is this problem, so likely are you to suffer from it, that it usually goes unnoticed. It doesn't even have a name. The writer Robertson Davies dubs it *acedia.*[31] Acedia used to be reckoned a sin, one of the seven deadly sins, in fact. Medieval theologians translated it as "sloth," but it is not physical torpor that makes acedia so deadly. It is the torpor of the soul, the indifference that creeps up on us as we age and grow accustomed to those we love, that poisons so much of adult life.

As we fight our way out of the problems of adolescence and early adulthood, we often notice that the defeats and setbacks that troubled us in our youth are no longer as agonizing. This comes as welcome relief, but it has a cost. Whatever buffers us from the turmoil and pain of loss also buffers us from feeling joy. It is easy to mistake the indifference that creeps over us with age and experience for the growth of wisdom. Indifference is not wisdom. It is acedia.

The symptom of this condition that concerns me is the waning of sexual attraction that so commonly comes between lovers once they settle down with each other. The sad fact is that the passionate attraction that so consumed them when they first courted dies down as they get to know each other well. In time, it becomes an ember; often, an ash. Within a few years, the sexual passion goes out of most marriages, and many partners start to look elsewhere to rekindle this joyous side of life. This is easy to do with a new lover, but acedia will not be denied, and the whole cycle happens again. This is the stuff of much of modern divorce, and this is the sexual disorder you are most likely to experience. I call it a disorder because it meets the defining criterion of a disorder: like transsexuality or S-M or impotence, it grossly impairs sexual, affectionate relations between two people who used to have them.

Researchers and therapists have not seen fit to mount an attack on acedia. You will find it in no one's nosology, on no foundation's priority list of problems to solve, in no government mental health budget. It is consigned to the innards of women's magazines and to trashy "how to keep your man" paperbacks. Acedia is looked upon with acceptance and indifference by those who might actually discover how it works and how to cure it.

It is acedia I wish to single out as the most painful, the most costly, the most mysterious, and the least understood of the sexual disorders. And therefore the most urgent.

12

Dieting: A Waist Is a Terrible Thing to Mind

I JUST HAD LUNCH. A really classy buffet—twenty-two dollars for all I could eat—my nemesis. I can't resist trying everything and then going back for more of the things that taste especially good. I realized after the very first plateful—shrimp, sashimi, and potato salad—that my stomach was full and I didn't need any more. But I kept going back: a plate of the cold cuts, rolls and butter, then some more shrimp and some smoked salmon, then the hot dishes—duck and onions, and blackened chicken with sausage—and a token bit of vegetable. Then the salads (the avocado-and-bacon was great) and the fresh fruit. Then I topped it off with three desserts: the white chocolate mousse, the carrot cake, and the cherry pie.

How do I feel now? Stuffed, certainly. But fat, ugly, unhealthy, and ashamed as well.

I have been watching my weight and restricting my intake—except for an occasional binge like this—since I was twenty. I weighed about 175 pounds then, maybe 15 pounds over my official "ideal" weight ("big-boned and barrel-chested," I told myself). I weigh 199 pounds now, thirty years later, about 25 pounds over the "ideal." "I've had a sedentary adulthood: writing, doing research, seeing patients, teaching," I tell myself, "and I only started exercising—a half-mile swim every day—last year." I have tried about a dozen regimes—fasting, the "Beverly Hills Diet," no carbohydrates, Metrecal for lunch, 1,200 calories a day, low fat, no lunch, no starches, skipping every other dinner. I lost 10 or 15 pounds on each in about a month.

I lied: I had to quit the Beverly Hills thing—all the pineapple and watermelon I could eat—because I got such bad diarrhea. The pounds always came back, though, and I have gained a net of about a pound a year—inexorably.

This is the most consistent failure in my life. It's also a failure I can't just put out of mind, like the failure to get rid of my slice at golf. There are too many reminders, every time I look in the mirror and every time I look at a tempting dish. In thirty years of dieting, this is what I've been trying to achieve:

- I want to be more attractive. I hate this two-inch spare tire.
- I want to stay healthy. My father had a stroke at just my age.
- I want to feel zestier. I am often tired and irritable.
- I want to feel that I am in control, not that I'm a grown man defeated by a carrot cake.

Pretty sound reasons. I think I should keep at it. Okay, no dinner tonight, only coffee (with saccharin) tomorrow morning, no dessert for the rest of the week.

Not so fast. I have spent the last few years reading the scientific literature, not the parade of best-selling diet books or the flood of women's magazine articles on the latest way to slim down. The scientific findings look clear to me, but there is not yet a consensus. I am going to go out on a limb in this chapter, because I see so many signs all pointing in one direction. What I have concluded will, I believe, soon be the consensus of the scientists. The conclusions surprise me. They will probably surprise you, too, and they may change your life.

Here is what the picture looks like to me:[1]

- Dieting doesn't work.
- Dieting may make overweight worse, not better.
- Dieting may be bad for health.
- Dieting may cause eating disorders—bulimia and anorexia.

Are You Overweight?

Here is an "ideal weight" chart. Are you above the "ideal" weight for your sex, height, and age? If so, you are "overweight." What does this really mean? "Ideal" weight is arrived at simply. Four million people, now dead, who were insured by the major life-insurance companies of America were once weighed and had their height measured. At what weight on average do people of a given height turn out to live longest? That weight is called "ideal," or "desirable." Anything wrong with that?

You bet. The real use of the table, and the reason your doctor takes it seriously, is that an "ideal" weight implies that, on average, if you slim down to yours, you will live longer. This is the crucial claim. Lighter

1983 METROPOLITAN LIFE INSURANCE HEIGHT AND WEIGHT TABLES[2]

Height	*Small Frame*	*Medium Frame*	*Large Frame*
MEN (ages 25–59, dressed in 5 pounds of clothes)			
		POUNDS	
5′2″	128–134	131–141	138–150
5′3″	130–136	133–143	140–153
5′4″	132–138	135–145	142–156
5′5″	134–140	137–148	144–160
5′6″	136–142	139–151	146–164
5′7″	138–145	142–154	149–168
5′8″	140–148	145–157	152–172
5′9″	142–151	148–160	155–176
5′10″	144–154	151–163	158–180
5′11″	146–157	154–166	161–184
6′0″	149–160	157–170	164–188
6′1″	152–164	160–174	168–192
6′2″	155–168	164–178	172–197
6′3″	158–172	167–182	176–202
6′4″	162–176	171–187	181–207
WOMEN (ages 25–59, dressed in 3 pounds of clothes)			
4′10″	102–111	109–121	118–131
4′11″	103–113	109–121	120–134
5′0″	104–115	113–126	122–137
5′1″	106–118	115–129	125–140
5′2″	108–121	118–132	128–143
5′3″	111–124	121–135	131–147
5′4″	114–127	124–138	134–151
5′5″	117–130	127–141	137–155
5′6″	120–133	130–144	140–159
5′7″	123–136	133–147	143–163
5′8″	126–139	136–150	146–167
5′9″	129–142	139–153	149–170
5′10″	132–145	142–156	152–173
5′11″	135–148	145–159	155–176
6′0″	138–151	148–162	158–179

people indeed live longer, on average, than heavier people, but how much longer is hotly debated.

But the crucial claim is unsound because weight (at any given height) has a normal distribution, *normal* both in a statistical sense and in the biological sense. Why is there a distribution of weights at all? Why don't all 64-inch-tall thirty-five-year-old women weigh 130 pounds? Some women fall on the heavy side of 130 pounds because they are heavy-boned, or buxom, or have slow metabolisms. Others fall there because they overeat and never exercise. In the biological sense, the couch potatoes can legitimately be called overweight, but the buxom, heavy-boned, slow people deemed overweight by the "ideal" table are at their natural and healthiest weight. If you are a 155-pound woman and 64 inches in height, you are "overweight" by around 15 pounds. This means nothing more than that the average 130-pound, 64-inch-tall woman lives somewhat longer than the average 155-pound woman of your height. It does not follow that if you slim down to 125 pounds, *you* will stand any better chance of living longer.

Here is an analogy. Imagine that fifty-year-old men who are gray-haired die sooner than fifty-year-old men who are not. If you are a gray-haired fifty-year-old, should you dye your hair? No, and for two reasons: First, whatever causes grayness may also cause dying sooner, and coloring your hair will add no time to your life because it doesn't undo the underlying cause of dying sooner. Second, health damage caused by repeatedly coloring your hair with chemicals might itself shorten your life.

In spite of the insouciance with which dieting advice is dispensed, no one has properly investigated the question of whether slimming down to "ideal" weight produces longer life. The proper study would compare the longevity of people who are at their "ideal" weight without dieting to people who achieve their "ideal" weight by dieting. Without this study, the common medical advice that you should diet down to your "ideal" weight is simply unfounded.[3]

This is not a quibble, for there is evidence that dieting damages your health and that this damage may shorten your life.

Myths of Overweight

The advice to diet down to your "ideal" weight in order to live longer is one myth of overweight. Here are some others:

Overweight people overeat. Wrong. Nineteen out of twenty studies show that obese people consume no more calories each day than non-obese people. In one remarkable experiment, a group of very obese people dieted down to only 60 percent overweight and stayed there. They needed one hundred fewer calories a day to stay 60 percent overweight than normal people needed to stay at normal weight. Telling a fat person that if she would change her eating habits and eat "normally" she would lose weight is a lie. To lose weight and stay there, she will need to eat excruciatingly less than a normal person, probably for the rest of her life.[4]

Overweight people have an overweight personality. Wrong. Extensive research on personality and fatness has proved little. Obese people do not differ in any major personality style from nonobese people. They are not, for example, more susceptible to external food cues (the fragrance of garlic bread, for example) than nonobese people.[5]

Physical inactivity is a major cause of obesity. Probably not. Fat people are indeed less active than thin people, but the inactivity is probably caused more by the fatness than the other way around.

Overweight shows a lack of willpower. This is the granddaddy of all the myths. When I am defeated by that piece of carrot cake, I feel like a failure: I should be able to control myself, and there is something morally wrong with me if I give in. Fatness is seen as shameful because we hold people responsible for their weight. Being overweight equates with being a weak-willed slob. We believe this primarily because we have seen plenty of people decide to lose weight and do so in a matter of weeks.

But almost everyone returns to the old weight after shedding pounds. Your body has a natural weight that it defends vigorously against dieting. The more diets tried, the harder the body works to defeat the next diet. Weight is in large part genetic. All this gives the lie to the "weak-willed" interpretation of overweight. More accurately, dieting pits the conscious will of the individual against a deeper, more vigilant opponent: the species' biological defense against starvation. The conscious will can occasionally win battles—no carrot cake tonight, this month without carbohydrates—but it almost always loses the war.

The Demographics of Dieting

We are a culture obsessed with thinness. How many times a day do you think about your weight? Each time you catch a glimpse of your naked body or your double chin in the mirror? Each time you touch your midriff bulge? Each meal? Each time you eat something tasty and want more? Every time you're hungry? My guess is that the average overweight adult (the large majority of us) thinks discontentedly about his or her body more than five times a day. By contrast, how many times a day do you think about your salary? My guess is once a day, or, if you are really strapped, about five times a day. Is being overweight as important as going broke?

You and I, and about 100 million other Americans, share this nagging discontent. In 1990, Americans spent more than $30 billion on the weight-loss industry, almost as much as the federal government spent on education, employment, and social services combined. These billions are poured into hospital diet clinics and commercial weight-loss programs, into health spas and exercise clubs, into 54 million copies of diet books. Ten billion dollars went for diet soft drinks. There were 100,000 jaw-wiring and liposuction operations at $3,500 each. More than $500 was spent on weight loss by each overweight adult in America. We would save this much if we could be convinced that we were not overweight or that there was nothing we could do about being overweight.[6]

The fashion industry, the entertainment industry, and women's magazines bombard us with female models of beauty and talent so thin as to represent almost no actual women in the population. We have gotten heavier and heavier, but the models have gotten thinner and thinner. From 1959 to 1978, the average *Playboy* centerfold became markedly more gaunt, and the average Miss America contestant dropped almost one-third of a pound a year. During the same twenty years, the average young American woman gained about the same amount. Both these trends have continued into the 1990s.[7]

The purveyors of weight loss are the children of those pioneering advertising campaigners who in the first half of this century created and then preyed upon insecurity ("He said that she said that he had halitosis"). The weight-loss industry's clout should not be underestimated. It has cornered the bulk of the self-improvement market and a sizable percentage of the American medical dollar. It is self-interested and powerful. It is pleased that the "ideal weight" tables put so many of us in the overweight category. It is delighted that Americans believe minor overweight is a serious health risk. It is ecstatic that men now find thin women sexier than voluptuous women. It thrives on the fact that Americans are so insecure in themselves and so desperately unhappy with their bodies. It has on its payrolls some of the most prominent scientists of appetite, who publish journal articles touting new, improved diets and exaggerating the health risks of overweight.

All this has created a general public that is discontent, even despairing, about their bodies, and willing—even eager—to spend a substantial portion of their earnings in the belief that they can and should become much thinner than they are. It is time for this to end.

The Oprah Effect

There is a professional consensus about two facts:

- You can lose weight in a month or two on almost any diet.
- You will almost certainly gain it back in a few years.

The American public watched in hopeful fascination as a daytime TV host, Oprah Winfrey, went on Optifast, which is, technically, a *VLCD* (*very-low-calorie diet*). She became slimmer and slimmer before our eyes: 180, 160, 150, 140, 120. In a matter of months, she lost 67 pounds and looked trim and petite. Oprah praised the diet, and Optifast's business soared. Over the next year, the viewing public watched in morbid fascination as Oprah went from 110 to 120 to 130, all the way back to 180. Embittered, Oprah condemned the diet, and Optifast's business shrank.

The "Oprah effect" was no surprise to the scientific community. Even before Oprah went on her VLCD, a definitive study of her diet had been published. Five hundred patients on Optifast began at an average of 50 percent over their "ideal" weight. More than half of these patients dropped out before treatment was complete. The rest, like Oprah, lost a great deal of weight—an average of 84 percent of their excess weight. An excellent result. Over the next thirty months, the patients, like Oprah, regained an average of about 80 percent. In another follow-up of VLCD, only 3 percent of the patients were considered successes after five years. In yet another study of VLCDs, 121 patients were followed for years after they lost 60 pounds on average. Half were back at their old weight after three years, 90 percent after nine years. Only 5 percent remained at their reduced weight. The best result I can find is a study in which 13 percent of subjects remained thin after three years.[8]

No other diet has been shown to work in the long run. There are about a dozen well-executed long-term studies involving thousands of dieters, and all of them show basically the same dismal result: Most people gain almost all their weight back in four to five years, with perhaps 10 percent remaining thin. The longer the follow-up, the worse the outcome. The trajectory points to complete failure after enough time elapses.[9] More telling than what is published is what is not published. There has been dead silence from the commercial programs. They have long-term weight figures on tens of thousands of their clients, but they have kept their findings secret. It doesn't take a Sherlock Holmes to figure out why.

A few diet experts take the view that enough is enough: Dieting is a cruel hoax, and it is time for Congress to intervene. Many sit glumly on the fence, perhaps awaiting the day of reckoning. But some respected experts call for new and more innovative diets with far more attention paid to maintenance. Drs. Kelly Brownell and Tom Wadden, two leading obesity researchers, have called for a national obesity campaign with the goal of a ten-pound loss by all overweight Americans.[10] These optimists have one plausible argument: Almost all the long-term failures are *patients*—obese people who go to hospital clinics. These may be the most hopeless cases, the terminally fat. Maybe diets will work better on the slightly overweight, the people who don't need to go to clinics, the people who have not repeatedly tried and failed.

I doubt it. Workplace and home-correspondence interventions have fared just as poorly as hospital clinics.[11] Maybe someone will discover a way to screen overweight people so that only the ones likely to succeed will be accepted for dieting programs. Maybe someone will have that new insight into maintenance that has thus far eluded everyone. But in the meantime, the clearest fact about dieting is that after years of research, after tens of millions of dieters, after tens of billions of dollars, *no one has found a diet that keeps the weight off in any but a small fraction of dieters.*[12]

Yo-yo Dieting

Rats permanently change the way they deal with food after they have been starved once. After they regain the weight, their metabolism slows. They like fatty foods more. They accumulate larger fat deposits. The more cycles of famine and feast, the better they get at storing energy. They may even rebound from starvation to a higher weight than ever before once food is abundant again.[13]

It looks as if people do the same thing. After dieting, people radically change the way they deal with food. Dieters become intensely preoccupied with food, thinking about it all day long, even dreaming about it. The body changes, hoarding energy. Normal activities—sitting and exercising—use up fewer calories in formerly obese women who have slimmed down than in matched controls who have never dieted. Even sleeping burns 10 percent fewer calories in the onetime obese. Less energy is given off in heat. Lethargy, a real energy saver, is common. Buttercream frosting tastes better than it used to. It may even take fewer calories for a dieter to put on a pound than for a normal person. So a sizable number of patients don't simply relapse, but wind up heavier than they were in the first place.[14]

In one study, the "lucky" 10 percent of formerly fat people who dieted and stayed thin ate an average of 1,298 calories a day to stay at their new weight, whereas normal controls ate 1,950 calories to stay at that same weight. This demonstrates that dieters may never again be able to eat normal amounts of food if they want to stay thin. Yo-yo dieting—taking weight off, putting it all on again, and then trying to take it off once more—is a Sisyphean battle. The second time obese patients go on a VLCD, they lose weight more slowly, yet they take in exactly the same number of calories as the first time.[15]

This makes biological sense. Imagine a species only recently emerged from 100,000 years of famine. During this epoch, weeks or even a whole season go by with almost nothing to eat. Then there is a big kill or a bumper crop. Everyone gorges and then rations what is left until the next big kill. An epoch of famine and feast produces strong evolutionary pressure for a creature who gorges and stores up a lot of fat during periods of plenty, but releases fat's life-sustaining energy with reluctance during shortages. The more the creature goes through the feast-famine cycle, the better it gets at storing fat and conserving energy.

Now imagine that this epoch suddenly ends and food is abundant. This creature eats a great deal and gets fat. Someone conceives a scheme to limit fat, and the creature voluntarily undereats. But its body can't tell the difference between self-imposed starvation and actual famine. So the hoary survival defenses kick in: The body defends its weight by refusing to release fat, by lowering its metabolism, and by insistently demanding food. The harder the creature tries not to eat, the more vigorous these defenses become.[16]

This creature is *Homo sapiens,* the departed epoch is the Pleistocene, the time is now, and the doomed scheme is dieting.

Bulimia and Natural Weight

A concept that makes sense of your body's vigorous defense against weight loss is *natural weight.* When your body screams "I'm hungry," slows its metabolism, makes you lethargic, stores fat, craves sweets and renders them more delicious than ever, and makes you obsessed with food, what it is defending is your natural weight. It is signaling that you have dropped into a range it will not accept. Natural weight prevents you from gaining too much weight or losing too much. When you eat too much for too long, the opposite defenses are activated and make long-term weight gain difficult. A group of prisoners was paid to add 25 percent to their body weight by eating twice their usual calories for six months. The first few pounds came on easily, but then there was no weight gain.[17]

There is also a strong genetic contribution to your natural weight. Identical twins reared apart weigh almost the same throughout their lives. When identical twins are overfed, they gain weight and add fat in lockstep and in the same places. The fatness or thinness of adopted children resembles their biological parents—particularly their mother—very closely, but does not at all resemble their adoptive parents. This suggests that you have a genetically given natural weight that your body wants to maintain. I don't know a formula for assigning a number to your natural weight, but it is probably considerably higher than your "ideal" weight. The average middle-aged American man, for example, weighs 16 percent more than his "ideal" weight.[18]

The idea of natural weight may help cure the new disorder that is sweeping young America. Hundreds of thousands of young women have contracted it. More than 5 percent of the young women to whom I teach Abnormal Psychology every fall complain of it. Two percent of adult women may have it in severe form.[19] It consists of bouts of binge eating and purging alternating with days of undereating. These young women are universally concerned with their body image. They are usually normal in weight or a bit on the thin side, but they are terrified of becoming fat. So they diet. They exercise. They take laxatives by the cup. Twice a week they find themselves at a buffet or in an ice-cream parlor. They gorge: four hot-fudge sundaes topped off with a banana split. Then they vomit and take more laxatives. This malady is called *bulimia nervosa* ("bulimia" for short).

Therapists are puzzled by bulimia, its causes and treatment. Debate rages about whether it is an equivalent of depression, or an expression of a thwarted desire for control, or a symbolic rejection of the feminine role. Almost every psychotherapy has been tried. Antidepressants and other drugs have been administered with some effect, but—with one exception, which I'll discuss shortly—little success has been reported.[20]

I don't think that bulimia is mysterious, and I think that it will be curable. I believe that bulimia is caused by dieting. The bulimic goes on a diet, and her body attempts to defend its natural weight. With repeated dieting, this defense becomes more vigorous. Her body is in massive revolt—insistently demanding food, storing fat, craving sweets, and lowering metabolism. Periodically, these biological defenses will overcome her extraordinary willpower (and extraordinary it must be even to approach an "ideal" weight, say, twenty pounds lighter than her natural weight). She will then binge. Horrified by what this will do to her figure, she vomits and takes laxatives to purge calories. Thus bulimia is a natural consequence of self-starvation to lose weight in the midst of abundant food.[21]

Every bulimic I have met is dieting. Systematic surveys of bulimics show that at least 80 percent are on diets immediately before bulimia starts. The epidemic is sweeping America right now because the thin ideal has become thinner and thinner over time as the average female body has gotten heavier and heavier. The ideal has so far outstripped the capacity to achieve it that the discrepancy between natural weight and "ideal" weight is so great as to produce binge eating on a massive scale. Women whose natural weights are most discrepant from their "ideal" weights will be most vulnerable.

One study observed twenty bulimics who binged an average of three times a week. Ten received a nutritionally adequate treatment diet for eight weeks consisting, unbeknownst to them, of at least 1,400 calories a day. All of them stopped binging. A control group of ten others ate a sham diet that was the equivalent of what they had been eating. They continued to binge, but when they were switched to the nutritionally adequate diet, all of them stopped binging completely. This suggests that dieting is a cause of bulimia and suggests a major strategy for therapy.[22]

The therapist's task is to get the patient to stop dieting and become comfortable with her natural weight. He should first convince the patient that her binge eating is caused by her body's reaction to her diet. Then he must confront her with a question: Which is more important, staying thin or getting rid of bulimia? By stopping the diet, he will tell her, she can get rid of the uncontrollable binge-purge cycle. Her body will now settle at her natural weight, and she need not worry that she will balloon beyond that point. For some patients, therapy will end there because they would rather be bulimic than "loathsomely fat." For these patients, the central issue—ideal weight versus natural weight—can now at least become the focus of therapy. For others, defying the social and sexual pressure to be thin will be possible, dieting will be abandoned, weight will be gained, and bulimia should end quickly.

These are the central moves of the cognitive-behavioral treatment of bulimia. There are more than a dozen outcome studies of this approach, and the results are good. There is about 60 percent reduction in binging and purging (about the same as with antidepressant drugs). But unlike drugs, there is little relapse after treatment. Attitudes toward weight and shape relax, and dieting withers. Two studies explicitly compared drugs and cognitive-behavioral treatment, and in both studies, drugs were less effective.[23]

The dieting theory cannot fully explain bulimia. Many people who diet don't become bulimic; some can avoid it because their natural weight is close to their "ideal" weight, and therefore the diet they adopt does not starve them.[24] In addition, bulimics are often depressed, since binging-purging leads to self-loathing. Depression may worsen bulimia by making it easier to give in to temptation. Further, dieting may just be another symptom of bulimia, not a cause. Other factors aside, I can speculate that dieting below your natural weight is a necessary condition for bulimia, and that returning to your natural weight and accepting that weight will cure bulimia.

There is a new and disheartening development in "eating disorders."

The Right Treatment

BULIMIA NERVOSA SUMMARY TABLE

	Antidepressant Drugs	*Cognitive-Behavioral Therapy*
Improvement	▲▲	▲▲
Relapse	▲	▲▲
Side Effects	▼▼▼	▼
Cost	inexpensive	inexpensive
Time Scale	weeks	weeks/months
Overall	▲◢	▲▲◢

Improvement

▲▲▲▲	= 80–100% markedly improved or symptom free
▲▲▲	= 60–80% markedly improved
▲▲	= at least 50% moderately improved
▲	= probably better than placebo
o	= probably useless

Relapse (after discontinuation of treatment)

▲▲▲▲	= 10% or fewer relapse
▲▲▲	= 10–20% relapse
▲▲	= moderate relapse rate
▲	= high relapse rate

Side Effects

▼▼▼▼	= severe
▼▼▼	= moderate
▼▼	= mild
▼	= none

Overall

▲▲▲▲	= excellent, clearly the therapy of choice
▲▲▲	= very good
▲▲	= useful
▲	= marginal
o	= probably useless

Dr. Robert Spitzer, a New York City psychiatrist who organized the writing of that useful document the *Diagnostic and Statistical Manual of the American Psychiatric Association* (*DSM-3* and *DSM-3-R*), is now trying to have "binge-eating disorder" added to *DSM-4*. He discovers this new malady in as many as 30 percent of those dieting in hospital weight-loss programs. They binge occasionally, but they don't purge, so they gain weight. From my point of view, many of these poor people are trying to slim down to weights far below their natural weight. Their bodies, like bulimics', are screaming for food. Perhaps their disorder is not binge eating but inappropriate dieting.[25]

In fact, we should consider a new category for *DSM-4*, "dieting disorder," defined as being within 20 percent of your "ideal" weight and ruining your life and health by dieting.

The idea of natural weight has another huge practical implication. Right now I'm drinking my morning coffee with three packets of artificial sweetener in it. I love sweet coffee, but I hate the nearly 50 calories in a tablespoon of sugar in each cup. I have been assuming—until now—that for each dose of artificial sweetener I consume, I will take in that many fewer calories each day. I am also afraid that if I stop drinking artificially sweetened beverages, I will gain weight. This is the hidden logic of the army of consumers that supports the $10 billion diet-soft-drink industry. With artificial sweetener in three cups of coffee, the savings is about 150 calories; two diet soft drinks means another 400 or so calories saved: That's around 550 calories a day I avoid; almost 4,000 calories a week, more than the equivalent of one pound of weight. But why haven't I lost a pound a week since I started using artificial sweeteners? (I calculate that I should now weigh less than zero and go floating off like a helium balloon.)

The answer, I suspect, is natural weight. I probably eat an extra 550 calories elsewhere each day to make up for the sugar I avoid. Those calories aren't in sugar, so my teeth aren't rotting out, but they might be in fat. I don't know if this is so, but I'm going to find out.[26]

Diet Pills

Diet pills suppress appetite, and they have one virtue: Unlike diets, taking pills requires no discipline. But pills create the same problem as dieting—rapid regaining of weight—and are more dangerous: In 1973, the Federal Drug Administration severely limited their use because the weight loss they produce (about two pounds per week) is small, and the health risks, including psychosis, addiction, heart attack, and death, are substantial.[27]

New drugs are developed every so often. The latest ones, fenfluramine and phentermine, show more promise. They produce substantial weight loss, and unlike their predecessors, they may readjust the "set point" of natural weight rather than just suppress appetite.

Michael Weintraub, an obesity researcher, coordinated a well-done study of these two drugs.[28] One hundred twenty-one participants, mostly women, started the study at over two hundred pounds. The study lasted four years: Those women receiving the drugs (coupled with behavior therapy and exercise) lost an average of thirty pounds and kept the weight off for as long as they took the drugs. As soon as they ceased taking the drugs, however, the weight returned.

These two drugs have some side effects—dry mouth, nervousness, sedation, vivid dreams, and depression—which are milder than the early appetite-suppressing drugs. The side effects are not trivial, though, and because of them, more than one-third of the patients dropped out without much benefit. Overall, however, one-third of the patients lost a good bit of weight and kept it off—a much better result than any diet has achieved. Future research on these drugs should determine the long-term effects of taking them, and how to reduce the side effects and therefore the dropout rate. The development of these drugs is promising, but until more research is completed I regard them as experimental.

Overweight vs. Dieting: The Health Damage

Being heavy carries some health risk. There is no definitive answer to how much, because there is a swamp of inconsistent findings. Distilling these findings is hazardous, but here is my best guess:[29]

- *Enormous obesity* (double "ideal" weight or more) may well cause premature death.
- *Substantial obesity* (30 to 100 percent above "ideal" weight) possibly causes health damage and may be associated with somewhat increased mortality.
- *Mild to moderate overweight* (10 to 30 percent above "ideal" weight) may possibly be associated with a marginal increase in mortality, particularly for those at risk for diabetes.
- *Underweight* is clearly associated with substantially greater mortality.

If you are overweight, you should ignore scare tactics like Optifast's desperate "Obesity is a death sentence" ad. Even if you could just wish pounds away, never to return, it is not certain you should. Being somewhat above your "ideal" weight may actually be your healthiest natural condition, best for your particular constitution and your particular metabolism. Of course, you can't wish pounds away, but you can diet them away with any popular diet, chosen at random. But the odds are overwhelming that most of the weight will return, and that you will have to diet it away again and again. From a health and mortality perspective, should you diet? *There is, probably, a serious health risk from losing weight and regaining it.*

There have been three large-scale studies of weight cycling and death. The first, a study of one million Americans, is often overlooked since it shows increased mortality with increased weight. But it also shows that men and women who lose more than ten pounds in five years have substantially more heart attacks and strokes than expected. This is true of the people who lose weight voluntarily (dieters) as well as the people who lose weight involuntarily because they are ill. In the second study, men who had at least one cycle of loss and regain are at double the risk for death from heart disease than men who progressively gain weight over twenty-five years. In the third study, more than five thousand men and women from Framingham, Massachusetts, were observed for thirty-two years. People whose weight fluctuated over the years had 30 to 100 percent greater risk for death from heart disease than people whose weight was stable. When corrected for smoking, exercise, cholesterol level, and blood pressure, the findings became more convincing, suggesting that weight fluctuation (the primary cause of which is presumably dieting) may itself increase the risk of heart disease.[30]

Being overweight is risky. But dieting is risky as well. Which risk is bigger? From a health perspective alone, should you diet or not?

I suspect, but I am not yet certain, that the weight-fluctuation hazard may be larger than the hazard of staying overweight. In the only study that directly compared the two risks, the Framingham study, the weight-cycling risk was shown to be markedly bigger than the overweight risk. If this result is replicated, and if dieting is shown to be the primary cause of weight cycling, it will convince me that you should not diet to reduce your risk of heart disease.

If you are coming into middle age and have gradually gained weight since your early twenties, you are probably tempted to diet for health reasons. Resist the temptation. Two exemplary studies show that you may have less health risk than those who have not gained weight. The Framingham people who gradually gained some weight over the years were at lower risk even than people whose weight was stable, and at much less risk than the yo-yoers. In a study of seventeen thousand Harvard alumni, men who gained fifteen pounds or more after graduating were at one-third *less* risk of death than everyone else. No one knows why, but a gradual gain in weight across your middle years seems normal and healthy.[31]

Depression and Dieting

Depression is yet another cost of dieting, because two root causes of depression are failure and helplessness. Dieting sets you up for failure. Because the goal of slimming down to your "ideal" weight pits your fallible willpower against untiring biological defenses, you will often fail. At first you will lose weight and feel pretty good about it. Any depression you had about your figure will disappear. Ultimately, however, you will probably not reach your goal; and then you will be dismayed as the pounds return. Every time you look in the mirror or vacillate over a white chocolate mousse, you will be reminded of your failure, which in turn brings depression. On the other hand, if you are one of the fortunate few who can keep the weight from coming back, you will probably have to stay on an unsatisfying low-calorie diet for the rest of your life. A side effect of prolonged malnutrition is depression. Either way, you are more vulnerable to it.

If you scan the list of cultures that have a thin ideal for women, you will be struck by something fascinating. All thin-ideal cultures also have eating disorders. They also have roughly twice as much depression in women as in men. (Women diet twice as much as men. The best estimate is that 13 percent of adult men and 25 percent of adult women are now on a diet.) The cultures without the thin ideal have no eating disorders, and the amount of depression in women and men in these cultures is the same. This suggests that around the world, the thin ideal and dieting not only cause eating disorders but also cause women to be more depressed than men.[32]

The problem of fat consciousness and depression starts shortly before puberty. Earlier, boys have at least as much depression as girls. When puberty starts, boys go from flabby to muscular, but girls, whose weight gain is primarily fat, go from lean to voluptuous. Boys move toward their ideal body, but girls move away from it. Soon after puberty, girls are twice as depressed as boys, and the girls who are most depressed are the ones most upset about their body.[33]

In a culture that glorifies being thin and young, many of us who are neither are discontents, vulnerable to continual messages that we are failures. It is just a few short steps from constantly feeling like a failure to becoming a depressed patient.

The Bottom Line

I have been dieting off and on for thirty years. I diet because I want to be more attractive, healthier, zestier, and more in control. How do these goals stack up against the facts?

Attractiveness. Losing weight will make me look more attractive. I am, however, a married man with four children, and I have pretty much gone out of the attracting business. If I were a twenty-five-year-old woman, however, this goal would loom much larger. In this society, the closer a young woman is to her "ideal" weight, the more attractive she is deemed. I do not approve, but these are the facts.

If your attractiveness is a high-enough priority to convince you to diet, keep three drawbacks in mind: First, the attractiveness you gain will be temporary. All the weight you lose and maybe more will likely come back in a few years. This will depress you. Then you will have to lose it again—and it will be harder the second time. Or you will have to resign yourself to being less attractive. Second, when women choose the silhouette figure they want to achieve, it turns out to be thinner than the silhouette that men label most attractive.[34] Third, you may well become bulimic, particularly if your natural weight is substantially more than your "ideal" weight.

On balance, if short-term attractiveness is your overriding goal, diet. But be prepared for the costs.

Health. If I diet, I am probably at increased risk for death. Losing and regaining weight probably increases my mortality risk, perhaps more than staying overweight or even allowing myself to gain more weight gradually. No one has ever shown that losing weight will increase my longevity.[35]

On balance, the health goal does not warrant dieting.

Zest. If I diet, I will have less bulk to carry around. I should be able to run and swim faster. But this advantage will vanish when I regain the weight. In addition, my metabolism will slow down in defense of my natural weight, and this is often manifested as lethargy. Worse, I may still be lethargic after the diet ends and the weight is regained. I now wonder if my lack of zest as I have gotten older isn't the consequence of dieting, not a consequence of the extra pounds. Is it possible that the celebrated "chronic fatigue syndrome" may stem in part from a history of dieting? My desire for more energy will probably not be well served by dieting.

Control. I want to be in control, but the second dessert tells me I am not. Wrong. I have simply been too quick to condemn myself on this score, because I didn't know the facts. I thought that my weight was under my control. But now I see that for thirty years my vacillating willpower has been pitted against an unceasing biological defense of my natural weight.

I would get a lot more done if I could sleep only six hours a night. But when I try this and find that I feel exhausted two hours earlier the next evening, I do not feel ashamed or weak of will. I know it is just my body insisting on making up the two hours' lost sleep. For many people, getting to an "ideal" weight and staying there is just as biologically impossible as going with much less sleep. This fact tells me not to diet, and defuses my feeling of shame. My bottom line is clear: I am not going to diet anymore.

Of course, there is something other than dieting that can help you achieve your goals.

Advice to the Overweight

Fitness vs. fatness. I just returned from my daily half-mile swim. I am really proud of myself today because I was able to sprint the last fifty yards. I have been swimming laps religiously for about a year. I have not lost any weight (in fact, I've gained a few pounds). But my hips are slimmer, my mood is less irritable, I sleep better, and I have more energy. I have also read the scientific literature on exercise. Achieving fitness is clearly more sensible than fighting fatness.

A surprisingly small amount of exercise may lower death risk significantly. In one study of ten thousand men and three thousand women, the least-fit 20 percent were shown to have far and away the highest death risk. Moving out of the least-fit fifth markedly lowered risk. This suggests that even modest exercise, as opposed to becoming fanatical, will produce the biggest reduction in risk. Confirming this, the death rate of the sedentary men in the Harvard alumni group I mentioned earlier is 30 percent higher than that of the men who exercise moderately. Statistically, moderate exercise—burning off 2,000 calories per week—produces two extra years of life. (Perhaps God does not subtract the time spent exercising from your allotted time on earth.) "Moderate exercise" translates into an hour of normal walking or a half hour of slow running or a half hour of swimming each day. Exercise also fights depression and increases self-esteem. Exercise seems to be a much bigger factor in mortality than overweight, and it is probably easier to keep doing over the years than dieting, since it is (almost) fun.[36]

Exercise alone will probably not take off weight. Coupled with a diet program, it may produce a bit better long-term weight loss. Whatever, exercise has its beneficial effects on health, whether or not you lose weight. But there is a danger that coupling exercise with the discouraging enterprise of dieting may cause you to give up on exercise, too—once the weight starts to come back.[37]

The makeup of your diet. It may be useless to try to eat less food, but it is useful to eat less *unhealthy* food: Fat and alcohol are to be watched. In this century, what Americans eat has become about 25 percent fattier, and fat in our food gets converted into fat on our bodies. Fast food, chocolate bars, and ice cream are high in fat. There is little to be said for any but modest drinking of alcohol, and lots to be said against it. Alcohol is very high in calories, addicting, and brain-damaging.[38]

Changing the composition of your diet may or may not take off weight. It is not known if the body will, in the long run, make up for the calories lost by a low-fat or a low-alcohol diet, but the chances are that cutting back on both is healthful anyway.

Eating only when hungry. Overeating, consuming more food than you need to sate your hunger, is more of a problem than overweight. Unlike overweight, you can curtail overeating. Most of us are out of touch with hunger. We eat when the clock tells us it is time to, not when we are hungry. We clean our plates, hungry or not. We gorge when things taste especially good, hungry or not.

Overeating may be yet another untoward consequence of dieting. Recall that Pleistocene ancestor after a famine. Eating only when hungry is a luxury he cannot afford. He becomes a hoarder, an overeater. His surviving the next famine might depend on his stuffing himself after

The Right Treatment

WEIGHT LOSS SUMMARY TABLE

	All Diets	*VLCD**	*Fenfluramine & Phentermine†*	*Diet Pills*	*Stomach Bypass (Very Obese Only)*
INITIAL LOSS	▲▲▲	▲▲▲▲	▲▲▲	▲▲	▲▲▲▲
DROPOUT RATE	▼▼▼	▼▼▼▼	▼▼	▼▼▼	not applicable
SUCCESS RATE	o	o	▲▲	o	▲▲▲
REGAIN	▼▼▼▼	▼▼▼▼	▼▼	▼▼▼▼	▼▼
SIDE EFFECTS	▼▼▼	▼▼▼	▼▼	▼▼▼▼	▼▼▼
COST		inexpensive		inexpensive	expensive
TIME SCALE FOR INITIAL LOSS	weeks	months	weeks	weeks	months
OVERALL	▲	▲	▲▲	o	▲▲▲‡

INITIAL LOSS

▲▲▲▲ = 80–100% lose 20 or more pounds
▲▲▲ = 60–80% lose 10–20 pounds
▲▲ = at least 50% lose some weight
▲ = probably better than nothing

DROPOUT RATE

▼▼▼▼ = 55% or more drop out
▼▼▼ = 40–55% drop out
▼▼ = 20–40% drop out
▼ = less than 20% drop out

REGAIN

▼▼▼▼ = 50% or more regain most of their weight
▼▼▼ = 30–50% regain most of their weight
▼▼ = 10–30% regain most of their weight
▼ = less than 10% regain

SIDE EFFECTS

▼▼▼▼ = severe
▼▼▼ = moderate
▼▼ = mild
▼ = none

SUCCESS RATE

▲▲▲▲ = 80% remain at the reduced weight 3 years later
▲▲▲ = 60% remain at the reduced weight 3 years later
▲▲ = 40% remain at the reduced weight 3 years later
▲ = 20% remain at the reduced weight 3 years later
o = 0–20% remain at the reduced weight 3 years later

OVERALL

▲▲▲▲	= excellent, clearly the therapy of choice
▲▲▲	= very good
▲▲	= useful
▲	= marginal to useless
o	= useless

*VLCD = very-low-calorie diet

†Insufficient research has been done on the safety and effectiveness of fenfluramine and phentermine. The table is my best guess about their effectiveness. I regard them as for experimental purposes only at this stage of development.

‡N.B.: Because the surgical patients, unlike patients in the other treatments, come entirely from a superobese group (100 percent or more of ideal weight), I have allowed "reduced weight" for them to mean a 60 percent loss in excess weight. On this liberal basis, gastric bypass gets two and a half upward pointers.

---

a big kill. He eats as much as he can whenever the opportunity presents itself. Former dieters become overeaters for just this reason. All the body knows is that it has once been starved. You change your approach to food, and overeat whenever lots of good food is available, even if you are not hungry. You have learned to ignore hunger in the interest of survival.

Here are a few steps for how you can stop overeating and get back in touch with hunger:[39]

- When you see something really tasty, ask yourself, "Do I need something in my stomach, or do I only want a taste in my mouth?" If just the taste, refuse.
- Halfway through the main course, stop for a full minute. Ask yourself, "Am I full?" If you are, wrap the rest of the food and end the meal. If not, repeat this three-quarters of the way through.
- Eat slowly and sip water frequently to slow down eating. Put your fork down between bites; this gives you a chance to consider if any more food is necessary to fill you up.

Finally, if you are an overeater, you probably eat all the food put before you. This is a very strong habit that must be broken. Excess food is essentially being thrown down the toilet or poured onto your midriff. I want you to do the *flushing exercise* to break this habit. Halfway through the main course of the next big meal you have at home, stop. Cut the rest of your food into pieces. Get the dessert, and cut it up too. Now flush it all down the toilet—this is where it will wind up, and this exercise allows you to skip the middleman.

Surgery for the very obese. Dieting has a poor outcome for the very obese. Most patients regain most of their weight in a few years, and this weight fluctuation itself carries a significant death risk. If you are very obese (double your "ideal" weight or more), you should consider surgery. The most successful operation is a stomach bypass (technically, a "Roux-en-Y gastric bypass"). This four-hour operation hooks your lower intestine to the top of your stomach. This is major surgery with a fair number of complications that must be corrected by more surgery. The mortality rate from the surgery is very low, below 1 percent, but do note that patients have a subsequent suicide rate of around 1 percent. The food you eat for the rest of your life must be soft, for it passes through your body less well digested. Appetite decreases, weight loss is dramatic, and, most important, the weight tends to stay off. In three- and five-year follow-ups of several hundred patients, the majority have done well. The patient who weighed three hundred pounds before surgery weighs only two hundred pounds five years later. Heart function also improves. Only about 15 to 20 percent fail completely and end up weighing close to their original weight. Gastric bypass is the only treatment of obesity with a documented satisfactory long-term outcome. The effect of this surgery on overweight people who are less than enormously obese is presently unknown, but given their desperation about overweight, I will not be surprised if moderately overweight Americans start to seek it out in the near future.[40]

A Word to the Professional

I intend this book for two audiences. It is primarily for the consumer. Millions of people are trying to make rational decisions about how to cope with their problems and what to do about their shortcomings. They consume self-improvement regimens, psychological treatment, and psychiatric treatment to the tune of many billions of dollars annually. There is presently no consumer's guide, nothing comprehensive and scientifically grounded, to tell the public which treatments work and which treatments fail, which problems can be conquered and which are intractable, which shortcomings can be improved and which cannot. Creating such a guide is my primary aim.

My second audience is the professional: the clinical and counseling psychologist, the psychiatrist, the social worker, the physician, the deliverer and designer of self-improvement programs. Dieting is a special case for us. It affects about half our clients, and it dwarfs all the rest of the problems we deal with by its sheer scale. For a half century we have been advising our clients to diet. Initially, our justification was sound: The "ideal weight" tables pointed to increased health risk with overweight. The situation has changed in the last twenty years. It is now clear that

- weight is almost always regained after dieting
- dieting has a number of destructive side effects including repeated failure and hopelessness, bulimia, depression, and fatigue
- losing and regaining weight itself presents a health risk comparable to the risk of overweight

When we encourage dieting, we are in danger of violating our oath to "do no harm." Help-givers should change their advice. We should tell our overweight clients that unless their only concern is short-term attractiveness, dieting is unlikely to work.

Commercial weight-loss plans, diet books, and magazine diets are under a more urgent obligation: They should warn their clients and their readers *emphatically* that any weight lost is likely to be regained. If commercial programs will not do this voluntarily, disclosure of their long-term success (or failure) rates and of their side effects should be a matter of law.

These steps will go a long way toward making our profession a more responsible one.

13

Alcohol

Poetry is the lie that makes life bearable.

R. P. Blackmuir (from a poetry lecture, Princeton University, spring 1959)

FIFTEEN YEARS AGO two pioneering graduate students at the University of Pennsylvania—Lauren Alloy and Lyn Abramson—conducted an experiment that yielded the most annoying results I have seen in my scientific lifetime. For a decade I kept hoping their findings would be overturned, but subsequent studies confirmed them.

Subjects were given differing degrees of control over the lighting of a light. For some, the action they took perfectly controlled the light: It went on every time they pressed a button, and it never went on if they didn't press. The others, though, had no control whatsoever: The light went on regardless of whether or not they pressed the button; they were helpless.

The people in both groups were asked to judge, as accurately as they could, how much control they had. Depressed people were very accurate. When they had control, they assessed it accurately, and when they did not have control, they said so. The nondepressed people astounded Alloy and Abramson: These subjects were accurate when they had control, but when they were helpless, they were undeterred—they still judged that they had a great deal of control. The depressed people knew the truth. The nondepressed people had benign illusions that they were not helpless when they actually were.

Alloy and Abramson wondered if maybe lights and button pushing did not matter enough, so they added money: When the light went on, the participants won money; when the light did not go on, they lost money. But the benign illusions of nondepressed people did not go away; in fact, they increased. Under one condition, where everyone had some control, the task was rigged so that everyone lost money. Here, nondepressed people said they had less control than they actually had. When the task was rigged so that everyone won money, nondepressed people said they had more control than they actually had. Depressed people, on the other hand, were rock solid, accurate whether they won or lost.

Supporting evidence confirms that depressed people are accurate judges of how much skill they have, whereas nondepressed people think they are much more skillful than others judge them to be (80 percent of American men think they are in the top half of social skills). Nondepressed people remember more good events than actually happened, and they forget the bad events. Depressed people are accurate about both. Nondepressed people believe that if it was a success, they did it, it is going to last, and, moreover, that they are good at everything; but if it was a failure, someone did it to them, it is going away quickly, and it was just this one little thing. Depressed people are evenhanded about success and failure. "Success has a thousand fathers, and failure is an orphan" is only true of the beliefs of nondepressives. In a follow-up study, Alloy found that nondepressed people who are realists go on to become depressed at a higher rate than nondepressed people who have these illusions of control.[1] Realism doesn't just coexist with depression, it is a risk factor for depression, just as smoking is a risk factor for lung cancer.

It is a disturbing idea that depressed people see reality correctly while nondepressed people distort reality in a self-serving way. As a therapist I was trained to believe that it is my job to help a depressed patient to both feel happier and see the world more clearly. I am supposed to be the agent of happiness as well as the agent of truth. But maybe truth and happiness antagonize each other. Perhaps what we have considered good therapy for a depressed patient merely nurtures benign illusions, making the patient think that her world is better than it actually is.

This possibility is more than just disturbing when you flesh it out. It is downright subverting of one of our most cherished beliefs about therapy: that the therapist is the agent of both reality and health. For what other problems does good mental health depend on deluding oneself? For what other problems does cure depend on nurturing illusions rather than facing facts? Maybe the tactics that relieve a problem and the truth about the problem are not the same.

Nowhere is the antagonism between the tactics of recovery and the truth better seen than in problems of substance abuse. This chapter is about alcohol. I will not discuss other recreational drugs or cigarettes at any length, but all of what I have to say applies to the abuse of these substances as well.

Alcohol and Alcoholism

- There is a disease called alcoholism.
- An alcoholic is powerless before this illness.
- Alcoholism is a physical addiction.
- Alcoholism is a progressive disease.
- Once an alcoholic, always an alcoholic.
- There is an addictive personality.
- One drink, and relapse is inevitable.

All of these statements are commonly believed. All of them are probably useful. People who abuse alcohol are better off believing them. People who try to help alcohol abusers can be more effective if they believe the statements to be true. Indeed, these beliefs are at the cornerstone of many self-help groups, including the granddaddy of all self-help groups, Alcoholics Anonymous.

Strangely, however, none of them is clearly true. At the very least, each is controversial; many scientists view these "truths" skeptically. Some view them as excusing misbehavior by relabeling it as a medical symptom (as *psychopathic* is substituted for *evil, kleptomaniac* for *thief, sexual deviant* for *rapist, pedophile* for *child molester, temporary insanity* for *murder*), others view them as political slogans, and others say they are blatant falsehoods.

My primary job is to see if alcohol abuse is curable. Along the way, however, I cannot avoid looking at these beliefs. I will not be able to settle the controversies about alcoholism as a disease, an addiction, a bad habit, or a sin. I do not have the final word about the addictive personality, nor about controlled drinking. I will give you my opinion about these issues, but opinion is all it is. No false modesty here: While

I am an authority on emotion, and an active researcher on sex and dieting, I am only an educated reader in the substance-abuse literature. I can give you the latest word, but my clinical and research experience in this field is limited.

Are You an Alcoholic?

> First the man takes a drink, then the drink takes a drink, then the drink takes the man.
>
> Japanese proverb

Do you have a problem with alcohol? Is it "abuse," or, worse, do you "depend" on drinking to get through the day? It will not surprise you to find out that the lines between handling liquor well, abusing alcohol, and being dependent on it are far from clear. As a rule of thumb, the more symptoms you have, the worse your problem. Take the following quiz:

MICHIGAN ALCOHOLISM SCREENING TEST

(adapted from Melvin Selzer, M.D.)

POINTS		YES	NO
0	0. Do you enjoy a drink now and then?		
2	1. Do you not feel you are a normal drinker? (By *normal,* I mean you drink less than or as much as most other people.)		
2	2. Have you ever awakened the morning after some night before and found that you could not remember part of the evening?		
1	3. Does your wife, husband, a parent, or another near relative ever worry or complain about your drinking?		
2	4. Can you not stop drinking without a struggle after one or two drinks?		

POINTS		YES	NO
1	5. Do you ever feel guilty about your drinking?		
2	6. Do friends or relatives think you are not a normal drinker?		
2	7. Are you not able to stop drinking when you want to?		
5	8. Have you ever attended a meeting of Alcoholics Anonymous?		
1	9. Have you ever gotten into physical fights when drinking?		
2	10. Has your drinking ever created a problem between you and your wife, husband, parent, or other relative?		
2	11. Has your wife, husband, or other family member ever gone to anyone for help about your drinking?		
2	12. Have you ever lost friends because of your drinking?		
2	13. Have you ever gotten into trouble at work or school because of your drinking?		
2	14. Have you ever lost a job because of your drinking?		
2	15. Have you ever neglected your obligations, your family, or your work for two or more days in a row because you were drinking?		
1	16. Do you drink before noon fairly often?		

POINTS		YES	NO
2	17. Have you ever been told you have liver trouble? Cirrhosis?		
*	18. After heavy drinking have you ever had delirium tremens (d.t.'s) *(5 points) or severe shaking *(2 points) or seen things that weren't really there *(2 points)?		
5	19. Have you ever gone to anyone for help about your drinking?		
5	20. Have you ever been in a hospital because of drinking?		
2	21. Have you ever been a patient in a psychiatric hospital or the psychiatric ward of a general hospital where drinking was part of the problem that resulted in hospitalization?		
2	22. Have you ever been arrested for drunk driving, driving while intoxicated, or driving under the influence of alcoholic beverages (2 points for each arrest)?		
2	23. Have you ever been arrested, or taken into custody for a few hours, because of other drunk behavior (2 points for each arrest)?		

Scoring. The scoring is simple. Total your points. There is no sharp cutoff, but a total of 5 points or more places you in the alcoholic—dependent on alcohol—category. Four points suggests that you abuse alcohol. Three points or less suggests no major alcohol problem. This test is conservative, a screening test, so it tends to call more people alcoholic than you would expect. If you score more than 3 points, you should attend very carefully to the sections that follow on recovery from alcoholism.

Is Alcoholism a Disease?

Is alcoholism a disease? There is no question about substance abuse that has produced more passionate controversy than this one. Alcoholics Anonymous insists that alcoholism is a disease and that the alcoholic is "powerless" before it. But for more than a hundred years, others have insisted that "drunkenness is a vice, not a disease," and that "alcoholism is no more a disease than thieving or lynching."[2]

For the scholar, this debate is a matter of truth and the sanctity of language. For the helper, this is a matter of helping tactics. Whatever, this is a subject that inevitably lends itself to give-and-take exchange:

Attack: Alcoholism, unlike a real disease, is not physical. If someone tells you there is a known metabolic deficiency, a known gene, or a known biochemical weakness that alcoholics have, hold on to your wallet. There is no such thing. Alcoholism is a social, economic, and interpersonal problem, not a physical pathology.

Rejoinder: Alcoholism is not a disease like malaria, with a specific germ or chemical abnormality as its cause; it is more like high blood pressure. Hypertension is bound up with social, interpersonal, and economic factors, and most hypertension is *essential*—it has no known physical cause. But it does have known physical consequences—heart attack and stroke—just as alcoholism brings cirrhosis of the liver and brain damage in its wake. Alcoholism, like many diseases, has strong heritability. Identical twins are more concordant than fraternal twins, and the offspring of biological parents who are alcoholic are several times more likely to become alcoholic, even if they are raised by teetotalers.[3]

Attack: Heritability does not cut much ice: Stupidity, ugliness, and criminality are inherited, but that does not make them diseases. You either have a real disease, like syphilis or schizophrenia, or you don't. But with alcoholism there is merely a continuum of alcohol consumed, with heavy drinkers at one extreme. So calling this extreme a disease is like calling very short people (midgets as opposed to dwarfs) diseased.

Rejoinder: Just as there is no clear dividing line with hypertension, there is none with alcoholism. All we can say is the more of it, the worse the problems tend to be.

Attack: This is an egregious instance of *victimology,* the art of transforming failures into victims. We are a society that does not take kindly to failure. Failures are felt to be vaguely immoral—lazy, stupid, mean, or obnoxious. But we have also become a gentler society in recent years—no longer are our classrooms appointed with dunce caps or our children's report cards replete with Fs (we now have "Unsatisfactory" and "Incomplete" instead). No longer can our kids go unpunished for taunting a retarded child as the "village idiot." We now deal with failures in a manner that tries to save them from the humiliations of the past. We relabel them victims, and of victims no ill can be said. Alcoholics are, in truth, failures, and their failure is a simple failure of will. They have made bad choices, and they continue to do so every day. By calling them victims of a disease, we magically shift the burden of the problem from choice and personal control, where it belongs, to an impersonal force—disease. This move erodes individual responsibility and even lends an aura of moral legitimacy to drunkenness. It magnifies the problem, making change less likely.

Rejoinder: Recall the Japanese proverb cited earlier. As alcoholism worsens, voluntary control gets weaker. Calling alcoholism a disease highlights how little control its victims come to have. Choice mattered at first, but in its later stages, alcoholics have almost no choice. A driver who chooses to speed down a freeway in a car with defective brakes and winds up spending years in casts made some bad early choices that had long-term disastrous consequences. But his broken neck and useless arm are now illnesses.[4]

AND SO the dispute continues through another half dozen attacks and rejoinders. There is a decent argument on each side: There are good reasons to call alcoholism a disease, but there are almost equally good reasons not to. The dispute is roughly a draw.

But a disease, unlike a triangle or a benzene ring, is not an object of science. *Disease* is not well defined; rather, it is a label that lies outside science itself and is used to introduce specific topics. It is a term like *cognition* as opposed to *short-term memory* in psychology, or *life* as opposed to *gene* in biology, or *cure* as opposed to *spinal-cord damage* in medicine. There is some latitude about whether or not to attach the label *disease* to alcoholism, and therefore I believe that other considerations come into play. Primarily, we should ask if people who label themselves *diseased* with alcoholism are better off. Are helpers of alcoholics more effective if they think they are treating a disease? Is change more likely?

Tactics. The way we explain our failures to ourselves, unlike the truth of the disease concept of alcoholism, is not merely academic. In fact, how we label our troubles has sweeping consequences. When we believe an explanation that is permanent, pervasive, and personal, we do much worse than when we explain our problems in temporary, local, and impersonal terms. For example, if we explain our unemployment as "I have no talent" (permanent, pervasive, and personal), we get depressed, we feel helpless, we don't look for a job, and our failure bleeds into the rest of our lives. If, on the other hand, we believe that the cause is the recession (temporary, local, and impersonal), we soon try to find another job, we fight off depression, we don't feel worthless or helpless, and we go on in the other domains of living. This is the main concern of my book *Learned Optimism,* and it applies directly to the disease concept of alcoholism.

When someone finds himself dependent on alcohol, and it finally dawns on him that his life, his family, his career, and everything else he values is in danger, how should that man explain this to himself? As it turns out, he doesn't have many choices. He can explain it as a disease. The other possibilities are to explain it as a vice, a result of bad choices and bad character, or as sin. Compare disease to vice. Disease is more temporary (it is often curable), whereas vice is more permanent (it stems from bad character, and character changes little if at all). A disease is more specific (it comes from an accidental biology and environment), whereas vice is global (it comes from being a bad person). A disease is impersonal, whereas a vice indicts you because *you* chose it.

The upshot is that a disease is a more optimistic explanation than vice, and optimism is about changeability. Pessimistic labels lead to passivity, whereas optimistic ones lead to attempts to change. It follows that alcoholics who label themselves as ill will be less depressed, less helpless, have higher self-esteem, and, most important, will try harder to change or be changed than alcoholics who label themselves bad people.

There is another benefit of the disease label: It is a ticket into the medical care system.

I come down on the side of the disease concept of alcoholism. Not because it is unimpeachably true (I doubt that), but because it is more hopeful than the alternative explanations available until recently. Alcoholics who see themselves as ill, and professionals who see their alcoholic clients as ill, are more likely to try to change this state of affairs than if they see immorality. The "disease" of alcoholism is one of the therapeutic illusions that can help make life bearable for alcoholics.

Alcoholics Anonymous, in my view, only gets it half right. By calling alcoholism a disease, AA makes change more likely than if it let its members believe they were vice-ridden or sinful—the main alternative explanations when AA was founded. But the modern era has invented some gentler alternatives: A "habit disorder," a "behavioral problem," even a "human frailty" are ways a sophisticated alcoholic could explain his failures now. Each of these is a markedly more optimistic label than "vice" or "sin," and probably more optimistic than "disease." Habits can change, behavioral problems are specific, and frailties come and go. These ways of looking at alcoholism promote more change than either the vice and sin views or the disease model.[5]

This contrast becomes sharper when you consider some of AA's famous twelve steps. Step one, for instance, has the alcoholic "powerless" before his disease. The disease is genetic and beyond his control. Only by relinquishing control to a "higher power" can recovery take place. The disease is always there, rendering him ever susceptible to relapse.

This framework cuts both ways. On the one hand, powerlessness is sometimes the stuff of religious conversion. The dark night of the soul can steel people to quit drinking in the face of enormous temptation and stick with this decision. On the other hand, a belief in powerlessness tends to undo the main virtue of the disease view, which is to move people out of sloth toward trying to change themselves. A sense of powerlessness often leads to passivity, helplessness, and hopelessness.

Is There an Addictive Personality?

Alcoholics are depressed, anxious, dependent, oral, filled with self-doubts and self-loathing, and they harbor a sense of inferiority. They are also pessimistic, self-defeating, paranoid, aggressive, and psychopathic, to name just a few of their worst personality characteristics. These facts have led investigators to claim that there is an addictive personality: some constellation of these traits. This means that people with such personalities are easy targets for addictive substances or behaviors. Take away the alcohol, and they will turn to crack, to sex, to gambling, or to cigarettes. It also implies that such people turn to alcohol to numb their emotional torments. You may be worried that you or someone close to you—displaying this constellation—is at risk.

This is a matter that has been dealt with definitively, though it took many years of work and a major methodological advance: long-term studies of the life span of alcoholics—prospective, "longitudinal" studies. The idea of an addictive personality is rooted in looking at alcoholics for only a short time, say a year, or even five years. When this is done, you see many of these so-called addictive traits. But it is absolutely crucial that these people are studied while they are abusing alcohol. Which comes first, the addictive traits or the abuse of alcohol? It could be that watching helplessly as alcohol destroys your life brings about anxiety, depression, crime, dependency, pessimism, inferiority feelings. Alternatively, it might also be that these traits bring about alcoholism.

Two landmark studies have looked at groups of men[6] over a period of forty or more years: from childhood—before any alcoholism—until late middle age. Both have been conducted by George Vaillant, a Harvard researcher, and my candidate for the most important psychoanalyst since Freud. In one study, the Harvard classes of 1939–44 were combed for their healthiest members. Five percent were chosen on the basis of extraordinarily good physical and mental health, as well as intellectual prowess. As undergraduates they were endlessly interviewed and took scores of psychological tests. These men have since been followed closely to this very day. Of the 252 men, 30 became abusers of alcohol. Vaillant asked how these 30 men differed, before they became alcoholic, from the other 222 men.

Before I report what he found, I want to mention his second study, whose subjects came from the opposite end of the American spectrum of opportunity: Boston's inner city. These men, too, were followed for forty years. Seventy-one of them became alcoholic; 260 did not. Again, Vaillant asked how the alcoholics differed from the rest before their alcoholism.

The results of the two studies were identical. There is no sign of an alcoholic personality. The men who became alcoholics differed in only two ways from the men who did not: They had more alcoholic relatives and they were more likely to be Northern European (particularly Irish). Emotional insecurity, depression, dependence, criminality while young, and the rest of the addictive panoply (in the absence of alcoholic parents) did not predict alcoholism.[7]

These results are a breath of fresh air. Before Vaillant's discovery, clinicians who looked at alcoholics only during the disease felt free to make such alarmist pronouncements as "The development of the disease process of alcoholism is inconceivable without underlying psychopathology."[8] Vaillant's discovery is that such pronouncements are simply wrong: It is alcoholism that produces the traits of depression, dependence, criminality, and so on. The only thing alcoholics have in common prior to their alcoholism is a dangerous susceptibility to alcohol, not underlying bad character or mental illness that merely displays itself in the guise of drunkenness.

The good news is that once alcohol abuse ends, so do these undesirable traits. The recovered alcoholic is no more depressive, psychopathic, pessimistic, or selfish than any of the rest of us. Since he may have missed two decades of his life, however, he is often less grown up in work, in emotional life, and in relationships than other men his age. As my closest childhood friend told me after recovering from twenty-five years of drug abuse, "Marty, I'm fifty going on twenty-five."

Is Alcoholism Progressive?

It is a central tenet of AA that alcoholism is not only a disease but a *progressive* disease. Like syphilis, which unchecked progresses from a sore on the penis to weakness of the limbs to insanity to death, alcoholism unchecked progresses from social tippling to abuse to addiction to death. Once someone genetically inclined to be alcoholic starts abusing alcohol, there can be only one of two outcomes: death from alcoholism or total abstinence. Is this picture true?

There is one sense in which alcoholism is certainly progressive. Alcohol produces *tolerance*—you need more and more of it to give you the same high. Tolerance, along with withdrawal—the craving that abstinence produces—is what it means to have an addiction. When someone claims that alcohol or heroin produces a physical addiction, they are wrong if they believe that there is some known chemical or biological pathology. Rather, "physical" addiction is a misnomer. All it refers to are *behavioral* facts: It takes more and more of the substance to work, and if you stop taking it, you will suffer withdrawal.[9]

But needing more and more alcohol is not what AA means by the claim that alcoholism is progressive. This claim means that the symptoms get worse with more alcohol. First come blackouts and frequent intoxication, then arrests, complaints from friends and relatives, and morning drinking. This is followed by repeated failures to stop drinking. Then come job loss and benders. Finally, after three to ten years, come convulsions, hospital treatment, and AA. This ends either with successful abstinence or with death.[10]

The same landmark study that answered the question of whether there is an addictive personality tells us whether alcoholism is progressive. Because the study provides an entire lifetime picture of the alcoholic—before, during, and after (if there is an after)—it maps out the whole course of alcoholism.

Here, AA gets it mostly right. Alcoholism is not inevitably progressive, but it usually is. Of the 110 inner-city alcoholics looked at over forty years, 73 followed a progressive course ending either in abstinence (about half) or extreme abuse and death (the other half). The remaining 37 did not show a progressive disease. These men recovered from alcoholism to social drinking or periodic heavy drinking without much in the way of adverse symptoms.

Vaillant has just obtained the fifty-year follow-up of these men. He now paints an even more complete picture: Early in life, alcoholism progresses. Drinking gets heavier and heavier from age 18 to age 30 to age 40. Then it begins to stabilize. Few alcoholics are worse at age 65 than they were at age 45. Middle age, if you manage to live that long, is usually self-correcting. Crime, obesity, schizophrenia, manic-depression, and alcoholism all tend to burn out in middle age. Vaillant states a "One-Third" rule for alcoholism: By age 65, one-third are dead or in awful shape, one-third are abstinent or drinking socially, and one-third are still trying to quit.[11]

Can you tell in advance if an alcoholic is headed for the progressive course or the rarer nonprogressive course? Those men headed for the progressive disease had the worst symptoms once they started drinking, they smoked more (two packs a day), and they spent more years feeling "out of control" of their drinking (fifteen versus four years).

Recovery

- What are your chances of recovering from alcoholism?
- Does treatment work?
- Does AA work?

These are very difficult questions to answer. I know of no other area of treatment research in which so much money has been spent and so little has been accomplished. To my mind, the lack of knowledge is a scandal. The right way to determine if treatment X (say, AA or a medication or an inpatient program) works is simple, in principle. Give a group of alcoholics treatment X. Give a control group, matched for factors relevant to recovery (like employment, emotional stability, severity, and social class), everything except treatment X. Then wait and see who shows a better outcome. This has been done for most of the problems we have looked at in this book. It has not been done for alcoholism.

There is one obstacle to good outcome studies of alcoholism: Researchers are dealing with a problem in which a cycle of recovery and relapse is repeated for years in its natural history. Illumination as to why relapse is so common begins with what does *not* protect you against relapse. George Vaillant, for instance, compared the childhoods of those alcoholics who relapsed time and again with the childhoods of those who became securely abstinent. All of the following do not predict who will become securely abstinent:

- good mothering
- high boyhood competence
- not coming from a multiproblem family
- high IQ
- good education
- no family alcoholism

This should shock those of you who believe in the importance of childhood experience (chapter 14 will shake your belief in this dogma further).

So many factors that seem to protect people against devastation by other psychological troubles fail to protect people against alcoholism because this problem, unlike other diseases, destroys three of the most important factors that facilitate recovery from any disease: ego strength, willpower, and social support. Alcohol damages the brain: Strong people with tenacious willpower are rendered weak and pliant. Alcohol renders "kings and geniuses no different from paupers and imbeciles." It is the "great leveler of human differences." Further, alcohol systematically destroys your loves and friendships. It robs you of social support by rendering you selfish, irresponsible, and out of control over anger and sadness. Without friends and family, the sufferers of any chronic disease have a worse course.[12]

If all these childhood factors fail to make recovery more likely, what succeeds? First, the fewer symptoms you have on the alcoholism quiz, the more likely it is that you will recover. After that, being married, having a job, being middle-aged, being well-educated, being white, and being middle-class all predict recovery. In short, social stability helps enormously. People who are in this category, rather than the "skid row" category, have twice the chance of recovering.[13]

Paradoxically, extreme severity helps recovery as well. When people are very badly threatened—with death, disfigurement, bankruptcy—they are ripe for conversion. Hitting bottom can, unmistakably, be a powerful force for dramatic change and recovery. Having a middling case of alcoholism, being a "heavy drinker," has the worst outcome. It is not mild enough to make recovery easy and not extreme enough to threaten life, family, and livelihood so shockingly as to jolt you into abstinence. Vaillant's Harvard men who were moderately alcoholic at forty still are as they enter old age. The mild cases and the extreme cases do better.[14]

What are the overall chances of recovery from severe alcoholism in the natural course of events? First, one major caveat: The chronic relapses of alcoholism mean that when researchers look for only a short time—say, for six months after any treatment—they will see a rosy picture. Perhaps as many as 65 percent of people treated are on the wagon for this long after treatment. Every alcoholic has gone on the wagon time and again. Trying to give it up and repeatedly failing is part of what it means to be alcoholic. But the real picture starts to emerge after a minimum of eighteen months. Studies that reveal true chances of recovery from alcoholism are the few very long-term studies.

Here are some representative statistics: Of 110 alcoholic men from the inner city whom George Vaillant followed for their lifetime, 49 (45 percent) became abstinent for at least a year. Of these 49, 21 (19 percent) became securely abstinent—on the wagon for at least three years. Of 100 clinically treated alcoholics Vaillant followed for twelve years after hospital discharge, 25 percent were stably abstinent, 21 percent were uncertain, 37 percent were dead, and 17 percent were still alcohol-dependent. Similar percentages emerge from a ten-year follow-up of British alcoholics. So the best estimates I can venture about the long-term chances of recovery from alcoholism are:[15]

- A substantial minority of alcoholics recover.
- About one in five will recover completely.
- About half will die prematurely or remain alcohol-dependent.
- Socially stable alcoholics have about double the chances of recovery.
- Very severe and very mild symptoms most suggest recovery.

When Vaillant compared the men who became abstinent with the men who died or remained alcoholic, he found four natural healing factors among those who recovered. First, the abstinent found a substitute dependency to sustain themselves: candy binges, compulsive eating, Librium, prayer and meditation, chain smoking, work, or a hobby. Second, the abstinent men were threatened with painful and disastrous medical consequences: Hemorrhaging, a fractured hip, seizures, and ghastly stomach problems all brought these men face-to-face with physical destruction (painless liver disease was not enough to drive the point home). Third, the men found a source of increased hope: Religious conversion and Alcoholics Anonymous (of which more in a moment) were typical. Finally, the men often found new love relationships, unscarred by the guilt and the devastation they had already inflicted on their wives. The more of these four healing factors the men were able to incorporate, the better their chances.

It is against this background of a natural healing process that formal treatment must be compared. Sadly, formal treatments work only marginally better than the natural rate of recovery.

Your first impulse, if you have the means, is probably to enter one of the many elaborate inpatient medical-treatment units for alcoholics. These programs are expensive and usually involve a team of helpers. The best ones offer a wide range of services: drying out (*detoxification*), counseling, behavior therapy, medical treatment for complications, aversion therapy, a comfortable setting, and AA-type groups. You can have all or some of these. Long-term outcome sometimes seems quite good: For example, one unit points with pride to a recent ten-year follow-up of two hundred former patients. Sixty-one percent were "completely" or "stably" remitted.[16] But the patients from this study were not from skid row—they were socially stable, and so could be expected to have roughly this good an outcome anyway. To determine if such programs do any better than natural recovery, a matched control group is required. This study lacked one, and, indeed, controlled-outcome studies of inpatient units are rare. The patients are usually paying customers, they don't want to be randomly put into a control group, and they will go elsewhere for treatment if so assigned.

However, there have been some attempts to do controlled studies. A particularly dramatic one was done in London fifteen years ago. One hundred married male alcoholics were randomly given either of two treatments. The first treatment was elaborate: a year of counseling and social work, an introduction to AA, aversion therapy with drugs, drugs to alleviate withdrawal, as well as free access to inpatient medical treatment. The second treatment was merely one session of advice, involving the drinker, his wife, and a psychiatrist. The psychiatrist told the couple that the husband had alcoholism and that he should abstain from all drinking. Further, he should stay in his job, and the couple should try to stay together. The theme was that recovery "lay in [the couple's] own hands and could not be taken over by others." Twelve months later, the two groups looked the same: About 25 percent from each group were doing better.[17]

George Vaillant found the same result when he compared his own program of intensive clinic treatment at the Cambridge (Massachusetts) Hospital to no treatment. His one hundred patients dried out, received medical and psychiatric consultation, halfway housing, an alcohol-education program, and twenty-four-hour walk-in counseling for themselves and their relatives. Two years later, one-third were improved and two-thirds were doing poorly. Vaillant pooled four more similar treatment studies and had roughly the same results: one-third improved, two-thirds doing poorly. Then he compared all these treatment outcomes to three pooled no-treatment studies. With no treatment, one-third improved and two-thirds did poorly.[18]

One study of 227 union workers newly identified as alcoholic contradicts these results. The workers were randomly assigned to either inpatient hospital treatment, or compulsory attendance at AA for a year without hospitalization (or they could choose no treatment). The hospital treatment, which lasted about three weeks, included drying out and AA meetings, and was aimed toward abstinence; afterward, these workers were required to attend AA three times a week for a year and to be sober at work. The compulsory AA group had the same constraints, but without hospitalization. Two years later, the hospitalization group was doing much better than the other two groups: It had twice as many abstainers (37 percent versus 17 and 16 percent), almost twice as many men who were never drunk, and only half as many who needed to be hospitalized again.[19]

Putting all this information together, I can recommend inpatient treatment, *but only marginally*. It is expensive, and there is only one decent study showing that it improves on the natural course of recovery; many studies, admittedly of lesser quality, contradict that study.

As for outpatient psychotherapy, there is no evidence that any form of talking therapy—not psychoanalysis, not supportive therapy, not cognitive therapy—can get you to give up alcohol. There has been only one small-scale study of behavior therapy. In it, alcoholics learned skills of how to control their drinking. The study had promising results, but little follow-up of this treatment has taken place.[20] Once abstinence has taken hold, however, talking therapy might help ease the difficult adjustment back into sobriety, responsible family life, and steady employment. Overall, recovery from alcohol abuse, unlike recovery from a compound fracture, does not depend centrally on what kind of inpatient or outpatient treatment you get, or whether you get any treatment at all.[21]

With regard to medications, the most widely used drug is Antabuse (disulfiram). Antabuse and alcohol don't mix: When an alcoholic takes a dose of Antabuse and then drinks alcohol, he becomes horribly nauseated and short of breath. This discourages alcohol drinking; but the alcoholic can always decide to eliminate Antabuse rather than alcohol. To avoid this, Antabuse is surgically implanted under the skin. In controlled studies, however, there is no difference in later drinking between alcoholics who have implanted Antabuse or a placebo. Both groups continue heavy drinking when the implantation ends.[22]

The use of Antabuse is but one in the larger portfolio of treatments that aim to produce an aversion to alcohol. In electrical aversion, shock is paired with taking a drink in the hope of making the taste of alcohol aversive; this treatment does not seem to work. In chemical aversion, drugs that make alcoholics sick to their stomach are paired with the taste of alcohol. There is better theoretical rationale for this move (recall the potency of the *sauce béarnaise* effect discussed in chapter 6, on phobias). Over thirty thousand alcoholics have received such treatments, but without clear effect—the treated groups do about as well as matched controls would be expected to do. Astonishingly, there has been only one study with random assignment to aversion or control. Overall, then, I cannot recommend aversion therapy for alcoholism. There is simply no scientifically worthy evidence that aversion treatment improves on the natural course of recovery.[23]

Naltrexone provides new hope for the successful medication of alcoholics. Joseph Volpicelli, an addiction researcher at the University of Pennsylvania, proposed that alcohol drinking stimulates the body's opiate system and so causes a high. By blocking the brain's opiate system chemically, the high should be blocked. In a twelve-week study of seventy male alcoholics, half got naltrexone (an opioid blocker) and half got a placebo. Fifty-four percent of the placebo-treated men relapsed, but only 23 percent of the naltrexone-treated men did. Most of the men had at least one drink during the study; the placebo-treated men went on to binge, but most of the naltrexone-treated men stopped after one drink—just what you'd expect if naltrexone had indeed blocked the high. A second study, at Yale, has replicated these effects. Caution is in order because of the lack of long-term follow-up, but this is the most promising development to date in the otherwise fruitless history of medication for alcoholics.[24]

THE SINGLE most frustrating question is whether Alcoholics Anonymous and the self-help groups that have spun off from it work. Alcoholics Anonymous cannot be evaluated with any certainty for several reasons. First, AA cannot be scientifically compared to the "natural course of recovery," my criterion for all the comparisons above, because the group itself is such a ubiquitous part of the natural course of recovery in America. Try to create a control group of alcoholics whose members do not already go to AA. When you do, you will find that they are usually less severely alcoholic than those who enter AA, and thus a useless control. Second, AA does not welcome scientific scrutiny. It promises anonymity to its members and inculcates loyalty to the group—two conditions that make long-term follow-up difficult and disinterested self-reporting unusual. AA bears more resemblance to a religious sect than to a treatment, a fact that is not irrelevant to its success. Third, the people who stay in AA and attend thousands of

The Right Treatment

ALCOHOLISM SUMMARY TABLE*

	Inpatient	*Psychotherapy*	*Aversion*	*AA*	*Naltrexone*†
IMPROVEMENT	▲	o	o	▲	▲▲
RELAPSE	▲	▲	▲	▲	?
SIDE EFFECTS	▼▼	▼	▼▼▼	▼	▼▼
COST	expensive	expensive	moderate	free	inexpensive
TIME SCALE	weeks/months	years	weeks/months	years	weeks
OVERALL	▲	o	o	▲	▲▲

IMPROVEMENT

▲▲▲▲ = 80–100% markedly improved or symptom free
▲▲▲ = 60–80% markedly improved
▲▲ = at least 50% moderately improved
▲ = probably better than placebo
o = probably not better than the natural course of recovery

RELAPSE (after discontinuation of treatment)

▲▲▲▲ = 10% or fewer relapse
▲▲▲ = 10–20% relapse
▲▲ = moderate relapse rate
▲ = high relapse rate

SIDE EFFECTS

▼▼▼▼ = severe
▼▼▼ = moderate
▼▼ = mild
▼ = none

OVERALL

▲▲▲▲ = excellent, clearly the therapy of choice
▲▲▲ = very good
▲▲ = useful
▲ = marginal
o = probably not better than the natural course of recovery

*Controlled-drinking-skills behavior therapy shows promise, but as yet the evidence is too scanty to recommend it.

†Naltrexone shows considerable promise, but no long-term study of relapse or side effects has yet been done. Because the initial reports look strong, I can, however, recommend naltrexone as an experimental treatment.

meetings tend to be the people who stay sober. This does not necessarily mean that AA is the cause. The causal arrow may go the opposite way: Drunkenness causes people to slink away in guilt, and being able to remain sober allows people to stay. Finally, AA is a sacred cow. Criticism of it is rare, and testimonial praise is almost universal. The organization has been known to go after its most trenchant critics as if they were heretics, and so criticism, even in the scientific literature, is timid.

Given this minefield, I will hazard an evaluation anyway. My best guess is that AA is only marginally effective overall, but that it may be quite effective for certain subgroups of alcoholics.

I start with the sad fact that there has not been a single, sound, controlled study of AA. This is unfortunate because AA is the most widespread treatment for alcoholism, and current practice among clinicians, ministers, and family doctors is to send most of their alcoholic clients directly to AA. Advocates publish glowing numbers from uncontrolled studies, but their methodology is so flawed that I am forced to dismiss them.

George Vaillant's inner-city men provide a sample—with no control group—followed for a very long time. Among the men who were ever abstinent and the 20 percent who became securely abstinent, more than one-third rated AA as "important." Indeed, AA was second only to "willpower" on this score. In another of his studies, Vaillant followed a clinic sample for eight years, and 35 percent became stably abstinent: Of these, two-thirds had become regular AA attenders. I cannot tell which causes which, but it is an often-repeated finding that of the one-third of alcoholics who have a good long-term outcome, many participate religiously in AA, attending hundreds of meetings a year.[25]

AA is not for everyone. It is spiritual, even outright religious, and so repels the secular-minded. It demands group adherence, and so repels the nonconformist. It is confessional, and so repels those with a strong sense of privacy. Its goal is total abstinence, not a return to social drinking. It holds alcoholism to be a disease, not a vice or a frailty. One or more of these premises are unacceptable to many alcoholics, and these people will probably drop out. For those who remain, however, my best guess is that many of them *do* benefit. It would be a mistake to be formulaic about who will find AA congenial. All sorts of unlikely types show up and stay—poets and atheists and loners. AA changes the character of some of those who stick with it. After all, it fills two of Vaillant's four criteria for bolstering recovery: It provides a substitute dependency, and it is a source of hope.

Total Abstinence

One of my closest friends, Paul Thomas, is a bartender. Paul is nothing if not fanatical. When he took up bridge, he became a Life Master in under two years. When he took up golf, he became a scratch golfer in a summer. When he fathered a Down's syndrome child, he became president of the Philadelphia chapter for helping Down's children. When he took up drinking, he drank for ten solid years. He has not touched a drop in the last fifteen years. When asked how he does it, he says he doesn't need reminders of hitting bottom because he sees them every day among his customers.

When I read the intensely passionate literature on whether total abstinence or a return to social drinking should be the goal of recovery, I decided to get his opinion. I had dinner with him at his bar. I told him that the literature showed, quite definitively, that a fraction of recovered alcoholics can return to social drinking. His view was uncomplicated. "I hope they keep this a secret from the rest."

Paul's reaction makes a good deal of sense to me. First, the facts: Some fraction of recovered alcoholics are able to return to drinking without major problems like binges, blackouts, and violence. Just how small this minority is is a matter of debate. George Vaillant found that between 5 and 15 percent of his alcoholics returned to social drinking. In a twenty-year follow-up of Swedish alcoholics, 25 percent had become social drinkers and only 20 percent were abstainers. Fewer than this percentage of severe alcoholics are likely to become social drinkers, and only the alcoholics with the fewest major problems seem able to take this route. When the most severe alcoholics recover, they do so by total abstinence. By Paul's logic, the possibility of social drinking should be kept secret from them.[26]

Controversy still reigns about whether—in the long run—controlled drinking works as well as abstinence. In 1972, two bold alcohol researchers, Mark and Linda Sobell, published successful results of a controlled-drinking program. Numerous defenders of AA scorched the Sobells. Mary Pendery and her colleagues, for example, argued that the Sobells' results, looked at more closely ten years later, were grim: For example, a number of the "successes" had died, probably of alcoholism. But in turn, Pendery has been attacked for failing to mention that in the Sobells' abstinence control group, a number had died in the ten intervening years. And so it goes. The issue is still unsettled.[27]

Surely, the goal of total abstinence has one main virtue. Believing in it keeps severe alcoholics on the path most likely to lead to recovery. Even if it is true that some alcoholics can recover and still drink a little, the goal of total abstinence, like the disease label, is probably a good tactic.

The goal of abstinence has one disadvantage, however. When the alcoholic believes that taking a single drink means he has fallen back into his old habit, one lapse can bring down his house of cards. A binge becomes very likely. In one study, the total-abstinence goal was compared to the controlled-drinking goal. After a year, the two groups had the same rate of abstinence—about one-third. But among the nonabstinent (the "failures"), the abstinence treatment resulted in three times as much drinking as the controlled-drinking approach.[28]

Many people who eventually recover from alcoholism slip occasionally along the way. Rather than viewing this as "I'm in relapse," "My disease has won," or "I've lost it," there is a more optimistic way of thinking. A slip can instead be seen as a temporary setback triggered by external events, not as a lack of willpower. Lapses are opportunities to learn better how to cope, not signs that the alcoholic is once more powerless before his disease.[29]

The abstinence goal accords with the myth that alcoholics suffer from uncontrollable drinking. But in the natural course of alcoholism, alcoholics frequently control their drinking—in the short run: Sometimes one drink leads to the next and the next, but on some occasions the alcoholic chooses to stop. Alcoholics frequently control how much they drink—not drinking right before a job interview, for example. Most alcoholics have gone on the wagon several times but have eventually fallen off. The problem is not that one drink *always* leads to loss of control, but that in the long run, most alcoholics start drinking again—even after repeated successful control of drinking. Alcoholism has immense momentum, but total loss of control is not an accurate description.

Change: Alcohol, Cigarettes, Drugs

Alcohol presents a picture similar to that of most commonly abused drugs: cigarettes, cocaine, and opiates. First, some people are very vulnerable to any one of these appetites, probably for genetic reasons. There is no evidence, however, of an "addictive" personality that is vulnerable to *all* of them. Second, in the natural course of things, if the abuse is severe, fewer than half (only a third for alcohol) will be able to give it up. This means the problem is certainly not incurable, but the outlook is not rosy. Third, no medical or psychological treatment yet devised much improves on the natural recovery rate. If your first impulse is to get expensive hospital treatment, psychotherapy, or medication, think again. There is no secret expertise about alcoholism. Family, friends, and support that provides pressure and hope—not the least being AA, religion, and work—and, crucially, the individual himself are the site of the cure.

Heavy drinking, it must always be remembered, is a way of life. When, for example, the alcoholic goes to a party, he sees the party in different terms than the rest of us do. "How well stocked is the bar?" "Isn't that my neighbor's brother-in-law? He will surely snitch." "I wonder if my old crony Tom is coming, so we can make the rounds afterward?" Heavy drinking is no less a way of life than bookishness for an intellectual, politics for a senator, or love of Jesus for a fundamentalist Christian. Giving it up is not a matter of doing without a hobby. It is closer to doing without the self.[30]

In America, slavery was once part of the southern way of life. It was believed to be constitutional, and southerners felt their sense of self violated when abolitionists tried to take it away. Yet slavery is a terrible institution. Wife beaters and their battered spouses have a way of life, one that is also terrible. Being a way of life does not make something right or good or benign.

Heavy drinking is a bad way of life. It destroys the individual and those he loves. There is nothing to be said in its favor. These are old saws. But what is new is the emerging fact that individuals cannot do all that much about this way of life once it has taken hold. After a lifetime of trying, about one-third of alcoholics escape it. One-third escaping such a debilitating condition is a real accomplishment, but it is the other two-thirds that constitute the major tragedy. Drugs (with the possible new exception of naltrexone), psychotherapy, AA, inpatient treatment, and willpower all show only the slightest victories—at best—for that two-thirds.

When a destructive institution like slavery or wife beating will not be overthrown by the individuals it most hurts, we are justified in appealing to something more powerful than the self to overthrow it. Just as there is a higher morality than individual choice that makes slavery and wife beating wrong, so too with alcoholism. Few of our problems cry out more clearly for social control.

Social control has been tried, you say, and it failed. I agree: Prohibition, although it decreased alcohol-related illness, was a tremendous failure, and I do not propose reviving it. But how much alcohol is consumed and the rate of alcoholism are very sensitive to less-sweeping social control. Liquor taxes, for example, are low. They have not kept up with inflation over the last forty years. It is estimated that doubling the present federal tax would cut cirrhosis deaths by six thousand per year, to say nothing of the number of lives it would save on the highways. Reducing the number of liquor stores and bars, restricting advertising, raising age limits, and curtailing profits from the sale and manufacture of alcohol would all cut heavy drinking.[31] When individuals are powerless to change a problem of the magnitude of alcoholism, it falls finally to the society to act.

IT HAS become fashionable to blame alcoholism on the way your parents raised you or on other misfortunes of childhood. The very unchangeability of alcoholism, in this view, testifies to the power that childhood events exert over adult life. In fact, all of the problems of adulthood examined in this book have been attributed to such events. In the next and final part, we look at whether your childhood exerts such a hold on your life today. At stake is nothing less than whether you are a prisoner of the past or are free to change.

PART FOUR

Growing Up—At Last

Freud considered that after age 45, psychoanalysis could do nothing for a neurotic: Jung was convinced that 45 was roughly the period of life when its immensely important second development began, and that this second period was concerned with matters which were, in the broadest sense, religious.

Many people are put off by this attitude. They want nothing to do with religion and are too lazy or too frightened to accept the notion that religion may mean something very different from orthodoxy. They attach themselves to the notion that Man is the center of all things, the highest development of life, and that when the individual consciousness is closed by death, that is, as far as they are concerned, the end of the matter. Man, as the instrument of some vastly greater Will, does not interest them, and they do not see their refusal as a limitation on their understanding.

Robertson Davies, "The Essential Jung"[1]

14

Shedding the Skins of Childhood

WHEN DOES TIME stop for you? Does it happen when you are making love, playing with your children, speaking at a meeting, looking at a masterpiece, or when you yourself are painting? Where are you truly at home—on a golf course in Maui, reading in your study, planting delphiniums, at a Springsteen concert, serving coffee in a shelter for the homeless?

These questions are not trivial. You must ask them and listen to your own answers. For they are pivotal in a transition that many of you are now making: the transition from the first season to the second season of your life.

There are, I believe, only two great seasons in life: the season of expansion and the season of contraction. This chapter is about these two seasons. The season of expansion begins at birth. Your overriding task in this season is to discover the demands of the world as you find it and to fit yourself to those demands: schooling, finding a mate, having children, embracing the values of your place and time, embarking on your life's work, and, if you are lucky, mastering it. Evolution has ensured that this will be an extrinsic season, your time for learning what is expected of you and then doing what is mandated from the outside.

I suspect that the average reader of this book is between the ages of thirty and forty-five. You, average reader, are now coming into "the height of your powers." You are roughly halfway through life. You are at the time when the first season ends and the second season begins.

In the second season, your life will be defined not so much by the outside world as by certain realities that have been coalescing inside you. Your task during the season of contraction centers around what you learned during the season of expansion. You discovered then the activities, objects, and people you love, things that were not means to any end but ends in themselves. When you sensed them and suspected what they meant, you probably postponed pursuing them. Their song has become more insistent lately. The second season allows you to postpone no longer. You will rearrange your life to fit what you have discovered you are. From now until very late in life, when so many of your options will narrow, you will pursue what your inner world demands.

What drives the transition from one season to the next can be—but rarely is—the sense of completion that comes from total success. Sometimes it is "topping out"—going as high as you can or want to. It can be your children grown to independence. But completions need not be the motive force: Failure, frustration, or sheer boredom can be marvelously productive in thrusting you from one stage to the next. Either way, the upheaval comes. You slowly and subtly stop doing what you used to do, stop being what you used to be, stop salivating to the old stimuli: You find an excuse to miss a party so that you can sit home in front of a fire with your spouse; you start wearing sneakers to work; you stop going to movies with subtitles; you let your *New Yorker* subscription lapse; you go to church for the first time since childhood. You become less and less what others expect.

Responding at last to what is intrinsic can mean self-indulgence, frivolity, or even emptiness. But it need not. An astonishingly large part of what is truly you coincides with old notions like duty, service, generosity, and nurturance: helping to build a community center—by both laying bricks and raising funds; running for office; guiding young people—your grandchildren—to maturity; giving back much of what you have so arduously won.

It is perilously easy to fail at making this transition—to allow what happened to you in the first season to cripple you in the second. But success is common, contrary to those who would have us believe we are prisoners of childhood. Growth—even huge leaps—occurs throughout adulthood. I dedicate what follows to your change and to your growth.

The Inner Child

The centerpiece of my discussion here is the philosophy of the "recovery movement," the widely popular view that adult problems are caused by childhood mistreatment. I criticize this view on both factual and moral grounds, though I am addressing it in order to be constructive. I want to underscore the theme of this book: that you can make major changes all throughout adulthood if you know the ways of changing that actually work.

Many failings of adult life are currently blamed on the misfortunes of childhood. Depression in mid-life is blamed on the punishment meted out by parents decades before. In her 1991 best-seller, Patti Davis, Ronald and Nancy Reagan's daughter, blames her current troubles on her parents. She highlights being slapped in the face by her mother when she was eight, and she blames both her mother and her father for not giving her enough love because they were too much in love with each other (this is the First Family, no less). In the larger society, inability to love is blamed on sexual abuse by an uncle, a father, or a brother. The talk shows buzz with tearful recountings of childhood incest and sexual molestation. Your beating up on your kids is blamed on your father beating up on you. Indeed, the basic premise of the recovery movement is that bad events in childhood cripple adult life. But, the movement promises us, this is curable. By coming to grips with those early traumas, we can restore our health and sanity.[1]

> *Farquhar is a troubled thirty-year-old; angry, depressed, and guilt-ridden. He remembers a time when he was three: He refused to go to bed and screamed "I hate you" to his mother. His father, enraged, grabbed him and shouted, "You have violated God's Fifth Commandment: 'Honor thy father and thy mother.' " Little Farquhar felt guilt and shame, and now grown-up Farquhar, wounded, still carries this "toxic guilt" around. By doing "inner child" exercises, Farquhar rids himself of this burden. He phones his father (now seventy-two) and discharges his anger. He relives all the pain and guilt, and in his mind he divorces his father and mother.*[2]

Here are the twin premises of the inner-child recovery movement:

- Bad events in childhood exert major influence on adulthood.
- Coming to grips with those events undoes their influence.

These premises are enshrined in film and theater. The biggest psychological hit of 1991 was the film version of Pat Conroy's lyrical novel *The Prince of Tides,* in which Tom Wingo (Nick Nolte), an alcoholic football coach, has been fired from his job, and is cold to his wife and little girls. He and his sister were raped twenty-five years before as kids. He tearfully confesses this to Dr. Susan Lowenstein (Barbra Streisand), a New York psychoanalyst, and thereby recovers his ability to feel, to coach, and to control his drinking. His sister, presumably, would also recover from her suicidal schizophrenia if she could only relive the rape. The audience is in tears. The audience seems to have no doubt about the premises.

But I do.

The Power of Childhood

It is an easy matter to believe that childhood events hold sway over what kind of an adult you become. The evidence seems to be right before your eyes. The kids of smart parents turn out to be smart; it must be all those books and good conversations. Kids from broken homes often divorce; they must have lacked good "role models" for how to love enough. Kids who were sexually abused often become frightened pessimists; little wonder, they found the world a frightful place. Kids of alcoholics often turn out alcoholic; they learned uncontrolled drinking at their father's knee. The kids of authoritarian parents turn out authoritarian. The kids of basketball players and musicians turn out to have these talents. Kids who were beaten by their parents beat up their own kids.

As persuasive as they seem, these observations are hopelessly confounded. Yes, these people did grow up in worlds in which they were nurtured in their parents' image, *but they also have their parents' genes.* Each of these observations supports a genetic interpretation as much as a childhood interpretation: smart genes, unloving genes, anxious genes, pessimistic genes, alcoholic genes, authoritarian genes, athletic and musical genes, violent genes. Why do the genetic interpretations sound so farfetched to the modern ear while the childhood interpretations sound so comfortably true?

The appeal of the child-rearing explanations has a theoretical dimension and a moral dimension. Freud assumed both that childhood events create adult personality and that their consequences can be undone by reliving—with great feeling—the original trauma. Sound familiar? It should, because the premises are just the same as those of the inner-child movement. Freud's premises may have undergone a steady decline in currency within academia for many years, but Hollywood, the talk shows, many therapists, and the general public still love them. The recovery movement marries Freud's basic premises to the confessional method of AA. The result is the most popular self-help movement of the 1990s.

Childhood trauma and catharsis do make good theater. But the appeal of the inner-child movement goes much deeper, for there is here a sympathetic moral and political message as well. Its appeal has its modern beginning with the defeat of the Nazis. The Nazis used the respectable science of genetics to bolster their theory of Aryan superiority. Genetically "inferior" people—Jews, Gypsies, Slavs, the retarded and deformed—were deemed subhuman and were sent to the death camps. In the wake of our victory over the Nazis, anything they used or misused was tainted. Nietzsche's philosophy, Wagner's operas, and authoritarianism all became suspect. American psychology, already environmental, now shunned genetics completely and became wedded to explanations of childhood personality and the dogma of human plasticity.

When stoked by this reaction to Nazism, the logic of the dogma of human plasticity is: Once we allow the explanation that Sam does better than Tom because Sam is genetically smarter, we start our slide down the slippery slope to genocide. After World War II, genetic explanations became explanations of last resort, for they had the fetid odor of fascism and racism about them. All this accorded well with our basic democratic ideal that all men are created equal.

The second aspect of the moral appeal of the inner-child movement is consolation. Life is full of setbacks. People we love reject us. We don't get the jobs we want. We get bad grades. Our children don't need us anymore. We drink too much. We have no money. We are mediocre. We lose. We get sick. When we fail, we look for consolation, one form of which is to see the setback as something other than failure—to interpret it in a way that does not hurt as much as failure hurts. Being a victim, blaming someone else, or even blaming the system is a powerful and increasingly widespread form of consolation. It softens many of life's blows.

Such shifts of blame have a glorious past. Alcoholics Anonymous made the lives of millions of alcoholics more bearable by giving them the dignity of a "disease" to replace the ignominy of "failure," "immorality," or "evil." Even more important was the civil rights movement. From the Civil War to the early 1950s, black people in America did badly—by every statistic. How did this get explained? "Stupid," "lazy," and "immoral" were the words shouted by demagogues or whispered by the white gentry. Nineteen fifty-four marks the year when these explanations began to lose their power. In *Brown v. Board of Education,* the Supreme Court held that racial segregation in schools was illegal. People began to explain black failure as "inadequate education," "discrimination," and "unequal opportunity."

These new explanations are literally uplifting. In technical terms, the old explanations—stupidity and laziness—are personal, permanent, and pervasive. They lower self-esteem; they produce passivity, helplessness, and hopelessness. If you were black and you believed them, they were self-fulfilling. The new explanations—discrimination, bad schools, lean opportunities—are impersonal, changeable, and less pervasive. They don't deflate self-esteem (in fact, they produce anger instead). They lead to action to change things. They give hope.

The recovery movement enlarges on these precedents. Recovery gives you a whole series of new and more consoling explanations for setbacks. Personal troubles, you're told, do not result as feared from your own sloth, insensitivity, selfishness, dishonesty, self-indulgence, stupidity, or lust. No, they stem from the way you were mistreated as a child. You can blame your parents, your brother, your teachers, your minister, as well as your sex and race and age. These kinds of explanations make you feel better. They shift the blame to others, thereby raising self-esteem and feelings of self-worth. They lower guilt and shame. To experience this shift in perspective is like seeing shafts of sunlight slice through the clouds after endless cold, gray days.

We have become victims, "survivors" of abuse, rather than "failures" and "losers." This helps us get along better with others. We are now underdogs, trying to fight our way back from misfortune. In our gentle society, everyone roots for the underdog. No one dares speak ill of victims anymore. The usual wages of failure—contempt and pity—are transmuted into support and compassion.

So the inner-child premises are deep in their appeal: They are democratic, they are consoling, they raise our self-esteem, and they gain us new friends. Small wonder so many people in pain espouse them.

Do Childhood Events Influence Adult Personality?

Flushed with enthusiasm for the belief that childhood had great impact on adult development, many researchers eagerly sought support. They expected to find massive evidence for the destructive effects of bad childhood events such as parental death, divorce, physical illness, beatings, neglect, and sexual abuse on the adulthood of the victims. Large-scale surveys of adult mental health and childhood loss were conducted. Prospective studies of childhood loss on later adult life were done (these take years and cost a fortune). Some evidence appeared—but not much. If your mother dies before you are eleven, you are somewhat more depressive in adulthood—but not a lot more depressive, and only if you are female, and only in about half the studies. A father's dying had no measurable impact. If you are firstborn, your IQ is higher than your sibs—but by less than one point, on average. If your parents divorce (we must exclude the studies that don't even bother with control groups of undivorced families), there is a slight disruptive effect on later childhood and adolescence. But the problems wane as children grow up, and they may not be detectable in adulthood.[3]

The major traumas of childhood, it was shown, may have some influence on adult personality, but the influence is barely detectable. These reports threatened one of the bulwarks of environmentalism. Bad childhood events, contrary to the credo, do not mandate adult troubles—far from it. There is no justification, according to these studies, for blaming your adult depression, anxiety, bad marriage, drug use, sexual problems, unemployment, beating up your children, alcoholism, or anger on what happened to you as a child.[4]

Most of these studies were methodologically inadequate anyway. They failed, in their enthusiasm for human plasticity, to control for genes. It simply did not occur to their devisers, blinded by ideology, that criminal parents might pass on criminal genes, and that both the felonies of criminals' children and how badly criminals mistreat their children might stem from genes rather than mistreatment. There are now studies that do control for genes: One kind looks at the adult personalities of identical twins reared apart; another looks at the adult personalities of adopted children and compares their personalities with those of their biological parents and of their adoptive parents.

All of these studies find massive effects of genes on adult personality, and only negligible effects of any particular events. Identical twins reared apart are far more similar as adults than fraternal twins reared together for the qualities of authoritarianism, religiosity, job satisfaction, conservatism, anger, depression, intelligence, alcoholism, well-being, and neuroticism, to name only a few. In parallel, adopted children are much more similar as adults to their biological parents than to their adoptive parents.

These facts are the latest, if not the last, word in the renascent nature-nurture controversy. They come from a convergence of large-scale studies using up-to-date measures. These studies find ample room for nongenetic influences on adult personality because less than half the variance is accounted for by genes. But researchers have not found any specific nongenetic influences yet (nongenetic influences can include fetal events, child rearing, childhood trauma, schooling, adolescent and adult events, and measurement error, among others). Some of these specific factors may yet emerge as important to adult personality, but to date, none have.[5]

If you want to blame your parents for your own adult problems, you are entitled to blame the genes they gave you, but you are not entitled—by any facts I know—to blame the way they treated you.

Childhood Sexual Trauma

There is one childhood trauma that is often singled out as a special destroyer of adult mental health: sexual abuse. What I am about to say on this subject can easily be misinterpreted, misquoted, and wrenched out of context. So this preface: I believe sexual abuse is evil. It should be condemned and punished. Abused children and adult survivors need help, but help that works—not "pop psychology" help.

Today I would be labeled a sexually abused child. Myron "molested" me every weekday for about a year when I was nine. I walked four blocks to School 16. On the corner, Myron sold the *Times Union* for a nickel. He dressed in dun-colored rags, was unshaven, and stammered badly. Today my colleagues would label him "a retarded adult with cerebral palsy." In the early 1950s, people in Albany, New York, labeled him a "bum" and a "dummy." But he and I had a special friendship. He kissed me and we hugged for a few minutes. He told me his troubles and I told him mine. Then I went off to fourth grade.

One day, Myron disappeared from his corner. I looked for him frantically, and a policeman on the beat nearby told me that Myron had "gone away." I was heartbroken. He hadn't even said good-bye.

Five years later, I saw Myron as I got off a bus to go to the Palace Theatre way downtown. "Myron!" I shouted joyously. He took one look at me and ran away as fast as his limp allowed. A pile of unsold newspapers, flapping in the cold winter wind, remained.

Today, of course, I can fill in the gaps. A passing neighbor must have seen Myron "molesting" (i.e., hugging and kissing) me. She told my parents. My parents told the police. The police told Myron that if they ever saw him with me again, they would send him to prison—or worse (Albany was not a gentle place in the 1950s). No one told me any of this.

I forgot about it until ten years ago, when child molesting became a much discussed topic. First came reports on incest among the poor, then alarming statistics on the middle class. There were warnings about uncles and stepfathers—since the molester was usually found to be a friend or a relative. Then one celebrity after another revealed that her father had abused her and left hideous psychological scars. Then therapists began to probe routinely for forgotten sexual abuse in therapy—and usually found it. Then, in lawsuits, grown-up children began to claim that they now remembered the parental abuse thirty years earlier that had ruined their lives.

A body of research grew up to bolster the public alarm. In a typical study, the mental health of adult women who are incest survivors is checked. The results are uniform: These women are more depressed, anxious, suicidal, drug-abusing, lonely, guilty, and sexually troubled than members of control groups.[6] The published interpretation is that sexual abuse in childhood caused the adult problems.

The curmudgeon speaks: In their zealotry, the authors of these articles abandon methodological niceties like adequate control groups and consideration of rival explanations. Often, the survivors in the studies are very self-selected. They are recruited because they are troubled adults: They are in therapy or in self-help groups, or they even, literally, answered an ad for "incest victims." It is no surprise that they have more problems than the control group. And the control groups are suspect, too (when there even is one); they fail to match the incest victims for the most obvious, critical variables. What these studies fail to control for (this is the unmentioned alternative) are genetic differences and other environmental differences confounded with incest. The kind of fathers, brothers, and uncles who abuse young children are men with major problems of their own. Incest victims, more often than not, come from very troubled families with much more mental illness than the control groups have. Some of the mental illness and some of the family problems are probably genetic. So it remains entirely possible that the depression, anxiety, anger, and sexual problems in the incest survivors do not come from incest. They may stem from some of the other nasty events so frequent in a dysfunctional family, or they may be genetic. Once the ideology is stripped away, we still remain ignorant about whether sexual abuse in childhood wreaks damage in adult life and, if so, how much.

Often forgotten is the child herself. What can we do to best contain the damage? What can we do that will best help the adult who was abused years before as a child?

In talking about post-traumatic stress disorder, my main conclusion was that awful events have lasting ill effects that therapy seems to do little to alleviate. Concentration camps, torture, brutal rape, all leave lasting scars. This is true when the event occurs in adulthood, and this is also true when the event occurs in childhood. But contrary to the inner-child premises, I know of no data that childhood trauma has more power than adult trauma.

My impression is that the natural healing of children is, on the whole, better than for adults. There have been several follow-up studies of sexually abused children, and each shows surprisingly good recovery. More than half the kids improve markedly within a year or two, and the number of kids with severe problems diminishes markedly. A few, tragically, get worse.[7]

Child sexual abuse varies in objective severity from brutal rape at one extreme to erotic fondling at the other. In post-traumatic stress disorder, objective severity, short of violence and life threat, does not determine how long the symptoms last and how intense they are. Suffering identical traumas, some adults are scarred for life while others are unchanged. A few are even strengthened. ("What doesn't kill me makes me stronger," says Nietzsche.) This is also true of children. Consistently, a quarter to a third of sexually abused kids show no symptoms, and contrary to theories of "repression" and "denial," these children stay symptom free. Our job as therapists and parents is to contain the damage. With our help, brutal assault need not get translated into full-blown PTSD, and mild fondling need not get escalated into PTSD.

If we do things to magnify the trauma in the child's mind, we will amplify the symptoms; if we do things to mute the trauma, we will reduce the symptoms. Natural healing occurs, but well-meaning parents, therapists, and courts of law can slow healing. Sometimes they even repeatedly rip the protective scar tissue off the wound. Children involved in lengthy criminal cases are ten times more likely to remain disturbed than children whose cases are resolved quickly.[8]

This is the message of my story about Myron. My parents and the police—in those unenlightened days—lowered the volume. They quietly got Myron off my street corner and scared him badly. If they got enraged or hysterical, I didn't know about it. They did not interrogate me about the intimate details. No emergency-room doctor probed my anal sphincter. I did not go to court. I was not sent to therapy to undo my "denial." I was not, years later, encouraged to rediscover what I had "repressed" and then to relive the trauma to cure my current troubles.

If your child is abused or if you were abused, my best advice is to turn the volume down as soon as possible. Reliving the experience repeatedly may retard the natural healing.

Thus the first inner-child premise—that childhood events have a major influence on adult personality—does not stand up to scrutiny. Only a few childhood events, like the death of your mother, have any documented influence on adult emotional life. And their influence is surprisingly small, particularly when compared to the effect of genes on adult personality. "Toxic shame" and "toxic guilt" in adulthood, instilled by parental abuse, are inventions of the recovery movement. When careful investigators look closely and analyze the route, they do not find evidence that shame and guilt cause the adult problems. There is some evidence that parental abuse leads to troubles in adulthood—bad marriages, for example—but not via guilt or shame. The cause is more drastic, as in the statistically well documented scenario in which bad parental abuse leads to a little girl's placement in a residential nursery. When she reaches puberty, she has no place to go. She escapes by teenage pregnancy or by an early, impulsive marriage, the sort that usually don't last. Then there are those instances in which a difficult girl causes ill-tempered parenting. That also results in her becoming a difficult grown-up. Such women marry mousy men, who withdraw from them. Their marriages then fall apart.[9]

Another fashionable candidate for major influence on adult personality is childhood sexual abuse. This case is, at best, unproven.[10] Traumatic events, like brutal sexual abuse, exert destructive effects on later life. But childhood trauma is not more destructive than adult trauma. If anything, children heal better than do adults. Put simply, the case for childhood trauma—in anything but its most brutal form—influencing adult personality is in the minds of the inner-child advocates. It is not to be found in the data.

The Flashbulb or the Snowball

Here is the single most surprising fact about child rearing and childhood events: Study after study has shown that the interfamilial variance in personality is about the same as the intrafamilial variance—once you control for genes. (Practice saying this and you can take the life out of any cocktail party.) Translated into English, this means that, on average, the personalities of any two children from the same family turn out to be about as different from each other as they are from the personality of any random child—once you control for genes.[11]

Childhood events seem so important because we have one and only one model in mind: the flashbulb. We have long assumed that these episodes explode brightly and so are foundational because they are so vivid. This model does not fit the facts. Here is a model that fits better: the snowball. When two rocks start rolling off the top of a snowy hill, very small initial differences get bigger and bigger as the snowballs gather momentum. A small depression on the hill can also alter the trajectory enormously. Small, early variations in direction and small deviations along the path develop into big differences by the time the snowballs have bumped their way to the bottom of the hill.[12]

Take Joan and Sarah, two little sisters, six and seven, growing up in the Marquez household. They share 50 percent of their genes and seem quite similar. They are slightly different in athletic ability. Joan is a bit stronger than Sarah. When it comes to choosing teammates for tug-of-war in the first grade, Joan always gets picked before Sarah. Sarah comes away from gym day after day feeling disheartened. But she is slightly more talented in music, and so she tries hard in choir. Joan skips choir to play softball. By the end of high school, Joan will be a star gymnast with Olympic ambitions and Sarah the lead soprano in local summer stock. Similar snowballing could eventuate from small differences in optimism, or in looks, or in how much the third-grade teacher liked them, or in how much they liked gardening with Daddy.[13]

In spite of their being taken to the opera once a month, learning to eat chèvre, gardening with Daddy, and taking tuba lessons, Joan and Sarah are no more likely both to like opera, chèvre, the tuba, or gardening than any two random kids—once you take genetic similarity into account. So even though they start with similar personalities and are raised in practically the same way—same parents, same teachers, same strict discipline, same church, same allowances—Sarah and Joan turn out to be very different adults.

Freedom and Depth

Childhood events—even childhood trauma—and childrearing appear to have only weak effects on adult life. Childhood, contrary to popular belief, does not seem, empirically, to be particularly formative. So, contrary to popular belief, we are not prisoners of our past. How we were raised—by martinets swatting our little fingers with rulers or by permissive parents of Spock (the pediatrician, not the Vulcan) persuasion; how we were fed—on demand or on schedule, on breast or on bottle; even mother's death, parents' divorcing, and being second-born exert, at most, small influences on what we are like as adults. We do not need to go through elaborate exorcisms, like ceremonially divorcing our parents, to change our lives.

As adults, we are indeed free to change. I believe that most of the hoary free-will controversy has been empty, full of false dichotomies and reifications: "Is all action strictly determined by the past, or is it sometimes a product of free choice?" "Do we have a faculty of free will?" "Can human beings participate in their own salvation, or is it a gift of God?"

I believe that these questions stem in large part from a misunderstanding about words. With opposites, we sometimes understand both words fully. Both members of the pair can be known separately. *Sweet* and *sour, smart* and *stupid,* are examples. Sweetness, sourness, smartness, and stupidity all exist, and have meanings definable without reference to their opposites. But sometimes we understand and can define only one member of a pair fully, and the other means nothing more than the absence of the first. We know what *embarrassed* means, but *unembarrassed* means nothing more than "not embarrassed." There is such a thing as embarrassment, but there is no such thing as unembarrassment. *Embarrassed* can be defined without reference to *unembarrassed,* but the reverse is not true. *Colored* and *colorless, finitude* and *infinity,* are like this. *Insanity* and *sanity, disease* and *health, abnormality* and *normality,* have generated disputes, with scholars manufacturing qualities of sanity or health or normality, when all these concepts amount to is the absence of insanity, the absence of disease, and the absence of abnormality.[14]

The attempt to define *free will* is the granddaddy of these pointless quests. We understand what it is to be *coerced.* It is to be a prisoner frog-marched down a hill. Coercion is something tangible. Freedom is the absence of coercion, nothing more.

Events from childhood do not coerce our personalities in adulthood. We are not frog-marched by parental spankings at age six into being guilt-ridden thirty-year-olds. Our genes do not coerce our adulthood. Unlike spankings, they have a substantial statistical effect on our personality, but we are not frog-marched into being alcoholics even if our biological parents are alcoholics. Even having the genetic predisposition, there are tactics we can adopt to avoid alcoholism. We can, for example, shun drinking altogether. There are many more teetotal people with alcoholic parents than you would expect there to be by chance alone.

Absent coercion, we are free. Freedom of the will, choice, the possibility of change, mean nothing more—absolutely nothing more—than the absence of coercion. This means simply that we are free to change many things about ourselves. Indeed, the main facts of this book—that depressives often become nondepressives, that lifelong panickers become panic free, that impotent men become potent again, that adults reject the sex role they were raised with, that alcoholics become abstainers—demonstrate this. None of this means that therapists, parents, genes, good advice, and even dyspepsia do not influence what we do. None of this denies that there are limits on how much we can change. It only means that we are not prisoners.

Catharsis

The first inner-child premise—that childhood events determine adult personality—is false. Now I want to turn to the second inner-child premise—that coming to grips with childhood abuse cures adult problems.

John Bradshaw, in his best-seller *Homecoming: Reclaiming and Championing Your Inner Child,* details several of his imaginative techniques: asking forgiveness of your inner child, divorcing your parent and finding a new one, like Jesus, stroking your inner child, writing your childhood history. These techniques go by the name *catharsis,* that is, emotional engagement in past trauma-laden events. Catharsis is magnificent to experience and impressive to behold. Weeping, raging at parents long dead, hugging the wounded little boy who was once you, are all stirring. You have to be made of stone not to be moved to tears. For hours afterward, you may feel cleansed and at peace—perhaps for the first time in years. Awakening, beginning again, and new departures all beckon.

Catharsis, as a therapeutic technique, has been around for more than a hundred years. It used to be a mainstay of psychoanalytic treatment, but no longer. Its main appeal is its afterglow. Its main drawback is that there is no evidence that it works.[15] When you measure how much people like doing it, you hear high praise. When you measure whether anything changes, catharsis fares badly. Done well, it brings about short-term relief—like the afterglow of vigorous exercise. But once the glow dissipates, as it does in a few days, the real problems are still there: an alcoholic spouse, a hateful job, early-morning blues, panic attacks, a cocaine habit. There is no documentation that the catharsis techniques of the recovery movement help in any lasting way with chronic emotional problems. There is no evidence that they alter adult personality. And, strangely, catharsis about fictitious memories does about as well as catharsis about real memories. The inner-child advocates, having treated tens of thousands of suffering adults for years, have not seen fit to do any follow-ups.[16] Because catharsis techniques are so superficially appealing, because they are so dependent on the charisma of the therapist, and because they have no known lasting value, my advice is "Let the buyer beware."

The Moral Dimension of Recovery Re-examined

I can find no support for the two basic assumptions of the recovery movement: that childhood abuse influences adult personality, and that cure by catharsis works. Even if the movement has no foundation, however, the appeal of taking on the victim label is still great. It is democratic, it is consoling, it raises our self-esteem, and it transforms others' contempt into compassion. Or does it?

It depends on the alternatives. If you are alcoholic, the disease label may once have helped you a great deal. The only alternative label used to be "bad person." Disease is curable, limited, and impersonal. Bad character is permanent, pervasive, and personal. Believing you are bad leads to helplessness, hopelessness, and self-hate. Believing you have a disease can lead to action, seeking out a cure, renewed hope, and some measure of self-esteem. If you are a black teenager, unemployed and facing jail, explaining your troubles as discrimination or bad schools may help for the same reason. The alternative labels, "stupid," "lazy," and "criminal," should you believe them, are self-fulfilling.

Depression, sexual troubles, anxiety, loneliness, and guilt are the main problems that drive consumers into the recovery movement. Explaining such adult troubles as being caused by victimization during childhood does not accomplish much. Compare "wounded child" as an explanation to some of the other ways you might explain your problems: "depressive," "anxiety-prone," or "sexually dysfunctional." "Wounded child" is a more permanent explanation; "depressive" is less permanent. As we saw in the first section of this book, depression, anxiety, and sexual dysfunction—unlike being a wounded child—are all eminently treatable. "Wounded child" is also more pervasive in its destructive effects: "Toxic" is the colorful word used to describe its pervasiveness. "Depression," "anxiety," and "sexually dysfunctional" are all narrower, less damning labels, and this, in fact, is part of the reason why treatment works.

So "wounded child" (unless you believe in catharsis cures) leads to more helplessness, hopelessness, and passivity than the alternatives. But it is less personal—your parents did it to you—than "depressive," "anxiety-prone," and "sexually dysfunctional." Impersonal explanations of bad events raise self-esteem more than personal ones. Therefore "wounded child" is better for raising your self-esteem and for lowering your guilt.

Self-esteem has become very important to Americans in the last two decades. Our public schools are supposed to nurture the self-esteem of our children, our churches are supposed to minister to the self-esteem of their congregants, and the recovery movement is supposed to restore the self-esteem of victims. Attaining self-esteem, while undeniably important, is a goal that I have reservations about. I think it is an overinflated idea, and my opinion was formed by my work with depressed people.

Depressed people, you will recall, have four kinds of problems: behavioral—they are passive, indecisive, and helpless; emotional—they are sad; bodily—their sleeping, eating, and sex are disrupted; cognitive—they think life is hopeless and that they are worthless. Only the second half of this last symptom amounts to low self-esteem. I have come to believe that lack of self-esteem is the least important of these woes. Once a depressed person becomes active and hopeful, self-esteem always improves. Bolstering self-esteem without changing hopelessness or passivity, however, accomplishes nothing. To put it exactly, I believe that low self-esteem is an *epiphenomenon,* a mere reflection that your commerce with the world is going badly. It has no power in itself. What needs improving is not self-esteem but your commerce with the world. So the one advantage of labeling yourself a victim—raised self-esteem—is minimal, particularly since victimhood raises self-esteem at the cost of greater hopelessness and passivity, and therefore worsens commerce with the world.

This is indeed my main worry about the recovery movement. Young Americans right now are in an epidemic of depression. I have speculated on the causes in the last chapter of my book *Learned Optimism,* and I will not repeat my conjectures here. Young people are easy pickings for anything that makes them feel better—even temporarily. The recovery movement capitalizes on this epidemic. When it works, it raises self-esteem and lowers guilt, but at the expense of our blaming others for our troubles. Never mind the fact that those we blame did not in fact cause our troubles. Never mind the fact that thinking of ourselves as victims induces helplessness, hopelessness, and passivity. Never mind that there are more effective treatments available elsewhere.

It is more important to focus on responsibility and being forward-looking.[17] Seeing ourselves as victims of childhood makes us prisoners of the past and erodes our sense of responsibility. All successful therapy has two things in common: It is forward-looking and it requires assuming responsibility. Therapy that reviews childhood endlessly, that does not focus on how to cope in the here and now, that views a better future as incidental to undoing the past, has a century-long history of being ineffective. All therapy that works for depression, anxiety, and sexual problems focuses on exactly what is going wrong now and on how to correct it. All this requires a heightened sense of responsibility for our problems and a commitment to hard work (and even homework) to make the future better. The past is touched upon, but usually to get insight into patterns of problems, not as a way to shuck off the blame.[18]

So I worry that the second season of people in "recovery" will be crippled—not by what actually happened to them in the first season, but by their seeing themselves as prisoners of their childhoods—victims helpless to begin anew in a new season.

The Uses of Childhood

I can endorse the goal of the recovery movement—mobilizing troubled adults to change problems they thought were unchangeable. But I cannot endorse either its premises or its methods. To me, these get in the way of my positive message: Growth and change are the rule, not the exception, throughout adult life. As you enter your second season, many of you are troubled—depressed, anxious, angry, or lonely. You may have become accustomed to your pain, but that does not make it an acceptable feeling to live with the rest of your life. And you need not. There are alternative and effective ways to change, and they have been detailed in Parts 2 and 3 of this book. They are not quick fixes, nor are they emotionally orgiastic, but they are worthwhile and they do last.

There is a third premise of the recovery movement that I *do* endorse enthusiastically: The patterns of problems in childhood that recur into adulthood are significant. They can be found by exploring your past, by looking into the corners of your childhood. Coming to grips with your childhood will not yield insight into *how* you became the adult you are: The causal links between childhood events and what you have now become are simply too weak. Coming to grips with your childhood will not make your adult problems go away: Working through the past does not seem to be any sort of cure for troubles. Coming to grips with your childhood will not make you feel any better for long, nor will it raise your self-esteem.

Coming to grips with childhood is a different and special voyage. The sages urged us to know ourselves, and Plato warned us that the unexamined life is not worth living. Knowledge acquired on this voyage is about patterns, about the tapestry that we have woven. It is not knowledge about causes. Are there consistent mistakes we have made and still make? In the flush of victory, do I forget my friends—in the Little League and when I got that last big raise? (People have always told me I'm a good loser but a bad winner.) Do I usually succeed in one domain but fail in another? (I wish I could get along with the people I really love as well as I do with my employers.) Does a surprising emotion arise again and again? (I always pick fights with people I love right before they have to go away.) Does my body often betray me? (I get a lot of colds when big projects are due.)

You probably want to know why you are a bad winner, why you get colds when others expect a lot of you, and why you react to abandonment with anger. You will not find out. As important and magnetic as the "why" questions are, they are questions that psychology cannot now answer. One of the two clearest findings of one hundred years of therapy is that satisfactory answers to the great "why" questions are not easily found; maybe in fifty years things will be different; maybe never. When purveyors of the evils of "toxic shame" tell you that they know it comes from parental abuse, don't believe them. No one knows any such thing. Be skeptical even of your own "Aha!" experiences: When you unearth the fury you felt that first kindergarten day, do not assume that you have found the source of your lifelong terror of abandonment. The causal links may be illusions, and humility is in order here. The other clearest finding of the whole therapeutic endeavor, however, is that change is within our grasp, almost routine, throughout adult life. So even if why we are what we are is a mystery, how to change ourselves is not.

Mind the pattern. A pattern of mistakes is a call to change your life. The rest of the tapestry is not determined by what has been woven before. The weaver herself, blessed with knowledge and with freedom, can change—if not the material she must work with—the design of what comes next.

15

Depth and Change: The Theory

IT IS TIME for a review and for the theory. When we survey all the problems, personality types, patterns of behavior, and the weak influence of childhood on adult life, we see a puzzling array of how much change occurs. From the things that are easiest to those that are the most difficult, this rough array emerges:

Panic	Curable
Specific Phobias	Almost Curable
Sexual Dysfunctions	Marked Relief
Social Phobia	Moderate Relief
Agoraphobia	Moderate Relief
Depression	Moderate Relief
Sex Role	Moderate Change
Obsessive-Compulsive Disorder	Moderate/Mild Relief
Sexual Preferences	Moderate/Mild Change
Anger	Mild/Moderate Relief
Everyday Anxiety	Mild/Moderate Relief
Alcoholism	Mild Relief
Overweight	Temporary Change
Post-Traumatic Stress Disorder (PTSD)	Marginal Relief
Sexual Orientation	Probably Unchangeable[1]
Sexual Identity	Unchangeable

Clearly, we have not yet developed drugs or psychotherapies that can change all these. I believe that success and failure stems from something other than inadequate treatment. Rather, it stems from the depth of the problem.

Depth, an old but elusive notion, is, I believe, the key. We all have experience of psychological states of different depths. Sometimes when I have been on the road for weeks and I come home fatigued, something strange happens to me in the middle of the night. It is called *depersonalization.* I wake up and can't remember. I don't know where I am. I can't remember what year it is, or even the season. I don't know what kind of car I drive. I don't know who is sleeping next to me. When the phenomenon is really extreme, I don't know how old I am. (But I always know that I am male.) This state passes in a few seconds, and my memories come flooding back to me—at least they have so far.

If you ask someone, out of the blue, to answer quickly "Who are you?" they will usually tell you—roughly in this order—their name, their sex, their profession, whether they have children, and their religion or race. Underlying this is a continuum of depth from surface to soul—with all manner of psychic material in between. Lest the purists among you be put off by my using the word *soul,* let me remind you of Freud's terminology. Freud's word for his subject matter was not *psyche* (as it has been rendered in English by his medical translators), or *mind* (as the modern cognitivists prefer), but *die Seele,* the soul—an entity connoting much more than cold cognition.

I believe that issues of the soul can barely be changed by psychotherapy or by drugs. Problems and behavior patterns somewhere between soul and surface can be changed somewhat. Surface problems can be changed easily, even cured. What is changeable, by therapy or drugs, I want to speculate, varies with the *depth* of the problem.

What exactly does *depth* mean? How do we know if we are dealing with a deep issue or a superficial one? Depth, as I intend it, has three aspects. The first is biological. The second has to do with evidence. The third concerns power.

The biological aspect of death is evolutionary. Is the state *prepared?* Prepared learning, you will recall from the *sauce béarnaise* phenomenon, occurs with but one experience, is not rational, is not conscious, is resistant to change, and is selective only for objects of adaptive significance. Phobias about animals and insects display these hallmarks and are, therefore, prepared. So are obsessions about infection or violence, fetishes about female legs or breasts, and depression over the death of a child. Biologically deep problems are prepared or even innate. Therefore they are represented genetically, and, as adaptive traits, they are heritable. There has been a long evolutionary history operating to promote the state. Manic-depression is an example. The cycling of energy with the seasons, from summer activity to winter hibernation, may be its evolutionary basis, and it is highly heritable.[2] That identical twins are more concordant for manic-depression than are fraternal twins provides evidence for the adaptive value of mood cycling.

The first claim of my theory is: To the extent that a psychological condition has biological underpinnings because it is prepared or heritable, it will be harder to change; to the extent that it is unprepared—simply a learned habit—it will be easier to change.

The evidentiary aspect of depth is about confirmation and disconfirmation: How easy is it to get evidence for the belief underlying the problem? The other side of the coin of evidence-gathering is even more important: How difficult is it to get evidence that will disabuse you of the belief? It is perilously easy to live our lives noticing only evidence in favor of our deep beliefs and to shun testing whether those beliefs are false. The thought underlying post-traumatic stress disorder—"The world is a miserable, unjust place, with no solace for me"—is easy to confirm. Just read the front page of this morning's newspaper. The thought underlying obsessive-compulsive problems—for example, "If I don't wash my hands thoroughly, I will contaminate my child"—will not get disconfirmed by someone who avoids testing it. The person with this thought washes her hands two hours a day. Her hands are always clean, and her child never gets contaminated. She will never get disconfirming evidence because she performs the ritual so frequently. So she will never find out that not washing her hands does not lead to contamination of her child.

So the second claim of my theory is: The easier a belief underlying a problem is to confirm and the harder it is to disconfirm, the harder it will be to change.

The third aspect of depth is the power of the belief underlying the problem. I use *power* in the sense of the power of a theory. A theory is said to have high power when it is general and so explains many of the facts about the world. Relativity theory—applicable to all of time and space—has high power. A theory has low power when it applies to only a few isolated facts. "There are a lot of ticks this year because it has been a dry summer" does not apply much beyond ticks and humidity, and so is of low power. Everything else being equal, we cling to a powerful theory more tenaciously than to a less powerful theory when we are confronted with exactly the same contrary evidence disputing both.

Some of our personal beliefs are powerful in just the same way a theory is powerful—they make sense of a great deal of our world. Being a socialist or believing in a benevolent God are but two of many possible examples. These beliefs permeate our understanding of what happens to ourselves and to others. They are deeply entrenched. Stalin's purges did not shake the beliefs of socialists very much, nor did the Black Death make God seem evil or indifferent to most believers. Other personal beliefs have low power. Believing that cars made in Detroit on Fridays have more defects because the workers are looking forward to the weekend explains only your windshield-wiper problem and little else in your life. The thoughts underlying our problems can be of high or low power. The belief that spiders are very dangerous is of low power, whereas the belief that I am an unlovable person or that I need to drink to get through the day has high power.

So the third claim of my theory is: To the extent that the belief underlying a problem has high power, it will be hard to change; to the extent that it has low power, it will be easier to change.

Added together, these claims may explain when a problem will change easily and when it will resist change. Let us reconsider the problems and see.

Transsexualism, the inversion of sexual identity, is, by these criteria, the deepest problem. It is biologically laid down in gestation. It is virtually undisconfirmable and pervades all of life. It is also totally unchangeable.

Sexual orientation (homosexuality and heterosexuality—not, to my way of thinking, problems, but simply patterns of behavior) is almost as deep. Part of its basis is probably laid down during gestation, and it probably has specific underpinning in the brain. Once orientation is adopted, evidence steadily mounts for it—you enjoy it and it fits. That a woman is attracted to members of her own sex is easy for her to confirm and hard for her to disconfirm, and this attraction is of high power—pervading much of what she does. While the desire itself resists change mightily, whom you perform with is a bit flexible.

Post-traumatic stress disorder is a disorder of the soul. It probably has little evolutionary basis and is not known to be heritable, but the underlying belief is powerful and readily confirmed. If, for instance, your child dies, you have been robbed, by a stroke of cruel fate, of what you hold most precious. Your worldview changes: This world is cruel, there is no justice, I have no future, there is no hope, and I wish I hadn't survived. There is pervasive reality to what you now believe, since your child is never coming back. All you have to do to confirm your new philosophy is turn on the eleven o'clock news. The cascade of bad events that usually follows in the wake of a tragedy further confirms your pessimism. Sometimes surprisingly good things happen and your view softens, but only reluctantly. Therapy and drugs might make you less afraid of the specific place of the tragedy. Little more, except for rape victims, has so far been accomplished in alleviating PTSD. You now *know* just how fragile all happiness is.

Weight is quite a deep matter. Dieting works only temporarily for more than 90 percent of "overweight" people. Your weight is defended by powerful biological and psychological processes that served your ancestors well through famine and hardship. Appetite and weight have layers of biological and psychological defense: brain centers firing, blood-sugar level dropping, metabolic slowdown, fatigue, fat storage, changing number and size of fat cells, intense food cravings, stomach rumbling, and binge eating. Natural selection has assured that we will be able to starve ourselves voluntarily only with the greatest of difficulty. The evidentiary criterion is not applicable to overweight, but the power criterion is. Your habits of eating are part of your way of life. Your styles of working, loving, and playing are often tied up with what, where, and how much you eat.

Alcoholism has some biological underpinnings. It is moderately heritable, and part of what it means to have a biological addiction is that cells living in an alcohol-laden environment become dependent on the presence of alcohol to function well. That I need a drink to get through this interview, or this class, or this date is hard to disconfirm—particularly when I don't abstain and find out that the date goes well anyway. Usually, I drink and it goes tolerably well, or I don't drink and I have the shakes. Alcoholism has power. It is a way of life. Like the intellectual who goes to a party and sees it in terms of her interests ("Isn't that guest politically naïve? How many books does the host have in the living room?"), so, too, the alcoholic ("How well stocked is the bar? Who will make the rounds with me afterward? Who knows my boss and might report my drinking heavily?"). Alcoholism is therefore not easy to change.

Everyday anxiety is not as deep as alcoholism. Fear and courage are basic facts of personality and genetics. They have a strong evolutionary basis ("It is safer in the cave"). Those of us born fearful and timid lead, for the most part, fearful and timid lives. We are assailed with frightening thoughts. These thoughts are hard to disconfirm if we manage to avoid the feared circumstances, and they are frequently confirmed (muggers *do* come out at night). That the world is a frightening place is a fairly powerful theory. This can be changed, but not easily. With discipline, drugs, and clever tactics in therapy, we can be steeled, at least a bit.

Pervasive **anger** is probably somewhat less deep than pervasive anxiety. It has a clear evolutionary value, and there is some evidence for its heritability. If you believe you are being trespassed against, you can usually find evidence for it: The targets of your anger *are* sometimes out to get you. But you will also get some disconfirmation too, since sometimes the targets of your anger turn out to be manifestly innocent. The belief in trespass is powerful when it is a general belief like "Others are out to get me" or "The world is full of people who only care about themselves." It is of low power when it is only a specific ("My boss is a jerk!") belief. The therapy evidence is far from conclusive, but anger seems somewhat—although not sweepingly—modifiable.

Sexual preferences (called *paraphilia* when disordered) are at middling depth. They seem to be evolutionarily prepared. They are easy to obtain confirming evidence for once adopted—they are great fun—but they are narrow beliefs influencing only your erotic life. Once adopted, they do not wane spontaneously, but they can be modified somewhat in therapy.

Obsessive-compulsive disorder also has middling depth. The thoughts and rituals seem to be evolutionarily prepared (cleaning and checking, dirt and violence, were all issues for pretechnological humans), and there is some evidence for heritability. The obsession is extremely hard to disconfirm: An efficient ritual ensures that you don't sit around to find out if your ritual—unperformed—results in disaster. But the obsessions are not powerful: They are limited to germs, violence, explosions, and the like. Therapy helps quite a bit but usually does not cure.

Sex role may have some brain and fetal-hormone contribution. When you are a child, evidence pours in to support your stereotyped beliefs, and they are powerful beliefs, organizing much of childhood. But the evidence and their power wanes dramatically with maturity, when you can better appreciate the virtues of tolerance, justice, and individuality. Sex roles are inflexible for young children, but increasingly flexible as children grow up.

Depression is also of middling depth. Sometimes the beliefs are distortions and are easy to disconfirm: for example, the belief of a wealthy woman that she is a bag lady.[3] But often the beliefs are based in reality; indeed, depressives are more accurate at judging their success and failure than nondepressives.[4] Sometimes depressive beliefs are of low power: "She doesn't love me"; "I'm a hopeless golfer." Sometimes they are powerful and pervasive: "I'm not worth loving"; "I'm a total failure." There is some mild heritability and possibly an evolutionary basis for staying in the cave and conserving energy for a while after a loss. At any rate, with therapy or drugs, moderate relief ensues, but your battle against depression—even then—can still be life-long.

Social phobia and agoraphobia lie nearer the surface. They make some evolutionary sense, and there is some evidence of mild heritability. The underlying beliefs are easy to confirm since they are not wildly inaccurate: Shy people *do* get embarrassed by others; if you have one of your panic attacks in public, it may very well be that you *will* be sick as a dog and no one will help you. If you avoid social gatherings or do not leave your apartment, these beliefs will not get disconfirmed. The social-phobic beliefs have moderate power: Seeing yourself as socially unskilled or unlikable may explain a fair amount of what happens to you. The agoraphobic belief that you will get ill and no one will help you has relatively low power. With therapy and drugs, some relief ensues for both, but not a complete cure.

Problems of **sexual performance** change quite easily with the right therapy, and I consider them problems near the surface. There is no biological basis for the sexual dysfunctions, but in the throes of one it is quite hard to disconfirm the belief "I am sexually inadequate," particularly during the vicious circle of spectatoring. These problems are not powerful beliefs, since they are confined to erotic and family life.

Specific phobias also lie near the surface. Spiders, for example, *are* dangerous: They bite, and very rare ones might even kill you. There is an evolutionary history pushing you to feel this way, but while prepared,

DEPTH OF THE DISORDERS AND BEHAVIOR PATTERNS (▲▲▲▲ = maximal contribution per factor)

	Biology	*Evidence*	*Power*	*Total*	*Changeability*
SEXUAL IDENTITY	▲▲▲▲	▲▲▲▲	▲▲▲▲	▲▲▲▲▲▲▲▲▲▲▲▲	unchangeable
SEXUAL ORIENTATION	▲▲▲	▲▲▲	▲▲▲	▲▲▲▲▲▲▲▲▲	probably unchangeable
PTSD	o	▲▲▲▲	▲▲▲▲	▲▲▲▲▲▲▲▲	little relief (mild relief for rape)
OVERWEIGHT	▲▲▲	▲	▲▲▲	▲▲▲▲▲▲▲	temporary change only
ALCOHOLISM	▲▲	▲▲	▲▲▲	▲▲▲▲▲▲▲	mild relief
ANGER	▲▲	▲▲▲	▲▲	▲▲▲▲▲▲▲	mild/moderate
EVERYDAY ANXIETY	▲▲	▲▲	▲▲	▲▲▲▲▲▲	mild/moderate
SEXUAL PREFERENCES	▲▲	▲▲	▲▲	▲▲▲▲▲▲	moderate/mild
OBSESSIVE-COMPULSIVE DISORDER	▲▲	▲▲▲▲	o	▲▲▲▲▲▲	moderate/mild
SEX ROLE					
CHILDREN	▲	▲▲▲	▲▲▲	▲▲▲▲▲▲▲	rigid
ADULTS	▲	▲	▲	▲▲▲	flexible
DEPRESSION	▲	▲▲	▲▲▲	▲▲▲▲▲▲	moderate
SOCIAL PHOBIA	▲	▲▲▲	▲▲	▲▲▲▲▲▲	moderate
AGORAPHOBIA	▲	▲▲▲	▲	▲▲▲▲▲	moderate
SEXUAL DYSFUNCTIONS	o	▲▲	▲▲	▲▲▲▲	almost curable
SPECIFIC PHOBIAS	▲▲	▲▲	o	▲▲▲▲	almost curable
PANIC	o	▲▲	o	▲▲	curable

the specific content of phobias is not heritable. The belief that spiders are dangerous is hard to disconfirm if you avoid spiders altogether and never find out that if endured, spiders are much more scared of you than you are of them. The belief is of low power—it explains only spiders. With therapy, this fear can be extinguished almost completely—but the phobia may reappear when rekindled by other troubles.

Panic lies at the surface. It turns out merely to be a mistaken belief that your heart racing is a symptom of heart attack, or that gasping for breath is a symptom of stroke. Very little else hinges on this belief, and so it is of low power. It is quite easy to disconfirm by showing a hyperventilating patient that his symptoms are symptoms of anxiety or overbreathing, not of heart attack. It does not seem to have a strong evolutionary history, and it is not heritable. When changed by therapy or evidence, panic is almost always cured.

A theory is defined not only by what it claims, but also by what it omits. Most theories of personality claim that childhood is powerful and that emotional traits are likewise strong. My theory denies both of these assumptions. There is no premise here about early learning being strong. My theory says that it does not matter *when* problems, habits, and personality are acquired; their depth derives only from their biology, their evidence, and their power. Some childhood traits are deep and unchangeable, but not because they were learned early and therefore have a privileged place. Rather, those traits that resist change do so either because they are evolutionarily prepared or because they acquire great power by virtue of becoming the framework around which later learning crystallizes. My theory also makes no claim about emotional learning being deep, and therefore traumatic learning has no privileged place in it. When emotional traits resist change, their unchangeability derives from either their biology, their evidence, or their power—not from trauma. I have spent the last thirty years investigating what we learn under trauma, and I am impressed by how very flexible such learning is. The omissions of early and traumatic learning are central to my theory, and fit well with the fact that the influence on adult life of childhood and its traumas is weak. In this way, the theory of depth carries the optimistic message that we are not prisoners of our past.

So I intend to revive an idea long neglected by scientists other than the Freudians: the idea of depth. I believe it is the key to change. Changing that which is deep requires mighty effort—massive doses of drugs or interminable therapy—and the attempt is likely, in the end, to fail. That which is near the surface changes much more readily.

When you have understood this message, you will never look at your life in the same way again. Right now there are a number of things that you do not like about yourself and that you want to change: your short fuse, your waistline, your shyness, your drinking, your glumness. You have decided to change, but you do not know what you should work on first. Formerly you would have probably selected the one that hurts the most. Now you will also ask which attempt is most likely to repay your efforts and which is most likely to lead to further frustration. You now know that your glumness, your shyness, and your anger are much more likely to change than your drinking, which is more likely to change than your waistline.

Some of what does change is under your control, and some is not. You can best prepare yourself to change by learning as much as you can about what you can change and how to make those changes. This has been the purpose of my book. Like all true education, learning about change is not easy; harder yet is surrendering some of our hopes. There are few shortcuts and no quick fixes to be had. You have heard the exhortations of the multibillion-dollar self-improvement industries and the therapy and medication guilds. Much of what you have heard from them has been false promises. Much of the optimism they have engendered has been unwarranted.

I have spent the last twenty-five years investigating optimism, and it is certainly not my purpose to destroy your optimism about change. But it is also not my purpose to assure everybody that they can change in every way. That would be yet another false promise. Optimism, the conviction that you *can* change, is a necessary first step in the process of all change. But unwarranted optimism, the conviction that you can change what in fact you cannot, is a tragic diversion. Years of frustration, self-reproach, giving up, and, ultimately, remorse follow. My purpose is to instill a new, warranted optimism about the parts of your life you can change and so help you focus your limited time, money, and effort on making actual what is truly within your reach.

Recall the "Serenity Prayer" that opened this book: the courage to change what you can change, the serenity to accept what you cannot change, and the wisdom to know the difference. Life is a long period of change. What you have been able to change and what has resisted your highest resolve might seem chaotic to you; for some of what you are never changes no matter how hard you try, and other aspects change readily. My hope is that this book has been the beginning of wisdom about the difference.

ACKNOWLEDGMENTS

NOTES

INDEX

ACKNOWLEDGMENTS

This book has been twenty-five years in its birthing. I began to worry about the collision between biological and environmental views of change when I was a graduate student at the University of Pennsylvania in the mid-1960s. Three people brought the importance of the issue home to me. The first was Dick Solomon, the very embodiment of the nurture side of the issue—an influential learning theorist who spent his career looking into the *tabula rasa* for the roots of emotion and emotional change. He was my Ph.D. adviser and my teacher. The second was Paul Rozin, then a young upstart with the unheard-of combination of a Ph.D. in biology and one in psychology. He thought the *tabula rasa* approach to learning made no sense. He was my teacher, too. The third person, John Garcia, put learning theory into evolutionary perspective. In a brilliant set of experiments, John had the temerity to propose that learnability itself has been the subject of natural selection. For John, the *tabula rasa* came with many instructions, defaults, and biases. I thought John was right, and began back then to write books and articles espousing this view.

Then the issue lay dormant within me for almost twenty years, as I myself evolved from learning theorist to clinical psychologist to social scientist. I read the burgeoning literature on change and watched the gulf grow wider between environmentalists and biological psychiatrists. As the gulf widened, however, there came the first major discoveries of methods of markedly changing many of the psychological disorders. Disorders that had resisted change now yielded to a variety of drugs and psychotherapies. There seemed to be a pattern in what changed and what did not change, in what changed with drugs as opposed to what changed with psychotherapy. This pattern seemed to be the same one I saw in the work of John Garcia.

The idea for writing a book on this topic was born in Kona Village, Hawaii, in the winter of 1990–91. It came out of conversations about our children with my wife, Mandy, and then with Michael Crichton, the novelist and essayist. Crichton and I both had two-year-old daughters (Taylor and Lara, respectively) and were caught up in the day-to-day tribulations of childrearing. We wondered about what things actually influenced our daughters and what elements of childrearing were wholly without effect. I reeled off my opinions about biological preparedness, sexual identity, phobias, and the *sauce béarnaise* phenomenon. Michael encouraged a book (we have the same publisher, Sonny Mehta of Alfred A. Knopf), and my agent, Richard Pine, was aglow with enthusiasm. And so was my editor, Jonathan Segal, who is not easily kindled.

I sought and received the advice and comments of many people—experts in the wide range of the disorders, drugs, psychotherapies, and self-improvement schemes—and I have tried to integrate that wisdom into this book. I extend my thanks to them now, with the customary absolution for the results. First, the people who read and commented on entire chapters or even longer swaths: Kelly Brownell (dieting), David Clark of Oxford University (anxiety), Michael Crichton (all), Edna Foa (PTSD and depth), Alan Kors (booters and bootstrappers), Alan Marlatt (alcoholism), John Money (sex), Robert Plomin (childhood), Jack Rachman (obsessions), Sandy Scarr (childhood), Amanda Seligman, my oldest daughter (all of Part 1), Joseph Volpicelli (alcoholism), George Vaillant (alcoholism), Fred Van Fleteren (booters and bootstrappers), and Terry Wilson of Rutgers University (dieting and alcoholism).

Several people have allowed me to reprint their questionnaires in the book: I thank Lisa Friedman Miller, Lenore Radloff, Melvin Selzer, and Charles Spielberger.

Jonathan Segal and Richard Pine each gave the manuscript several readings and improved it each time, not only sentence by sentence but in substance. Heather Smay read the manuscript as it evolved and was my tireless research assistant. My secretaries, Elise McMahon and Terry Silver, were helpful in ways too diverse to number.

So many conversations, so many constructive comments, so many memos and letters, so much time freely given, so much exchange of ideas—I am sure I have inadvertently omitted some who helped, but my thanks to Jeff Albert, Lauren Alloy, Lori Andiman, Mike Bailey, Paul Baltes, Jon Baron, Aaron Beck, Mary Bell, Beth Brezner, Kevin Brownlee, Greg Buchanan, David Buss, Dan Chirot, Billy Coren, Paul Crits-

Cristoph, Rob DeRubeis, Harold Dibble, Ken Dodge, Maureen Eisenberg, Albert Ellis, David Featherman, Alan Feingold, Pamela Freyd, Alan Fridlund, Lisa Friedman, Jim Fries, Don Fusting, Judy Garber, Joan Girgus, Henry Gleitman, Lila Gleitman, David Goldberg, Ruben Gur, T. George Harris, Peter Herman, Tom Hirst, Steve Hollon, Janet Hyde, Lisa Jaycox, Charlie Jesnig, Martin Katahn, Gerald Klerman, John LaRosa, Bruce Larsen, Lester Luborsky, David Lykken, Alan Mann, Isaac Marks, Jack Maser, Dennis McCarthy, Nigel McCarthy, Jeff Meckstroth, Shirlee Meckstroth, Bob Miller, Sue Mineka, Paul Monaco, Peter Muehrer, Susan Nolen-Hoeksema, Gabriele Oettingen, Dan Oran, James Pennebaker, Chris Peterson, Arthur Pine, Chris Prokop, Judith Rapoport, Karen Reivich, Richard Rende, Bob Rescorla, Sam Revusky, Chris Risley, Judy Rodin, Dave Rosenhan, Mollie Rosenhan, Julie Rubenstein, Marvin Sachs, Harold Sackeim, Robert Schuller, Peter Schulman, Barry Schwartz, David Seligman, Irene Seligman, Paul Soloway, David Spiegel, John Stickney, Mickey Stunkard, Paul Thomas, Lou Tice, Joseph Volpicelli, Peter Whybrow, George Wilson, Camille Wortman, and the students in Psychology 709 in the spring semesters of 1992 and 1993.

The most special thanks go to my wife, Mandy McCarthy Seligman, not only for reading and commenting on all of this book (except this part), but for her unflagging good cheer and boundless love. And to Nicole Seligman, my two-year-old. The writing of the book began on or about the day of her conception, and the first draft was finished the day she took her first steps. Her buoyancy and the sunshine she radiates made even the hardest parts easier.

M.E.P.S.
July 1993

NOTES

A serious scholar writing for the general public walks a tightrope between readability and responsibility. My way of presenting the scholarship underlying the book is to offer these endnotes. These are intended for my scholarly audience and those of you who want to read further.

CHAPTER 1 *What Changes? What Doesn't Change?*

1. M. Seligman and J. Hager, eds., *The Biological Boundaries of Learning* (New York: Appleton-Century-Crofts, 1972).
2. M. Seligman, *Helplessness: On Depression, Development, and Death* (San Francisco: Freeman, 1975); M. Seligman, *Learned Optimism* (New York: Knopf, 1991).
3. Copyright by Lisa Friedman Miller. I thank her for her generosity in letting me use it here.

CHAPTER 2 *Booters and Bootstrappers*

1. This version is taken from the *Passover Haggadah,* distributed by Maxwell House Coffee, 1981.
2. Even the more psychological books of the Bible—Job and Psalms, for example—are peculiar, seen from a modern perspective, in what mental states are present and what mental states are absent. There is some emotion—anger, grief, and joy; but less cognition—expectation, belief, inference, problem solving; and almost nothing of human will—decision, intention, choice, and preference. What Aristotle called *conation* is almost absent from the Scriptures (see Deuteronomy 30:19 and Isaiah 65:12 for two rare exceptions).

   I used a concordance to bear out this impression. Since I am a far cry from a biblical scholar, I am not sure my observation would bear closer scrutiny. If it is true, however, I take the question of why this might be so to be a great historical question.
3. The skeptical reader should spend some time with the stark account of Abraham's sacrifice in Genesis 22: 1–13. Abraham's absence of mentation is striking.
4. Pico's *Oration* (1486), translated by D. Brooks-Davies and S. Davies, quoted in S. Davies, *Renaissance Views of Man* (Manchester: Manchester University Press, 1978), 62–82.

   I have been unable to find a history of free will. I hope that a scholar will someday be moved to undertake such a history. A history of free will, unlike, say, the history of empiricism, would be more than an airy exercise in the history of a philosophical notion. If I am right, what a given historical period believes about free will reflects, and may even affect, how active or passive that culture is, how helpless and how despairing that culture is.

This section of my book, along with this note and the note below on human participation in grace, is my bare sketch of such a history.

Pico was far from the first to articulate the concept of free will. Dante wrote, "A light is given you to know good and evil, and free will (*"e libero voler"*), which if it endure fatigue in its first battles with the heavens, afterwards, if it is well nurtured, it conquers completely" (canto 16, *Purgatory*). Before Dante, Aquinas endorsed it, more than halfheartedly.

It was clearly put forth one thousand years before Pico by Pelagius in his lost work *De Libero Arbitrio.* Unfortunately for Pelagius, he had the most towering of opponents, the luminescent Saint Augustine. Augustine, for most of his life, held that humans could indeed will evil, but that when they will good, it is merely by the irresistible action of divine grace.

Augustine's conception traces back to the Stoic Seneca's view that fate and human freedom are compatible. And Seneca's view, in turn, traces back another century to Cicero. The Golden Age Greeks had a lively interest in free will versus fate, and this contrasts instructively with the debate's absence from the Bible. The issue of free will is Greco-Roman in origin, not Judeo-Christian.

At any rate, Augustine's opposition to Pelagius may have set back the idea of free will for a millennium or so, since save for Aquinas and Dante, it did not seem to reemerge with any force until Pico. See Marianne Djuth's "Stoicism and Augustine's Doctrine of Human Freedom After 396," in J. Schnaubelt and F. Van Fleteren, eds., *Collectanea Augustiniana* (New York: Peter Lang, 1990), for an illuminating account of this hoary dispute at the close of the fourth century.

5. From the point of view of advocates of human choice, Luther's *On the Bondage of the Will* (1525) makes chilling reading. He angrily rebutted the Dutch theologian Erasmus's view of God (*On the Freedom of the Will,* 1524) as a father who lifts a fallen toddler. The father, Erasmus explained, does almost everything, but the toddler has some small agency of his own. The new Protestantism was a backward step on the road to belief in human agency when contrasted to the emerging Catholic humanists such as Erasmus.

6. There are two related theological disputes. The first concerns free will. The second is whether humans participate in their own salvation, in "grace." It is the attitude toward this second issue that probably best reflects what people believe about the power or impotence of human agency.

Grace, *gratis* in Latin, means "freely given"—by God, of course. In this original meaning, humans do not participate at all—receiving grace is entirely God's will. Pelagius, in addition to believing in free will, believed that we do participate in grace. This is part of the Pelagian heresy: There *are* things humans can do to achieve salvation. Saint Augustine waffled on free will, occasionally endorsing the notion that humans could choose good as well as evil. But he clearly believed that humans do not participate in achieving grace. Thomas Aquinas, while closer to Pelagius on the subject of free will, also believed that humans do not participate in grace.

The possibility that humans participate in their own grace—and the accompanying leap forward in the belief in the potency of human agency—came from Erasmus, Arminius, and Wesley. This belief was simply without an effective voice throughout the Middle Ages and the early Renaissance.

7. From "The General Deliverance," in J. Wesley, *Sermons,* vol. 2 (New York: Emory and Waugh, 1831), 50.
8. From "The Means of Grace," in J. Wesley, *Sermons,* vol. 1 (New York: Emory and Waugh, 1831), 135–47.

9. The Jackson speech is quoted in Alice Felt Tyler's important *Freedom's Ferment* (Minneapolis: University of Minnesota Press, 1944), 22. Tyler portrays the first half of the nineteenth century as centrally driven by the idea of the perfectibility of humankind.
10. Letter of Freud to Wilhelm Fliess, 14 November 1897. From the *Complete Letters of Sigmund Freud to Wilhelm Fliess, 1887–1904* (Cambridge, Mass.: Belknap, 1985), 281. It is significant, however, that in concert with the therapist's agency, the patient must "work through" his problems. The patient is never viewed as wholly passive, but he is not viewed as capable of unaided self-improvement. Most of the booters also have the individual at least cooperating in his elevation, but not being the primary motive force. It is like Erasmus's toddler, with some little agency, guided by God, with most of the agency.
11. From Bruce Kuklick's brilliant *Churchmen and Philosophers* (New Haven: Yale University Press, 1985), 227. Kuklick traces the history and influence of American Protestantism on American social consciousness.
12. J. B. Watson, *Behaviorism* (New York: People's Institute Publishing, 1924), 237.
13. It is astonishing to me that this stream of thought, which I believe is the religious manifestation of the idea of the potency of individual agency, seems to be beneath the notice of academics. I cannot find a learned treatise in social science that even *cites* these thinkers, much less takes them seriously. Serious they are.

CHAPTER 3 *Drugs, Germs, and Genes*

1. This and all other case histories in this book are collages, with the details somewhat fictionalized to protect the identity of those concerned.
2. A review of the only five well-done controlled studies of the antipsychotics can be found in P. Keck, B. Cohen, R. Baldessarini, and S. McElroy, "Time Course of Antipsychotic Effects of Neuroleptic Drugs," *American Journal of Psychiatry* 146 (1989): 1289–92. Across these five studies, roughly 50 percent reduction of symptoms is reported. A useful general review of rate of effectiveness is in R. Spiegel, *Psychopharmacology,* 2d ed. (New York: Wiley, 1989).
3. Nathan Kline's militant brief about the discovery of the first antidepressant drugs, "Monoamine Oxidase Inhibitors: An Unfinished Picaresque Tale," in F. J. Ayd and H. Blackwell, eds., *Discoveries in Biological Psychiatry* (Philadelphia: Lippincott, 1970), makes for delicious reading.
4. Quantifying the effect of the antidepressants is not simple. Unlike the antipsychotics, there have been a large number of good outcome (double-blind, placebo-controlled) studies of the tricyclics. But depression goes away on its own in time, and so there is a high rate of remission with just a placebo, perhaps as high as 45 percent. A drug has to outperform the placebo to work, and this happens in only about two-thirds of outcome studies. Different studies quantify improvement in many different ways, and this also makes comparison difficult. A consensus figure is that about 65 percent of patients improve noticeably with the tricyclics. See, for example, the useful review by Phillip Berger, "Antidepressant Medications and the Treatment of Depression," in J. Barchas, P. Berger, R. Ciaranello, and G. Elliot, eds., *Psychopharmacology* (New York: Oxford University Press, 1977), 174–207. For a good recent study, see K. White, W. Wykoff, L. Tynes, L. Schneider, et al., "Fluvoxamine in the Treatment of Tricyclic-Resistant Depression," *Psychiatric Journal of the University of Ottawa* 15 (1990): 156–58.

   A useful general review of rate of effectiveness is in Spiegel, *Psychopharmacology.*
5. See, for example, J. Hall, "Fluoxetine: Efficacy Against Placebo and by Dose—An Overview," *British Journal of Psychiatry* supplement 3 (1988): 59–63.

6. This little-known story is narrated by John Cade in his "The Story of Lithium," in Ayd and Blackwell, *Discoveries in Biological Psychiatry,* 218–29.
7. Lithium is more effective on the manic side of manic-depressive illness than it is for the depression. It is preventative of manic episodes as well, if taken regularly. It has toxic side effects (both cardiac and gastrointestinal) and so must be monitored carefully. See R. Sack and E. De Fraites, "Lithium and the Treatment of Mania," in Barchas et al., *Psychopharmacology,* 208–25. One of the major problems of prescribing lithium is that many manic patients won't take it. They feel good—very good—and they often don't want medication.

   See also H. Johnson, K. Olafsson, J. Andersen, P. Plenge, et al., "Lithium Every Second Day," *American Journal of Psychiatry* 146 (1989): 557, for a recent study on effective administration.
8. The discovery and early history of the minor tranquilizers (as the anxiolytics are called) is narrated candidly by Frank Berger, "Anxiety and the Discovery of Tranquilizers," and by Irvin Cohen, "The Benzodiazepines," in Ayd and Blackwell, *Discoveries in Biological Psychiatry,* 115–29 and 130–41, respectively.
9. The most optimistic recent estimate I know of concerning "percentage effectiveness" of the antipsychotics is: complete eradication of delusions and hallucinations, 22.5 percent; partial improvement, 60 percent; no improvement, 17.5 percent. This is from J. Chandler and G. Winokur, "How Antipsychotic Are the Antipsychotics? A Clinical Study of the Subjective Antipsychotic Effect of the Antipsychotics in Chronic Schizophrenia," *Annals of Clinical Psychiatry* 1 (1989): 215–20.
10. I volunteered to be a subject for David Rosenhan's classic study "On Being Sane in Insane Places," *Science* 179 (1973): 250–58. Rosenhan and I went into Norristown State Hospital together. He was ill-treated, as expected. I was wonderfully treated. This tale is worth a whole chapter itself—but in some other volume.
11. J. Wegner, F. Catalano, J. Gibralter, and J. Kane, "Schizophrenics with Tardive Dyskinesia," *Archives of General Psychiatry* 42 (1985): 860–65; ACNP-FDA Task Force, "Medical Intelligence—Drug Therapy," *New England Journal of Medicine* 130 (1973): 20–24. Fine recent coverage of tardive dyskinesia is in C. Gualtieri, *Neuropsychiatry and Behavioral Pharmacology* (New York: Springer-Verlag, 1991).
12. G. Cooper, "The Safety of Fluoxetine—An Update," *British Journal of Psychiatry* 153 (1988): 77–86; J. Wernicke, "The Side-Effect Profile and Safety of Fluoxetine," *Journal of Clinical Psychiatry* 46 (1985): 59–67; M. Teicher, C. Glod, and J. Cole, "Emergence of Intense Suicidal Preoccupation During Fluoxetine Treatment," *American Journal of Psychiatry* 147 (1990): 207–10.

    For a recent review of antidepressant side effects generally, see G. Beaumont, "Adverse Effects of Antidepressants," *International Clinical Psychopharmacology* 5 (1990): 61–66, and S. Preskorn and G. Jerkovich, "Central Nervous System Toxicity of Tricyclic Antidepressants: Phenomenology, Course, Risk Factors, and the Role of Drug Monitoring," *Journal of Clinical Psychopharmacology* 10 (1990): 88–95.

    The jury is still out on both the safety and the relative effectiveness of Prozac.
13. P. Tyrer, S. Murphy, D. Kingdon, et al., "The Nottingham Study of Neurotic Disorder: Comparison of Drug and Psychological Treatment," *Lancet,* 30 July 1988, 235–40, contends that the anti-anxiety drugs are clinically useless for neurotic disorders. A useful general review of rate of effectiveness is in Spiegel, *Psychopharmacology,* 15–19, 25–29.
14. J. Roache, "Addiction Potential of Benzodiazepines and Non-Benzodiazepine Anxiolytics," in *Advances in Alcohol and Substance Abuse* 9 (1990): 103–28, provides a balanced view. For an alarmist view, see S. Olivieri, T. Cantopher, and J. Edwards, "Two Hundred Years of Anxiolytic Drug Dependence," *Neuropharmacology* 25 (1986): 669–70. For a

more complacent view of the safety of anti-anxiety drugs, see A. Nagy, "Possible Reasons for a Negative Attitude to Benzodiazepines as Antianxiety Drugs," *Nordisk Psykiatrisk Tidsskrift* 4 (1987): 27–30. My best guess is that taken regularly, the anti-anxiety drugs tend to become impotent and addictive.

J. Tinklenberg, "Anti-Anxiety Medications and the Treatment of Anxiety," in Barchas et al., *Psychopharmacology,* 226–42, provides useful descriptive data.

15. For a recent upbeat review of lithium and its side effects, see J. Jefferson, "Lithium: The Present and the Future," *Journal of Clinical Psychiatry* 5 (1990): 4–8. Lithium is being used more and more on unipolar depression as well as on manic-depression. The data are suggestive, but the side effects are still definitely a danger.

16. K. Dodge, J. Bates, and G. Pettit, "Mechanisms in the Cycle of Violence," *Science* 250 (1990): 1678–83, is a "politically correct" article notable for the completeness of its environmental theorizing on the cycle of abuse, and its complete absence of genetic theorizing.

17. D. Buss, "Sex Differences in Human Mate Preferences: Evolutionary Hypotheses Tested in 37 Cultures," *Behavioral and Brain Sciences* 12 (1989): 1–49, discusses cogently the evolution of sexual attractiveness. See especially the quoted comment within by N. Thornhill on the evolution of feminine beauty. See also D. Buss, "Evolutionary Personality Psychology," *Annual Review of Psychology* 42 (1991): 439–91, for related theorizing.

18. Ludwig Wittgenstein, in *Philosophical Investigations* (London: Blackwell, 1953), paragraphs 77–83, sets the stage for this argument by showing that nouns in ordinary language have no *necessary* feature that defines them. Rather, nouns like *games* consist of a family resemblance of overlapping elements. Inasmuch as evolution selects traits like beauty, intelligence, and motor coordination, which have no necessary defining feature, the problem of finding their underlying genetic structure will be identical to the problem of finding a necessary condition defining a word. To say that these traits are *polygenic* (determined by many genes) is to miss the point.

On my analysis, then, these traits are not interestingly genetic—the combination of genes that underlie them is too large and overlapping. But they are heritable, nonetheless.

19. One quibble concerning personality traits in identical twins reared apart rises from selective placement by adoption agencies. When identical twins are separated and put up for adoption, agencies might place them similarly. So the offspring of religious parents might go to religious homes, and the offspring of rich parents to rich homes. When similarity of placement is quantified, however, this doesn't seem to count for much of the observed similarity.

Another quibble concerns how long the twins were reared together before separation. If they are not put up for adoption until late in childhood, the whole argument falls, and similarity could result either from genes or rearing. Most good twins-reared-apart studies, therefore, look only at twins separated early in the first year of life.

What is not a quibble is the possibility that personality is only indirectly heritable—that "nature works via nurture." So we will see below that optimism is heritable: Identical twins are more concordant for it than fraternal twins. But optimism is produced by lots of success (and pessimism by lots of failure) in life. Success and failure, in turn, are caused by characteristics like looks, strength, and motor coordination, all of which are physical and heritable. Identical twins are more concordant for these characteristics (both twins are similar on massiveness or runtiness) than are fraternal twins. So what might be directly heritable are physical characteristics that produce the personality trait, with the personality trait actually wholly caused by the environment. This argument applies to all molar personality characteristics.

T. Bouchard, D. Lykken, M. McGue, N. Segal, A. Tellegen, "Sources of Human Psychological Differences: The Minnesota Study of Twins Reared Apart," *Science* 250 (1990): 223–28, apart from being a classic experiment, is also articulate on this point. While these findings are sometimes dismissed as "gene-environment covariation," such dismissal misses the point. It is the environment that is primarily causal here, not the genes—and intervening to break the gene-environment covariation shows this.

Much of the future of environmental treatments for biologically loaded problems may be discovering ways *to break the gene-environment covariation.*

20. The best source for the details of this monumental study is Bouchard, et al., "Sources of Human Psychological Differences." I highly recommend it to the curious reader. It is of high scope and quality.

Some people still have the preconception that IQ is not at all genetic. They are wrong. If someone tells you this, they are either scientifically illiterate or ideologically blinded. Don't buy a used car from them. The identical-twin and adoptive data on IQ are massive and compelling: At least half (and in the Bouchard study, 75 percent) of the variance in IQ is genetic. What "intelligence" means, however, and what it predicts about achievement in life is much murkier.

The television-viewing study is R. Plomin, R. Corley, J. DeFries, and D. Fulker, "Individual Differences in Television Viewing in Early Childhood: Nature as Well as Nurture," *Psychological Science* 1 (1990): 371–77. The religiosity study is N. Waller, B. Kojetin, T. Bouchard, D. Lykken, and A. Tellegen, "Genetic and Environmental Influences on Religious Interests, Attitudes, and Values," *Psychological Science* 1 (1990): 138–42. The last four personality factors are from an analysis of the California Personality Inventory: T. Bouchard and M. McGue, "Genetic and Rearing Environmental Influences on Adult Personality: An Analysis of Adopted Twins Reared Apart," *Journal of Personality* 58 (1990): 263–92.

21. See N. Pedersen, G. McClearn, R. Plomin, J. Nesselroade, J. Berg, and U. DeFaire, "The Swedish Adoption/Twin Study of Aging: An Update," *Acta Geneticae Medicae et Gemellologiae* 40 (1991): 7–20. R. Plomin, M. Scheier, C. Bergeman, N. Pedersen, J. Nesselroade, and G. McClearn, "Optimism, Pessimism, and Mental Health: A Twin/Adoption Analysis," *Personality and Individual Differences* 13 (1992): 921–30, presents the optimism piece of it.

22. See B. Hutchings and S. Mednick, "Criminality in Adoptees and Their Adoptive and Biological Parents: A Pilot Study," in S. Mednick and K. Christiansen, eds., *Biosocial Bases of Criminal Behavior* (New York: Gardner, 1977), 127–42.

For similar logic applied to divorce, see M. McGue and D. Lykken, "Genetic Influence on Risk of Divorce," *Psychological Science* 3 (1992): 368–73. Divorce is partly heritable and seems to result partly from heritable characteristics that the two parties bring to their union.

23. It is not only the nonheritable half of personality that can change. The heritable half is made up of both directly genetic effects and "gene-environment covariance." This last bit of jargon is very important. "Gene-environment covariance" refers to the effective events in the environment that produce a trait but that are correlated with genes, and so do not appear to be environmental effects. So, for example, being very tall is heritable. Playing basketball professionally is also heritable. This is because tall people get into environments—eighth-grade basketball teams, for example—in which they excel and that reward them. They go on to become top basketball players. The genes don't directly get you to the NBA; success at basketball does. Success at basketball is the effective environmental cause—but it is correlated with the genes for tallness.

Gene-environment covariance can be broken by intervention, allowing change to occur even in the heritable fraction of personality. Tall people who don't get the opportunity to play basketball in high school don't get into the NBA. Another example of gene-environment covariance is crime. Crime is partly heritable, and psychopathic kids tend to alienate their parents and teachers. Their parents and teachers usually give up on them because they are so nasty. The kids, lacking a relationship with an adult, turn to the streets. This makes them street-smart criminals. If the parents persist and don't reject the kid—breaking the covariance—they may prevent the kid from becoming a criminal.

I thank David Lykken for this example. Its implications are profound.

CHAPTER 4 *Everyday Anxiety*

1. Judith Rapoport, in *The Boy Who Couldn't Stop Washing* (New York: Dutton, 1989), calls attention to trichotillomania—the disorder of pulling at your hair, twirling it, picking pimples, and extreme self-grooming. When severe, baldness and skin irritation result. She argues that it is a biological disorder related to obsessive-compulsive disorders and that it can be relieved with an antidepressant drug, Anafranil (clomipramine), that also relieves obsessive-compulsive disorder. While I don't agree that either trichotillomania or obsessive-compulsive disorder is a "brain" disorder, both do have biological *correlates.* I believe that the two are related to each other, and that both are related to the evolution of grooming, in the large sense.
2. Randolph Nesse uses the oil-light metaphor in "What Good Is Feeling Bad? The Evolutionary Benefits of Psychic Pain," *The Sciences* (1991): 30–37.
3. Developed by Charles Spielberger in collaboration with G. Jacobs, R. Crane, S. Russell, L. Westberry, L. Barker, E. Johnson, J. Knight, and E. Marks. I have selected the trait-anxiety questions, inverting some of the scoring of the negatively worded items for easy self-scoring. Dr. Spielberger has kindly provided comparison norms as well.
4. Benson's suggested technique (as explained in *The Relaxation Response* [New York: Morrow, 1975]) combines progressive relaxation, nasal breathing, and meditation. See E. Jacobson's classic *Progressive Relaxation* (Chicago: University of Chicago Press, 1938) for the original technique. Neither of these is a quick "how to" manual, however.

   The single best quick technique is called *applied relaxation training.* It is based on a therapy developed by Lars Goren-Ost ("Applied Relaxation: Description of a Coping Technique and Review of Controlled Studies," *Behaviour Research and Therapy* 25 [1987]: 397–410). A simple five-page "how to do it" is found in the appendix of D. Clark, "Anxiety States: Panic and Generalized Anxiety," in K. Hawton, P. Salkovskis, J. Kirk, and D. Clark, eds., *Cognitive Behaviour Therapy for Psychiatric Problems: A Practical Guide* (Oxford: Oxford University Press, 1989), 92–96. This technique takes you from progressive relaxation to relaxing while engaged in everyday activities.
5. For a meta-analysis (composite analysis of many studies), see K. Eppley, A. Abrams, and J. Shear, "Differential Effects of Relaxation Techniques on Trait Anxiety: A Meta-analysis," *Journal of Clinical Psychology* 45 (1989): 957–74. In their review of seventy studies, TM does best, exceeding progressive relaxation and other relaxation and meditation techniques, which all reduce trait anxiety as well. Recent evidence also suggests benefits of meditation for even the severely anxious patient: See J. Kabat-Zinn, A. Massion, J. Kristeller, et al., "Effectiveness of Meditation-Based Stress Reduction Program in the Treatment of Anxiety Disorders," *American Journal of Psychiatry* 149 (1992): 937–43. See also G. Butler, M. Fennell, P. Robson, and M. Gelder, "Comparison of Behavior Therapy and

Cognitive Behavior Therapy in the Treatment of Generalized Anxiety Disorder," *Journal of Consulting and Clinical Psychology* 59 (1991): 167–75.

6. My one warning about meditation and relaxation concerns depression. I do not recommend either of these techniques if you are highly depressed (see chapter 8). Both relaxation and meditation work by lowering autonomic nervous system arousal. Highly depressed people (who are not agitated) need autonomic revving-up, and not dampening, since lowering arousal further can feed into their depression. Adverse effects of TM are not unknown, but the majority of practitioners report no adverse effects at all. See L. Otis, "Adverse Effects of Transcendental Meditation," in D. Shapiro and R. Walsh, eds., *Meditation: Classic and Contemporary Perspectives* (New York: Aldine, 1984), 201–8.

CHAPTER 5 *Catastrophic Thinking*

1. You might wonder about my choice of sex for case histories. When there is a clear prevalence for females, as there is for panic (two to one, women versus men), I choose *she.* If there is a clear prevalence for males, I use *he.* If there is no difference, I will use *he* and note the prevalence.
2. It has become fashionable to claim that the distinction between the biological and the psychological is not meaningful. It is all a pseudoquestion of historic interest only, some writers tell us. Or we're told that there is no deep distinction between mind and body. "Reductionists" tell us that all psychological events are ultimately biological, but that we just don't know the biology of them yet. "Interactionists" tell us that all psychological events are just the interaction of environmental events and biology.

   I plead agnosticism.

   Both reductionism and interactionism are philosophical positions, unproven matters of faith. One or the other might turn out to be correct—in a thousand years. It may ultimately turn out, for example, that cognitive therapy works because it changes the trait of pessimism that is located in a presently unknown chemical pathway in the hippocampus. Such a possibility, however, is completely unhelpful to the consumer trying to decide if cognitive therapy or imipramine is the best thing for her depression *now.* Such a possibility is completely irrelevant to the scientist trying to find out *now* if pessimism is a risk factor for depression.

   Right now, 1994, there are clear and useful distinctions between the biological and the psychological. Psychological events are measured at the molar level, the level of the whole intact person: Feelings, thoughts, traits, and behaviors are examples. Biological events don't require a whole person for measurement; they are specified molecularly: Neural firings, endorphin changes, and dexamethasone suppression are examples. When something is primarily psychological, this means that it can be treated by interventions involving the whole person—cognitive therapy, psychoanalysis, hypnosis, behavior therapy, meditation, or day care, for example. When something is primarily biological, this means that intervention can successfully occur at the molecular level: drugs, surgery, or electroconvulsive shock, for example.

   When someone tells you that there is no biological/psychological distinction, that the nature/nurture dispute is settled or passé, or that there is no mind/body distinction, keep a close eye on your wallet. That someone is stating an article of faith, one that is unhelpful to any actual scientist or consumer of therapy and, worse, that is intellectually anesthetic.
3. This is a highly reliable finding, shown in dozens of studies. See, for example, M. Liebowitz, J. Gorman, A. Fryer, et al., "Lactate Provocation of Panic Attacks," *Archives of General Psychiatry* 41 (1984): 764–70; and J. Gorman, M. Liebowitz, A. Fryer, et al., "Lactate

Infusions in Obsessive-Compulsive Disorder," *American Journal of Psychiatry* 142 (1985): 864–66.

4. See S. Torgersen, "Genetic Factors in Anxiety Disorders," *Archives of General Psychiatry* 40 (1983): 1085–89; and R. Crowe, "Panic Disorder: Genetic Considerations," *Journal of Psychiatric Research* 24 (1990): 129–34.
5. See D. Charney and G. Heninger, "Abnormal Regulation of Noradrenergic Function in Panic Disorders," *Archives of General Psychiatry* 43 (1986): 1042–54; and E. Reiman, M. Raichle, E. Robins, et al., "The Application of Positron Emission Tomography to the Study of Panic Disorder," *American Journal of Psychiatry* 143 (1986): 469–77.
6. See, for example, S. Svebak, A. Cameron, S. Levander, "Clonazepam and Imipramine in the Treatment of Panic Attacks," *Journal of Clinical Psychiatry* 51 (1990): 14–17; and G. Tesar, "High-Potency Benzodiazepines for Short-term Management of Panic Disorder: The U.S. Experience," *Journal of Clinical Psychiatry* 51 (1990): 4–10.
7. The proceedings of this conference are published in S. J. Rachman and J. Maser, eds., *Panic: Psychological Perspectives* (Hillsdale, N.J.: Erlbaum, 1988).
8. Parallel examples can be generated for fear of going crazy and fear of losing control, two other common contents of a panic attack. In each case, the first bodily sensations are misinterpreted as a sign of insanity or of losing control. The vicious cycle of misinterpreting mounting anxiety symptoms as further evidence of imminent cataclysm then starts.
9. This dialogue is adapted from D. Clark, "Anxiety States: Panic and Generalized Anxiety," in K. Hawton, P. Salkovskis, J. Kirk, and D. Clark, eds., *Cognitive Behaviour Therapy for Psychiatric Problems: A Practical Guide* (Oxford: Oxford University Press, 1989), 76–77.
10. For relapse with Xanax (alprazolam), see, for example, J. Pecknold, R. Swinson, K. Kuch, C. Lewis, "Alprazolam in Panic Disorder and Agoraphobia: Results from a Multicenter Trial: III. Discontinuation Effects," *Archives of General Psychiatry* 45 (1988): 429–36. A very informative lay article about Xanax, "High Anxiety," appeared in *Consumer Reports* January 1993, 19–24.
11. On 25–27 September 1991, NIMH brought the leading figures in panic together again for a "consensus" meeting, a trial by jury of the panic therapies. Their conclusion was equivocal and disappointing. The numbers presented agree very closely with my summary table. In spite of this, the jury did not explicitly compare the cognitive therapies to the drug therapies, and therefore no mention was made of the superiority of the cognitive treatment to drugs. I can only speculate as to what interests were served by this, but I think their conclusions were pusillanimous and a disservice to the general public. See "National Institutes of Health Consensus Development Statement. Treatment of Panic Disorder. September 25–27, 1991." See especially J. Margraf, D. Barlow, D. Clark, and M. Telch, "Psychological Treatment of Panic: Work in Progress on Outcome, Active Ingredients, and Follow-up," *Behaviour Research and Therapy* 31 (1993): 1–8.

    Since my conclusions are not as yet universally accepted, I want to list the main outcome studies that document the unusually powerful effects of the cognitive treatment:

    D. Clark, M. Gelder, P. Salkovskis, A. Hackman, H. Middleton, and P. Anastasiades, "Cognitive Therapy for Panic: Comparative Efficacy." Paper presented at the annual meeting of the American Psychiatric Association, New York City, May 1990.

    A. Beck, L. Sokol, D. Clark, B. Berchick, and F. Wright, "Focussed Cognitive Therapy of Panic Disorder: A Crossover Design and One Year Follow-up" (manuscript, 1991).

    L. Michelson and K. Marchione, "Cognitive, Behavioral, and Physiologically-based Treatments of Agoraphobia: A Comparative Outcome Study." Paper presented at the annual meeting of the American Association for the Advancement of Behavior Therapy, Washington, D.C., November 1989.

L. Ost, "Cognitive Therapy Versus Applied Relaxation in the Treatment of Panic Disorder." Paper presented at the annual meeting of the European Association of Behavior Therapy, Oslo, September 1991.

J. Margraf and S. Schneider, "Outcome and Active Ingredients of Cognitive-Behavioural Treatments for Panic Disorder." Paper presented at the annual meeting of the American Association for the Advancement of Behavior Therapy, New York City, November 1991.

CHAPTER 6 *Phobias*

1. Through mistranslation, the CS and CR have become known as the "conditioned" stimulus and response. Condition*al* (that is, the conditional stimulus only acquires its properties conditionally, upon pairing with the US and the UR) is the actual meaning of the adjective, however.
2. J. Garcia and R. Koelling, "Relation of Cue to Consequence in Avoidance Learning," *Psychonomic Science* 4 (1966): 123–24.
3. For the detailed discussion and debate about these five problems, start with M. Seligman and J. Hager, eds., *The Biological Boundaries of Learning* (New York: Appleton-Century-Crofts, 1972).
4. The anesthesia experiment can be found in D. Roll and J. Smith, "Conditioned Taste Aversion in Anesthetized Rats," in Seligman and Hager, *The Biological Boundaries of Learning,* 98–102.

   Garcia tried his experiment with coyotes who made a habit of killing sheep. He laced ground lamb with nonlethal doses of poison. When the coyotes recovered, not only did they hate the taste of lamb, but they ran away from sheep! Lambs would actually chase them around the barnyard. When around lamb meat, the coyotes urinated on it and buried it. They didn't treat lamb meat as a mere signal that sickness was on its way; rather, they came to hate and fear sheep in themselves. See C. Gustavson, J. Garcia, W. Hankins, and K. Rusiniak, "Coyote Predation Control by Aversive Conditioning," *Science* 184 (1974): 581–83.

   Pavlovian conditioning is defined operationally: pairing of CS and US that results in a CR. This operational definition masks a basic distinction between two different processes that can be engaged.

   The first is bloodless and intellectual: A CS is treated as a mere signal for the US. Dogs salivated to the sight of Pavlov because they expected to be fed. Pavlov himself had not become like food.

   The second is deeper: The CS actually takes on the properties of the US, and becomes aversive in and of itself. Coyotes urinating on lamb meat, trying to bury it, and treating lambs as if they were dominant coyotes all indicate that the lamb has taken on aversive properties in itself. Unlike ordinary Pavlovian conditioning, whatever occurs during taste aversion does not occur at a rational level. Prepared CS-UR relationships, in my view, create conditioning at this deeper level.
5. L. Robins, J. Helzer, M. Weissman, et al., "Lifetime Prevalence of Specific Psychiatric Disorders at Three Sites," *Archives of General Psychiatry* 41 (1984): 949–58; I. Marks, "Epidemiology of Anxiety," *Social Psychiatry* 21 (1986): 167–71.
6. Until the early 1960s, psychoanalysis was the therapy used by default. The discovery of systematic desensitization and of flooding ended this. It is worth reading Freud's famous "Little Hans" case, which originated the Oedipal theory of phobias. See S. Freud, "Analysis of a Phobia in a Five-Year-Old Boy," in *The Complete Works of Sigmund Freud,* vol. 10, trans. J. Strachey (London: Hogarth Press, 1974), 5–100; and, for a demolition of Freud's

argument, J. Wolpe and S. J. Rachman, "Psychoanalytic 'Evidence': A Critique Based on Freud's Case of Little Hans," *Journal of Nervous and Mental Disease* 131 (1960): 135–47. See also H. Laughlin, *The Neuroses* (Washington, D.C.: Butterworth, 1967), 545–606, on phobias, for the analytic view at this time. The "never easy" comes from Laughlin. This view of phobias is—at last and deservedly—a dead horse.

7. L. Ost, U. Steiner, and J. Fellenius, "Applied Tension, Applied Relaxation, and the Combination in the Treatment of Blood Phobia," *Behaviour Research and Therapy* 27 (1989): 109–21. More recent reports suggest close to 100 percent cure with this procedure.
8. There are few noncase report studies of cognitive therapy for phobias. Those that exist show gains, but behavior therapy is added, so it is not possible to sort out any additional usefulness of the cognitive component. There are undeniable cognitive distortions in phobias, but I doubt that they can be countered directly by cognitive techniques. See G. Thorpe, J. Hacker, L. Cavallaro, and G. Kulberg, "Insight Versus Rehearsal in Cognitive-Behaviour Therapy: A Crossover Study with Sixteen Phobics," *Behavioural Psychotherapy* 15 (1987): 319–36.
9. In one study, 79 percent of agoraphobic patients who received cognitive therapy plus extinction for panic were panic free, as against only 39 percent with extinction alone. In L. Michelson and K. Marchione, "Cognitive, Behavioral, and Physiologically-based Treatments of Agoraphobia: A Comparative Outcome Study." Paper presented at the annual meeting of the American Association for the Advancement of Behavior Therapy, Washington, D.C., November 1989.

   R. Mattick and L. Peters, "Treatment of Severe Social Phobia: Effects of Guided Exposure With and Without Cognitive Restructuring," *Journal of Consulting and Clinical Psychology* 56 (1988): 251–60, suggest possible benefits of cognitive therapy with social phobias as well.
10. There are about a half dozen reasonably well done recent studies of the effects of various drugs on social phobias. See J. Gorman and L. Gorman, "Drug Treatment of Social Phobia," *Journal of Affective Disorders* 13 (1987): 183–92; A. Levin, F. Scheier, and M. Liebowitz, "Social Phobia: Biology and Pharmacology," *Clinical Psychology Review* 9 (1989): 129–40; M. Versiani, F. Mundim, A. Nardi, et al., "Tranycypromine in Social Phobia," *Journal of Clinical Psychopharmacology* 8 (1988): 279–83; M. Liebowitz, J. Gorman, A. Fryer, et al., "Pharmacotherapy of Social Phobia: An Interim Report of a Placebo-Controlled Comparison of Phenelzine and Atenolol," *Journal of Clinical Psychiatry* 49 (1988): 252–57; J. Reich and W. Yates, "A Pilot Study of the Treatment of Social Phobia with Alprazolam," *American Journal of Psychiatry* 145 (1988): 590–94; and M. Liebowitz, R. Campeas, A. Levin, et al., "Pharmacotherapy of Social Phobia," *Psychosomatics* 28 (1987): 305–8.

    Most of these studies show a 60 to 75 percent level of improvement with drugs (the MAO inhibitors are particularly effective). Unfortunately, most of these studies do not report what happens to the patients after drugs are discontinued. Those that do (Versiani et al., "Tranycypromine in Social Phobia"; Reich and Yates, "A Pilot Study") report very high relapse rates. R. Noyes, D. Chaudry, and D. Domingo, "Pharmacologic Treatment of Phobic Disorders," *Journal of Clinical Psychiatry* 47 (1986): 445–52, review this literature and conclude with two major cautions: A high dropout rate with drugs and a high relapse rate after drug discontinuation are likely. It is on this basis that I conclude that the drugs have only a cosmetic effect on social anxiety.
11. See C. Zitrin, D. Klein, M. Woerner, and D. Ross, "Treatment of Phobias I: Comparison of Imipramine Hydrochloride and Placebo," *Archives of General Psychiatry* 40 (1983): 125–38, versus I. Marks, S. Gray, D. Cohen, et al., "Imipramine and Brief Therapist-Aided

Exposure in Agoraphobics Having Self-Exposure Homework," *Archives of General Psychiatry* 40 (1983): 153–62.

This is still rather a heated controversy, with the benefits of antidepressants alone and of exposure (extinction) alone in some doubt. One serious worry is the high relapse rate, perhaps over 50 percent, when drugs are stopped (see R. Noyes, M. Garvey, B. Cook, and L. Samuelson, "Problems with Tricyclic Anti-Depressant Use in Patients with Panic Disorder or Agoraphobia," *Journal of Clinical Psychiatry* 50 [1989]: 163–69). Similarly, extinction therapy alone has some lasting benefit five years after termination, with about 50 percent of patients doing well, but few completely well (see P. Lelliott, I. Marks, W. Monteiro, et al., "Agoraphobics 5 Years After Imipramine and Exposure: Outcome and Predictors," *Journal of Nervous and Mental Diseases* 175 [1987]: 599–605). So each alone has some lasting benefit but is far from a cure.

The combination of exposure and antidepressants looks like the least controversial treatment of choice. Improvement rate may be as high as 90 percent with the combination (see J. Ballenger, "Pharmacotherapy of the Panic Disorders," *Journal of Clinical Psychiatry* 47 [1986]: 27–32). In a particularly well executed study, only the combination group improved, with the agoraphobes who had either tricyclics alone or exposure alone not improving significantly (see M. Telch, S. Agras, C. Taylor, et al., "Combined Pharmacological and Behavioural Treatment for Agoraphobia," *Behaviour Research and Therapy* 23 [1985]: 325–35). For other well-executed combined drug-and-exposure studies, see M. Mavissakalian and L. Michelson, "Two-Year Follow-up of Exposure and Imipramine Treatment of Agoraphobia," *American Journal of Psychiatry* 143 (1986): 1106–12.

For a quantitative review of the drug and psychotherapy literatures in agoraphobia, see R. Mattick, G. Andrews, D. Hadzi-Pavlovic, and H. Christensen, "Treatment of Panic and Agoraphobia: An Integrative Review," *Journal of Nervous and Mental Disease* 178 (1990): 567–76.

12. This case history comes from Isaac Marks, the leading contemporary British investigator of phobias.
13. See M. Seligman, "Preparedness and Phobias," *Behavior Therapy* 2 (1971): 307–20; and S. J. Rachman and M. Seligman, "Unprepared Phobias: Be Prepared," *Behaviour Research and Therapy* 14 (1976): 333–38.
14. A. Ohman, M. Fredrikson, K. Hugdahl, and P. Rimmo, "The Premise of Equipotentiality in Classical Conditioning: Conditioned Electrodermal Responses to Potentially Phobic Stimuli," *Journal of Experimental Psychology: General* 105 (1976): 313–37. For an articulate dissenter from the Ohman experiments and from the preparedness theory of phobias, see R. McNally, "Preparedness and Phobias: A Review," *Psychological Bulletin* 101 (1987): 283–303.
15. L. Ost and K. Hugdahl, "Acquisition of Phobias and Anxiety Response Patterns in Clinical Patients," *Behaviour Research and Therapy* 21 (1981): 623–31
16. S. Hygge and A. Ohman, "Modelling Processes in Acquisition of Fear: Vicarious Electrodermal Conditioning to Fear-Relevant Stimuli," *Journal of Personality and Social Psychology* 36 (1978): 271–79. For a beautifully done parallel experiment in nonhuman primates, see S. Mineka, M. Davidson, M. Cook, and R. Keir, "Observational Conditioning of Snake Fear in Rhesus Monkeys," *Journal of Abnormal Psychology* 93 (1984): 355–72.
17. Snakes and spiders make for stronger CSs than guns and knives, although the latter are more dangerous in cultural—but not evolutionary—fact than the former. See E. Cook, P. Hodes, and P. Lang, "Preparedness and Phobias: Effects of Stimulus Content on Human Visceral Conditioning," *Journal of Abnormal Psychology* 95 (1986): 195–207.

CHAPTER 7 *Obsessions*

1. As remembered from "What Do We Plant?," by Henry Abbey (1842–1911).
2. So catchy is this ditty that I read it once in fifth grade (some forty years ago) and it has stayed with me—intact—ever since, making monthly appearances on my jingle channel. Mark Twain, "Punch, Brothers, Punch" (1876), in *The Complete Humorous Sketches and Tales of Mark Twain,* ed. Charles Neider (Garden City, N.Y.: Doubleday, 1961), 303.

   Ethical considerations forbid my telling you the lyrics of the even catchier jingles.
3. D. Barlett and J. Steele, *Empire: The Life, Legend, and Madness of Howard Hughes* (New York: Norton, 1979), 233.
4. S. J. Rachman and R. Hodgson's classic book *Obsessions and Compulsions* (New York: Appleton-Century-Crofts, 1980) remains the definitive behavioral work on the topic. The questionnaire from this book is reproduced with minor changes.
5. Judith Rapoport, *The Boy Who Couldn't Stop Washing* (New York: Plume, 1990), 90–91. The evidence for heritability that follows comes from M. Lenane, S. Swedo, H. Leonard, et al., "Psychiatric Disorders in First Degree Relatives of Children and Adolescents with Obsessive Compulsive Disorder," *Journal of the American Academy of Child and Adolescent Psychiatry* 29 (1990): 407–12.
6. S. Turner, D. Beidel, and R. Nathan, "Biological Factors in Obsessive-Compulsive Disorders," *Psychological Bulletin* 97 (1985): 430–50; L. Baxter, M. Phelps, J. Mazziotta, et al., "Local Cerebral Glucose Metabolic Rates in Obsessive-Compulsive Disorder: A Comparison with Rates in Unipolar Depression and Normal Controls," *Archives of General Psychiatry* 44 (1987): 211–18; R. Rubin, J. Villanueva-Meyer, J. Ananth, et al., "Regional Xenon 133 Cerebral Blood Flow and Cerebral Technetium 99m HMPAO Uptake in Unmedicated Patients with Obsessive-Compulsive Disorder and Matched Normal Control Subjects," *Archives of General Psychiatry* 49 (1992): 695–702.

   The latest studies show normalization of brain function with Anafranil (clomipramine) treatment, fluoxetine treatment, and behavior therapy. See C. Benkelfat, T. Nordahl, W. Semple, et al., "Local Cerebral Glucose Metabolic Rates in Obsessive-Compulsive Disorder," *Archives of General Psychiatry* 47 (1990): 840–48; L. Baxter, J. Schwartz, K. Bergman, et al., "Caudate Glucose Metabolic Rate Changes with Both Drug and Behavior Therapy for Obsessive-Compulsive Disorder," *Archives of General Psychiatry* 49 (1992): 681–89; S. Swedo, P. Pietrini, H. Leonard, et al., "Cerebral Glucose Metabolism in Childhood-Onset Obsessive-Compulsive Disorder," *Archives of General Psychiatry* 49 (1992): 690–94.
7. Both Judith Rapoport, in *The Boy Who Couldn't Stop Washing,* and Isaac Marks and Adolf Tobena, in "Learning and Unlearning Fear: A Clinical and Evolutionary Perspective," *Neuroscience and Biobehavioral Reviews* 14 (1990): 365–84, have argued for an evolutionarily prepared substratum of OCD.
8. For recent studies of Anafranil (clomipramine), see M. Jenike, L. Baer, P. Summergrad, et al., "Obsessive-Compulsive Disorder: A Double-Blind, Placebo-Controlled Trial of Clomipramine in 27 Patients," *American Journal of Psychiatry* 146 (1989): 1328–30; R. Katz, J. DeVeaugh-Geiss, P. Landau, "Clomipramine in Obsessive-Compulsive Disorder," *Biological Psychiatry* 28 (1990): 401–14; M. Pato, T. Piggott, J. Hill, et al., "Controlled Comparison of Buspirone and Clomipramine in Obsessive-Compulsive Disorder," *American Journal of Psychiatry* 148 (1991): 127–29; and M. Mavissakalian, B. Jones, S. Olson, J. Perel, "Clomipramine in Obsessive-Compulsive Disorder: Clinical Response and Plasma Levels," *Journal of Clinical Psychopharmacology* 10 (1990): 261–68. See M. Trimble, "Worldwide Use of Clomipramine," *Journal of Clinical Psychiatry* 51 (1990): 51–54, for a review of eleven double-blind studies. Overall, slightly fewer than 50 percent of the

patients are improved to subclinical levels, and perhaps 25 percent are almost symptom free.

For side effects and the high relapse rate after drug discontinuation, see M. Pato, R. Zohar-Kadouch, J. Zohar, D. Murphy, "Return of Symptoms After Discontinuation of Clomipramine in Patients with Obsessive-Compulsive Disorder," *American Journal of Psychiatry* 145 (1988): 1521–25, which shows an 80 percent relapse rate; T. Piggott, M. Pato, S. Bernstein, et al., "Controlled Comparisons of Clomipramine and Fluoxetine in the Treatment of Obsessive-Compulsive Disorder," *Archives of General Psychiatry* 47 (1990): 926–32, which shows a comparable effect for fluoxetine to clomipramine and comparable high relapse after drug discontinuation; and J. Greist, "Treating the Anxiety: Therapeutic Options in Obsessive-Compulsive Disorder," *Journal of Clinical Psychiatry* 51 (1990): 29–34.

For an articulate critique of the biological viewpoint, see P. DeSilva and S. J. Rachman, *Obsessive-Compulsive Disorder: The Facts* (Oxford: Oxford University Press, 1992), 53–54.

9. The woodworking-film experiment was reported by M. Horowitz, "Intrusive and Repetitive Thoughts After Experimental Stress," *Archives of General Psychiatry* 32 (1975): 1457–63.
10. This case is adapted from I. Marks, S. J. Rachman, and R. Hodgson, "Treatment of Chronic Obsessive-Compulsive Neurosis by *in Vivo* Exposure," *British Journal of Psychiatry* 127 (1975): 349–64.
11. J. Greist, "Treatment for Obsessive Compulsive Disorder: Psychotherapies, Drugs, and Other Somatic Treatment," *Journal of Clinical Psychiatry* 51 (1990): 44–50. For a complete review of the dozen or more outcome studies of behavior therapy for OCD, see Rachman and Hodgson, *Obsessions and Compulsions*, 299–358; and DeSilva and Rachman, *Obsessive-Compulsive Disorder*, 53–54.

CHAPTER 8 *Depression*

1. I have spent most of my life writing about depression. Much of the material in this chapter is adapted from other things I have written, particularly from chapter 4, "Ultimate Pessimism," in *Learned Optimism* (New York: Knopf, 1991), 54–70.
2. See Seligman, *Learned Optimism*, for the grand tour of explanatory style. Detailed reviews of explanatory style and depression, and extensive bibliographies, can be found in C. Peterson and M. Seligman, "Causal Explanations as a Risk Factor for Depression: Theory and Evidence," *Psychological Review* 91 (1984): 347–74; in P. Sweeney, K. Anderson, and S. Bailey, "Attributional Style in Depression: A Meta-analytic Review," *Journal of Personality and Social Psychology* 50 (1986): 974–91; and in L. Abramson, G. Metalsky, and L. Alloy, "Hopelessness Depression: A Theory-Based Process-Oriented Sub-Type of Depression," *Psychological Review* 96 (1989): 358–72.
3. L. Robins, J. Helzer, M. Weissman, H. Orvaschel, E. Gruenberg, J. Burke, and J. Regier, "Lifetime Prevalence of Specific Psychiatric Disorders in Three Sites," *Archives of General Psychiatry* 41 (1984): 949–958G; G. Klerman and M. Weissman, "Increasing Rates of Depression," *Journal of the American Medical Association* 261 (1989): 2229–35.
4. G. Klerman, P. Lavori, J. Rice, T. Reich, J. Endicott, N. Andreason, M. Keller, and R. Hirschfeld, "Birth-Cohort Trends in Rates of Major Depressive Disorder Among Relatives of Patients with Affective Disorder," *Archives of General Psychiatry* 42 (1985): 689–93.
5. The finding that depression now starts younger comes from the elegant mathematization of the data from a study by T. Reich, P. Van Eerdewegh, J. Rice, J. Mullaney, G. Klerman,

and J. Endicott, "The Family Transmission of Primary Depressive Disorder," *Journal of Psychiatric Research* 21 (1987): 613–24.

6. P. Lewinsohn, P. Rohde, and J. Seeley, "Birth-Cohort Changes in the Occurrence of Depression: Are We Experiencing an Epidemic of Depression?" *Journal of Abnormal Psychology* 102 (1993): 110–20.
7. This is an area so obscured by ideology that you should be guided to the best *disinterested* study. I recommend the very careful review of the topic by S. Nolen-Hoeksema, "Sex Differences in Depression: Theory and Evidence," *Psychological Bulletin* 101 (1987): 259–82. A longer version is S. Nolen-Hoeksema, *Sex Differences in Depression* (Stanford, Calif.: Stanford University Press, 1990). An exhaustive bibliography of the topic and of the controversy discussed in the next few paragraphs of chapter 8 can be found there.
8. The most detailed argument for the close symptom correspondence of learned helplessness and *DSM-3*-diagnosed depression is made by J. Weiss, P. Simson, M. Ambrose, A. Webster, and L. Hoffman, "Neurochemical Basis of Behavioral Depression," *Advances in Behavioral Medicine* 1 (1985): 253–75. This paper and the important work of Sherman and Petty (below) also lay out the powerful brain-chemistry and pharmacological similarities between learned helplessness and depression (see A. Sherman and F. Petty, "Neurochemical Basis of Antidepressants on Learned Helplessness," *Behavioral and Neurological Biology* 30 [1982]: 119–34).
9. Three psychologists have made the major contributions to the recent study of rumination: Julius Kuhl, Susan Nolen-Hoeksema, and Harold Zullow. See J. Kuhl, "Motivational and Functional Helplessness: The Moderating Effect of State- Versus Action-Orientation," *Journal of Personality and Social Psychology* 40 (1981): 155–70; H. Zullow, "The Interaction of Rumination and Explanatory Style in Depression." Master's thesis, University of Pennsylvania, 1984; and Nolen-Hoeksema, *Sex Differences in Depression.*
10. M. McCarthy, "The Thin Ideal, Depression, and Eating Disorders in Women," *Behaviour Research and Therapy* 28 (1990): 205–15.
11. J. Girgus, S. Nolen-Hoeksema, M. Seligman, G. Paul, and H. Spears, "Why Do Girls Become More Depressed Than Boys in Early Adolescence?" Paper presented at the meeting of the American Psychological Association, San Francisco, August 1991.
12. S. Hollon, R. DeRubeis, and M. Evans, "Combined Cognitive Therapy and Pharmacotherapy in the Treatment of Depression," in D. Manning and A. Frances, eds., *Combined Pharmacotherapy and Psychotherapy in Depression* (Washington, D.C.: American Psychiatric Press, 1990), 35–64. In one well-publicized study, eleven patients who responded well to imipramine took the drug continuously for five years, and only one became depressed. Of nine patients given a placebo, five became depressed. See D. Kupfer, E. Frank, J. Perel, et al., "Five-Year Outcome for Maintenance Therapies for Recurrent Depression," *Archives of General Psychiatry* 49 (1992): 769–73. This suggests that if antidepressant drugs work for you and curtail depression, stay on them even when you're feeling fine, to prevent recurrence.
13. For a review of the effectiveness of ECS, see M. Fink, *Convulsive Therapy: Therapy and Practice* (New York: Raven Press, 1979). There is now a whole journal, *Convulsive Therapy,* devoted to ECS. For a cautious view, see J. Taylor and J. Carroll, "Current Issues in Electroconvulsive Therapy," *Psychological Reports* 60 (1987): 747–58. For recent findings, see D. Devanand, H. Sackeim, and J. Prudic, "Electro-convulsive Therapy in the Treatment-Resistant Patient," *Psychiatric Clinics of North America* 14 (1991): 905–23.
14. A. Beck, *Cognitive Therapy and the Emotional Disorders* (New York: New American Library, 1976), 233–62.
15. The basic reference to the NIMH collaborative study is I. Elkin, M. Shea, J. Watkins, S.

Imber, et al., "National Institute of Mental Health Treatment of Depression Collaborative Research Program: General Effectiveness of Treatments," *Archives of General Psychiatry* 46 (1989): 971–82. The reader should be warned that this is still a guild "hot potato" and that even now the data are disputed and are in the process of being reanalyzed.

The latest findings are about recurrence: M. Shea, I. Elkin, S. Imber, et al., "Course of Depressive Symptoms over Follow-up," *Archives of General Psychiatry* 49 (1992): 782–87; and M. Evans, S. Hollon, R. DeRubeis, et al., "Differential Relapse Following Cognitive Therapy and Pharmacotherapy for Depression," *Archives of General Psychiatry* 49 (1992): 802–8. Both of these major studies find that cognitive therapy fares better than drug treatment (which is tapered off during follow-up) on preventing recurrence of depression. But there is still considerable recurrence even in the cognitive-therapy groups, with drugs showing about 50 percent recurrence over two years and cognitive therapy about 30 percent recurrence.

16. Elkin et al., "National Institute of Mental Health Treatment of Depression Collaborative Research Program," 971–82.
17. G. Klerman, M. Weissman, B. Rounsaville, and E. Chevron, *Interpersonal Psychotherapy of Depression* (New York: Basic Books, 1984).

CHAPTER 9 *The Angry Person*

1. Developed by Charles Spielberger in collaboration with G. Jacobs, R. Crane, S. Russell, L. Westberry, L. Barker, E. Johnson, J. Knight, and E. Marks. I have selected the trait-anger questions, inverting some of the scoring of the negatively worded items for easy self-scoring.
2. R. Ardrey, *The Territorial Imperative* (New York: Atheneum, 1966).
3. J. Hokanson, "The Effects of Frustration and Anxiety on Aggression," *Journal of Abnormal Psychology* 62 (1961): 346; J. Hokanson and M. Burgess, "The Effects of Three Types of Aggression on Vascular Processes," *Journal of Abnormal and Social Psychology* 65 (1962): 446–49; R. Williams, J. Barefoot, and R. Shekelle, "The Health Consequences of Hostility," in M. Chesney and R. Rosenman, eds., *Anger and Hostility in Cardiovascular and Behavioral Disorders* (New York: McGraw-Hill, 1985), 173–85.
4. S. Greer and T. Morris, "Psychological Attributes of Women Who Develop Breast Cancer: A Controlled Study," *Journal of Psychosomatic Research* 19 (1975): 147–53; M. Watson, S. Greer, L. Rowden, C. Gorman, et al., "Relationship Between Emotional Control, Adjustment to Cancer and Depression and Anxiety in Breast Cancer Patients," *Psychological Medicine* 21 (1991): 51–57.
5. D. Spiegel, J. Bloom, H. Draemer, and E. Gottheil, "Effect of Psycho-Social Treatment on Survival of Patients with Metastatic Breast Cancer," *Lancet* 2 (1989): 888–91.
6. S. Greer and T. Morris, "Psychological Attributes of Women Who Develop Breast Cancer," found higher rates of breast cancer for both anger suppressors and exploders. There is one very serious statistical problem in this study. With a complex trait like Type C, there is a technique called *partial correlation* that can tell us what the active ingredient—anger suppression, helplessness, or lack of fighting spirit—is in the higher rates of cancer. These authors consistently fail to use it.

   See M. Seligman, *Learned Optimism* (New York: Knopf, 1991), 167–78, for the documentation of the cancer link to helplessness, hopelessness, and depression. As things stand, my best guess is that any Type C link to breast cancer operates through helplessness, and not through anger suppression.
7. Williams et al., "The Health Consequences of Hostility," in Chesney and Rosenman, *Anger and Hostility in Cardiovascular and Behavioral Disorders,* 173–85; K. Matthews, D. Glass,

R. Rosenman, and R. Bortner, "Competitive Drive, Pattern A, and Coronary Heart Disease: A Further Analysis of Some Data from the Western Collaborative Group Study," *Journal of Chronic Diseases* 30 (1977): 489–98; G. Ironson, C. Taylor, M. Boltwood, et al., "Effects of Anger on Left Ventricle Rejection Fraction in Coronary Artery Disease," *American Journal of Cardiology* 70 (1992): 281–85.

8. J. Hokanson and M. Burgess, "The Effects of Status, Type of Frustration, and Aggression on Vascular Processes," *Journal of Abnormal and Social Psychology* 65 (1962): 232–37; J. Hokanson and R. Edelman, "Effects of Three Social Responses on Vascular Processes," *Journal of Abnormal and Social Psychology* 71 (1966): 442–47.
9. You might ask why regular exercise—e.g., marathon running—decreases your risk of heart attack, since it raises heart rate. During the actual running of the marathon, your heart rate goes way up. But your resting heart rate level during the other twenty-one hours of the day goes down. Indeed, this may be the main benefit of exercise. Your total number of beats per year is now lower, and you don't reach your beat allotment until later in life.
10. M. Weissman and E. Paykel, *The Depressed Woman* (Chicago: University of Chicago Press, 1974), 138–53.
11. K. Dodge and N. Crick, "Social Information-Processing Bases of Aggressive Behavior in Children," *Personality and Social Psychology Bulletin* 16 (1990): 8–22. Dodge's work is pioneering and has generated an intervention program for conduct disorder in schools.
12. S. Nolen-Hoeksema, J. Girgus, and M. Seligman, "Depression in Children of Families in Turmoil" (unpublished manuscript). I want especially to exempt my valued colleagues, Joan Girgus and Susan Nolen-Hoeksema, from any responsibility for my speculation that less parental fighting will lower the amount of depression in children.
13. See chapter 8 of my *Learned Optimism,* on which this discussion of parental turmoil is based. Three other important references are J. Wallerstein and S. Blakeslee, *Second Chances: Men, Women, and Children a Decade After Divorce* (New York: Ticknor & Fields, 1989) (but see R. Forehand, "Parental Divorce and Adolescent Maladjustment: Scientific Inquiry vs. Public Information," *Behaviour Research and Therapy* 30 [1992]: 319–28, for a critique of such studies as Wallerstein and Blakeslee's); E. Hetherington, M. Cox, and C. Roger, "Effects of Divorce on Parents and Children," in M. E. Lamb, ed., *Nontraditional Families* (Hillside, N.J.: Erlbaum, 1982); and E. Cummings, D. Vogel, J. Cummings, and M. El-Sheikh, "Children's Responses to Different Forms of Expression of Anger Between Adults," *Child Development* 60 (1989): 1392–1404.
14. S. Feshbach, "The Catharsis Hypothesis and Some Consequences of Interaction with Aggression and Neutral Play Objects," *Journal of Personality* 24 (1956): 449–62; L. Berkowitz, "Experimental Investigations of Hostility Catharsis," *Journal of Consulting and Clinical Psychology* 35 (1970): 1–7. Carol Tavris's discussion of the catharsis view in her excellent book *Anger: The Misunderstood Emotion* (New York: Touchstone, 1989) is particularly lucid.
15. Raymond Novaco, *Anger Control* (Lexington, Mass.: D. C. Heath, 1975), 52–67. This is a good book for the professional, detailing one small-scale outcome study and a variety of cognitive-behavioral techniques for controlling anger.
16. This example is from L. Powell and C. Thoreson, "Modifying the Type A Pattern: A Small Group Treatment Approach," in J. A. Blumenthal and D. C. McKee, eds., *Applications in Behavioral Medicine and Health Psychology: A Clinician's Source Book* (Sarasota, Fla.: Professional Resource Exchange, 1987), 171–207.
17. Novaco, *Anger Control,* 8–12. See also A. Goldstein and H. Keller, *Aggressive Behavior: Assessment and Intervention* (New York: Pergamon, 1987), 139–44.

    Several investigators are presently developing new strategies for anger control. These are summarized in D. Goleman, "Strategies for Lifting Spirits Are Emerging from Studies," *New York Times*, 30 December 1992, C6.

18. Sharon Bower, *Assert Yourself* (Boston: Addison-Wesley, 1975).

CHAPTER 10 *Post-traumatic Stress*

1. The case of Hector and Jodi is adapted and modified to protect the privacy of the family. The case comes from the files of Dr. Camille Wortman, the leading researcher on the long-term consequences of bereavement.
2. E. Lindemann, "The Symptomatology and Management of Acute Grief," *American Journal of Psychiatry* 101 (1944): 141–48.
3. D. Lehman, C. Wortman, and A. Williams, "Long-term Effects of Losing a Spouse or Child in a Motor Vehicle Crash," *Journal of Personality and Social Psychology* 52 (1987): 218–31.
4. J. Kluznik, N. Speed, C. Van Valkenberg, and R. Magraw, "Forty-Year Follow-up of United States Prisoners of War," *American Journal of Psychiatry* 143 (1986): 1443–45.
5. Reliable statistics for unreported rape are hard to get, and increasingly they are becoming ideologically obfuscated. L. Gise and P. Paddison, "Rape, Sexual Abuse, and Its Victims," *Psychiatric Clinics of North America* 11 (1988): 629–48, make the one-in-three lifetime guess.

   The official diagnostic criteria for PTSD are now softening, particularly in response to the "Rape Trauma Syndrome." No longer will the criteria include such language as "beyond the ordinary range of human loss." *DSM-4*'s description of a qualifying event will probably be "actual or threatened death or injury, or a threat to the physical integrity of oneself or others." See *DSM-4 Options Book* (Washington, D.C.: American Psychiatric Association, 1991), H-17.
6. This case is adapted from S. Bowie, D. Silverman, S. Kalick, and S. Edbril, "Blitz Rape and Confidence Rape: Implications for Clinical Intervention," *American Journal of Psychotherapy* 44 (1990): 180–88. They distinguish between a blitz rape, which involves an unknown assailant attacking out of the blue, and a confidence rape, which involves someone you know. Their data is based on one thousand rape victims. Unfortunately, they do not tell us if the prognoses for PTSD and recovery differ with the two kinds of rapes.
7. B. Rothbaum, E. Foa, D. Riggs, T. Murdock, and W. Walsh, "A Prospective Examination of Post-Traumatic Stress Disorder in Rape Victims," *Journal of Traumatic Stress* 5 (1992): 455–75.
8. The classic modern paper about reaction to rape, its typology, and its duration is A. Burgess and L. Holmstrom, "Adaptive Strategies and Recovery from Rape," *American Journal of Psychiatry* 136 (1979): 1278–82. B. Rothbaum et al., "A Prospective Examination of Post-Traumatic Stress Disorder in Rape Victims," present the most complete picture of the sequelae in the first three months following rape. S. Girelli, P. Resick, S. Marhoefer-Dvorak, and C. Hutter, "Subjective Distress and Violence During Rape: The Effects on Long-term Fear," *Violence and Victims* 1 (1986): 35–46, report prognosis to be a function of distress, not violence. D. Kilpatrick, B. Saunders, A. Amick-McMullan, et al., "Victim and Crime Factors Associated with the Development of Crime-Related Post-Traumatic Stress Disorder," *Behavior Therapy* 20 (1989): 199–214, in contrast, report that life threat and violence best predict chronic PTSD.

   D. Kilpatrick, B. Saunders, L. Veronen, C. Best, and J. Von, "Criminal Victimization: Lifetime Prevalence, Reporting to Police, and Psychological Impact," *Crime and Delinquency* 33 (1987): 479–89, report the seventeen-year follow-up.

9. A. Feinstein and R. Dolan, "Predictors of Post-Traumatic Stress Disorder Following Physical Trauma: An Examination of the Stressor Criterion," *Psychological Medicine* 21 (1991): 85–91.
10. L. Weisaeth, "A Study of Behavioural Responses to Industrial Disaster," *Acta Psychiatrica Scandinavia* 80 (1989): 13–24; A. McFarlane, "The Aetiology of Post-Traumatic Morbidity: Predisposing, Precipitating, and Perpetuating Factors," *British Journal of Psychiatry* 154 (1989): 1221–28; Z. Solomon, M. Kotler, and M. Mikulincer, "Combat-Related Posttraumatic Stress Disorder Among Second-Generation Holocaust Survivors: Preliminary Findings," *American Journal of Psychiatry* 145 (1988): 865–68; Z. Solomon, B. Oppenheimer, Y. Elizur, M. Waysman, "Exposure to Recurrent Combat Stress: Can Successful Coping in a Second War Heal Combat-Related PTSD from the Past?" *Journal of Anxiety Disorders* 4 (1990): 141–45; U. Malt and L. Weisaeth, "Disaster Psychiatry and Traumatic Stress Studies in Norway," *Acta Psychiatrica Scandinavia* 80 (1989): 7–12.
11. T. Yager, R. Laufer, and M. Gallops, "Some Problems Associated with War Experience in Men of the Vietnam Generation," *Archives of General Psychiatry* 41 (1984): 327–33, present grim statistics on the aftermath of the Vietnam War for veterans. These authors are not the skeptics.
12. K. Erikson, *Everything in Its Path: Destruction of Community in the Buffalo Creek Flood* (New York: Simon and Schuster, 1976), movingly narrates the destruction of an Appalachian community and the plight of the dispossessed survivors. What Erikson fails to make clear, however, is that the survivors who so wrenchingly told him their awful stories were in the middle of suing the Pittston Company for the ruin of their lives and the dissolution of their community.
13. J. Frank, T. Kosten, E. Giller, and E. Dan, "A Randomized Clinical Trial of Phenelzine and Imipramine for Posttraumatic Stress Disorder," *American Journal of Psychiatry* 145 (1988): 1289–91; J. Davidson, H. Kudler, R. Smith, et al., "Treatment of PTSD with Amitriptyline and Placebo," *Archives of General Psychiatry* 47 (1990): 250–60. For a review of twenty drug studies for PTSD, see M. Friedman, "Toward Rational Pharmacotherapy for Posttraumatic Stress Disorder: An Interim Report," *American Journal of Psychiatry* 145 (1988): 281–85.
14. James Pennebaker, *Opening Up* (New York: Morrow, 1990), 37–51, 94–97. I recommend this book to all students of PTSD.
15. E. Foa, B. Rothbaum, D. Riggs, and T. Murdock, "Treatment of Post-Traumatic Stress Disorder in Rape Victims," *Journal of Consulting and Clinical Psychology* 59 (1991): 715–23.
16. Foa et al., "Treatment of Post-Traumatic Stress Disorder in Rape Victims." Other studies that suggest some relief produced by cognitive and behavioral treatment of PTSD are E. Frank, B. Anderson, B. Stewart, C. Dacu, et al., "Efficacy of Cognitive Behavior Therapy and Systematic Desensitization in the Treatment of Rape Trauma," *Behavior Therapy* 19 (1988): 403–20; and P. Resick, C. Jordan, S. Girelli, C. Hutter, et al., "A Comparative Outcome Study of Behavioral Group Therapy for Sexual Assault Victims," *Behavior Therapy* 19 (1988): 385–401.

    An easy-to-follow manual for such exposure therapy is H. Moore, *Traumatic Incident Reduction: A Cognitive-Emotional Resolution of the Post-Traumatic Stress Disorder (PTSD)* (Clearwater, Fla., 1991). Patients are cycled repeatedly through a mental viewing of the precipitating incident, until the response becomes "lighter." Using TIR, Moore reports dramatic improvement in a brief time, but what is needed is a well-controlled outcome test of these procedures.
17. Edna Foa, personal communication, 18 July 1992. Foa is a professor at the Medical

College of Pennsylvania, Department of Psychiatry, Center for the Treatment and Study of Anxiety. Because this is the pioneering center in the treatment of rape, and because so few centers are presently treating rape effectively, I include the center's phone number: (215) 842-4010.

The study is mentioned in E. Foa and D. Riggs's comprehensive "Post-Traumatic Stress Disorder in Rape Victims," *American Psychiatric Press Review of Psychiatry* 12 (1992): 273–303. See also P. Resick and M. Schnicke, "Cognitive Processing Therapy for Sexual Assault Survivors," *Journal of Consulting and Clinical Psychology* 60 (1992): 748–56.

CHAPTER 11 *Sex*

1. Sexologists refer to these layers as *gender* identity, *gender* role, and the like. I find the word *gender* in such usage unpalatable. Pronouns, but little else, can be properly said to have gender. This is more than a grammarian's reservation, however: *Gender* in place of *sex* is a desiccating word, a eunuch word. Like the *id* of Freud's translators in place of his original *das Es, gender* dries up the vital fluids that pulsate through erotic life.

   John Money, a modern pioneer in research on sexuality, is most responsible for introducing *gender* to mean more than what pronouns have. Underlying his attempt is the distinction between sex—your genital configuration—and gender—your status as male and female, a much broader idea than what is dictated by your genitals. As laudable as this distinction may be, sexology has become a field with impenetrable jargon ("Let's do it, let's fall in limerence"). For a history and apologia for some of this jargon, see J. Money, "The Concept of Gender Identity Disorder in Childhood and Adolescence After 37 Years." Paper presented at a conference on gender identity and development, St. George's Hospital, London, March 1992.
2. D. Barlow, G. Abel, and E. Blanchard, "Gender Identity Change in a Transsexual: An Exorcism," *Archives of Sexual Behavior* 6 (1977): 387–95.
3. In the only well-documented report of psychotherapy changing sexual identity that I can find, three yeoman behavior therapists attempted very intensive therapy to change, piece by piece, the feminine motor behaviors, role behaviors, masturbation, and fantasies in sequence over the course of many months. Three transsexual men were so treated. In only one of the three cases was clear long-term success obtained. See D. Barlow, G. Abel, and E. Blanchard, "Gender Identity Change in Transsexuals," *Archives of General Psychiatry* 36 (1979): 1001–7.
4. B. Kuiper and P. Cohen-Kettenis, "Sex Reassignment Surgery: A Study of 141 Dutch Transsexuals," *Archives of Sexual Behavior* 17 (1988): 439–57; M. Ross and J. Need, "Effects of Adequacy of Gender Reassignment on Psychological Adjustment: A Follow-up of Fourteen Male-to-Female Patients," *Archives of Sexual Behavior* 18 (1989): 145–53.
5. I want to call the reader's attention to an alternative theory: R. Pillard and J. Weinrich, "The Periodic Table Model of the Gender Transpositions: Part I. A Theory Based on Masculinization and Defeminization of the Brain," *The Journal of Sex Research* 4 (1987): 425–54, is an oddly brilliant attempt to explain the variations in sexual identity and behavior with two simple principles: masculinization and defeminization, both influenced by genes, hormones, and nurture. So speculative is this theory (and mine as well) that I leave it to future research to pass judgment.
6. J. Money and J. Dalery, "Iatrogenic Homosexuality: Gender Identity in Seven 46XX Chromosomal Females with Hyperadrenocortical Hermaphroditism Born with a Penis, Three Reared as Boys, Four Reared as Girls," *Journal of Homosexuality* 1 (1976): 357–71; J. Money, M. Schwartz, and V. Lewis, "Adult Heterosexual Status and Fetal Hormonal

Masculinization and Demasculinization: 46XX Congenital Virilizing Adrenal Hyperplasia and 46XY Androgen-Insensitivity Syndrome Compared," *Psychoneuroendocrinology* 9 (1984): 405–14; J. Money, "Sin, Sickness, or Status?" *American Psychologist* 42 (1987): 384–99.

7. V. Lewis and J. Money, "Gender Identity/Role: GI/R Part A: XY (Androgen-Insensitivity) Syndrome and XX (Rokitansky) Syndrome of Vaginal Atresia Compared," in L. Dennerstein and G. Burrows, eds., *Handbook of Psychosomatic Obstetrics and Gynecology* (New York: Elsevier, 1983), 51–60.
8. Sexologists lump the homosexual-versus-heterosexual "choice" into the same category ("sexual-object choice") as the "choice" of body parts, fetishistic objects, and erotic situations (S-M, pedophilia, flashing, etc.). I break these into two separate categories, sexual orientation and sexual preferences, because I think they are different processes. The homosexual/heterosexual "choice" is deeper, dictated earlier in life, and more inflexible than the sexual preferences for body parts, inanimate objects, and arousing situations.
9. S. Levay, "A Difference in Hypothalamic Structure Between Heterosexual and Homosexual Men," *Science* 253 (1991): 1034–37. Further evidence for differing brain structures in a nonreproductively related area was found by L. Allen and R. Gorski, "Sexual Orientation and the Size of the Anterior Commissure in the Human Brain," *Proceedings of the National Academy of Sciences* 89 (1992): 7199–7202. Here the anterior commissure was significantly larger in homosexual men than in heterosexual women, who in turn had more tissue here than heterosexual men had.
10. The examples that follow are not intended to be hormonally or anatomically accurate; they are merely schemata to illustrate what the architecture underlying separate processes for identity, sexual organs, and orientation would have to be like.
11. The breakthrough article speculating roughly in this way is L. Ellis and M. Ames, "Prenatal Neurohormonal Functioning and Sexual Orientation: A Theory of Homosexuality-Heterosexuality," *Psychological Bulletin* 101 (1987): 233–58. So provocative was this piece that I was forced to change an entire course in midstream to discuss it at length when it came out in 1987.

    For the literature on twins and homosexuality, see E. Eckert, T. Bouchard, J. Bohlen, and L. Heston, "Homosexuality in Monozygotic Twins Reared Apart," *British Journal of Psychiatry* 148 (1986): 421–25. M. Bailey and R. Pillard, "A Genetic Study of Male Sexual Orientation," *Archives of General Psychiatry* 48 (1991): 1089–96, is the landmark study in this area. While this points directly to a genetic in addition to a fetal-hormone mechanism, homosexuality still might be entirely fetal in origin. Identical twins do not have identical intrauterine environments. One twin is often bigger than the other. Could it be that identical twins do not get identical hormonal baths? No one knows yet.

    It is possible that bisexuality—or, strictly speaking, the capacity for bisexuality—has as its substratum just a bit of androgen insufficiency in utero. Future research will tell. But it is important that most of the development of bisexuality is in adolescence and adulthood, not in utero. People not infrequently become actively bisexual when exposed to homosexuality during their teens and twenties. For this reason I include bisexuality as a sexual preference, and exclusive homosexuality as a sexual orientation.
12. Evidence is not completely lacking. A. Ehrhardt, H. Meyer-Bahlburg, L. Rosen, et al., "Sexual Orientation After Prenatal Exposure to Exogenous Estrogen," *Archives of Sexual Behavior* 14 (1985): 57–75, found increased bisexuality and homosexuality among women whose mothers had taken DES, which has masculinizing effects, during pregnancy.

    In the genetic study of lesbianism, unlike the study of male homosexuality, sisters were just as concordant for lesbianism as fraternal twins, suggesting no clear role for fetal hormones. M. Bailey, R. Pillard, M. Neale, and Y. Agyei, "Heritable Factors Influence Sexual Orientation in Women," *Archives of General Psychiatry* 50 (1993): 217–23.

13. In the original study (M. Feldman and M. MacCulloch, "The Application of Anticipatory Avoidance Learning to the Treatment of Homosexuality. 1. Theory, Technique, and Preliminary Results," *Behaviour Research and Therapy* 2 [1966]: 165–83), the authors found marked improvement in 58 percent of the men who started therapy and 69 percent of the men who completed therapy. In an automated follow-up, only 31 percent of the men who started therapy and 42 percent of the completers improved markedly. "Heterophobes" and men completely indifferent to women did not improve. See S. James, A. Orwin, and R. Turner, "Treatment of Homosexuality. 1. Analysis of Failure Following a Trial of Anticipatory Avoidance Conditioning and the Development of an Alternative Treatment System," *Behavior Therapy* 8 (1977): 840–48. See also N. McConaghy, M. Armstrong, and A. Blaszczynski, "Controlled Comparison of Aversive Therapy and Covert Sensitization in Compulsive Homosexuality," *Behaviour Research and Therapy* 19 (1981): 425–34. They also find about 50 percent success, but argue that no change in sexual orientation has occurred. The best overall review is H. Adams and E. Sturgis, "Status of Behavioral Reorientation Techniques in the Modification of Homosexuality: A Review," *Psychological Bulletin* 84 (1977): 1171–88.
14. R. Baenninger, "Some Consequences of Aggressive Behavior: A Selective Review of the Literature on Other Animals," *Aggressive Behavior* 1 (1974): 17–37.
15. T. Templeman and R. Stinnett, "Patterns of Sexual Arousal and History in a 'Normal' Sample of Young Men," *Archives of Sexual Behavior* 20 (1991): 137–50.
16. This is the view propounded by Richard von Krafft-Ebing. His *Psychopathia Sexualis* (New York: Physicians' and Surgeons' Book Company, 1922) is a great and eminently readable compilation. I number him with Freud, Kinsey, Masters and Johnson, and John Money among the great liberators in this field.
17. For example, see D. Raphling, "Fetishism in a Woman," *Journal of the American Psychoanalytic Association* 37 (1989): 465–91. The S-M study is N. Breslow, L. Evans, and J. Langley, "On the Prevalence and Roles of Females in the Sadomasochistic Subculture: Report of an Empirical Study," *Archives of Sexual Behavior* 14 (1985): 303–17.
18. I recommend the first chapter of the explosive *Sexual Personae* (New York: Vintage, 1991), by the bête noire of feminism, Camille Paglia, for the view that promiscuity is normal in men but an illness in women. As for evidence, see David Buss's cross-cultural studies about sexual attractants in men versus women, reported in his "Sex Differences in Human Mate Preferences: Evolutionary Hypotheses Tested in 37 Cultures," *Behavioral and Brain Sciences* 12 (1989): 1–49.
19. W. Marshall, A. Eccles, and H. Barbaree, "The Treatment of Exhibitionists: A Focus on Sexual Deviance Versus Cognitive and Relationship Features," *Behaviour Research and Therapy* 29 (1991): 129–35; B. Maletzky, " 'Assisted' Covert Sensitization in the Treatment of Exhibitionism," *Journal of Consulting and Clinical Psychology* 42 (1974): 34–40.
20. A thorough review is found in J. Bradford, "Organic Treatment for the Male Sexual Offender," *Annals of the New York Academy of Sciences* 528 (1988): 193–202.
21. There are large literatures on all these points. Two good reviews are A. Huston, "The Development of Sex Typing: Themes from Recent Research," in *Developmental Review* 5 (1985): 1–17; and M. Sedney, "Development of Androgyny: Parental Influences," *Psychology of Women Quarterly* 11 (1987): 31–326. The classic in this field is E. Maccoby and C. Jacklin, *The Psychology of Sex Differences* (Stanford, Calif.: Stanford University Press, 1974).

22. See the Sedney and Huston reviews (cited immediately above) for good coverage of the studies that try and fail to coax young children into androgyny.
23. H. Meyer-Bahlburg, J. Feldman, P. Cohen, and A. Ehrhardt, "Perinatal Factors in the Development of Gender-Related Play Behavior: Sex Hormones Versus Pregnancy Complications," *Psychiatry* 51 (1988): 260–71; S. Berenbaum and M. Hines, "Early Androgens Are Related to Childhood Sex-Typed Toy Preferences," *Psychological Science* 3 (1992): 203–6. J. Money and A. Ehrhardt, *Man and Woman, Boy and Girl* (Baltimore: Johns Hopkins University Press, 1972), is an excellent general reference for the precursor studies.
24. J. Reinisch, unpublished study cited in C. Gorman, "Sizing Up the Sexes," *Time* (20 January 1992), 45–46.
25. The most comprehensive recent overview is J. Hyde, "Meta-analysis and the Psychology of Gender Differences," *Signs: Journal of Women in Culture and Society* 16 (1990): 55–73.
    The spatial score may have a biological component. Astonishingly, women's scores go up by between 50 and 100 percent when their estrogen level is low, and men's scores go up when their testosterone level is low. See I. Silverman and M. Eals, "Sex Differences in Spatial Abilities: Evolutionary Theory and Data," in J. Barko, L. Cosmides, and J. Tooby, eds., *The Adaptive Mind: Evolutionary Psychology and the Generation of Culture* (Oxford: Oxford University Press, 1992), 487–503. It is also intriguing that while men are better at rotating three-dimensional objects (perhaps related to navigating the savannah while hunting), women are apparently better at the spatial task of remembering the place of objects (perhaps related to foraging).
26. J. Hall, *Nonverbal Sex Differences: Communication Accuracy and Expressive Styles* (Baltimore: Johns Hopkins University Press, 1984).
27. Alan Feingold of Yale University has written a landmark article on this topic, containing exhaustive data reanalysis of the major ability tests: "Sex Differences in Variability in Intellectual Abilities: A New Look at an Old Controversy," *Review of Educational Research* 62 (1992): 61–84.
28. A. Feingold, "Sex Differences in Variability in Intellectual Abilities."
29. There is an alternate explanation of the narrowing of sex differences: renorming. Every few years, the big test makers (ETS, California Achievement, etc.) renorm their tests to try to make them better and "fairer." To do this, they sometimes throw out items on which there is a sex difference or a race difference and substitute items that do not differ empirically. If this is what is going on in the reduction of the ability-score differences, it is sheer artifact. The ability differences remain, but we can no longer see them as clearly.
30. W. Masters and V. Johnson, *Human Sexual Inadequacy* (Boston: Little, Brown, 1970), is a classic, but too technical to be a good read. H. Kaplan, *The New Sex Therapy* (New York: Brunner-Mazel, 1974), is a better choice for the layman. For a skeptical view, see B. Zilbergeld and M. Evans, "The Inadequacy of Masters and Johnson," *Psychology Today* 14 (1980): 28–43.
31. I adopt the usage of *acedia* from Robertson Davies's essay "The Deadliest Sin of All," in *One Half of Robertson Davies* (New York: Viking, 1977), 62–68. Much of what follows derives from this brilliant essay.

CHAPTER 12 *Dieting*

1. This is a truly voluminous subject, full of articles that contradict one another, and peopled by scientists and clinicians caught in a conflict between an emerging truth about the ineffectiveness of dieting on the one hand, and making a living on the other.

I want to single out two major pieces of work about dieting, both unpopular: The first is J. Polivy and P. Herman, *Breaking the Diet Habit* (New York: Basic Books, 1983). Although a decade old now and out of print, its basic contentions on the ineffectiveness and dangers of dieting continue to be borne out in this fast-moving field. The second is the most up-to-date, scholarly review of dieting: D. Garner and S. Wooley, "Confronting the Failure of Behavioral and Dietary Treatments for Obesity," *Clinical Psychology Review* 11 (1991): 729–80. Both are whistle-blowing (though possibly overstated) and ahead of their time. I lean on them strongly in this chapter. They are must reads for all students in this field, and if taken to heart they will go a long way toward making psychology a more responsible profession.

Finally, the consumer should consult the splendid "Diets: What Works—What Doesn't," *Consumer Reports,* June 1993, 347–57.

2. The Metropolitan Life table is adapted from E. Weigley, "Average? Ideal? Desirable? A Brief Overview of Height-Weight Tables in the United States," *Journal of the American Dietetic Association* 84 (1984): 417–23.
3. The argument that being over your "ideal" weight means that you would live longer if you dieted down to your "ideal" weight is a non sequitur of the first magnitude. It astonishes me that serious physicians have been dispensing such advice for decades. Technically speaking, it is a fallacious argument on two grounds: First, it confuses correlation and cause. Some third variable may cause people at their "ideal" weight both to have that weight *and* to live longer. Second, it ignores the health cost of dieting to get to a lower weight, which in itself could offset the health benefit of being at that lower weight.

   There is something else to be said against the Met Life "ideal" weights. Met Life charged about 20 to 30 percent extra in life-insurance premiums to the overweight. A good number of the overweight policyholders were willing to pay an extra premium because they knew something was wrong with their health that the company didn't. This means that the overweight people that Met Life insured were probably unhealthier than people of the same weight who didn't try to get insurance. Policyholders systematically select against the company, and the result of this is that the "ideal" weight figure is probably markedly too low.
4. J. Garrow, *Energy Balance and Obesity in Man* (New York: Elsevier, 1974), and S. Wooley, O. Wooley, and S. Dyrenforth, "Theoretical, Practical, and Social Issues in Behavioral Treatment of Obesity," *Journal of Applied Behavior Analysis* 12 (1979): 3–25, review these studies. K. Brownell and T. Wadden, "The Heterogeneity of Obesity: Fitting Treatments to Individuals," *Behavior Therapy* 22 (1991): 153–77, is a useful general source debunking the myths of overweight.

   New studies of doubly labeled water challenge the view that the obese don't overeat, however. According to such studies, obese people underreport how much they eat by 30 percent. See D. Schoeller, "Measurement of Energy Expenditure in Free-Living Humans by Using Doubly Labeled Water," *Journal of Nutrition* 118 (1988): 1278–89.
5. R. Striegel-Moore and J. Rodin, "The Influence of Psychological Variables in Obesity," in K. Brownell and J. Foreyt, eds., *Handbook of Eating Disorders* (New York: Basic Books, 1986), 99–121.
6. "What's Ahead? The Weight Loss Market," *Obesity and Health* (July 1989), 51–54. J. LaRosa, *Dieter Beware: The Complete Consumer Guide to Weight Loss Programs* (Valley Stream, N.Y.: Marketdata Enterprises, 1991), is a useful if unselective compendium of the facts and financial doings of the diet industry.
7. D. Garner, P. Garfinkel, D. Schwartz, and M. Thompson, "Cultural Expectations of Thinness in Women," *Psychological Reports* 47 (1980): 483–91; R. Jeffrey, S. Adlis, and

J. Forster, "Prevalence of Dieting Among Working Men and Women: The Healthy Worker Project," *Health Psychology* 10 (1991): 274–81.

8. M. Hovell, A. Koch, C. Hofstetter, et al., "Long-term Weight Loss Maintenance: Assessment of a Behavioral and Supplemented Fasting Regimen," *American Journal of Public Health* 78 (1988): 663–66; T. Andersen, K. Stokholm, O. Backer, and F. Quaade, "Long-term (5-Year) Results After Either Horizontal Gastroplasty or Very-Low-Calorie Diet for Morbid Obesity," *International Journal of Obesity* 12 (1988): 277–84; D. Johnson and E. Drenick, "Therapeutic Fasting in Morbid Obesity: Long-term Follow-up," *Archives of Internal Medicine* 137 (1977): 1381–82; P. Stalonas, M. Perri, and A. Kerzner, "Do Behavioral Treatments of Obesity Last? A Five-Year Follow-up Investigation," *Addictive Behavior* 9 (1984): 175–83. T. Wadden, A. Stunkard, and J. Liebschutz, "Three-Year Follow-up of the Treatment of Obesity by a Very Low Calorie Diet, Behavior Therapy, and Their Combination," *Journal of Consulting and Clinical Psychology* 56 (1988): 925–28, found that six out of forty-five patients maintained weight loss completely after three years.

   The most complete source is "Methods for Voluntary Weight Loss and Control," proceedings of a National Institutes of Health conference, 30 March–1 April 1992, along with its staggering 1,119-item bibliography ("Methods for Voluntary Weight Loss and Control," in *Current Bibliographies in Medicine* [CBM 92-1] [Washington, D.C.: U.S. Government Printing Office, 1992].

9. See Garner and Wooley, "Confronting the Failure of Behavioral and Dietary Treatments," for a review and bibliography of all the long-term follow-up studies. See also M. Holmes, B. Zysow, and T. Delbanco, "An Analytic Review of Current Therapies for Obesity," *Journal of Family Practice* 28 (1989): 610–16.

10. K. Brownell and T. Wadden, "Etiology and Treatment of Obesity: Understanding a Serious, Prevalent, and Refractory Disorder," *Journal of Consulting and Clinical Psychology* 60 (1992): 505–17, are representative of the group that remains undaunted by the poor long-term results of dieting. They call for more realistic goals—reasonable weight rather than "ideal" weight—better screening for really motivated clients, and more research on maintenance. They write articles on a "balanced" view of dieting in response to the data in this chapter. I admire their dogged persistence, but I do not share their optimism about the future of the dieting industry. There is little reason to hope that ten-pound losses will be maintained any better than twenty-five-pound losses are. There is little reason to believe that people who suffer through diet after diet are unmotivated, and there is even less reason to expect any breakthrough about maintenance.

    Brownell and Wadden assert that the public good will not be served if people come to believe "(a) diets do not work; (b) dieting is more dangerous than staying heavy; and (c) excess weight is a trivial risk factor." This statement astonishes me. Brownell and Wadden are two of the investigators whose very research makes these propositions so plausible. Rather than hoping to chill debate about whether dieting is useless or even harmful, I believe it is very much in the public interest to *provoke* such debate.

11. See R. Jeffrey, J. Forster, and T. Schmid, "Worksite Health Promotion: Feasibility Testing of Repeated Weight Control and Smoking Cessation Classes," *American Journal of Health* 3 (1989): 11–16; and R. Jeffrey, W. Hellerstedt, and T. Schmid, "Correspondence Programs for Smoking Cessation and Weight Control: A Comparison of Two Strategies in the Minnesota Heart Health Program," *Health Psychology* 9 (1990): 585–98.

12. The serious scholar should read "Methods for Voluntary Weight Loss and Control" (see note 9, above). The upshot is that no known diet keeps weight off in the long run, except for a very small minority of dieters.

13. The rat model of yo-yo dieting was developed by K. Brownell, M. Greenwood, E. Stellar,

and E. Shrager, "The Effects of Repeated Cycles of Weight Loss and Regain in Rats," *Physiology and Behavior* 38 (1986): 459–64. The increased metabolic efficiency is well replicated, but whether yo-yo rats rebound to a higher weight is still controversial. See R. Contreras and V. Williams, "Dietary Obesity and Weight Cycling: Effects on Blood Pressure and Heart Rate in Rats," *American Journal of Physiology* 256 (1989): 1209–19. See R. Keesey, "The Body-Weight Set Point," *Postgraduate Medicine* 83 (1988): 115–27, and Garner and Wooley, "Confront the Failure of Behavioral and Dietary Treatments," for reviews.

In spite of all the press on yo-yo dieting, I believe that more animal research is still needed to determine which effects of yo-yoing are reliable.

14. G. Blackburn, G. Wilson, B. Kanders, et al., "Weight-cycling: The Experience of Human Dieters," *American Journal of Clinical Nutrition* 49 (1989): 1105–9; E. Drenick and D. Johnson, "Weight-Reduction by Fasting and Semi-Starvation in Morbid Obesity: Long-term Follow-up," in G. Bray, ed., *Obesity: Comparative Methods of Weight Control* (London: John Libbey, 1980), 25–34; C. Geissler, D. Miller, and M. Shah, "The Daily Metabolic Rate of the Post-Obese and the Lean," *American Journal of Clinical Nutrition* 45 (1987): 914–20.

I do not believe that the human literature on this issue is yet conclusive. The rat literature and the human literature have replicated increased metabolic efficiency during starvation and dieting. But what happens after weight is regained is less certain: I would like to see replications of whether weight overshoots to higher levels in rats and humans. I would also like to see a longitudinal study with long-term follow-up looking at metabolic efficiency after weight regain along the lines of the cross-sectional study of Geissler et al., "The Daily Metabolic Rate." See also Garner and Wooley, "Confront the Failure of Behavioral and Dietary Treatments."

15. Geissler et al., "The Daily Metabolic Rate"; Blackburn et al., "Weight-cycling."
16. P. Brown and M. Konner, "An Anthropological Perspective on Obesity," *Annals of the New York Academy of Sciences* 499 (1987): 29–46.
17. E. Sims, "Experimental Obesity, Diet-Induced Thermogenesis, and Their Clinical Implications," *Clinics in Endocrinology and Metabolism* 5 (1976): 377–95.
18. Sims, "Experimental Obesity"; A. Stunkard, J. Harris, N. Pedersen, and G. McClearn, "The Body-Mass Index of Twins Who Have Been Reared Apart," *New England Journal of Medicine* 322 (1990): 1483–87; A. Stunkard, T. Sorenson, C. Hanis, et al., "An Adoption Study of Human Obesity," *New England Journal of Medicine* 314 (1986): 193–98. The correlation is stronger for the lean than for the obese, indicating that environmental factors may play more of a role in obesity. See R. Price and A. Stunkard, "Commingling Analysis of Obesity in Twins," *Human Heredity* 39 (1989): 121–35; C. Bouchard, A. Tremblay, J. Despres, et al., "The Response to Long-term Overfeeding in Identical Twins," *New England Journal of Medicine* 322 (1990): 1477–82. For the relation between "ideal" weight and actual weight, see A. Keys, "Overweight, Obesity, Coronary Heart Disease and Mortality," *Nutrition Reviews* 38 (1980): 297–307.
19. The best prevalence statistics come from C. Fairburn and S. Beglin, "Studies of the Epidemiology of Bulimia Nervosa," *American Journal of Psychiatry* 147 (1990): 401–8.
20. Antidepressant drugs have some positive effects. They do better than a placebo at reducing binging and purging, with about a 60 percent reduction in frequency. But most patients still have the symptoms at the end of treatment, with only 22 percent, on average, symptom free. Once antidepressants are stopped, rate of relapse is very high. For a review of the antidepressants in bulimia, see C. Fairburn, W. S. Agras, and G. T. Wilson, "The Research on the Treatment of Bulimia Nervosa: Practical and Theoretical Implications," in G.

Anderson and S. Kennedy, eds., *The Biology of Feast and Famine: Relevance to Eating Disorders* (New York: Academic Press, 1992), 318–40.

21. This is not an original proposal. It is the interpretation put forward by Polivy and Herman in *Breaking the Diet Habit,* Garner and Wooley in "Confront the Failure of Behavioral and Dietary Treatments," and Jane Wardle. See particularly J. Polivy and C. P. Herman, "Dieting and Binging: A Causal Analysis," *American Psychologist* 40 (1985): 193–201; and J. Wardle, "Compulsive Eating and Dietary Restraint," *British Journal of Clinical Psychology* 26 (1987): 47–55.

    In putting forward a similar theory both of anorexia and bulimia, Peter Slade calls the bulimic a "failed anorexic," failed in that the anorexic can keep dieting without giving in to binging. See P. Slade, "Towards a Functional Analysis of Anorexia Nervosa and Bulimia Nervosa," *British Journal of Clinical Psychology* 21 (1982): 167–79. See M. Boskind-Lodahl and J. Sirlin, "The Gorging-Purging Syndrome," *Psychology Today* (March 1977), 50–52, 82–85, for a survey of the rate of dieting just before bulimia starts. For two epidemiological studies linking dieting quite tightly to eating disorders, see G. Patton, E. Johnson-Sabine, K. Wood, et al., "Abnormal Eating Attitudes in London Schoolgirls—A Prospective Epidemiological Study: Outcome at Twelve Month Follow-up," *Psychological Medicine* 20 (1990): 383–94; and K. Kendler, C. MacLean, M. Neale, et al., "The Genetic Epidemiology of Bulimia Nervosa," *American Journal of Psychiatry* 148 (1991): 1627–37. Dieters are at least eight times more likely to get an eating disorder than nondieters.

22. I take my hat off to S. Dalvit-McPhillips, "A Dietary Approach to Bulimia Treatment," *Physiology and Behavior* 33 (1984): 769–75. It is a shame that this paper has remained obscure.

23. See Fairburn and Beglin, "Studies of the Epidemiology of Bulimia Nervosa," for a complete review of the cognitive-behavioral studies, and C. Fairburn, R. Jones, R. Peveler, et al., "Three Psychological Treatments for Bulimia Nervosa," *Archives of General Psychiatry* 48 (1991): 463–69, for an exemplary outcome study. For a fine antidepressant drug study, see U. McCann and W. S. Agras, "Successful Treatment of Nonpurging Bulimia Nervosa with Desimpramine: A Double-Blind, Placebo-Controlled Study," *American Journal of Psychiatry* 147 (1990): 1509–13. The two outcome studies that explicitly compare drugs and cognitive-behavioral therapy are J. Mitchell, R. Pyle, E. Eckert, et al., "A Comparison Study of Antidepressants and Structured Intensive Group Psychotherapy in the Treatment of Bulimia Nervosa," *Archives of General Psychiatry* 47 (1990): 149–57; and W. S. Agras, E. Rossiter, B. Arnow, et al., "Pharmacologic and Cognitive-Behavioral Treatment for Bulimia Nervosa: A Controlled Comparison," *American Journal of Psychiatry* 149 (1992): 82–87.

24. C. Telch, W. Agras, and E. Rossiter, "Binge Eating Increases with Increasing Adiposity," *International Journal of Eating Disorders* 7 (1988): 115–19. See G. T. Wilson, "Short-term Psychological Benefits and Adverse Effects of Dieting and Weight Loss," paper delivered at the NIH conference "Methods for Voluntary Weight Loss and Control" (1991), for the argument that dieting may be necessary but not sufficient for bulimia.

25. J. Brody, "Study Defines 'Binge Eating Disorder,'" *New York Times,* 27 March 1992, A16.

26. There is an inconclusive small literature about the effect of artificial sweeteners on weight gain. Some researchers have shown that rats gain weight with artificial sweeteners, but some have shown the reverse. It's the same with human subjects. (See *Appetite* 11 [1988]: supplement 1.) No one has attempted the right study: a long-term follow-up of overweight people who are put on (or taken off) artificial sweeteners. It would cost about $5 million to do this study and find out if the $10-billion-a-year diet-food industry is a scam.

27. L. Craighead, A. Stunkard, and R. O'Brien, "Behavior Therapy and Pharmacotherapy for Obesity," *Archives of General Psychiatry* 38 (1981): 763–68.
28. This study may prove to be a watershed, shifting the treatment of obesity from dietary (too ineffective) or surgical (too radical) to pharmacological. It was published in eight articles as "Long-term Weight Control: The National Heart, Lung, and Blood Institute Funded Multimodal Intervention Study," *Clinical Pharmacology and Therapeutics* (supplement) (May 1992), 581–646.
29. This footnote could be a chapter in length, but I am going to resist. Rather, I will be selective and highlight just the best studies to guide the student of this topic as to why I come to the conclusions I do:

Enormous Obesity (100 percent above "ideal" weight): E. Drenick, S. Gurunanjappa, F. Seltzer, and D. Johnson, "Excessive Mortality and Causes of Death in Morbidly Obese Men," *Journal of the American Medical Association* 243 (1980): 443–45, followed two hundred extremely fat young men for ten years. They found that fifty died. Indeed, among the 25- to 34-year-olds, there was twelve times the expected death rate. But their subjects were people who had lost and regained weight from therapeutic fasts. It is just possible that dieting itself, not morbid obesity, contributed to sudden death.

Substantial Obesity (30 to 100 percent above "ideal" weight): Choosing the low cut point is the most difficult and controversial part of distilling this large literature. Thirty percent overweight looks to me to be approximately the point at which some danger begins. The "Pooling Project" combined data for 12,381 men from eight different American populations who had been followed for five to ten years. Looking at first heart attack, the inflection point seems to be at 30 percent over "ideal" weight. This is a conservative estimate, however, since it can be argued from these data sets that there is no increase at all in coronary risk with weight. See The Pooling Research Project Research Group, "Relationship of Blood Pressure, Serum Cholesterol, Smoking Habit, Relative Weight and ECG Abnormality to Incidences of Major Coronary Events: Final Report of the Pooling Project," *Journal of Chronic Diseases* 31 (1978): 201–306; E. Barrett-Connor, "Obesity, Atherosclerosis, and Coronary Artery Disease," *Annals of Internal Medicine* 103 (1985): 1010–19.

The other essential source is Ancel Keys's curve fitting of more than a dozen large-scale studies of body mass and coronary heart disease. His curves show two inflection points: one at the 30 percent overweight locus and the other at underweight. Importantly, the direction of the slope with mild overweight (0 to 30 percent) is downward, with more weight up to about 30 percent associated with less risk. See A. Keys, "Overweight, Obesity, Coronary Heart Disease."

See also E. Hammond and L. Garfinkel, "Coronary Heart Disease, Stroke, and Aortic Aneurysm," *Archives of Environmental Health* 19 (1969): 167–82. This is a landmark prospective study of one million people, and it shows increased risk with body weight. But the body weight at which the risk begins is in the upper 20 percent of the population, which seems to correspond to about the 30 percent overweight cut point.

One consoling note to people in this category: This amount of overweight probably does put you at risk in and of itself. Overweight correlates with high blood pressure and serum cholesterol. If your blood pressure is normal, if your cholesterol is normal, if you exercise moderately, and if you don't smoke, your risk of heart attack is not increased by being overweight. See the classic A. Keys, C. Aravanis, H. Blackburn, et al., "Coronary Heart Disease: Overweight and Obesity as Risk Factors," *Annals of Internal Medicine* 77 (1972): 15–27.

Diabetes mellitus, in contrast to coronary heart disease, presents a clearer picture of risk with moderate overweight. In one prospective study, risk went up 1,000 percent with moderate obesity and 3,000 percent with 45 percent obesity. See K. Westlund and R. Nicholaysen, "Ten-Year Mortality and Morbidity Related to Serum Cholesterol," *Scandinavian Journal of Clinical and Laboratory Investigations* 30 (supplement 127) (1972), 3. See also A. Rimm, L. Werner, B. Van Yserloo, and R. Bernstein, "Relationship of Obesity and Disease in 73,532 Weight-Conscious Women," *Public Health Reports* 90 (1975): 44–51. My conclusion is that if diabetes runs in your family, you should be more attentive to overweight as a risk factor than if heart disease runs in your family.

Mild to Moderate Overweight (10 to 30 percent above "ideal" weight): I have chosen my language carefully here—"possibly associated with a marginal increase in mortality"—because for every study that shows some health risk in this category, there is at least one that shows no health risk.

The thrust of the Keys and Barrett-Connor reviews is that there is little or no more heart-attack incidence in this range. Indeed, these people may be at lower risk than 0 percent overweight people.

On the other hand, the gray eminence is the Met Life "ideal weight" table, which in spite of its flaws is well entrenched in the public mind. More modern data supporting the view that even a little overweight is a health risk are found in J. Manson, G. Colditz, M. Stampfer, et al., "A Prospective Study of Obesity and Risk of Coronary Heart Disease in Women," *New England Journal of Medicine* 322 (1990): 882–89, which found risk starting at 10 percent overweight among female nurses; and T. Wilcovsky, J. Hyde, J. Anderson, et al., "Obesity and Mortality in the Lipid Research Clinics Program Follow-up Study," *Journal of Clinical Epidemiology* 43 (1990): 743–52, which found risk at low levels of overweight with men but not women. See also the National Institutes of Health Consensus Development and Conference Statement "Health Implications of Obesity," *Annals of Internal Medicine* 103 (1985): 147–51, which echoes the view that even a little overweight is bad. I find this report overly alarmist, and the tone is considerably moderated by the more recent National Research Council, "Obesity and Eating Disorders," in National Academy of Sciences, National Research Council, *Diet and Health Risk: Implications for Reducing Chronic Disease Risk* (Washington, D.C.: National Academy Press, 1989), 563–92.

Nonetheless, there has never been a study that shows anything but a very small statistical increase of coronary risk in the 10 to 30 percent range of overweight.

Underweight: See Keys, "Overweight, Obesity, Coronary Heart Disease"; S. Blair, H. Kohl, R. Paffenbarger, et al., "Physical Fitness and All-Cause Mortality: A Prospective Study of Healthy Men and Women," *Journal of the American Medical Association* 262 (1989): 2395–2401; R. Paffenbarger, P. Hyde, A. Wing, and C. C. Hsiesh, "Physical Activity, All-Cause Mortality, and Longevity of College Alumni," *New England Journal of Medicine* 314 (1986): 605–13. The mortality risk of the underweight, unlike that of the mild and moderately overweight, is strong, and it is not attributable to smoking or to subclinical disease. See also P. Sorlie, T. Gordon, and W. Kannel, "Body Build and Mortality: The Framingham Study," *Journal of the American Medical Association* 243 (1980): 1828–31.

One final caveat: No one has ever done the right kind of study to find out if overweight really causes premature death or poor health. The methodologically right study would randomly assign individuals to different weight levels and see who dies when. It seems likely that for ethical reasons this study will never be done in humans. All of the above studies are therefore distant second-best evidence.

30. Hammond and Garfinkel, "Coronary Heart Disease, Stroke, and Aortic Aneurysm"; P. Hamm, R. Shekelle, and J. Stamler, "Large Fluctuations in Body Weight During Young

Adulthood and the Twenty-Five-Year Risk of Coronary Death in Men," *American Journal of Epidemiology* 129 (1989): 312–18; L. Lissner, P. Odell, R. D'Agostino, et al., "Variability of Body Weight and Health Outcomes in the Framingham Population," *New England Journal of Medicine* 324 (1991): 1839–44; L. Lissner, C. Bengtsson, L. Lapidus, et al., "Body Weight Variability and Mortality in the Gothenburg Prospective Studies of Men and Women," in P. Bjorntorp and S. Rossner, eds., *Obesity in Europe 88* (London: Libbey, 1989), 51–56.

I use the word *probably* to describe the health risk of dieting. These four studies support it, and their findings do not come out of the blue. A number of smaller-scale studies of humans point to the same health risk for weight cycling, and so does the rat literature. See Garner and Wooley, "Confront the Failure of Behavioral and Dietary Treatments," for references and a selective review. But I judge the risk "probable," not "certain," because two studies fail to find weight variability associated with mortality: L. Lissner, R. Andres, D. Muller, and H. Shimokata, "Body Weight Variability in Men: Metabolic Rate, Health, and Longevity," *International Journal of Obesity* 14 (1990): 373–83; and J. Stevens and L. Lissner, "Body Weight Variability and Mortality in the Charleston Heart Study" (letter to the editor), in *International Journal of Obesity* 14 (1990): 385–86.

31. R. Paffenbarger et al., "Physical Activity, All-Cause Mortality." This paper is a classic, head and shoulders better in quality than the literature that precedes it.
32. M. McCarthy, "The Thin Ideal, Depression, and Eating Disorders in Women," *Behaviour Research and Therapy* 28 (1990): 205–15. See Jeffrey et al., "Prevalence of Dieting Among Working Men and Women," for dieting statistics. T. Wadden, A. Stunkard, and J. Smoller, "Dieting and Depression: A Methodological Study," *Journal of Consulting and Clinical Psychology* 54 (1986): 869–71, find that dieting, when measured from the beginning to the end, decreases depression among obese women who lost forty-five pounds on average. But when looked at from week to week, depression fluctuated wildly, with half the women getting noticeably more depressed occasionally.
33. J. Girgus, S. Nolen-Hoeksema, M. Seligman, G. Paul, and H. Spears, "Why Do Girls Become More Depressed Than Boys in Early Adolescence?" Paper presented at the meeting of the American Psychological Association, San Francisco, August 1991.
34. A. Fallon and P. Rozin, "Sex Differences in Perceptions of Desirable Body Shape," *Journal of Abnormal Psychology* 94 (1985): 102–5.
35. The closest any study has ever come concerns lowering blood pressure. If you are obese and your blood pressure is high, even a small amount of weight loss (10 percent of your weight) will probably lower it. See G. Blackburn and B. Kanders, "Medical Evaluation and Treatment of the Obese Patient with Cardiovascular Disease," *American Journal of Cardiology* 60 (1987): 55g–58g. What is still unknown is: When the lost body weight returns, how much will blood pressure increase, and what will the health damage be then? In any case, blood pressure is quite a fallible predictor of health.

    I find this study methodologically outdated. With what is known about the likelihood of weight regain after dieting, I believe that any claim about health benefit and weight loss can no longer be made on the basis of a "snapshot" study like Blackburn and Kanders's. The question is not the momentary benefit after dieting, but the net health effect of dieting followed by regaining the weight.
36. S. Blair et al., "Physical Fitness and All-Cause Mortality"; J. Holloway, A. Beuter, and J. Duda, "Self-Efficacy and Training for Strength in Adolescent Girls," *Journal of Applied Social Psychology* 18 (1988): 699–719; Paffenbarger et al., "Physical Activity, All-Cause Mortality."

    Again, this is probable but not certain, and I have used the qualifiers *seems* and *probably* to describe the beneficial effects on heart disease of taking up exercise. One study involving over eight thousand Swedish men found twice the risk for physically inactive men, which confirms the above studies. But when that study controlled for the factors correlated with exercise (occupation, diabetes, family history of coronary disease, and mental stress), the beneficial effect of exercise, in itself, disappeared. This finding is important because no one has yet done a large-scale random-assignment study of exercise and heart disease. So it is still unknown if exercising will prevent heart attack or if unchangeable factors that correlate with exercising prevent heart attack. See S. Johansson, A. Rosengren, A. Tsipogianni, et al., "Physical Inactivity as a Risk Factor for Primary and Secondary Coronary Events in Goteborg, Sweden," *European Heart Journal* 9 (supplement L) (1988): 8–19.

Dr. Ralph Paffenbarger of Stanford University recently reported that it is never too late to take up exercise. Based on a study of 10,000 Harvard alumni, he finds that men who start exercising between ages 45 and 54 live ten months longer, on average, than sedentary men; taking up exercise between ages 55 and 64 adds nine months, starting between 65 and 74 adds six months, and starting between 75 and 84 adds two months. See "Exercise to Live Longer, by 10 Months, That Is," *The New York Times,* 25 February 1993, B7.

37. The outstanding review of this large literature is G. Bray, "Exercise and Obesity," in C. Bouchard, R. Shepard, T. Stephens, et al., eds., *Exercise, Fitness, and Health. A Consensus of Current Knowledge* (Champaign, Ill.: Human Kinetics, 1990), 497–510. See also J. Foreyt and G. Goodrick, "Factors Common to Successful Therapy for the Obese Patient," *Medicine and Science in Sports and Exercise* 23 (1991): 292–97; and L. Ekelund, W. Haskell, J. Johnson, et al., "Physical Fitness as a Predictor of Cardiovascular Mortality in Asymptomatic North American Men," *New England Journal of Medicine* 319 (1988): 1379–84. S. Kayman, W. Bruvold, and J. Stern, "Maintenance and Relapse After Weight Loss in Women: Behavioral Aspects," *American Journal of Clinical Nutrition* 52 (1990): 800–807, found in a retrospective study that 90 percent of women who had dieted on their own and not regained weight exercised regularly, but that only 34 percent of relapsers did.
38. National Academy of Sciences, National Research Council, *Diet and Health Risk: Implications for Reducing Chronic Disease Risk,* 159–258, 431–64. Martin Katahn's popular *T-Factor Diet: Lose Weight Safely and Quickly Without Counting Calories or Even Cutting Them* (New York: Norton, 1989) is a useful guide to avoiding fatty foods. R. Stamler, J. Stamler, F. Gosch, et al., "Primary Prevention of Hypertension by Nutritional-Hygienic Means: Final Report of a Randomized, Controlled Trial," *Journal of the American Medical Association* 262 (1989): 1801–7.
39. These steps come from the last chapter of Polivy and Herman, *Breaking the Diet Habit,* 190–211.
40. C. Yale, "Gastric Surgery for the Morbidly Obese," *Archives of Surgery* 124 (1989): 941–46, followed 537 patients who underwent one of three kinds of surgery. In a five-year follow-up, gastric bypass was better than vertical-banded gastroplasty (VBG), which was much better than unbanded gastrogastrostomy. J. Hall, J. Watts, P. O'Brien, et al., "Gastric Surgery for Morbid Obesity: The Adelaide Study," *Annals of Surgery* 211 (1990): 419–27, followed 310 patients for three years, with similar outcomes. Cardiac function seems to improve after such surgery. See A. Alaud-din, S. Meterissian, R. Lisbona, et al., "Assessment of Cardiac Function in Patients Who Were Morbidly Obese," *Surgery* 108 (1990): 809–20.

CHAPTER 13 *Alcohol*

1. See my *Learned Optimism* (New York: Knopf, 1991), chapter 6, for a review of the evidence on this fascinating and robust illusion of control. The most recent piece showing realism as a risk factor for depression is L. Alloy and C. Clements, "Illusion of Control: Invulnerability to Negative Affect and Depressive Symptoms After Laboratory and Natural Stressors," *Journal of Abnormal Psychology* 101 (1992): 234–45.
2. "Drunkenness a Vice, Not a Disease" is the title of an 1882 pamphlet by J. E. Todd (Hartford, Conn.: Case, Lockwood, and Brainard). The parallel to thieving and lynching comes from E. J. McGoldrick, *The Management of the Mind* (Boston: Houghton Mifflin, 1954).
3. There have been at least ten heritability studies of alcoholism that converge on a substantial genetic risk. These are reviewed by D. Goodwin, "Alcoholism and Heredity," *Archives of General Psychiatry* 36 (1979): 57–61. The most complete review is in C. Cloninger and H. Begleiter, eds., *Genetics and Biology of Alcoholism* (Banbury Report Number 33) (Cold Spring Harbor, N.Y.: Cold Spring Harbor Press: 1990).
4. George Vaillant, in his landmark and courageous book *The Natural History of Alcoholism* (Cambridge, Mass.: Harvard University Press, 1983), uses this metaphor in his illuminating argument for retaining the medical model of alcoholism. It is, along with James Orford's sober *Excessive Appetites: A Psychological View of Addictions* (New York: Wiley, 1985), one of the two must reads in the field of alcoholism.
5. See G. A. Marlatt and J. Gordon, *Relapse Prevention* (New York: Guilford, 1985), for the argument that twelve-step programs and the disease concept are more pessimistic and imply greater chronicity than a "biopsychosocial model," which defines the problem as a "habit disorder." While these latter concepts are available and plausible to educated and sophisticated people, I cannot judge how plausible they are to the less sophisticated alcoholic.
6. All major studies of the natural history of alcoholism are about men. There is not a single one about women. While considerably fewer women are alcoholic, given the large absolute numbers of female alcoholics, there is a serious need for knowledge about the course of recovery among women.
7. See Vaillant, *The Natural History of Alcoholism,* 74–90; W. Beardslee, L. Son, and G. Vaillant, "Exposure to Parental Alcoholism During Childhood and Outcome in Adulthood: A Prospective Longitudinal Study," *British Journal of Psychiatry* 149 (1986): 584–91; and R. Drake and G. Vaillant, "Predicting Alcoholism and Personality Disorder in a 33-Year Longitudinal Study of the Children of Alcoholics," *British Journal of Addiction* 83 (1988): 799–807.
8. The quote comes from M. Tyndel, "Psychiatric Study of One Thousand Alcoholic Patients," *Canadian Psychiatric Association Journal* 19 (1974): 21–24. See also C. Vaillant, E. Milofsky, R. Richards, and G. Vaillant, "A Social Casework Contribution to Understanding Alcoholism," *Health and Social Work* 12 (1987): 169–76.
9. Someday the notion of "physical addiction" may come to have a specific physical, rather than just a behavioral, meaning. There is evidence that the brain may lose plasticity—the ability to make choices—as alcoholism gets worse. There is also evidence that when brain cells live in alcohol for a time, they change: They acclimate to an alcoholic medium and function better with alcohol than without it. See A. Urrutia and D. Gruol, "Acute Alcohol Alters the Excitability of Cerebellar Purkinje Neurons and Hippocampal Neurons in Culture," *Brain Research* 569 (1992): 26–37; D. Gruol, "Chronic Exposure to Alcohol During Development Alters the Membrane Properties of Cerebellar Purkinje Neurons in Culture," *Brain Research* 558 (1991): 1–12. Repeated doses of alcohol might even produce brain-cell "kindling" of the sort that Robert Post has hypothesized for cocaine, for stress,

and for depression. See R. Post, "Transduction of Psychosocial Stress into the Neurobiology of Recurrent Affective Disorder," *American Journal of Psychiatry* 149 (1992): 999–1010. But at present, the "physical" part of addiction is mostly hypothetical.

10. A. Pokorny, T. Kanas, and J. Overall, "Order of Appearance of Alcoholic Symptoms," *Alcoholism: Clinical and Experimental Research* 5 (1981): 216–20, lay out the steps of the progression, based on retrospective data.
11. This latest data and theory are contained in a personal communication from George Vaillant, July 1992.
12. See Vaillant, *The Natural History of Alcoholism,* 170–71, for a lucid discussion of the who and why of relapse.
13. F. Baekland, L. Lundwall, and B. Kissim, "Methods for the Treatment of Chronic Alcoholism: A Critical Approach," in R. Gibbons, Y. Israel, H. Kalant, et al., eds., *Research Advances in Alcohol and Drug Problems,* vol. 2 (New York: Wiley, 1975), 247–327; D. Armor, J. Polich, J. Michael, and H. Stanbul, *Alcoholism and Treatment* (Santa Monica, Calif.: The Rand Corporation, 1976); R. Rychtarik, D. Foy, W. Scott, et al., "Five to Six Year Follow-up of Broad Spectrum Behavioral Treatment for Alcoholism: Effects of Controlled Drinking Skills," *Journal of Consulting and Clinical Psychology* 55 (1987): 106–8.
14. George Vaillant, personal communication, July 1992.
15. G. Vaillant, "What Can Long-term Follow-up Teach Us About Relapse and Prevention of Relapse in Addiction?" *British Journal of Addiction* 83 (1988): 1147–57. G. Edwards, "As the Years Go Rolling By: Drinking Problems in the Time Dimension," *British Journal of Psychiatry* 154 (1989): 18–26, found that out of the ex-patients followed for a decade, 18 died (250 percent above expectation), 33 had good outcomes, 11 were equivocal, and 56 had bad outcomes.
16. The single best study I can find of elaborate hospital-based treatment is G. Cross, C. Morgan, A. Mooney, et al., "Alcoholism Treatment: A Ten-Year Follow-up Study," *Alcoholism: Clinical and Experimental Research* 14 (1990): 169–73. Its results are good: 61 percent remission. Crucially, however, it lacks the matched control group. J. Wallace, "Controlled Drinking, Treatment Effectiveness, and the Disease Model of Addiction: A Commentary on the Ideological Wishes of Stanton Peele," *Journal of Psychoactive Drugs* 22 (1990): 261–84, argues articulately for the effectiveness of such units, but given only one study with a matched and randomly assigned control group that finds positive results (see note 19, below), I cannot in good conscience recommend such treatment as reliably more effective than natural healing.

    This is not just an academic quibble. If this were a new treatment area, controlled study would not yet be mandatory. But this is a problem that costs the United States $100 billion or more annually and for which elaborate and expensive treatment has been going on for more than four decades. Fully cognizant of the practical problems, I nevertheless believe that controlled long-term studies are overdue.

    The most complete reviews of controlled studies of alcoholism have been reported by William R. Miller of the University of New Mexico. On the whole, he is less optimistic than I am about AA and more optimistic about behavioral training (marital therapy, self-control training, and social skills training). My reservations about the behavioral modalities concern the need for large groups and very-long-term follow-up. Otherwise our reviews coincide. See H. Holder, R. Longabaugh, W. Miller, and A. Rubonis, "The Cost Effectiveness of Treatment for Alcoholism: A First Approximation," *Journal of Studies on Alcoholism* 52 (1991): 517–40; W. Miller, "The Effectiveness of Treatment for Substance Abuse: Reasons for Optimism," *Journal of Substance Abuse Treatment* 9 (1992): 93–102.
17. J. Orford and G. Edwards, *Alcoholism—A Comparison of Treatment with Advice, with a*

Study of the Influence of Marriage (Oxford: Oxford University Press, 1977). See also Herbert Fingarette's discussion of this study in his *Heavy Drinking* (Berkeley: University of California Press, 1989), 70–95.

18. Chap. 8 of Vaillant, *The Natural History of Alcoholism,* is must reading for all who would not have their hearts broken and rebroken by the chronic relapses of their patients and relatives. See also National Institute on Alcohol Abuse and Alcoholism, "Seventh Special Report to the U.S. Congress on Alcohol and Health" (Washington, D.C.: Public Health Service, 1990) (DHHS publication number ADM 90-1656); and W. Miller and R. Hester, "Inpatient Alcoholism Treatment: Who Benefits?" *American Psychologist* 41 (1986): 794–805.
19. This study stands alone as being methodologically adequate and as supporting the usefulness of hospital treatment. See D. Walsh, R. Hingson, D. Merrigan, et al., "A Randomized Trial of Treatment Options for Alcohol-Abusing Workers," *New England Journal of Medicine* 325 (1991): 775–82. If replicated, it may be a watershed for inpatient alcoholism treatment.
20. E. Chaney, M. O'Leary, and G. Marlatt, "Skill Training with Alcoholics," *Journal of Consulting and Clinical Psychology* 46 (1978): 1092–1104. This seems like a promising treatment package, and it should be followed up on a large scale. It is, however, too small-scale and tentative to warrant recommendation now.
21. See chapter 12, "The Place of Expert Help" in J. Orford, *Excessive Appetites,* for a telling review of psychotherapy and alcoholism.
22. The full range of psychotropic drugs have been tried in alcoholism. None seem to work. See J. Halikas, "Psychotropic Medication Used in the Treatment of Alcoholism," *Hospital and Community Psychiatry* 34 (1983): 1035–39; and J. Sinclair, "The Feasibility of Effective Psychopharmacological Treatments for Alcoholism," *British Journal of Addiction* 82 (1987): 1213–23.

    There have been two apparent exceptions, neither of which, however, has worked out when large-scale controlled studies were done.

    The first apparent exception was Antabuse (disulfiram). For the best studies of Antabuse (double blind, placebo controlled) see J. Johnsen, A. Stowell, J. Bache-Wing, et al., "A Double-Blind Placebo Controlled Study of Male Alcoholics Given a Subcutaneous Disulfiram Implantation," *British Journal of Addiction* 82 (1987): 607–13; and J. Johnsen and J. Morland, "Disulfiram Implant: A Double-Blind Placebo Controlled Follow-up on Treatment Outcome," *Alcoholism: Clinical and Experimental Research* 15 (1991): 532–38.

    The second apparent exception was lithium: In the first well-done study, a 67 percent abstinence rate after one year in a controlled, random-assignment design was found. See J. Fawcett, D. Clark, C. Aagesen, et al., "A Double-Blind Placebo-Controlled Trial of Lithium Carbonate Therapy for Alcoholism," *Archives of General Psychiatry* 44 (1987): 248–56. These results were promising, and were thought to be independent of lithium's effect on manic-depression, until a major replication was undertaken: A double-blind study of 457 male alcoholics, both depressed and not depressed, showed no effect of lithium on alcohol drinking. See W. Dorus, D. Ostrow, R. Anton, et al., "Lithium Treatment of Depressed and Nondepressed Alcoholics," *Journal of the American Medical Association* 262 (1989): 1646–52.
23. The aversion treatments make up a large literature. The best recent reviews are found in the debate between Terry Wilson and Ralph Elkins. See G. T. Wilson, "Chemical Aversion Conditioning as a Treatment for Alcoholism: A Reanalysis," *Behaviour Research and Therapy* 25 (1987): 503–16; R. Elkins, "An Appraisal of Chemical Aversion (Emetic Therapy) Approaches to Alcoholism Treatment," *Behaviour Research and Therapy* 29

(1991): 387–413; G. T. Wilson, "Chemical Aversion Conditioning in the Treatment of Alcoholism: Further Comments," *Behaviour Research and Therapy* 29 (1991): 415–19. The lone controlled study is D. Cannon, T. Baker, and C. Wehl, "Emetic and Electric Shock Alcohol Aversion Therapy: Six- and Twelve-Month Follow-up," *Journal of Consulting and Clinical Psychology* 49 (1981): 360–68.

I have to remark, again, that it is little short of a scandal that the therapies for alcoholism that patients have had for decades—inpatient hospitalization, aversion, and AA—do not have large-scale, random-assignment, controlled studies to document their alleged effectiveness. This is particularly scandalous when there is so much precedent showing that in this area, controlled studies usually suggest that treatment does not improve on the natural recovery rate.

24. J. Volpicelli, A. Alterman, M. Hayashida, and C. O'Brien, "Naltrexone in the Treatment of Alcohol Dependence," *Archives of General Psychiatry* 49 (1992): 876–80; S. O'Malley, A. Jaffee, G. Chang, et al., "Naltrexone and Coping Skills Therapy for Alcohol Dependence," *Archives of General Psychiatry* 49 (1992): 881–87.

25. Here are the three most useful sets of references as to whether AA works.

First, two studies in addition to Vaillant's that show better prognosis for people who attend more AA meetings: M. O'Leary, D. Coastline, D. Haddock, et al., "Differential Alcohol Use Patterns and Personality Traits Among Three Alcoholics Anonymous Attendance Level Groups: Further Considerations of the Affiliation Profile," *Drug and Alcohol Dependence* 5 (1980): 135–44; V. Giannetti, "Alcoholics Anonymous and the Recovering Alcoholic: An Exploratory Study," *American Journal of Drug and Alcohol Abuse* 8 (1981): 363–70.

Second, the only studies that actually use a randomized assignment to treatment: One (K. Ditman, G. Crawford, C. Forgy, et al., "A Controlled Experiment on the Use of Court Probation for Drunk Arrests," *American Journal of Psychiatry* 124 [1967]: 160–63) shows no difference among AA, clinic attendance, and no treatment; another (J. Brandsma, M. Maultsby, and R. Welsh, *Out-Patient Treatment of Alcoholism* [Baltimore, Md.: University Park Press, 1980]) shows that AA does worse (more dropouts) than insight therapy, behavior therapy, or paraprofessional behavior therapy. Both these studies use court-referred involuntary subjects. They strongly suggest that AA is not useful for such subjects, on average, but they do not bear directly on the effectiveness of AA with voluntary subjects. A third randomized-assignment study, Walsh et al., "A Randomized Trial of Treatment Options," assigned alcoholic workers to AA or to hospital-based detoxification (but with a strong AA component) and found that those assigned to AA alone did most poorly.

Third, some studies that look at AA effectiveness with voluntary attenders, but with substandard methods: D. Smith, "Evaluation of a Residential AA Program," *International Journal of the Addictions* 21 (1986): 33–49; AA World Services, "Analysis of the 1980 Survey of the Membership of AA" (unpublished report, New York, 1981); G. Alford, "Alcoholics Anonymous: An Empirical Outcome Study," *Addictive Behaviors* 5 (1981): 359–70.

This literature is usefully reviewed by B. McCrady and S. Irvine, "Self-Help Groups," in R. Hester and W. Miller, eds., *Handbook of Alcoholism Treatment Approaches* (New York: Pergamon, 1989).

26. When data first came to light that some alcoholics could recover and still tipple, AA attacked in full force. For the beginnings of the *scientific* debate, see M. Sobell and L. Sobell, "Second Year Treatment Outcome of Alcoholics Treated by Individualized Behaviour Therapy," *Behaviour Research and Therapy* 14 (1976): 195–215, versus M. Pendery, I. Maltzman, and L. West, "Controlled Drinking by Alcoholics? New Findings and a

Re-evaluation of a Major Affirmative Study," *Science* 217 (1982): 169–75. "Alcoholics could die because of this," AA spokesmen were quoted as saying. That at least a few alcoholics recover through controlled drinking is now widely accepted. G. Nordstrom and M. Berglund, "A Prospective Study of Successful Long-term Adjustment in Alcohol Dependence: Social Drinking Versus Abstinence," *Journal of Studies on Alcohol* 48 (1987): 95–103; J. Orford and A. Keddie, "Abstinence or Controlled Drinking in Clinical Practice: A Test of the Dependence and Persuasion Hypothesis," *British Journal of Addiction* 81 (1986): 495–504; G. Edwards, A. Duckitt, E. Oppenheimer, et al., "What Happens to Alcoholics?" *Lancet* (30 July 1983), 269–71.

For the data that less-severe alcoholics recover through controlled drinking and that more-severe alcoholics recover through abstinence, see Vaillant, *The Natural History of Alcoholism*, 221–35.

27. M. Sobell and L. Sobell, *Individualized Behavior Therapy for Alcoholics: Rationale, Procedures, Preliminary Results, and Appendix* (California Mental Health Research Monograph no. 13) (California Department of Mental Hygiene, 1972); Pendery et al., "Controlled Drinking by Alcoholics?" See especially H. Fingarette's lucid discussion on pages 124–29 of *Heavy Drinking*, and the references in note 26, above.
28. See chapter 2, "Can Alcoholics Control Their Drinking?" of H. Fingarette's lucid little book *Heavy Drinking;* and A. Marlatt, "The Controlled Drinking Controversy," *American Psychologist* 38 (1983): 1097–1110.
29. S. Curry, G. A. Marlatt, and J. Gordon, "Abstinence Violation Effect: Validation of an Attributional Construct with Smoking Cessation," *Journal of Consulting and Clinical Psychology* 58 (1987): 145–49; and G. A. Marlatt and S. Tapert, "Harm Reduction: Reducing the Risk of Addictive Behaviors," in J. Baer, G. A. Marlatt, and R. McMahon, eds., *Addictive Behaviors Across the Lifespan: Prevention, Treatment and Policy Issues* (Newbury Park, Calif.: Sage, 1993), 243–73.
30. See chapter 5, "Heavy Drinking as a Way of Life," in Fingarette, *Heavy Drinking.*
31. See chapter 7, "Social Policies to Prevent and Control Heavy Drinking," in Fingarette, *Heavy Drinking.*

PART FOUR *epigraph*

1. In J. S. Grant, ed., *The Enthusiasms of Robertson Davies* (New York: Penguin, 1990), 235–36.

CHAPTER 14 *Shedding the Skins of Childhood*

1. P. Davis, *The Way I See It* (New York: Putnam, 1992), 33–42.
2. Adapted from John Bradshaw's immensely popular *Homecoming: Reclaiming and Championing Your Inner Child* (New York: Bantam, 1990), 227, 239.
3. Useful reviews: **Divorce:** R. Forehand, "Parental Divorce and Adolescent Maladjustment: Scientific Inquiry vs. Public Information," *Behaviour Research and Therapy* 30 (1992): 319–28. This review is a good corrective to the alarmist popular literature on divorce. It seems to be conflict, and not divorce per se, that does the harm. **Parental Death:** G. Brown and T. Harris, *Social Origins of Depression* (London: Tavistock, 1978). **Birth Order:** R. Galbraith, "Sibling Spacing and Intellectual Development: A Closer Look at the Confluence Models," *Developmental Psychology* 18 (1982): 151–73. **Adversity (generally):** A. Clarke and A. D. Clarke, *Early Experience: Myth and Evidence* (New York: Free Press, 1976); M. Rutter, "The Long-term Effects of Early Experience," *Developmental Medicine and Child Neurology* 22 (1980): 800–815.

4. When investigators actually go and look, rather than just declare that we are products of childhood, the lack of strong continuity from childhood to adulthood is what hits you between the eyes. This is a major discovery of life-span developmental psychology. "Change" is at least as good a description as "continuity" for what happens to us as we mature. For good reviews of this very large literature, see M. Rutter, "Continuities and Discontinuities from Infancy," in J. Osofsky, ed., *Handbook of Infant Development,* 2d ed. (New York: Wiley, 1987), 1256–98; H. Moss and E. Sussman, "Longitudinal Study of Personality Development," in O. Brim and J. Kagan, eds., *Constancy and Change in Human Development* (Cambridge, Mass.: Harvard University Press, 1980), 530–95; G. Parker, E. Barrett, and I. Hickie, "From Nurture to Network: Examining Links Between Perceptions of Parenting Received in Childhood and Social Bonds in Adulthood," *American Journal of Psychiatry* 149 (1992): 877–85; and R. Plomin, H. Chipuer, and J. Loehlin, "Behavior Genetics and Personality," in L. Pervin, ed., *Handbook of Personality Theory and Research* (New York: Guilford, 1990), 225–43.

   Especially instructive is the finding that divorce itself is heritable. If you have an identical twin who divorces, your chances of divorce increase sixfold, whereas a divorced fraternal twin only increases your chances of divorce twofold. See M. McGue and D. Lykken, "Genetic Influence on the Risk of Divorce," *Psychological Science* 3 (1992): 368–73.
5. The twin studies and adoptive studies are cited in chapter 3. See especially R. Plomin and C. Bergeman, "The Nature of Nurture: Genetic Influence on 'Environmental Measures,' " *Behavioral and Brain Sciences* 14 (1991): 373–427. For other important studies, see S. Dinwiddie and R. Cloninger, "Family and Adoption Studies in Alcoholism and Drug Addiction," *Psychiatric Annals* 21 (1991): 206–14; T. Bouchard and M. McGue, "Genetic and Rearing Environmental Influences on Adult Personality: An Analysis of Adopted Twins Reared Apart," *Journal of Personality* 68 (1990): 263–82; A. Heath, L. Eaves, and N. Martin, "The Genetic Structure of Personality: III. Multivariate Genetic Item Analysis of the EPQ Scales," *Personality and Individual Differences* 12 (1988): 877–88.

   There continues to be a flourishing field investigating childhood antecedents of adult problems. Occasionally reliable effects emerge, but what astonishes me—given the heritability literature—is the absence of any genetic theorizing in this field. So, for example, there are two recent, otherwise competent studies that find (1) correlations between mothers' treatment of children and the children's later criminality, and (2) correlations between childhood trauma and later suicidal attempts. Both interpret the childhood events as causal. Both fail to explore the possibility that the adult behavior and what happened in childhood result from third, genetic variables. These studies are H. Stattin and I. Klackenberg-Larsson, "The Relationship Between Maternal Attributes in the Early Life of the Child and the Child's Future Criminal Behavior," *Development and Psychopathology* 2 (1990): 99–111; and B. van der Kolk, C. Perry, and J. Herman, "Childhood Origins of Self-Destructive Behavior," *American Journal of Psychiatry* 148 (1991): 1665–71. Editors beware.
6. A. Browne and D. Finkelohr, "Impact of Child Sexual Abuse: A Review of the Research," *Psychological Bulletin* 99 (1986): 66–77; and K. Alter-Reid, M. Gibbs, J. Lachenmeyer, et al., "Sexual Abuse of Children: A Review of the Empirical Findings," *Clinical Psychology Review* 6 (1986): 249–66, both provide good reviews. J. Herman, D. Russell, and K. Trocki, "Long-term Effects of Incestuous Abuse in Childhood," *American Journal of Psychiatry* 143 (1986): 1293–96, is a good example of the genre.

   In one of the only studies to play off family pathology against the effect of childhood sexual abuse per se, no long-term effect of childhood sexual abuse could be found over and above associated family pathology. See M. Nash, T. Hulsey, M. Sexton, T. Harralson, and W. Lambert, "Long-term Sequelae of Childhood Sexual Abuse: Perceived Family Environment, Psychopathology, and Dissociation," *Journal of Consulting and Clinical Psychology* 61 (1993): 276–83. This leads to the curmudgeonly skepticism in the next paragraph.

7. D. Finkelhor, "Early and Long-term Effects of Child Sexual Abuse: An Update," *Professional Psychology: Research and Practice* 5 (1990): 325–30.
8. See D. Finkelhor, "Early and Long-term Effects of Child Sexual Abuse," for a recent review.

   Three longitudinal studies are R. Gomes-Schwartz, J. Horowitz, and A. Cardarelli, *Child Sexual Abuse: The Initial Effects* (Newbury Park, Calif.: Sage, 1990); A. Bentovim, P. Boston, and A. Van Elburg, "Child Sexual Abuse—Children and Families Referred to a Treatment Project and the Effects of Intervention," *British Medical Journal* 295 (1987): 1453–57; J. Conte, "The Effects of Sexual Abuse on Children: Results of a Research Project," *Annals of the New York Academy of Sciences* 528 (1988): 310–26.

   For the better prognosis in children than in adults, see R. Hanson, "The Psychological Impact of Sexual Assault on Women and Children: A Review," *Annals of Sex Research* 3 (1990): 187–232.

   For ripping off the scars and even manufacturing them out of whole cloth, see D. Kent, "Remembering 'Repressed' Abuse," *APS Observer* 5 (1992): 6–7.

   For the effect of lengthy litigation, see D. Runyan, M. Everson, D. Edelsohn, et al., "Impact of Legal Intervention on Sexually Abused Children," *Journal of Pediatrics* 113 (1988): 647–53.
9. The first scenario is from D. Quinton and M. Rutter, *Parenting Breakdown: The Making and Breaking of Intergenerational Links* (Aldershot, Eng.: Gower, 1988), 93–108. The second scenario is from A. Caspi and G. Elder, "Emergent Family Patterns: The Intergenerational Construction of Problem Behaviors and Relationships," in R. Hinde and J. Stevenson-Hinde, eds., *Relationships Within Families: Mutual Influences* (Oxford: Clarendon Press, 1988), 218–40.
10. There is one disorder that seems to fit the inner-child premises well: multiple personality. This typically seems to begin with severe childhood abuse—rape or attempted murder—from which the child withdraws by creating another personality to endure it. This tactic relieves pain, and so, when further trauma strikes, new personalities are created. See E. Bliss, "Multiple Personalities: Report of Fourteen Cases with Implications for Schizophrenia and Hysteria," *Archives of General Psychiatry* 37 (1980): 1388–97. Fortunately, this disorder is quite rare, and there is no evidence that this kind of etiology applies to ordinary depression, anxiety, or other common adult problems.
11. For a good review of this large literature, see R. Plomin and D. Daniels, "Why Are Children in the Same Family So Different from One Another?" *Behavioral and Brain Sciences* 10 (1987): 1–60, and R. Plomin, "Environment and Genes," *American Psychologist* 44 (1989): 105–11. For some of the literature on the small effects of child rearing on adult personality, see M. Heinstein, "Behavioral Correlates of Breast-Bottle Regimes Under Varying Parent-Infant Relationships," *Monographs of the Society for Research in Child Development* 28 (1963); J. Whiting and I. Child, *Child-Training and Personality* (New Haven: Yale University Press, 1953).
12. I thank my good friend Barry Schwartz for these colorful metaphors, which he uses in Psychology 1 at Swarthmore College. But I wish he would remember new minor forcing. See M. Rutter, "Pathways from Childhood to Adult Life," *Journal of Child Psychology and Psychiatry* 30 (1989): 23–51, for an elaborate discussion of many possible models and paths.
13. My discussion of the influence of the childhood environment on adult personality has glossed over an important distinction for human-behavior geneticists: the distinction be-

tween "shared" and "unshared" environments. Joan and Sarah share certain experiences—being upper-middle-class, gardening with Daddy, and Catholicism, for example. They also have an unshared environment: Joan was molested at age ten, Sarah had appendicitis, and Sarah secretly hates gardening. Shared and unshared environments turn out to have very different influences on adult personality. The shared childhood environment—church, school, rearing techniques, socioeconomic status—has virtually no effect on adult personality. Identical twins reared apart are just as similar, maybe more similar, in adult personality than identical twins reared together. Conversely, adopted sibs raised in the same household are no more similar than if they had been raised separately. This means that shared environment in childhood adds nothing.

The whole kit and caboodle that conventional American developmental psychology bet on came up with a bust.

The unshared childhood environment is more promising. It probably accounts for between 15 and 50 percent of the variance in adult personality—probably not as much as genes, but a substantial amount. Before we environmentalists get too excited once again, however, let me say some of what "unshared environment" includes: big events like sexual abuse (which warms the hearts of environmentalists); small events like missing one ballet class; how you interpret, perceive, or remember big or small events; differing bodily reaction to events; parents' loving you more or less than they did your sib; fetal hormones; childhood illnesses; and good old error of measurement—anything at all that you and your sib are not identical for. It is, unfortunately, a wastebasket category that contains three-quarters of psychology.

No specific piece of unshared environment in childhood has yet to be shown to have any effect at all on adult personality once genes are controlled. In the correct kind of design, J. Loehlin and R. Nichols, *Heredity, Environment, and Personality* (Austin: University of Texas Press, 1976), looked at over seven hundred pairs of identical twins. They isolated about fifty pairs in which one had saliently different events from the other during childhood—one had a serious illness but the other did not, one got spanked a lot, but the other did not, and so on. None of these differences produced any detectable differences in later personality.

To sum up: Genes have a big effect on adult personality. Surprisingly, childrearing techniques, schools, socioeconomic status, and religion do not have a detectable effect. Idiosyncratic experience—traumatic or nontraumatic events, differential treatment by parents, peculiar turn of mind—should in theory have a noticeable effect, but it has yet to be demonstrated.

This is a difficult but illuminating literature. I recommend that the serious student start with R. Plomin and D. Daniel's classic "Why are Children in the Same Family So Different from One Another?" *Behavioral and Brain Sciences* 10 (1987): 1–16, along with the very high quality "peer commentary" that follows. It also has a first-rate bibliography. Then read J. Dunn and R. Plomin, *Separate Lives: Why Siblings Are So Different* (New York: Basic Books, 1990).

More recent papers include A. Tellegen, D. Lykken, T. Bouchard, et al., "Personality Similarity in Twins Reared Apart and Together," *Journal of Personality and Social Psychology* 54 (1988): 1031–39; L. Baker and D. Daniels, "Nonshared Environmental Influences and Personality Differences in Adult Twins," *Journal of Personality and Social Psychology* 58 (1990): 103–10 (showing small but significant nonshared influences—father's strictness and mother's warmth—the only specific ones in the whole literature); J. Loehlin, J. Horn, and L. Willerman, "Heredity, Environment, and Personality Change: Evidence from the Texas Adoption Project," *Journal of Personality* 58 (1990): 221–43; T. Bouchard and M.

McGue, "Genetic and Rearing Environmental Influences on Adult Personality: An Analysis of Adopted Twins Reared Apart," *Journal of Personality* 58 (1990): 263–92. All of this heralds nothing less than a revolution in the study of how personality develops.

14. J. L. Austin, "A Plea for Excuses," in *Philosophical Papers* (Oxford: Clarendon Press, 1961), 123–52.

15. The research literature on the effectiveness of catharsis (also called *abreaction*) is very thin. For the most complete recent review, see I. Marks, "Emotional Arousal as Therapy: Activation vs. Dissociation," *European Psychiatry* 6 (1991): 161–70.

    On the negative side, see, for example, M. Stern, E. Plionis, and L. Kaslow, "Group Process Expectations and Outcome with Post-Myocardial Infarction Patients," *General Hospital Psychiatry* 6 (1984): 101–8; M. Lieberman, I. Yalom, and M. Miles, *Encounter Groups: First Facts* (New York: Basic Books, 1973); A Bohart, "Toward a Cognitive Theory of Catharsis," *Psychotherapy—Theory, Research, and Practice* 17 (1980): 192–201; R. Baron, "Countering the Effects of Destructive Criticism: The Relative Efficacy of Four Interventions," *Journal of Applied Psychology* 75 (1990): 235–45; and R. Edelmann and S. Hardwick, "Test Anxiety: Past Performance and Coping Strategies," *Personality and Individual Differences* 7 (1986): 255–57.

    On the positive side, see M. Nichols, "Outcome of Brief Cathartic Psychotherapy," *Journal of Consulting and Clinical Psychology* 42 (1974): 403–10; and H. Bierenbaum, A. Schwartz, and M. Nichols, "Effects of Varying Session Length and Frequency in Brief Emotive Psychotherapy," *Journal of Consulting and Clinical Psychology* 44 (1976): 790–98.

    In general, when it comes to how much patients like it, catharsis is rated highly. When it comes to measures of how well they do, catharsis fares badly.

    There is something to be said for disclosure of traumatic events, as opposed to catharsis per se. Evidence is mounting that not keeping trauma secret helps physical health. See, for example, J. Pennebaker, J. Kielcolt-Glaser, and J. Glaser, "Disclosure of Traumas and Immune Function: Health Implications for Psychotherapy," *Journal of Consulting and Clinical Psychology* 56 (1988): 239–45; and M. Greenberg and A. Stone, "Emotional Disclosure About Traumas and Its Relation to Health: Effects of Previous Disclosure and Trauma Severity," *Journal of Personality and Social Psychology* 63 (1992): 75–84. But disclosure to others does not equal catharsis, which is disclosure to the self.

    There may indeed be something to catharsis, but after 100 years its effects remain undocumented and underresearched, and its adherents seem to have largely given it up. So I am not prepared to condemn it outright as a method, just to caution the reader. I do find it scary to see such an unfounded method recurrently creep into such "pop" therapies for seriously troubled people as the encounter groups of the 1960s and 1970s, and the recovery groups of the 1990s.

16. I tried in vain to find any follow-up data at all from the recovery movement. John Bradshaw's office didn't have any (25 June 1992) and referred me to Mary Bell at the Center for Recovering Families in Houston. They were hoping to start such a study.

17. Two excellent critiques of the recovery movement: W. Kaminer, *I'm Dysfunctional, You're Dysfunctional: The Recovery Movement and Other Self-Help Fashions* (Reading, Mass.: Addison-Wesley, 1992); and D. Rieff, "Victims, All? Recovery, Co-dependency, and the Art of Blaming Somebody Else," *Harper's*, October 1991. See also J. Leo, "The It's-Not-My-Fault Syndrome," *U.S. News & World Report*, 18 June 1991.

18. These remarks about the importance of therapy being forward-looking, rather than focused on the past, should not be construed as an indictment of all psychodynamic therapy. One of the most welcome developments in modern psychoanalysis is the technique of looking

in detail at what past conflicts, current conflicts, and conflicts right in therapy have in common. This is done in order to isolate the core conflictual pattern and to deal with the future. (See L. Luborsky, *Principles of Psychoanalytic Theory: A Manual for Supportive-Expressive Treatment* [New York: Basic Books, 1984].) This is, to my way of thinking, a major advance.

CHAPTER 15 *Depth and Change*

1. I use the locution *unchangeable* and not *incurable* because I want to emphasize that I do not believe that homosexuality (when egosyntonic) is a disease in need of cure.
2. Peter Whybrow has argued that bipolar depression has its roots in seasonal demands on activity expenditure and activity conservation. P. Whybrow, *The Hibernation Response* (New York: Avon, 1988).
3. But not to be forgotten is the classic story of a "Cotard" patient. Cotard is an extreme form of depression in which you believe you are dead. One Cotard patient was queried about whether dead people bleed. He said, "Of course not." His therapist then stuck him with a pin.

   "I guess dead people do bleed" was his response. Disconfirmation evaded.
4. L. Alloy and L. Abramson, "Judgment of Contingency in Depressed and Nondepressed Students: Sadder but Wiser?" *Journal of Experimental Psychology: General* 108 (1979): 441–85.

INDEX

Permissions Acknowledgments

Grateful acknowledgment is made to the following for permission to reprint previously published material:

Consulting Psychologists Press, Inc.: Items from "State–Trait Anxiety Inventory" from *Self-Evaluation Questionnaire—Form Y* by C. D. Spielberger, R. L. Gorsuch, R. E. Lushene, P. R. Vagg, and G. A. Jacobs, copyright © 1977 by Charles D. Spielberger. Modified and reprinted by permission of the publisher, Consulting Psychologists Press, Inc., Palo Alto, CA 94303. All rights reserved. Further reproduction is prohibited without the publisher's written consent.

Liveright Publishing Corporation and W. W. Norton & Company Ltd.: "O sweet spontaneous" from *Complete Poems, 1904–1962,* by E. E. Cummings, edited by George J. Firmage, copyright © 1923, 1925, 1926, 1931, 1935, 1938, 1939, 1940, 1944, 1945, 1946, 1947, 1948, 1949, 1950, 1951, 1952, 1953, 1954, 1955, 1956, 1957, 1958, 1959, 1960, 1961, 1962 by E. E. Cummings. Copyright © 1961, 1963, 1966, 1967, 1968 by Marion Morehouse Cummings. Copyright © 1972, 1973, 1974, 1975, 1976, 1977, 1978, 1979, 1980, 1981, 1982, 1983, 1984, 1985, 1986, 1987, 1988, 1989, 1990, 1991 by the Trustees for the E. E. Cummings Trust. Rights in the U.K., copyright © 1951 by the Trustees for the E. E. Cummings Trust, administered by W. W. Norton & Company Ltd., London. Reprinted by permission of the publishers.

New Directions Publishing Corporation: "The Mind Is an Ancient and Famous Capitol" from *Selected Poems: Summer Knowledge* by Delmore Schwartz, copyright © 1959 by Delmore Schwartz. Reprinted by permission of New Directions Publishing Corporation.

University of Pennsylvania, Department of Psychology: Items 10–20 from Part Two of "State–Trait Anger Expression Inventory (STAXI)" by Charles D. Spielberger, copyright © 1979, 1986, 1988 by Psychological Assessment Resources, Inc. Reprinted by permission.

A Note About the Author

Martin E. P. Seligman, Ph.D., is Kogod Professor and Director of Clinical Training in Psychology at the University of Pennsylvania in Philadelphia. He is currently president of the division of clinical psychology of the American Psychological Association. The author of six previous books, including *Learned Optimism* and *Helplessness,* he is one of the world's leading authorities on motivation.

A Note on the Type

The text of this book was set in a face called Times Roman, designed by Stanley Morison for *The Times* (London), and first introduced by that newspaper in 1932.

Among typographers and designers of the twentieth century, Stanley Morison (1889–1967) was a strong forming influence, as typographical adviser to the English Monotype Corporation, as a director of two distinguished English publishing houses, and as a writer of sensibility, erudition, and keen practical sense.

In 1930 Morison wrote: "Type design moves at the pace of the most conservative reader. The good type-designer therefore realises that, for a new fount to be successful, it has to be so good that only very few recognise its novelty. If readers do not notice the consummate reticence and rare discipline of a new type, it is probably a good letter." It is now generally recognized that in the creation of Times Roman, Morison successfully met the qualifications of this theoretical doctrine.

Composed by ComCom, a division of
Haddon Craftsmen, Allentown, Pennsylvania
Printed and bound by The Haddon Craftsmen,
Scranton, Pennsylvania
Designed by Anthea Lingeman